ALSO BY MICHAEL SHELDEN

Friends of Promise:
Cyril Connolly and the World of Horizon

George Orwell: The Authorized Biography

GRAHAM GREENE
THE ENEMY WITHIN

GRAHAM GREENE

THE ENEMY WITHIN

MICHAEL SHELDEN

RANDOM HOUSE

NEW YORK

Originally published in Great Britain by William Heinemann Ltd., London, in 1994

Library of Congress Cataloging-in-Publication Data
Shelden, Michael.
Graham Greene : the enemy within / Michael Shelden.
p.   cm.
Includes bibliographical references and index.
ISBN 0-679-42883-6
1. Greene, Graham, 1904–1991—Biography. 2. Novelists,
English—20th century—Biography. I. Title.
PR6013.R44Z842   1995
823′.912—dc20   94-34172

Manufactured in the United States of America on acid-free paper
2 4 6 8 9 7 5 3
First U.S. Edition

CONTENTS

GRAHAM GREENE
THE ENEMY WITHIN

DECEPTION AND DETECTION

A ll good novelists have tasted the joy of deception, but Graham Greene was addicted to it. He was not content to practice the ordinary deceits of fiction writing. He made deception a way of life, habitually disguising his true intentions in his personal affairs as well as in his art. Beneath his various masks, the real Graham Greene was carefully hidden.

The world thought it knew him. He wrote three of the most widely praised, and widely read, novels of the century—*Brighton Rock* (1938), *The Power and the Glory* (1940), and *The Heart of the Matter* (1948). These works have been translated into dozens of languages and are often assigned as texts in college courses. Literary scholars have analyzed his artistic methods, and his political and religious views have been the subjects of frequent discussion in both popular and academic journals. John Updike wrote that parts of *The Power and the Glory* were worthy of Dostoevsky, and William Faulkner praised Greene's novel *The End of the Affair* (1951) as "one of the best, most true and most moving novels of my time, in anybody's language."

The many films of his novels helped to build his reputation. They gave the impression that he was not only an intellectually fascinating character but also a dashing figure of adventure—a sort of British

Hemingway. *The Quiet American* (1958) deals with the early stages of the war in Indochina, *Our Man in Havana* (1959) takes a comical look at spies operating in Cuba, and *The Comedians* (1967) focuses on the evils of Papa Doc Duvalier's Haiti. Greene's fame as a globe-trotting author began with the success of *The Third Man* (1949), which was filmed largely on location in Vienna. It is a dark thriller set in a bombed-out city occupied by the armies of four nations and features an international cast that includes Orson Welles, Joseph Cotten, Trevor Howard, and Alida Valli.

For at least thirty years Greene's friends and admirers expected him to win the Nobel Prize, but every year they were disappointed. On the surface, he seemed the perfect candidate. He had created a large body of distinguished work, beginning with his novels of the 1930s, and had dealt with a wide range of "serious" issues. He was honored by the good and the powerful in many countries. The French awarded him the Legion of Honor and named him a commander of the Order of Arts and Letters. He was given the medal of the city of Madrid, the Jerusalem Prize, the Shakespeare Prize of Hamburg, and the Pietzak Award of Poland. In his native country he was granted honorary degrees from both Cambridge and Oxford, and the queen made him a member of the Order of Merit, a rare distinction for a writer—Henry James was one of the previous literary members. All these awards seemed only to raise expectations that Greene would eventually receive literature's highest prize—the Nobel. His final chance came in 1990, the last full year of his life. But the award went to the Mexican author Octavio Paz.

When I began work on this biography, I intended it to be a very favorable portrait of a novelist who deserved all the prizes the world could give him. I wanted to trace each step of his career with sympathy and to point out his virtues as both a writer and a human being. But along the way, I kept uncovering unpleasant facts, and my understanding of Greene's life and art gradually changed. I found a haunted character with many startling secrets, and I began to see that his work used an elaborate code to address these secrets. As more and more pieces of the code were broken, I realized that Greene was not the man he pretended to be, and that his work, too, has a disturbing underside to it, a side that reflected his personality even as he deceived us about it.

To give an accurate account of Greene's career, I have had to pursue the story in a way similar to that of a detective trying to solve an old case. The result—this book—bears more resemblance to a mystery story than to a traditional biography. What emerges from my search for the "hidden" Greene is the figure of a great artist with a devilish imagination and a heart full of darkness. No prize could do justice to the complexity of his art, which blends messages of brutal horror with techniques of great beauty and subtlety. While he belongs among the major British authors of the century, he is the strangest member of the group, and the truth behind his life and work is likely to shock earnest admirers and prize givers alike.

Greene sought and found pleasure for pleasure's sake in nearly every part of the world, and he created a vast body of work that glorifies subversiveness as a virtue. About his personal pursuit of pleasure, he was always less than candid, but he was plainspoken about his faith in subversiveness. His most important statement on the latter subject is a speech called "The Virtue of Disloyalty." It was delivered in 1969, when Greene was awarded the Shakespeare Prize by the University of Hamburg. Appropriately, it attacks both Shakespeare and prize giving.

The writer's duty, Greene says, is to make trouble for any dominant power, to force complacent authorities and submissive followers to confront difficult questions. He emphasizes the importance of writers becoming "grit in the State machinery," but the speech makes it clear that disloyalty is necessary against anything that may be considered a part of the establishment—churches, universities, businesses, social and cultural groups, even great literary figures such as Shakespeare. His assumption is that if any of these institutions or people are truly deserving, they can survive the criticism directed against them. Otherwise, no one will suffer unduly except the pretentious, the humorless, the dogmatic, the corrupt.

The trouble with the virtue of disloyalty is that it can easily shift toward vice. Greene was disloyal to the core, and the truth is that he often acted in a cruel fashion—in both word and deed. He planned and carried out deceptions and betrayals in both his professional and his private affairs, and these actions reveal, in varying degrees, his capacity for cleverness and wisdom, mischief and frivolity, vengeance and malice. His victims included members of his family and close friends and allies, as well as big governments, institutions, and journalists. Some of his conduct was so subtle that the act of betrayal was never apparent to the victim. And because he was also capable of being a generous and entertaining companion, those who were close to him found it difficult to imagine that his belief in disloyalty and subversion could ever affect them.

Greene's story "The Destructors" (1954) provides an example of his pattern of betrayal; in this case the victim was his wife, Vivien. The story itself is a frightening tale about a young gang of boys who methodically tear apart a grand eighteenth-century house that is temporarily vacant. The boys use hammers, chisels, and saws to rip out the handsome old staircase, the fine paneling, the beautiful parquet floor. By the time the owner returns from a brief holiday, the place is gutted. But before he can inspect the damage, the boys waylay him, lock him in an outdoor toilet, and continue their vandalism until the foundation of the house is weakened and the entire structure creaks, ready to collapse at any moment. With the help of an unsuspecting adult whose vehicle accidentally strikes one of the few remaining supports, the walls come crashing down and rubble is scattered everywhere. The gang make their escape, delighted with their work. The unfortunate owner is released from the dark privy, surveys the damage, and bursts into tears as he struggles to comprehend why anyone would deliberately ruin his home.

After the story was published in *Picture Post,* the magazine was overwhelmed by thousands of letters from readers who were offended by its graphic description of wanton destruction. One angry reader complained of the author, "He must be such a cruel man—such a sadist." Asked for his response, Greene calmly remarked, "Something must have just gone wrong in the writing. I meant it to be funny." The perverse determination and stupidity of the vandals have their amusing side, but "funny" is hardly the term for the overall effect of the story, with its unsparing depiction of a beautiful house subjected to a slow, painful demolition.

Greene was well aware that at least one reader would find "The Destructors" especially painful. In all its essentials, the house resembles one in London that Greene had shared with Vivien and their two young children in the late 1930s. The house was damaged in the blitz, and the couple never returned to it. By the time "The Destructors" appeared, they had been legally separated for several years, but Vivien still had a sentimental attachment to the house, regarding it as the best home of their married life. She was in no doubt about the meaning of the story. "People wrote to the paper and complained about it," she recalled in an interview. "They said it was cruel. It was to me very cruel. . . . It was as if he enjoyed the destruction. I could recognize that it was my house, our house. It was a beautiful house. Seventeen-fourteen, it was built. I felt the story was a repudiation of the responsibility of family."

Greene knew how his wife felt about the house they had shared, and he also knew that she had a romantic fascination for old houses in general. In later life this fascination grew into a passion for collect-

ing antique dolls' houses. In fact, Vivien eventually became a prominent authority on the hobby. By presenting the disintegration of their
marriage in terms of a literal breaking up of a home, Greene was striking a blow that he knew his wife would feel. But it is important to
recognize that he did not spare himself. The story links him to the
irrational, childish destructiveness of the home wreckers and also to
the undignified suffering of the owner trapped in a privy. "Old
Misery" is the nickname he gives to the poor fellow, and it is indeed
"old misery" that Greene unearthed in this tale about a bad marriage
that he had escaped but could not forget. Returning to it in his imagination, he needlessly opened old wounds and inflicted new ones.

As "The Destructors" makes clear, the ultimate betrayal for Greene
was self-betrayal. From an early age he understood that a part of him
seemed determined to destroy everything good that came into his
world, even to the point of tempting him to take his own life. When
he was still in his twenties, he found a quotation that summed up his
inner conflict. In *Religio Medici* Sir Thomas Browne wrote, "There
is another man within me that's angry with me." Greene was so
impressed by the expression that he adapted it for the title of his first
novel, *The Man Within* (1929). In context, Browne's words refer to
a struggle against a personal demon: "We carry private and domestic
enemies within, public and more hostile adversaries without. The
Devil that did but buffet Saint Paul, plays methinks at sharp with
me." Browne's "another man" is his good side, the conscience that
tries to hold back the demon: "He rebukes, commands, and dastards
me. . . . For the heavens are not only fruitful in new and unheard of
stars, the earth in plants and animals, but men's minds also in villainy
and vices."

During a long life Greene's "another man" had much to contend
against, and he must have been forced on many occasions to retreat
in the face of overwhelming opposition from the "private and domestic enemies within." The battle is a familiar one, but Greene's inner
struggle was much more complex and intense than most. And he was
expert at conveying the full force of such battles in his fictional world.
Readers are not exempt from his list of targets. Most writers grow
weary of trying to meet the expectations of their audiences and are
tempted to see readers as tyrants who need to be disobeyed. Greene
was expert at frustrating such expectations without appearing to be
too rebellious. He liked to make villains sympathetic, innocent characters guilty, and heroes weak. He found beauty in ugly settings and
ugliness in the most attractive places. He wrote serious novels disguised as thrillers, created religious tales filled with doubt, a love story

filled with hate, an autobiography that barely mentions his wife and children, a travel book in which the mental journey is more important than the physical one, and a play in which one of the two major characters says only "yes" and "no."

Greene's bibliography is full of surprises. When he was still in his twenties, he wrote a particularly revealing little work that has never attracted much attention. It is a racy literary biography of John Wilmot, earl of Rochester, the Restoration author of "A Satire Against Reason and Mankind" and "The Imperfect Enjoyment." The book is as much a personal document about Greene as it is a biography of Rochester; it reflects Greene's deep identification with the dark life and unconventional values of his subject. He began the book with the knowledge that he and Rochester had a good many things in common. Both were tall and slender, Oxford educated, restless, wickedly funny, fond of strong drink, and highly oversexed. Both were poets, a fact that is easily forgotten now—Greene's first book was a small collection of poems called *Babbling April* (1925). Both were married men who sheltered their young wives in the country so they could pursue more vigorously the delights of London's prostitutes. After working during the day on his biography in the British Museum, Greene did research of another sort at night in the capital's backstreets.

Unfortunately, Greene had to wait forty years before the finished work could appear in print. When he wrote the biography, in the early 1930s, its sexual content was so strong that commercial publishers shied away. Greene's discussion of Rochester's poem "Signor Dildoe" was sufficient in itself to merit prosecution for obscenity in those days, when *Lady Chatterley's Lover* and *Ulysses* were available only in smuggled copies. By the 1970s, however, the biography was deemed safe for public consumption and was published in a lavishly illustrated edition. The book was called *Lord Rochester's Monkey;* Greene's title refers to the nobleman's disdainful comment on the absurd pretentiousness of his fellow men: "Most human affairs are carried on at the same nonsensical rate, which makes me . . . think it a fault to laugh at the monkey we have here, when I compare his conditions with mankind."

Although the poetry now seems tame by the standards of our time, some readers have wondered why Graham Greene—the celebrated Catholic novelist and serious social critic—would devote a good part of his early career to researching and writing an unmarketable book about a poet who composed subversive lyrics on sexual and political themes. One expert tried to clear up the matter by explaining that the nobleman eventually turned to Catholicism and made a "death-bed repentance." But Greene makes a point of saying that Catholicism "never" held any appeal for Rochester. Near the end of Rochester's life, when he was suffering from the ravages of what appears to have been syphilis, he did repent, but it was to the Anglican religion that he turned. He even talked his wife into renouncing her Catholic faith so that she could join him in the established Church.

What is so striking about Greene's book is that it shows no admiration for the act of repentance. The biographer portrays his subject as a determined and talented sinner who, in a moment of weakness, was somehow tricked into accepting God. Greene indicates no respect for the earnest Dr. Gilbert Burnet, who went to great lengths to give religious instruction to the dying poet. He calls him a "clever, cunning churchman" and finds his religious arguments unconvincing in comparison with Rochester's comments on the joys of the flesh. Although Greene admits that his subject's mind was troubled by "the confusion of love and lust and death and hate," this difficult condition is made to seem preferable to the cold clarity of salvation. In the last pages of the biography, as Rochester takes his final breath, God enters like a "thief" and snatches the poet's fragile soul before Satan has a fair chance to claim it as rightfully his.

This is a curious piece of work for a biographer who called himself a Catholic, especially because it was completed only a few years after Greene had joined the Church. But, of course, the writer was not a conventional Catholic, a conventional biographer, or a conventional man. Sin rarely left Greene's mind, and, as did Rochester, he often found himself experiencing the confusion of love and lust and death and hate. This sense of a shared predicament was the greatest motivation for Greene's interest in Rochester's story, and it is the driving force behind the biography. There was certainly no money to be had from it—a limited edition was the best that Greene could have hoped for. And he was not inspired by a love of literary scholarship. Although he did a remarkable job of research for someone who was young and inexperienced, he made little effort to find new material and accepted unreliable sources without question.

Greene's desire to see Rochester in a certain light was more important to him than accuracy. He wanted to write about a subject whose passionate nature was torn between loving sin and loathing it, and whose greatest joy came from subverting accepted standards in art, morality, religion, and politics. To a considerable extent, Lord Rochester was such a man. He used solemn religious phrases to make sexual puns (Greene calls this habit "tender blasphemy"), and he wrote outrageous parodies of traditional poetic forms. Rochester attacked politicians and priests with enthusiasm, deriding them for creating "false freedoms, holy cheats, and formal lies / Over their fellow slaves to tyrannise." He ruthlessly satirized King Charles II, who was not only his sovereign but also his friend and protector: "His sceptre and his prick are of a length; / And she may sway the one who plays with th' other." Whenever he had stirred up too much trouble, he liked to fool enemies and friends by hiding behind various masks—roaming the streets as a beggar, acting the part of an innkeeper, and advertising himself as a physician specializing in the treatment of female complaints.

Like so many characters in Greene's fiction, Rochester was "man enough" to seek his own damnation. Accordingly, Greene surrounds him with self-righteous bullies and gives God a walk-on part as an abductor who crashes the death scene to steal the vulnerable soul. As biography or theology, the book is a travesty—an affront to serious scholars and divines everywhere. But it must also be said that it is a brilliant travesty, one that is perfectly in keeping with Rochester's irreverent character at the height of his glory. Greene's portrait of God as a thief is the kind of tender blasphemy that Rochester himself employed, and the whole idea of bringing God into the scene is an assault on conventional biography, which holds that things are true only if they can be documented. Greene's fanciful scene may have nothing to do with Rochester's real death, but its subversiveness is true to his understanding of the poet's character and of his own.

Lord Rochester's Monkey cannot be dismissed as a young man's folly—one of those inconsequential oddities that pop up in the bibliographies of even the most serious writers. It was written at a crucial stage in Greene's career, when he was still struggling to make his name and when he could ill afford to divert his attention from the obligations of a three-novel contract with his publisher, Heinemann. It was a book that he had to write—regardless of whether anyone wanted to read it—because understanding Rochester was a way of understanding himself. It was also a way of justifying the path he was determined to take in his life and art—a path not unlike Rochester's before illness and God intervened.

II

Because of Greene's deception, readers developed all kinds of misleading ideas about him. He created the impression that he rarely granted interviews and that he would never appear on television, yet he gave more interviews than perhaps any other major English author—well over a hundred, some of them quite extensive, including one that is book length—and he made a number of television appearances in foreign countries. Many of these interviews were intricate exercises in subterfuge. He was prepared to give only so much of himself away, and it was rare that anyone tricked him into making an unintentional revelation. He once wrote that Henry James was "not unaware of the legend he was creating," and the same can be said of Greene.

In a profile from 1978, V. S. Pritchett described Greene as "genially subversive" and suggested an appropriate maxim for such men: "The world is too complacent. Let us catch it out." As a way of quietly warning the complacent world, Pritchett indicated that Greene's famous fear of boredom provided a convenient mask: "Boredom! The most ingenious, inventive and exciting of our novelists, rich in exactly etched and moving portraits of real human beings . . . is he really bored? Or is he putting on a defensive mask?" As an old friend, Pritchett knew that Greene enjoyed a life full of interest and material comfort. The novelist was able to travel as often and as far as he liked, and to go in style, staying at the best hotels and dining at the best restaurants. From the 1960s until his death in 1991, Greene's principal residence was a small apartment on the French Riviera, but he also kept a larger apartment in Paris and a beautifully landscaped villa in Anacapri. When he visited London he invariably stayed at the Ritz.

In the middle of interviewing Greene for the profile, Pritchett made a deep penetration into the vast territory of the novelist's reserve. He coaxed Greene into admitting that one of the most famous stories about his youth might have been overdramatized. In the original version of the story, a steely young Greene spins a live round in the chamber of his older brother's revolver, puts the barrel to his ear, and pulls the trigger. About this well-known account of Greene's youthful fascination with Russian roulette, Pritchett wrote: "Now he confesses to the suspicion that the bullets in the chamber of the revolver were probably harmless. Unlikely that live bullets were left lying about."

Countless journalists and critics have eagerly accepted the dramatic version, yet if they had taken a close look at an early version of the story, published in 1946 as "The Revolver in the Corner Cupboard," they would have noticed not only that Greene is vague about whether the bullets were real or blanks but also that his description of the "tiny" revolver suggests something closely resembling a starter's pistol. All of this makes sense; his brother was keenly athletic and might well have kept such an innocent item of the playing fields in an unlocked cupboard of his bedroom. But apparently readers like a novelist to be aggressively suicidal, so Greene eliminated the hint about the blanks when he later included the story in his autobiography. Few people seemed to notice the changes. Even Pritchett's article did little to dim the enthusiasm for the image of Greene risking death with a loaded firearm.

Whether the Russian roulette account is true or not, Greene's attraction to suicide was genuine. But it may not be insignificant that he waited twenty years to advertise the fact, and to give it a glamorous edge. When "The Revolver in the Corner Cupboard" first appeared, Greene was at work on the novel meant to relaunch his career after the interruption of the war years. The main issue raised by that novel—*The Heart of the Matter*—is suicide. And so the news that the author himself had contemplated blowing his brains out did not hurt the huge publicity that swirled around the novel after its publication in 1948. By 1951 *Time* magazine had picked up the story and was reporting it as unquestionable fact in a cover article on Greene, dramatically announcing, "At seventeen, he tried the most drastic cure for boredom he could think of: Russian roulette." Noting elsewhere in the article that Greene was a "reserved" man who "would like to have it thought that there is nothing very interesting . . . in his own life," the *Time* reporter did not pause to ask why such a private man would be so willing to reveal that he had been a suicidal teenager. Forty years later the story was so widely accepted that it found a place even in the obituary pages of *The New York Times,* where it was presented in such bland terms that one could almost imagine the young man casually toying with the weapon as he walked down a crowded street: "Mr. Greene took the revolver with him to [Oxford] and continued to play Russian roulette."

Some people seemed almost eager to be misled by Greene, as the amusing case of the Anglo-Texan Society demonstrates. In 1953 Graham Greene and his wealthy friend John Sutro picked up two charming ladies from Texas in the lounge of Edinburgh's Caledonian Hotel. After a couple of memorable evenings in the company of these Texans, Greene was in such a pleasant mood—helped along by a large quantity of Black Velvet—that he suggested to Sutro the formation of the Anglo-Texan Society, with himself as president and his friend as vice president. They quickly composed a solemn letter to *The Times* that announced the launch of the society and asked for new members to help encourage stronger ties between Texas and England. Wisely, they did not specify how close they wished those ties to be. They expected an odd reply or two but were amazed when dozens of letters arrived, including one from Sir Hartley Shawcross—the attorney general of Great Britain. Events moved rapidly, and the society soon found itself with a large and distinguished membership. A barbecue was held on the outskirts of London, and hundreds of Texans turned up, along with the U.S. ambassador, whom the governor of Texas had asked to serve as the official Texas ambassador for the event. Many of the guests arrived in double-decker London buses hired for the occasion, with signs proudly proclaiming, "Texas from Piccadilly Circus."

It was a good joke that took on an extraordinary life of its own, and Greene was delighted to stand back and watch so many innocent followers celebrating his bogus institution. After a decent passage of time, he relinquished the presidency to an eminently respectable member of the House of Lords and allowed the society to drift along without any further encouragement from him. But the episode is an instructive one for the author's trusting admirers. Anyone who writes about Greene must think carefully before accepting his comments at face value, although it is probably impossible to avoid being caught in at least a few of the many traps that he laid for the unwary. The procession of buses taking the eager Anglo-Texan supporters to their barbecue is not unlike the parade of writers who have rushed into print with earnest speculations on dubious autobiographical remarks by Greene. We are all potential subscribers to some version of the Anglo-Texan Society and at any moment can find ourselves boarding the wrong bus.

An amazingly large number of people took the wrong bus in 1984, when it was announced that a "lost" novel of Greene's had been discovered in Los Angeles. Press reports throughout the world said that Greene had written *The Tenth Man* when he was under contract to MGM in 1944 and that it had been gathering dust in a Hollywood vault ever since, forgotten even by its author. Greene did his best to promote this story, telling one journalist that the discovery had caught him completely by surprise: "I didn't take it seriously at first because I thought it was no more than a sketched idea. But when it reached me I saw it was a short novel of some sixty thousand words. I had obviously written and revised it very thoroughly." Even an inexperienced journalist should have expressed some doubt that a novelist could so easily forget 60,000 words of a book with a title that closely resembles that of such a famous work as Greene's own *The Third Man* (1950). No one seriously challenged the author's comments. Forty years is a long time, and perhaps it is reasonable to expect that a prolific writer would lose track of such an old manuscript. But there was nothing wrong with Greene's memory, and the novel had not been lost.

A quick inspection of the standard bibliography of Greene's work, published in 1979 and available at any good research library, would have shown an inquisitive reporter that a manuscript copy of *The Tenth Man* was listed as one of his unpublished pieces. As befits a past president of the Anglo-Texan Society, Greene had sold the copy—along with many other papers—to the University of Texas. Included with the manuscript is a letter from Greene's literary agent to a book collector who was interested in the work. The collector had written to Greene asking about the possibility of publishing it, and Greene had instructed his agent to reply that MGM held the copyright. The agent also mentioned that several copies of the manuscript seemed to be in circulation. No indication was given that either the author or his agent had ever considered the work "lost." The letter is dated March 30, 1967.

The "discovery" of *The Tenth Man* allowed Greene to have some fun at the expense of journalists who think only in terms of headlines. And, of course, there was always the added benefit of increased sales from the publicity. Greene may have been a cunning manipulator of his public image, but unlike so many others who possess that skill, he could also produce books of real literary merit. In his best novels he portrays private worlds of intense disaffection that expose the raw nerves of their inhabitants. These worlds are constantly on the edge of collapse, threatened by characters whose sense of disloyalty is so powerful that they cannot help subverting everything in sight. Violent passions take hold of them and seem to rage without reason. The urge to kill runs rampant in *Brighton Rock;* jealous hatred drives away all other emotions in *The End of the Affair* (1951); and the desire for self-destruction thrives on an energy of its own in *The Heart of the Matter*. In these books the "grit" of disloyalty clogs the brain's machinery and brings it to a shuddering breakdown.

Yeats spoke eloquently of a world in which "things fall apart; the centre cannot hold," but few writers can rival Greene's ability to capture the confusion and terror of living in such a world. His eye missed nothing. He saw the cracks waiting to open up, the towers beginning to lean. The monstrously evil Pinkie Brown, in what is perhaps Greene's greatest novel, *Brighton Rock,* slouches toward the bright lights of Brighton with nothing but destruction in mind. At his approach the innocent laughter and music of the resort town are transformed into the hollow background noise of a nightmare, and all images become distorted, as though reflected in a broken mirror.

If such a place as hell exists, Greene's destabilized worlds offer a good preview of it. He spent a lot of time thinking about hell, and it shows. In *The Power and the Glory* hell seems to have taken over a large part of Mexico. But Greene knew that he could find the flames rising to greet him wherever he cared to look. As Sir Thomas Browne observed, "Surely though we place Hell under the earth, the Devil's walk and purlieu is about it; men speak too popularly who place it in those flaming mountains, which to grosser apprehensions represent Hell. The heart of man is the place the Devil dwells in." It is Greene's ability to penetrate our hearts of darkness that makes him a writer of enduring importance. The visits he made to distant parts of the world were never as meaningful as his ongoing explorations of the more obscure places in the human imagination—his longest journey without maps.

My purpose in this biography is to retrace that journey. It is not a tour of every aspect of Greene's work, nor a strict chronological account of the life, but a pursuit of the brilliantly subversive man behind the public mask—the enemy within. The trail is occasionally serpentine, and a few dark patches were, for me, impenetrable. Greene is never easy to follow. He spoke as an expert when he wrote that Henry James "had a marvelous facility for covering up his tracks." The one great advantage is that Greene could not resist dropping clues now and then. The trick is to separate the real clues from all the false leads. The best ones are right under our noses—in the pages of his books.

CHAPTER TWO

I SPY

Graham Greene's family had no shortage of spies. The most distinguished was his uncle Sir William Graham Greene, a career civil servant at the Admiralty who was given "special duty in the military, political and secret branch" and who later helped establish the Naval Intelligence Department. The least distinguished was Graham's oldest brother—Herbert—who served as a well-paid spy for the Imperial Japanese Navy in the 1930s. His job was to collect information on America's military and economic strength from sources within England. To be fair to the competition, he kept both the British and the American governments informed of his activities, although he did not bother to let his Japanese employers know of his generosity. He also found time to do some spying during the Spanish Civil War, but the identity of the service that employed him is uncertain. When he was publicly accused of working for General Franco, he declared that he favored neither side in the war and added cryptically, "There are many countries to-day interested in Spain."

At the beginning of the Second World War, Graham's younger sister, Elisabeth, joined the Secret Intelligence Service (better known as MI-6) and later married a colleague, Rodney Dennys, who held a series of important positions in SIS—including that of Paris station chief. In 1941 Elisabeth recruited Graham into the regular ranks of the service, and he served as a full-time officer until 1944. His younger brother, Hugh, may also have done a little spying, especially in the late 1930s, when he was the *Daily Telegraph* correspondent in Nazi Berlin. In any case, Hugh shared the family's fascination for espionage, as can be seen from the anthology that he and Graham edited in 1957, *The Spy's Bedside Book*. As an epigraph for their volume, they agreed on a long quotation from Balzac that begins, "The trade of a spy is a very fine one," and ends with praise for the thrill of taking risks.

One of Graham's cousins, Benjamin Greene, was either a very careless spy or a very stupid political agitator. In the early months of the war, he was suspected of helping Nazi agents in Britain and spent seven months in prison for "hostile associations." He was held without trial, and some of the government evidence against him was false, but it is true that he was—at the very least—a Nazi sympathizer with highly questionable contacts at home and abroad. He gave speeches in praise of Germany after the invasion of Poland and warned England against the danger of "Jewish and American capitalists." After reading Ben Greene's *The Truth About the War* (1939), Clement Attlee called it "one of the nastiest pieces of pro-Hitler propaganda that I have met for a long time." It did not help the suspect's cause that he had made contact with the Anglo-German Fellowship on a visit to Germany in 1936 and had returned with translations of Hitler's speeches supplied to him by the fellowship. It was also unhelpful that one of his sisters was living in Nazi Germany and was in love with a German count.

Surely one spy per family is more than enough, so why did so many Greenes get caught up in the business?

One clue may lie in the character of Graham's father, Charles Henry Greene, who was also Sir William Graham Greene's brother, and Ben Greene's uncle and headmaster. As far as anyone can tell, Charles Greene was never involved in professional spying, but he did cultivate a good breeding ground for spies in a peaceful corner of Hertfordshire, where he ran a little amateur espionage operation of his own. As the first post-Edwardian headmaster of Berkhamsted School, Charles was deeply fearful that the 500 boys in his charge would be infected by modern licentiousness. He was obsessed by the idea that boys were always looking for opportunities to foul the Temple of the Body by masturbating or doing something "worse." They needed to be watched, carefully watched: spied on. Through a well-organized network of masters, matrons, and prefects, the boys were kept under almost constant surveillance. The headmaster's little contingent of spies was extremely diligent. As one former pupil recalled: "It was taken for granted that any boys left alone and unoccupied for more than a few minutes were going to get up to vicious mischief, with the result that efforts were made to fill every interstice of every day with public and communal activities."

The hope of success was slight for any boy who wanted to make more than eye contact with the local girls. To deter them, a dark warning was given: "There is a whole army of women living on the lusts of men." Boys were routinely interrogated to discover whether they posed any threat to the strict moral order of the place. Charles Greene was especially eager to discourage masturbation. He would ask bewildered younger boys about their knowledge of the act and would closely question older boys to find out whether masturbation had become a habit with them. He often prowled the grounds looking for suspicious conduct and would reprimand boys who were standing around with their hands in their pockets. There was always the possibility that they were warming more than their hands.

In spite of such vigilance, the awful pleasures of sex kept tempting the boys to misbehave in the darkness of their beds or in lavatories and changing rooms. Whenever an offender was caught, Charles Greene took decisive action. Quietly but swiftly, the parents were called to the school, and the boy was sent into permanent exile. In the wake of such incidents, the headmaster would assemble the boys and warn them that he had lost none of his resolve and would not rest until he had put a stop to all illicit activity. On one of these occasions, he declared that he "would rather . . . that the school should cease to exist than that it should become—as might well happen unless the evil were promptly scotched—a hotbed of unmentionable vice."

It is hardly surprising that Graham Greene was unhappy at his father's school. The puritanical restrictions were bad enough, but being the headmaster's son made everything much worse. His father expected him to be not only an exemplary pupil but also a loyal spy in the surveillance network. The son gave the father an extra pair of eyes in the relentless battle to thwart the growth of vice. But it was a battle that could end only in defeat for the son. If he reported misdeeds to the headmaster, the boys would hate him. If he kept silent, he would be disobeying his father. On both sides of the green baize door—the border between home and school—his loyalty was suspect. Did he owe allegiance to the boys or to the masters? The only way to make life bearable was to play one side against the other, pretending to serve both. Forced to assume the part of the double agent, he learned to appreciate, at a very early age, the virtue of disloyalty.

Spying could even be fun, he discovered, if the spy learned to serve his own interests first.

The pressure on Graham to be loyal to his father was enormous. Charles Greene believed strongly in making the most of family connections and owed much of his success to that belief. Despite a lackluster personality, an erratic teaching style, and a poor academic record at Oxford (he took a Third Class degree in the Honours School of Classical Moderations, and a Second Class in History), Charles had little trouble rising to the top at Berkhamsted, thanks to family influence. He joined the teaching staff in 1888, shortly after finishing his education, and became the devoted right-hand man of the school's most famous headmaster, Dr. Thomas Fry, whose wife happened to be Charles Greene's first cousin. The family connection grew tighter, and a bit more confusing, in 1896, when the young assistant master wed another first cousin—Marion Raymond Greene.

From the union of Charles and Marion came six more Greenes. Born on October 2, 1904, the future novelist—whose full name was Henry Graham Greene—was the fourth child. His older siblings were Molly, Herbert, and Raymond, and the "babies" of the family were Hugh and Elisabeth. The tribe soon received further reinforcements from Charles's rich brother, Edward, who brought his wife and six children to Berkhamsted and took up permanent residence in the town's largest house, a mile from the school. Everywhere young Graham looked there were Greenes. And, because they tended to be unusually tall, they were hard to overlook. His mother was six feet tall, his brother Hugh eventually reached six feet, six inches, and his uncle Edward's son Ben—the Nazi sympathizer—was six feet, eight inches. In this crowd of Berkhamsted giants, Graham grew to the rather modest height of six feet, two inches.

When Dr. Fry decided to leave Berkhamsted for an appointment as dean of Lincoln, he seems to have used all his influence to make certain that Charles succeeded him. An advertisement for the job appeared in the press, but it allowed candidates only eighteen days to complete their applications, virtually guaranteeing that Charles would face minimal competition. Even so, the Board of Governors showed considerable resistance to Fry's chosen man, whose qualifications were not outstanding. He had no experience outside Berkhamsted and could point to no major works accomplished on his own initiative. The good doctor's influence prevailed in the end, but it took three rounds of balloting to win the board's approval. After the decision was announced, one pupil spotted Charles in the school quadrangle "literally dancing with joy."

Without Fry's help at this critical time, Charles's career would have suffered a major setback, and it is conceivable that he would have felt unable to stay on at Berkhamsted under another man. In that case Graham might have been spared the burden of being a headmaster's son, which may help explain why such violent abuse is hurled at Fry in Graham's autobiography. He calls him "sinister" and "sadistic" and accuses him of flogging boys for trivial reasons. Fry's admirers are still fuming over these charges, arguing not only that they are false but that the novelist was never in a position to know the truth. And they are right. Graham was only six when Fry left Berkhamsted.

Charles was never heard to say a bad word against his predecessor. He knew only too well how lucky he was to have the headmaster's job, and perhaps his subsequent campaign to enforce a rigid moral discipline was simply a reflection of his own sense of inadequacy—an awareness that he was a vulnerable leader who needed to keep tight control over everything. By all accounts he was a man of good intentions and high ideals, but he lacked grace and confidence. It was easy to provoke him, and he was often guilty of overreacting. A recent history of the school includes a revealing anecdote about a time when he suddenly lost his temper in the main hall. While delivering a long rebuke to the boys, he noticed that one was giggling: " 'Go to my study,' thundered Charles, and as the boy passed by him on his way out, caught him a stinging blow on the cheek. This was unprecedented, and the rest of us waited awestruck to hear what further doom the wretched offender had met. Back he came, looking far from amused; and all he said was, 'He apologised.' "

Charles was essentially a shy man who never found it easy to cope with outbursts of emotion. He seemed most at ease when he was alone in his study reading for pleasure or quietly playing chess by the fire. One boy who was considered the school's best chess player was occasionally invited to join him in a game and was amazed at the transformation that occurred in the headmaster's normally stern demeanor. "When the craving for chess came on him, he had to play; in the fire of this passion, rules, regulations and routine were reduced to ashes." Lost in the world of precise squares and orderly moves, where logic rules all, Charles Greene forgot the messy world of intractable boys and unmentionable vice, and the thousand ways that his authority could be undermined. He became, if only for a few hours, content.

It was the father at the chessboard or the father reading poetry in his study who appealed to Graham. These sides of the man were glimpsed only in rare moments, but they made an important impression on the son, whose lifelong love of serious poetry began in his father's study. Charles's favorite poet was Browning. He looked to the writer's work for the kind of sentiments that could bolster his own faith in a world governed by clear, unchanging laws. But while he was praising "God's in His heaven— / All's right with the world," his son was discovering another Browning in such masterpieces as "My Last Duchess," "Fra Lippo Lippi," and *The Ring and the Book*. The father was so certain of Browning's correctness that he took no notice of how much excitement an intelligent boy could find in the poet's inspired descriptions of shadowy love, randy priests, and cold-blooded murderers.

Although Charles Greene believed that he was teaching moral absolutes to his family and his pupils, his inflexible approach and uncertain manner created a muddled atmosphere in which everything seemed open to question. His methods encouraged doubt and suspicion, not faith. And all his rules simply aroused strong desires to break rules and to seek out forbidden things. Some boys were so uncritical that they accepted everything they were told, but, of course, Graham was not such a boy. And neither was his good friend Claud Cockburn. Looking back on his days at the school, Cockburn concluded, "As a direct result of all this supervision and ordering about, one of the most valuable lessons my school taught me was how to break other people's rules."

The low point in Charles Greene's career came on November 11, 1918—Armistice Day. The end of four years of war should have given rise to many hours of celebration by the boys and the staff, but the headmaster managed to turn this great event into something that embarrassed everyone connected with the school. The trouble started with Charles's misguided attempt to teach his pupils a lesson in humility. The dead deserved to be honored in silence, he declared, and the living must go on with the hard business of creating a better world. There was no time to waste in frivolous celebrations, so there was no reason to give the school a day off. Let the rest of the world rejoice with song and drink; the disciplined minds at Berkhamsted would calmly go back to their books and work all day. As intransigent as ever, Charles refused to modify his noble plan, and the result was a full-scale revolt.

He was betrayed by some of his trusted spies. Determined to give the school a holiday, several prefects secretly encouraged a large gang of rowdy young men from a nearby training camp to storm the school and lead the pupils away on a victory march down the High Street. On the journey to the school, the gang was joined by various towns-

people and some boisterous members of the Women's Army
Auxiliary Corps. When the crowd arrived at the gates, the prefects let
them in, and the school was overrun with revelers. The headmaster
tried to call for order but was shouted down. A small collection of
drunks in the mob suggested that he should be chucked into the
Berkhamsted Canal. Under the circumstances it seemed advisable for
him to make a hasty retreat to the relative safety of his study. The
dreaded forces of anarchy made him a laughingstock, and in all the
confusion many of the pupils escaped to the High Street to enjoy a
brief period of freedom.

The next day the shaken headmaster assembled the boys and subjected them to a long, angry lecture, which ended with the threat of
a mass expulsion. But in the end only a few boys were punished.
Charles wisely recognized that he could not afford to make a bigger
fool of himself by taking wholesale revenge for his defeat. His attempt
to force humility on the boys ended in his own painful humiliation,
but he appears not to have taken this lesson to heart. He went on
enforcing all his cherished rules, railing against the modern urge to
rebel and the spread of such dangers as "the pernicious and destructive doctrines of Marx and Lenin." Many years later his novelist son
found some redeeming artistic value in the incident, using it as the
basic model for the "rag" arranged by the loutish Buddy Fergusson
and his fellow medical students in *A Gun for Sale* (1936).

At home Charles experienced his greatest failure with his eldest
son, Herbert, who learned all the wrong lessons from life as the son
of an amateur spymaster. Anyone who has read Herbert's *Secret
Agent in Spain* (1938) will know that the author's story does not
inspire confidence in his sanity. His character in the book is a strange
combination of a self-righteous crusader and a prankish schoolboy,
and the result is a ludicrous figure who undertakes absurd adventures
with a sense of great purpose. The book is probably the only espionage tale dedicated to a bishop ("To the Right Reverend the Lord
Bishop of Bath and Wells"). Herbert makes dangerous trips into the
middle of the fighting in Spain yet claims not to know which power
he is spying for, saying only that his contact is a man in London
named Y, who "is neither a Spaniard nor a Jap." Almost everyone in
his supporting cast is identified by an initial—B, J, X, Capt. A,
Monsieur W, and so on. The mysterious Y hands him top-secret documents that must reach someone else with only an initial for a name,
and he races off to Spain to do his master's bidding, worrying that
other spies are following him every step of the way. Police officers
search him, a dark-eyed beauty slips him a suspicious envelope, and

gunfire crackles in the distance, but the dashing hero completes his mission and escapes all this intrigue to savor the pleasures of life at his cottage in good old Plumpton, East Sussex.

Herbert did go to Spain, and he was involved in some sort of spying, but it is hard to believe that anyone took him as seriously as he took himself. His book is full of unintentionally funny episodes and comments. In his early days as a spy for Japan in London, he met with his contact in a Japanese restaurant and realized halfway through the meal that the waiter was paying him too much attention. With only his intuition to guide him, he concluded that the waiter was "an important member of the Japanese Secret Service" who had been sent to give him "a good 'look over.' " Why this would be necessary the book does not take up, but the author is delighted that he apparently passed the test and adds proudly, "Fortunately I was not forced to use chopsticks, an art which I have never mastered."

The book contains not the slightest hint that Herbert found anything comic or tragic in his freelance spying. He wears a smug look in the photograph next to the title page—a casual shot showing him seated with some scruffy characters at a pavement café near the Spanish frontier. A foolish sense of pride is evident throughout, but the best example can be found on an early page which features a coded message that looks like an eye chart, with letters and numerals mixed together. In his foreword the author patiently explains that it contains key facts about Y and some events in Spain. He invites the reader to break the code but boasts that it is unbreakable and that the key is "in the safe custody of the Westminster Bank." No reader seems to have risen to this challenge, but the message may be nothing more than a fancy version of the menu at his Japanese restaurant.

Herbert's family knew that he had a weak hold on reality and did their best to keep him at a distance. He drank heavily, gambled, lost good jobs, and went in and out of debt on a regular basis. He was always trying to get money from his family, and they came to dread his letters and calls. After Graham became a successful writer, Herbert pestered him for help in finding publishers and film producers who would consider one of his many projects for winning fame and fortune, an example of which was a proposed booklet on Sabena Airlines. In return, Herbert offered what he believed to be hot tips for the stock market—he was especially keen on the long-term prospects of Vacuum Brakes and Hudson Bay Shares. Graham gave Herbert some financial help but could not resist toying with him occasionally. As a Christmas present in 1953, he sent him a Watney's "Toast Token" for a free beer.

Except for Herbert, all Charles Greene's sons were successful. Hugh became director general of the BBC, and Raymond was a famous mountain climber and respected physician. In younger days Graham was so embarrassed by Herbert's string of misfortunes that he wanted him to disappear permanently. On more than one occasion he expressed the hope that Herbert would shoot himself—for the good of the family. Their father, however, had a weak spot for his oldest boy and did not want to be too critical of him, but that may be because he recognized a little too much of himself in Herbert—the overblown pride, the shaky idealism, the preoccupation with spying, the clumsy efforts to impress. Charles had always tried to play it safe in life, but if he had taken some risks beyond the cozy Greeneland of Berkhamsted, he probably would have failed as miserably as Herbert.

There was even a bit of Herbert in Charles's most successful son. Graham could laugh at his brother's mad ideas or wish that the failures were less conspicuous, but he had almost suffered the same fate. Until his late teens Graham was the brother who had seemed least likely to succeed. He was the one who frightened his parents by showing suicidal tendencies, he was the one who tried running away from home and the one who was so unstable at sixteen that he was put in the care of a psychoanalyst for six months. He survived these troubles, of course, but it is easy to see why he resented his brother so much. Herbert was the failure that Graham might have become, the living reminder of everything he had escaped. In any event, there was one thing the brothers would always have in common. It was a weakness that Graham would never outgrow—the temptation to spy.

II

It is impossible to make sense of Greene's life until one acknowledges the extent of his devotion to spying. Right up to his last days he insisted that his only real experience as a spy came in the early 1940s, when he served the war effort as a small fish swimming in the murky backwaters of the Secret Intelligence Service. And the implication was that he had done this work only because it was his wartime duty. His loyal readers knew that he was fascinated by espionage and that his literary work showed a sharp understanding of the spy's world, but most people accepted that his attachment to the subject simply reflected the creative needs of the novelist. It gave him something to write about. He could leave the real work to the professionals.

It helped that he was so famous for his independent political views.

He was obviously his own man, and it was difficult to imagine that Greene would want to give his services to any government. In the 1950s and beyond, his widely publicized attacks on American foreign policy made him seem so politically high-minded that few people dared to think he would dirty his hands with the nasty business of spying. And why would a famous and prosperous novelist want to get too close to such a business? He could easily do without the extra money and the extra trouble.

More important, how could the author of *Our Man in Havana* (1958) see any great value in the spy's job? No book has ever made spies look so ridiculous. At a difficult time in the Cold War, when everyone was worried that spies were helping to move the world toward nuclear war and when Ian Fleming was working hard to make the public believe in suave operatives such as James Bond, Greene was portraying secret agents as bumbling amateurs. His "intelligence" experts cannot tell the difference between drawings of secret weapon components and illustrations from a vacuum cleaner manual. In his novel the crafty M of the Ian Fleming stories becomes a comic figure called simply the Chief, who is as gullible as a six-year-old, eagerly swallowing false information because it looks so irresistible. And instead of the ruggedly handsome Bond, the hero is the unremarkable middle-aged salesman James Wormold. Herbert Greene might have been perfectly at home in such inept company, but his literary brother seemed too superior for playing spy games of any kind.

With Graham Greene, solid evidence has always been hard to come by. He planned it that way. Even if his statements had been scrutinized closely all along, they would have been difficult to credit or discredit. In 1980 the literary historian Paul Fussell wrote of Greene: "There are hints that he's been engaged in more espionage than we have known about, for sometimes he has the greatest trouble explaining his motives for being in a certain place at a certain crucial time." Fussell could not solve any of these mysteries, but he was one of the few people to question seriously the flimsy excuses that Greene usually offered for being in strange places at strange times. He was only a restless traveler, he said, looking for an escape from his chronic sense of boredom. Or he was curious to see a new place. Or he was merely looking for something new to write about.

But Fussell was correct about the hints. They are everywhere in Greene's autobiographical writings. He says that he went to Estonia in May 1934 for a fortnight's holiday, having flown there in a small airplane from Latvia. For a relatively obscure young novelist with limited funds and a wife and new baby at home, this was a most unusual—and costly—holiday spot. When he was on his way back to England, a revolution broke out in the capital of Latvia while he was wasting time waiting for a train at the central station, and he claims not to have seen a thing. A number of years later, he wrote a film treatment for a spy drama set in Estonia in the 1930s, although he never tried to explain why he would connect the subject of espionage with his innocent springtime holiday in lovely Estonia.

The pattern was the same in 1948, when he showed up in Prague just in time for the Communist overthrow of the government. He had been in Vienna gathering material for the screenplay of *The Third Man* and said he found himself in Prague "quite by accident." He was headed to Rome, but it seems that the only way he could fly from Vienna to Rome was by way of Prague. And there had been no reason to suspect trouble in the city, because the Austrian papers had given him no warning of it. All this sounds plausible if you assume that Greene, whose knowledge of German was slight, would be getting his news from Austrian papers rather than from Continental editions of English papers, which were full of news about the growing crisis in the Czech capital. Or that the only way to reach Rome was to begin by flying almost 200 miles in the opposite direction. A train journey would have been better.

It should be obvious that his story is false, but if anyone had said so while he was still living, Greene would have come up with all sorts of convincing denials, and his loyal defenders would have expressed their indignation at such "baseless speculation." The cherished myth of Greene's lucky adventures was worth a stout defense. Nevertheless, he was being deceptive, and there is hard evidence to prove it in this case. It can be found in his correspondence with the woman he loved at the time, Catherine Walston. She saved everything, including over a thousand letters from Greene. In the ones that he sent from Vienna, he tells her a week ahead of his departure that he is going to Prague and makes it clear that he intends to spend several days there. He also communicates the hope that the revolution will not take place before he arrives.

Was it really necessary to lie about this visit? The letters do not explain why he wanted to keep his intentions secret, but if he intended to go as a spy, it made sense to arrive in the easy disguise of the globetrotting writer just passing through. That was exactly the disguise he adopted on his first trip to French Indochina, in 1951, although he pushed the limits of credibility to the extreme on that occasion. He traveled to the country after a long visit to Malaya, where his brother Hugh was helping perpetuate British colonial rule as the head of the psychological warfare campaign against Communist rebels. According to Greene, he added Hanoi to his itinerary because he wanted to visit an old friend on the way home. It was several hundred miles out of his way, but the thing that made the French colonial authorities suspicious was the identity of his friend, Trevor Wilson. Officially, Wilson was the British consul in Hanoi. Most of his time, however, was devoted to his job as station chief for SIS, and several of his actions had caused the French to keep a close eye on him. He and Greene had served together as wartime intelligence officers, and the French were aware of this connection, partly because Wilson had worked with their forces in Algeria during the war. They did not interfere with Greene during his first trip, but when he returned to the country later in the year, the Sûreté did their best to follow him—sometimes with comic effect.

The list of Greene's questionable visits could go on and on—Moscow, Warsaw, East Berlin, Bucharest, Havana, Belgrade. Long before air travel was affordable for ordinary people, he was accumulating thousands of air miles each year dashing from one foreign capital to the next. In 1957 alone his journeys covered, according to his own estimate, 44,000 miles. He seemed to be always on the move, and, after years of such traveling, he surprised no one by showing up in the most unlikely places. It is little wonder that, by the end of the 1950s, he had an impressively large collection of those miniature alcohol bottles distributed on commercial flights. Journalistic assignments covered some of his expenses, but such frequent flying required a more generous kind of backing. At least one patron was the organization that Greene privately called "the best travel agency in the world"—the Secret Intelligence Service.

Thanks to a new spirit of openness about certain intelligence matters, the British Cabinet Office agreed in 1993 to give me a briefing based on the records of Greene's service with SIS. The decision was taken following my approach to Mr. William Waldegrave, MP, who had—in August 1992—invited historians and researchers to identify particular closed government records to which they would value greater access.

As the briefing confirmed, Greene joined SIS in 1941—in July, to be exact—and was officially known as Officer 59200, the same code number given to Wormold's immediate superior in *Our Man in Havana*. He held a position in Section V, the unit responsible for counterespionage. After spending fourteen frustrating months as a station chief in West Africa, he came back to England and worked directly under a future defector to the Soviet Union—Kim Philby—at the Section V office. He resigned his position as an officer of the secret service on May 9, 1944, but did not cut all his ties with the old firm. He continued to serve SIS informally until the early 1980s. In exchange for expenses he gave his help to the organization in many places—most notably, Vietnam, Poland, China, and Russia. And whether a particular trip was funded by SIS or not, he routinely gave its officers information from his foreign visits when he believed it might be useful.

From the 1950s until the late 1970s, one of his close contacts in the service was Maurice Oldfield, who became the director general in 1973. At the time Greene first visited Trevor Wilson in Vietnam, Oldfield was helping supervise intelligence operations in the Far East from an office in Singapore. Among other things Greene was used to recruit local agents during his trips to Vietnam and Laos. With people such as Oldfield, it was easy to make arrangements for assisting the service. Over lunch or a drink, Greene could report on anything that he found of interest or could get instructions for a job that needed doing. A great deal of this work was done without putting anything on paper for the official records and without mentioning Greene by name as an operative. But that was certainly the way he preferred to manage things, keeping clear of the bureaucracy and remaining free to come and go as he pleased. It is worth finishing the Balzac sentence Greene quoted in *The Spy's Bedside Book:* "The trade of the spy is a very fine one, when the spy is working on his own account."

Often Greene's main contact was not even an officer of the service but another independent operative. In the early postwar years this contact was primarily the filmmaker Alexander Korda, who had a long history of helping the secret service. The evidence of their connection is revealed primarily in unofficial sources. In September 1951, for example, Greene wrote to Catherine Walston that Korda had approached him, on behalf of the service, to undertake an unspecified mission, and that a meeting was being arranged to brief him. This appears to have been related to Greene's earlier stay in Vietnam, because within two months of the briefing he was back in Vietnam and remained there for several weeks. The following summer he and Korda joined forces for a boyish adventure as seagoing spies in the Adriatic. Using ample supplies of cash from the secret service, they cruised along the Yugoslav coast in the filmmaker's yacht, *Elsewhere,* and made detailed photographs of several strategic points. As part of their cover, they had some "innocent" guests onboard, including the distinguished chairman of the CBS television network, William Paley, and his wife, Babe.

Details about Korda's espionage work have been slow to emerge, but they make an intriguing story and help to explain some mysteries about Greene's activities. Although he won considerable fame and fortune from such film productions as *The Private Life of Henry VIII* (1933), *Things to Come* (1936), and *The Third Man,* Korda had a secret fascination for the backstage world of power politics and was eager to play some part in it. With a big studio and a cast of international stars at his command, he found it easy to win friends and influence people in high places. It also helped that he was willing to put big political names on the payroll for doing little or no work. Winston Churchill was his most famous employee. The great man was supposedly used as a scriptwriter, but none of his work ended up on the screen. Credit was given, however, to Sir Robert Vansittart—the former permanent undersecretary at the Foreign Office—for a most improbable contribution: song lyrics for the soundtrack of *The Thief of Bagdad* (1940). Korda became so carried away with this kind of generosity that his payroll included, at one time, the sons of three former or future prime ministers—Anthony Asquith, Randolph Churchill, and Oliver Stanley.

Having friends in high places was good for business. Korda's London Films company received an enormous amount of investment capital from Prudential Assurance, which was pressured into making the commitment by Conservative politicians. This money, in turn, enabled Korda to serve the interests of the British Empire by creating a series of imperial epics—*Sanders of the River* (1935), *The Drum* (1938), and *The Four Feathers* (1939). And the great public appeal of these well-financed films helped to make Korda the most famous, and most powerful, British filmmaker of the 1930s. He was everything a great movie mogul is supposed to be—brash, brilliant, cunning, and extravagant. "He really wanted to be Prince Metternich," Orson Welles said of Korda, "and he was better casting for it than Prince Metternich himself."

In the best Metternich tradition, Korda enjoyed spying and was eager to help his powerful friends keep an eye on the world. Equally eager to employ him was the redoubtable figure of Col. Claude Dansey, the wartime deputy director of SIS. The far-flung empire of London Films provided some of Dansey's agents with suitable cover for their intelligence work, and Dansey himself eventually became a director of his friend's company. Before America entered the war, Korda used his resources to help one of Dansey's men—William Stephenson—set up an office in New York for gathering intelligence. Partly in recognition of his assistance to British Security Coordination, as the New York office was called, Korda was knighted in 1942. It was also said that he had helped to prepare the way for the Allied invasion of North Africa by using a "bogus" film project to photograph long sections of the North African coastline.

Greene did some film work for Korda before the war, but they did not get to know each other well until 1947–48, when Korda's company made *The Fallen Idol* from Greene's screenplay. At one point in the 1930s, when he was writing a regular column on the cinema for *The Spectator,* Greene was perhaps the harshest critic of Korda's films and seemed to relish opportunities to ridicule new productions. But Korda worked persistently to win the writer's friendship, and it may have been Colonel Dansey who helped bring them closer together. Not long after the colonel's death, Greene took over a flat at 5 St. James's Street that Dansey had used as a favorite hideaway. His move into this place provides a good illustration of the tight circle into which Greene had been drawn. Before Dansey took the flat, it had belonged to his agent—and Korda's associate—William Stephenson (better known as the Man Called Intrepid). And three decades later it served as the model for the St. James's Street home of Greene's fictional spymaster Colonel Daintry in *The Human Factor,* where it is described as a place Daintry "found through the agency of another member of the firm."

Greene's visit to Prague in 1948—ostensibly a scouting trip for Korda's production of *The Third Man*—is an excellent example of the kind of spying he was able to do for the secret service. As the Korda archives at the British Film Institute show, Greene's travel arrangements to Vienna and Prague were made by an employee of London Films named Col. John Codrington. He was expert at cutting through travel restrictions imposed by the British government after the war and made sure that Korda's people had all the documents and currency they needed for overseas travel. This is not surprising because he had also been one of Dansey's top agents and knew the right strings to pull. Dansey had arranged Codrington's employment at London Films in the 1930s, and, apparently, the cover worked for many years.

Likewise, Greene's own cover was perfect for his adventure in Prague. Because he was a novelist of growing international prominence, and a writer on assignment for the great Alexander Korda, his ramblings were unlikely to raise suspicion, even during a crisis. He could pretend to be a harmless author, not a spy, and could easily be forgiven for wandering the streets in search of local color or of some curious literary connection that only he could appreciate. And there were publishers who wanted to see him, writers who wanted to discuss their works with him, admiring Catholics who wanted him to sign books. With so many reasonable excuses available, he could go almost anywhere and talk his way out of tight spots. Such freedom allowed him to do any number of valuable tasks for his employers back home—deliver messages and receive them, interview dissidents, recruit local contacts, identify the strengths and weaknesses of various factions, report on security measures.

Greene was especially helpful to the service in the 1950s. He was in regular contact with Rodney Dennys, Maurice Oldfield, and other important officers, such as Nicholas Elliott. In 1952 Greene wrote to Elliott proposing a rendezvous in Austria with a mysterious Hungarian woman, and in the same year he volunteered to spy during a visit to Finland. "He would be glad to help us in Finland in any way he can," an officer of the service noted at the time, although the methods and objectives of Greene's missions were not always specific. By the 1950s SIS had dealt with him often enough to know how and when his literary "cover" could be put to good use. Before the novelist's trip to Vietnam in 1955, an officer briefed him on the intelligence requirements in the area. The opinion seemed to be that Greene was amateurish but useful. He was described as adopting a dilettante approach to spying while remaining an enterprising and unconventional traveler whose visits to Indochina proved of assistance to the local station. Regarding his proposed visit to Finland, another SIS officer observed that Greene's assistance did not come free: "Bear in mind the fact that he would certainly wish to be remunerated for any out-of-pocket expenses. Despite the money he makes out of making the great British public worry about its soul, he is extremely mercenary."

One of Greene's most interesting missions in the 1950s was to spy on the Catholic Pax organization in Poland, which was Soviet backed. The ultimate purpose of Pax seems to have been to create divisions in the Polish Church. Greene was invited to visit Poland in November 1955, and although officials of Pax assumed that he wanted to see their good work in behalf of Catholicism, he was in fact reporting all the details of his contacts to SIS. The service asked him to keep in touch through the embassy in Warsaw and stressed that his main mission was to gather "the views of as many individuals as he [could] obtain"—views that might illuminate the depth of Soviet control over life and religion in Poland.

Greene made four trips to Moscow in the late 1950s, and there is evidence to suggest that he was working on each occasion for SIS. As Nicholas Elliott later acknowledged in an interview, Greene was always willing to keep his eyes open on behalf of the service and to suggest valuable contacts. During the Second World War, the official sources offer a great deal of information about his operations. For the postwar period, exact details are harder to obtain, with a few fascinating exceptions—most notably, his work with Trevor Wilson in Vietnam and a solo mission to China in 1957. Both these adventures will be taken up later chapters. Greene was by no means an important figure in the world of espionage, and most of his help was simply providing a novelist's insight into places where ordinary agents might not be allowed. He was indeed a dilettante, but he could play the game well when he wanted to, and it is abundantly clear that SIS valued him as an informant.

Perhaps the real significance of Greene's long relationship with SIS is that it calls into question his image as a trusted friend of international socialism. As his literary fame grew, and as his anti-American comments increased, Greene found it easier to gain access to such leaders as Fidel Castro, Ho Chi Minh, and Gen. Omar Torrijos. He was able to learn a great deal from these visits that might have been of interest to Maurice Oldfield and other old friends in the service. His cover was so good that none of the dictators seemed to suspect him of being anything besides a friendly literary man with a soft spot for their style of political leadership. He informed SIS of his interview with Ho in 1955, and there is every reason to believe that he passed along information about his meetings with Castro and Torrijos.

People who knew him well were not so ready to accept his carefully developed cover. "[Greene] is a great one for practical jokes," Evelyn Waugh wrote to a friend in 1960. "I think also he is a secret agent on our side and all his buttering up of the Russians is 'cover.' " Waugh knew that his friend had shown little interest in the Left when they were younger and had, in fact, been associated with men who favored the Right. The principal investor in Greene's magazine *Night and Day* was Victor Cazalet, Conservative member of Parliament, who was busy in the late 1930s defending Franco. In the very month that the magazine was incorporated, Cazalet was campaigning widely for the British public to rally to Franco's cause, declaring, "I . . . trust and pray that General Franco will win a victory for civilisation over Bolshevism." In the mid-1940s Greene spent four years as Douglas Jerrold's deputy at the publishing house of Eyre & Spottiswoode. Jerrold had also been a prominent British apologist for Franco, calling him "an ardent Christian . . . fighting for social justice." During the time that Greene worked for him, Jerrold continued to fight for his faith in what one of the directors of Eyre & Spottiswoode proudly called "real Toryism." In 1945 Greene told his mother that he planned to vote for the Tory candidate in the general election, and he spoke contemptuously of the Socialists.

In the 1950s Greene suddenly changed. He began spending a lot of time with Communists, visiting the Soviet Union, and arranging clandestine meetings with Castro's supporters in the last days of Batista's rule. In the early 1960s he received a guided tour of the recently completed Berlin Wall from one of its East German guards. After returning from this last trip, Greene praised the improving conditions of life in East Germany and criticized the materialistic people who went over the wall simply to be able to buy more consumer goods. Coming from a man with a villa in Anacapri, this criticism may have sounded hollow, but such remarks were certain to make it even easier to return for another close inspection of the wall's defenses.

Criticizing America was much more fun than praising Communists, and it was just as effective in establishing Greene's credentials as someone sympathetic to victims of American imperialism. The foreign policy blunders of successive American governments made them easy targets for Greene's wit, and much of his criticism was not only accurate but full of conviction. *The Quiet American* is a devastatingly precise prediction of the way self-righteous American champions of democracy would create havoc in Vietnam. Unfortunately, the Americans who should have read the novel were probably put off by the high praise the Soviet press gave it. *Pravda* called its publication "the most remarkable event" in recent British literary history. American newspapers and magazines reacted with outrage that the British novelist had won favor in Russia for portraying a young American patriot as a dangerous meddler. To combat this kind of Communist propaganda, the *Saturday Evening Post* took off the gloves and gave the author its toughest punch: "Graham Greene is an opium smoker, and some readers may wonder whether the preposterous statements in his book came to him in a pipe dream." Of course, it helped Greene that neither his Russian champions nor his American critics knew that his experiences in Vietnam were partly funded by the British secret service.

III

Greene was always finding new ways to create some useful confusion about his political views. The high point in this game came in 1967, when he announced in a letter to *The Times* that, if the choice had to be made between living in the Soviet Union or living in the United States, he would take the Soviets. The pleasure of making such a statement lay in the knowledge that it would cause rumblings in all the right places but that it would never have to be put to the test. For this resident of Antibes, who was unlikely to end up in Omaha or Odessa against his will, it was like saying, "Forced to choose between going to Venus or going to Mars, I would choose Mars." Instead of laughing at such a wild idea, various pundits tried to explain why the author preferred the simple virtues of communism to the harsh realities of capitalism.

The writer Mervyn Jones got a more accurate view of Greene's preferences when he ran into him a few weeks after the controversial statement was published. Greene was in a Jerusalem hotel sharing a drink with an old colleague from SIS, Malcolm Muggeridge, when Jones was asked to join them. As Greene sipped a glass of whiskey, Jones asked whether he was serious about choosing the Soviet Union over America: "'God forbid that I'd ever have to live in either,' he said, but Malcolm declared that he was dodging the question. A gleam was discernible in his pale blue eyes. 'Well,' he said, 'if I lived in the Soviet Union I'd be able to smuggle my books out, like Solzhenitsyn. That would be worth it, wouldn't it?' "

For the next twenty years, people kept asking about his statement, and he grew weary of making up new explanations. It was like being forced to tell the same joke over and over again. The main purpose of his original letter deserves comment, however, because it was anti-Soviet. He was trying to protest the imprisonment of two Soviet writers, whose cases genuinely interested him, but, to avoid seeming too critical, he added the false compliment about Soviet life and explained that his protest was motivated by his "affection" for the country. He was doing his best to be the well-intentioned, but independent, comrade. The Russians may not have been impressed, but that sort of ambiguity did not hurt Greene's image in the increasingly important battleground of the Third World.

It was only a year after publication of *The Times* letter that he gave his important speech "The Virtue of Disloyalty," and that year also saw his highly sympathetic introduction to Kim Philby's memoir, *My Silent War*. "Buttering up the Soviets" was an understandable ploy for a spy such as Greene, but his open enthusiasm for disloyalty, and for the virtues of his treacherous ex-chief, was guaranteed to raise a few suspicions about the loyalty of old 59200. In fact, he was carefully interrogated after Philby defected to Moscow in 1963, and, although the head of the internal investigation felt that Greene knew more about Philby's treason than he would admit, he was cleared of any complicity in the case.

Greene's relationship with Philby will be taken up in greater detail in a later chapter, but it is fair to speculate at this stage on whether Greene also played the double agent in his work for SIS. As a British spy, he was never important enough to be a major risk, but he could have made some real trouble—or conspired to let others make it—if he had wanted to. Morality would not have stopped him. The comments on Philby in Greene's introduction reinforce this notion, because he specifically rules out "moral judgments," explaining that they "are singularly out of place in espionage." Defending Philby was not an abstract game. People died because of Philby's treachery, yet Greene was ready to seek some rationalization for their deaths. Dismissing the phrase "He sent men to their deaths" as a cliché, he argues that Philby's actions were no worse than those of any battle commander. The analogy is shaky, however; most commanders do not make a habit of shooting their men in the back.

Although he grants Philby the virtue of "serving a cause and not himself," he says almost nothing about the nature of that commitment. What fascinated Greene was not the loyalty to another "cause" but the "craftsman's pride" with which Philby managed his intricate plan of deception. It is almost as though he regarded his former boss as a kind of novelist who was expert at spinning plots and subplots in all directions while managing to make everything conform to a grand outline.

The novelist as double agent was a favorite analogy for Greene. He wanted to suggest that all good makers of fiction are practiced deceivers who sustain suspense by constantly betraying readers' expectations. And he also meant that novelists must betray their characters, creating the illusion of life for them, then wrestling to keep them within the overall design, even when that design dictates their deaths. "Killing off a character" was a phrase that Greene took to heart. The more "real" the character becomes, the harder it is to carry out the necessary execution.

These imaginary betrayals were real enough to Greene, who spent so much of his life painstakingly building his fictional worlds. There was no reason to avoid betraying something as imaginary as the State. The idea of Great Britain—as opposed to the reality of friends in London or family in the country—never seemed to matter much to him, and, after he left it for the warmth of the Mediterranean, he always liked to say that the only things he really missed were English sausages and beer. After twenty-five years of living abroad, he chose to be buried abroad as well, in the superbly neutral ground of Switzerland.

This less than honorable schoolboy of Berkhamsted—this young quisling, to use his term—grew to love what he called "spying for spying's sake." He did not care for countries or politics, no matter how often he may have pretended to. His concerns were always much more fundamental, much closer to the things that drive individual lives—fear, hate, love, revenge, greed, pity, pride, faith, doubt. These are the things that he understood, and for any of these basics he could have justified the sacrifice of patriotism, as indeed he does in the novel inspired by Philby's case, *The Human Factor*. His common theme is the "rage of personality," a phrase he borrowed from Henry James, and it has nothing to do with establishing political commitments or upholding social responsibilities. It is about the blinding, uncontrollable pull that all those awkward human factors exert on some lives, the force that makes it impossible for the "personality" to sustain any connection beyond itself. Loyalty is like an infection that such a person must fight off or succumb to. Thus the warning from Joseph Conrad in the epigraph to *The Human Factor:* "I only know that he who forms a tie is lost. The germ of corruption has entered into his soul."

The whole truth about Greene's spying can never be known, but the important thing to establish here is its deep influence on the way that he approached the real world and his fictional one. More evidence from both worlds will be considered in later chapters, and perhaps the combination of the two will produce the best "hint of an explanation." But if the key lies anywhere, it is in Greene's fiction. Like all good literature, his work is a code for readers to decipher, except that in his case the code was the work of a trained professional. Part of his routine as an intelligence officer in West Africa was to prepare coded messages for transmission to his superiors, and he worked tirelessly to give them his special literary touch. Struggling to find an artful use for an odd word on his secret list—"eunuch"—he came up with this terse message: "As the chief eunuch said I cannot repeat cannot come." (In later years this was one of Maurice Oldfield's favorite anecdotes about Greene.)

Greene's pleasure in creating messages that might amuse only him can be seen in his affectionate portrait of modest Wormold laboring over the book that serves as his code source—a copy of Charles and Mary Lamb's *Tales from Shakespeare*. As he gets the hang of the game, Wormold is overwhelmed by the fun of it all and cannot resist the chance to work his message into these appropriate words from

Twelfth Night: "But I will draw the curtain and show the picture. Is it not well done?" The code here is a double one; it also alerts the reader that Greene is busy encoding messages and that we would do well to attend closely to the words passing rapidly before our eyes.

Greene's books explain him better than anything else. The problem for the reader is to focus on them with the same intensity that he brought to writing them. And nothing can ever be taken for granted. With this particular author, cover stories are an art form.

CHAPTER THREE

SECRET GARDEN

Henry Graham Greene took a special interest in the uncle who shared his middle name. Sir William Graham Greene hovered in the distant background of his nephew's life for almost half a century. A lifelong bachelor, he served the Admiralty faithfully for thirty-six years, and his reward was a long, exceedingly comfortable retirement at his country home, Harston House, in Cambridgeshire. The old fellow seemed indestructible. At the age of eighty-nine, he fell under a train but escaped serious injury by lying flat against the ground while the cars passed over him. Undaunted, he brushed himself off and continued his journey, later explaining to his nephew that "the chief interest of the experience was the opportunity to view a . . . train from a completely novel angle." Several months later he survived a fall from a tree after trying to cut down a branch. When death came at last, in 1950, he was ninety-three, and it was a chair that dealt the final blow, tripping him up on his lawn.

His beloved Harston House passed to another family but not before his nephew had given serious consideration to buying it. The place greatly appealed to Graham, and not merely because it held memories of a venerable relation. Throughout most of his childhood he had spent his annual summer holidays at the house and had found some rare moments of happiness playing in its lush garden, which was protected by a tall brick wall. There was a special walk shaded by thick laurel bushes, and beyond it lay an orchard and a pond with a tiny island in the middle. The garden was large enough to serve as an excellent setting for a favorite game that he would take to a higher level of play in adulthood, hide-and-seek. And, naturally, he was also fond of making long imaginary journeys to the wild places of the earth, using the orchard and the untidy little pond as convenient substitutes for Africa, India, and the American West.

Best of all, Harston was the one spot on earth where he was able to enjoy an extended holiday from his father. After the long months of work, Charles welcomed a chance for some vigorous outdoor activity in the Lake District or on the Continent. His wife and younger children were packed off to Harston. Sir William would usually spend the summer elsewhere, so the only adult with the authority to impose serious restrictions on Graham's pleasure was his mother. And she was a relatively lax guardian. Her husband's values were not unlike her own, but she lacked his enthusiasm for spying. She was an aloof, fastidious woman who preferred not to delve into the less pleasant aspects of life. As a mother she was more courteous than loving. As long as her children were not causing too much disruption to the orderly arrangement of her world, she was content to leave them to the care of their nanny or other family servants.

Looking back on his early childhood, Greene described his mother's occasional appearances in the nursery as "state visits." One of Graham's cousins recalled that Marion Greene could easily intimidate children: she was "very awe inspiring, very tall, very dignified and rather frightening." But since she kept her distance so much of the time, Graham was able to enjoy more freedom, and, as he grew older, he came not only to appreciate her remoteness but to respect her sedate charm. While his father always seemed to be looking for faults, his mother gave him a mild sense of acceptance, simply by not being too intrusive. He received little in the way of warmth from her—no impulsive hugs and kisses—but he claimed in later life that this did not bother him. It was enough that she made so few demands. Yet it is also true that there is a hint of resentment in his public comments about her, a feeling that her help was missing when it was needed most and that she was intolerant of anything outside her narrow view of life.

In the spaciousness of Harston and its grounds, Graham could easily disappear and pretend that he was entirely on his own—something impossible to do in the busy environment of his father's school. His favorite fantasy was that the whole place belonged to him, and he enjoyed getting to know every inch of "his" terrain. When his mother tried to recruit a special playmate for him one summer, he was not pleased, regarding the visitor as an intruder on his sacred ground. The chief merit of the place was that it offered solitude. In time, his brother Hugh became a trusted companion, and the two found several ways to create the kind of mischief that would have been unthinkable at Berkhamsted. One of their favorite pranks was to hide all the chamber pots in the house. A parlor maid of the time—Mrs. Rivers—remembered having to keep up a constant search for missing chamber pots, occasionally finding a full one that had been sitting at the back of a cupboard for a day or two.

More productive exercises also engaged Graham. It was at Harston that he learned to read a complete book on his own, and the importance of that feat would always give the place a magical quality in his imagination. He made the breakthrough by retiring to a secret spot in the attic and carefully deciphering the pages of his chosen text, *Dixon Brett, Detective*. The thrill of making meanings from all those new words on each page was so great that he wanted to keep his skill a secret, as though the pleasure would be even greater if he practiced it only on the sly. It was also a way of enjoying the freedom to choose what he read. As soon as his father discovered his skill, he would have to begin reading all the things that were supposed to be good for him, and no doubt the headmaster would not give him anything half as stimulating as *Dixon Brett, Detective*.

He found an odd sort of freedom in killing things. Told to find snails in the garden and dispose of them, he carried out his mission with considerable zest. He put them in a bucket, poured salt on them, and watched them turn into foam. For every hundred snails he destroyed, he received a small amount of money. There was also cash to be had from eliminating cabbage white butterflies. These killing sprees gave him such satisfaction that he made a great game out of them in adulthood. During his wartime stay in Sierra Leone, he enjoyed a "glorious" slaughter when he managed to kill more than 300 flies in four minutes. Everyone hates flies, but it takes a special person to time a mass murder of the pests, and then to do a body count. According to Malcolm Muggeridge, Greene also liked to buy ant farms and wipe them out with boiling water.

With no hint of irony, Greene recalls in his autobiography that, on one occasion in childhood, he tried "very hard to kill" his older brother Raymond. His chosen weapon was a croquet mallet, and his method of attack was to strike a blow on Raymond's skull. For the most part, however, he preferred not to cause serious bodily harm to blood relatives. Throughout his early years his brothers and sisters and cousins were practically his only playmates. He was always overly suspicious of outsiders, and there were more than enough young Greenes to keep him entertained when he felt the need for company. He later boasted that the Greene children could be entirely self-sufficient. "We didn't need anyone else," he claimed.

Besides Hugh, his great friend in the family was uncle Edward's son "Tooter" Greene. The two boys played with tin soldiers and clockwork trains, and shared fantasies of becoming explorers or military heroes. They collected stamps together, and for real excitement they would climb up to the roof of Edward Greene's big house in Berkhamsted and sit for hours surveying the landscape. They played games on the lawn—often with the other children in the family—and at Christmas all the Greenes came together for a long celebration, eating big meals and amusing themselves with charades and musical chairs. On such occasions Graham could let down his guard, at least among the children.

But nothing could match the pleasure of being alone at Harston. There he was free to ponder his troubles in silence and to imagine all kinds of escapes from the tyranny of adults and the disappointments of school life. Although he was careful to guard his privacy at Harston, he did find one adult whose company he enjoyed. This was Sir William's gardener, Ernest Northrop, who was in his thirties when Graham knew him best. An oil portrait of Northrop painted by one of Sir William's sisters still hangs in Harston House and shows him with a rugged but friendly face. Northrop and his wife, who was the cook, spent most of their working lives in Sir William's employ and were still serving him at the time of his death. As much as Graham liked to think that the garden was his personal territory, he knew that Ernest Northrop was the real master of it and was happy to learn its mysteries from him. No doubt it was also refreshing to spend time with an adult who was unconnected with any aspect of schoolteaching. In fact, Northrop was young Graham's only meaningful contact with an ordinary working man.

In 1952, when he was a well-established novelist, Greene returned to Harston to see how the place was doing under its new owners and decided to pay a call on his old friend Ernest. He brought along Catherine Walston's sister, Bonté, who was staying nearby. Before they went to the gardener's little cottage, Greene took Bonté on a brief guided tour of the garden, showing her the pond, the "Dark Walk" with its laurel bushes, the "caves of vines," all of which still seemed to retain an air of mystery from his childhood adventures.

When they reached Ernest's place, both husband and wife came out to welcome Greene with obvious "joy" in their faces, according to Bonté's memory of the visit. It was clear that they regarded him as one of their family, and Greene himself seemed remarkably at ease in their company.

Ernest Northrop died several years after this visit and would rate scant attention were it not for the fact that he is the key to a major obsession in Greene's work, and an important missing link in the novelist's biography. The loyal old gardener has never been mentioned by name in any biographical commentary on Greene, and the only place where Greene refers directly to him is in the short story "Under the Garden," which was first published in 1963. In that work Northrop is used a model for Javitt, the most bizarre figure in all Greene's fiction. The tale is full of clues about Greene's life and illustrates how the "real" stories he told about himself may be less reliable than the encoded messages of his fiction.

The main character in "Under the Garden"—William Wilditch—is a middle-aged man whose occupation is vaguely described as gathering "facts." He is a spy of a sort who has wandered the world doing odd jobs for anyone who wants information—governments, newspapers, corporations. When he is stricken with a serious lung problem, he seeks a peaceful retreat at Winton Hall, the country home that an old bachelor uncle used to loan out to Wilditch's mother for summer holidays. The place is now owned by a brother, who puts him up in a room where a lot of old books and papers from their childhood are gathering dust. In this collection he discovers a short story that he wrote in his teens about finding buried treasure on the island of Winton Hall's garden pond. Reading it after the passage of so many years, he is ashamed that he had falsified the real events of the adventure, which were much more outrageous than he could have described at the time to his school and family audience. What he had given them was only a "cover story," as he calls it, so he resolves to write out the true version one night, and the result occupies most of Greene's tale.

Wilditch claims that what he really discovered was a cave under the island, inhabited by a filthy, one-legged, garrulous old man whose only bed is a pile of potato sacks and whose chair is a lavatory seat. The man's sole companion is his wife, who spends most of her time preparing the regular supply of broth that he slurps from a dog's bowl. He goes by a name that he admits is false—Javitt—and fires a steady barrage of questions and comments at young Wilditch, who is both terrified and enchanted by him. "Forget all your schoolmasters," he shouts and launches into mini-lectures on the beauty of cats, the relation of time to "fucking," the correct way to fold a newspaper, the sexy smell of fish, and the working of his bowels. Javitt is everything that Wilditch's very proper mother would disapprove of, but the more the young boy listens to him, the more he likes what he hears. Although some things sound like wisdom and others like nonsense, the overall effect is intoxicating—a display of verbal fireworks that the boy cannot resist.

It hardly matters whether the boy understands Javitt's wild words. The pleasure comes from simply listening to a voice that is so uninhibited, so free from the cool restraint, the boring rectitude of parents and schoolteachers. Many of Javitt's remarks are unashamedly scatological, and the boy is delighted to hear the forbidden word *shit* used openly. As the perfect souvenir for his young visitor, Javitt offers a golden chamber pot but advises the boy to say that it was discovered accidentally in "an old cupboard"—a joke inspired, no doubt, by Greene's own youthful game of leaving smelly surprises for the Harston maids.

However unsavory his appearance and surroundings may be, Javitt is the complete master of his small kingdom under the garden, and he takes pride in surviving on his own terms. In freedom he has found enough beauty to compensate for his ugly features, and that beauty is embodied in the appropriately elusive figure of his lovely daughter, who roams the larger world above and whose photographs capture the boy's heart. He vows to spend his life in search of her, and Javitt gives him unusually clear advice on how to find this free spirit. The main thing, he says, is to survive, and that means following one basic rule: "Be disloyal." Under no circumstances can any concessions be made to authority. "If you have to earn a living, boy, and the price they make you pay is loyalty, be a double agent." With these words in mind, the boy begins his long search for freedom by suddenly deserting his strange host. He waits for him to fall asleep, quietly ties the old man's hands, and makes his getaway. But not before Javitt has awakened and smiled with approval. "You're learning fast," he says.

After finishing this account of his childhood adventure, Wilditch finds that he has spent all night working on his story, and, as he looks up from his desk, he hears a familiar sound in the morning air. His uncle's gardener, Ernest, is pushing a wheelbarrow down the gravel path leading to the garden. Although he wants to believe his story really happened, he sees that his image of the subterranean king is the sort of fantasy that a child might weave around the figure of the kindly gardener, whose manner and appearance immediately suggest a more subdued and respectable version of Javitt. The result of his overnight labor is a tale that is true, but only in the sense of re-creating faithfully a childhood dream that had scrambled and exaggerated various bits and pieces of reality. The basis of the dream becomes clearer when Wilditch goes down to renew his acquaintance with the gardener and hears echoes of Javitt's words in Ernest's conversation. Moreover, he is reminded that his mother disapproved of the gardener's independent ways and that the wild look of the garden offended her sense of propriety. "Too much shrubbery," she complained. So much thick shrubbery gave the young Wilditch a world like Javitt's, a special escape "under the garden." And whenever his mother could not find him, it was always Ernest who had been able to locate his hiding places. When the "missus" was not pestering the gardener about filling more sacks of potatoes for the kitchen, she was pestering him to keep track of the boy.

By returning to the place where he first learned the trick of surviving on his own, Wilditch is vaguely searching for something to revive his spirits in the face of advancing age and declining health. But the visit only adds to his sense of unease. Ernest is not the magical hero of the dream—he simply tended the garden that helped to create the boy's illusion of freedom. Wilditch taught himself the lesson of disloyalty, and he cannot help wondering whether it was a lesson worth learning. It helped him survive but did not free him from anything. The past still has him firmly in its grip, as he demonstrates by trying so hard to recapture old scenes from childhood. All his years of wandering have only brought him back to the place where his wandering began.

Wilditch's doubts started with his health problems—a bad bout of pneumonia from which he was slow to recover and a lingering suspicion that he might develop lung cancer. Like his fictional creation, Greene suffered these problems in his middle age. They began in 1960, when he came down with a nasty case of double pneumonia after returning from one of his visits to Moscow. He collapsed at home in London and required an ambulance. For two weeks he was confined to a hospital bed and was later subjected to a painful bronchoscopy because his doctors feared that he might have lung cancer. The medical procedure allowed examination of his lungs through the use of a long metal instrument inserted down his throat. It is described in grim detail at the beginning of "Under the Garden."

Among other things fiction offers writers a convenient way of telling the truth without having to admit it, and Greene was never willing to admit that he shared Wilditch's sentimental attachment to a magic garden. Of course, their cases are not identical. If anything Greene's attachment to Harston was much greater than the story suggests. In book after book he found a reason to include one or more aspects of the garden. As he pointed out to Bonté on their visit, Harston provided the model for the garden of the sanatorium in *The Ministry of Fear* (1943). The red brick wall, the orchard, the pond, and the island—they are all in the novel. Even Ernest makes a brief appearance as the unnamed gardener who is often heard in the distance pushing his wheelbarrow along the paths. Ernest also pops up in the early pages of Greene's first novel. Andrews, the main character in *The Man Within,* recalls a family gardener who kept him entertained in childhood with odd stories about seeds turning into "winkle dust" and about the smell of pine coffins coming up from old graveyards.

This is a lot of trouble to go to simply for the sake of honoring a childhood memory. Giving cameo parts to a favorite gardener may have amused the novelist, but what does it do for the novels? It is tempting to conclude that the magic garden and its overseer are merely good-luck charms that the superstitious novelist threw into the books at random, but their purpose is more substantial than that, and the clue to Greene's intentions can be found in another object from Harston. That object is conspicuously absent from Wilditch's tale but is present in both *The Ministry of Fear* and *The Man Within.* It is the small potting shed where Ernest kept all his tools and supplies and where—the evidence suggests—young Graham Greene put a cord around his neck and ended his life. Or would have done, if Ernest had not intervened.

II

The exact reasons for Greene's suicidal feelings will be discussed in the next chapter, but it is worth establishing first that he came closer to dying than he ever acknowledged directly. In Greene's case suicide by hanging makes sense—a great deal more sense than suicide by Russian roulette. But it does not make a pretty story, or one that is as dramatic. The limp figure of the hanged man is pathetic, an image of the trembling coward who dies in a dark corner, feet kicking above the overturned chair. A novelist would hesitate to send a hero to such a mean, shameful death. It is much better to take a bullet in the brain, especially for the male of the species, who tends to find a perverse kind of glory in blasting away his skull. This was certainly the preferred method in the adventure stories that Greene devoured as a boy. At the beginning of a tale featuring one of Greene's boyhood idols—Raffles, "the amateur cracksman"—the hero's sidekick bravely responds to financial ruin by preparing to shoot himself in the head. All the details of the scene would have been familiar to Greene, who was so fascinated by Raffles that he later wrote a play about him, *The Return of A. J. Raffles* (1975), and who lived—for a dozen years—at the same fashionable Piccadilly address that Raffles helped to make famous, Albany. Here is the thrilling scene in the chambers at Albany as the desperate friend explains to the reader why he was tempted to shoot himself in front of Raffles:

> The barrel touched my temple, and my thumb the trigger. Mad with excitement as I was, ruined, dishonoured, and now finally determined to make an end of my misspent life, my only surprise to this day is that I did not do so then and there. The despicable satisfaction of involving another in one's destruction added its miserable appeal to my baser egoism; and had fear or horror flown to my companion's face, I shudder to think I might have died diabolically happy with that look for my last impious consolation.

Fortunately, Raffles saves his friend, but this is the kind of talk that would make Russian roulette seem diabolically glamorous to an impressionable boy. There was also the example of a favorite story called "The Suicide Club" (1882), which was the work of Marion Greene's distant cousin Robert Louis Stevenson. Revolvers are not featured in the story, but the members of the Suicide Club play a game that has all the bravado of Russian roulette. They gather regularly at a secret location in London, and their president deals cards to each member—the one who receives the ace of spades must die; the one who gets the ace of clubs must arrange the necessary murder and carry it out. "The trouble of suicide is removed in that way," a member called Mr. Malthus explains, adding that the game also has its "delights," because "it combines the excitement of a gaming-table, a duel and a Roman amphitheatre." Malthus plays the game so infrequently that he is regarded as only an honorary member. "Envy me—envy me, sir," he tells a newcomer. "I am a coward." Greene liked this quotation so much that he went out of his way to mention it in *Lord Rochester's Monkey* and *The Lawless Roads* (1939). As Greene appreciated, the remark is ironic. When the next game is played, Mr. Malthus draws the fatal ace of clubs.

But it is infinitely more exciting to play such a game of chance with a loaded revolver, and this idea also came to Greene from a book, or so he said in later years. He was unsure of the author but thought it might have been someone named Ossendowski. Several years ago the critic Julian Symons went to the trouble of reading Ferdinand Ossendowski's *Beasts, Men and Gods* (1922)—an adventurous tale of "escapes from the Bolsheviks in Siberia and Mongolia after the Russian Revolution." Symons discovered that it was a popular work during the time Greene was supposedly experimenting with his brother's small pistol and that the first part of the book has the promising title "Drawing Lots with Death"—but, alas, Symons found that it contained no stories of Russian roulette.

Whatever the source of inspiration, Greene's tale has all the right ingredients for a good cover story. It makes the confused young man's wish for self-destruction look almost respectable. The hero of Greene's "The Revolver in the Corner Cupboard" is cunning and resourceful, and does not really mean to kill himself. It is simply the rashness of youth that makes him toy with the weapon. Even the melodrama of the situation is tempered by the calm adult voice of the narrator, who looks back on the folly of his youth from the sympathetic but wiser perspective of age. He makes us want not only to believe the story but to share his indulgent view of the boy's reckless spirit.

Nothing could have given Greene a better way to put an acceptable face on an ugly secret and to deflect any interest in uncovering it. Stifling all talk of suicide would have been difficult. Everyone in the family knew about the boy's occasional suicide threats, and rumors were bound to spread. But the sad story of a botched hanging in a dirty potting shed was something that he could never openly acknowledge. There was no way to fashion an acceptable public image out of that. So it made sense, in later years, to boast about the kind of suicide attempt that would do credit to a distant relative of Robert Louis Stevenson. A brave admission about Russian roulette might well put an end to any embarrassing speculation about other possibilities, especially if the tale gave the world what it wanted to hear. In this regard it is worth noting that Wilditch's "cover story"— the earlier, respectable version of his adventures on the island—was inspired by his reading of Stevenson and was called "The Treasure on the Island."

But Greene could not resist the desire to subvert cover stories with coded ones. And so, in the early novels, he began scattering hints of the trauma in the potting shed. In the opening pages of his very first novel, a hunted man is driven to hide in a small structure that resem-

bles a "potting shed," with "a pile of sacking" in one corner. In
Stamboul Train (1932) the wounded Dr. Czinner escapes from his
pursuers to a "shed," where he tries to hide behind piles of "fat
sacks." This trick does not work, and the doctor's place of refuge
becomes his place of execution. In *A Gun for Sale* the wanted criminal Raven hides from the police in a railway workman's "shed" and
tries to keep warm under a blanket of empty sacks. (For good measure, he is accompanied by a woman who will betray him and who
chats with him about a fortune-telling friend who used "those cards
with queer pictures on them. The Hanged Man. . . ." In *Brighton
Rock* Pinkie flees from a rival gang who have slashed his face and
hands, and, with "blood clotting on his neck," he hides briefly in a
garage that served its owner as "a kind of potting shed." In *The
Confidential Agent* (1939) the foreign agent whose name is given
only by the initial D.—in the best manner of Herbert Greene—finds
a temporary hiding place in—where else?—a garden shed.

Like the code in Herbert's *Secret Agent in Spain,* these scattered
references to Harston would have been impossible for any outsider to
understand in the 1930s, assuming that any reader of the time would
have bothered to look for such things in the work of a thriller writer.
It was a secret that could be safely hinted at, like the mysterious references to a woman named Glover in *The Confidential Agent.* Just as
it pleased Greene to find a reason to mention his lover from that
period—Dorothy Glover—so it was mildly exciting to plant a few
clues about a darker secret from the distant past. But in the 1950s,
after the Russian roulette story was safely established, he took the risk
of giving the game away in a play he brazenly called *The Potting Shed*
(1957).

Of course, Greene was always free to deny that there was anything
autobiographical in his play about a middle-aged writer trying to
come to terms with a childhood attempt at suicide. The writer, James
Callifer, has suppressed the event in his memory, and the play takes
him through a series of painful efforts to reconstruct what happened
in the potting shed at the family home, "Wild Grove." His emotionally cold mother wants to deny that anything happened and that the
rumors about young James having an "accident" were spread by the
talkative old gardener, whom the mother never trusted because of his
fondness for telling "fairy stories." The gardener—Mr. Potter—is no
longer living, but James confronts Mrs. Potter and demands to know
the truth. The family "hushed it up," and Mrs. Potter is the only one
willing to say what happened in that old potting shed at the end of
the "Dark Walk."

She explains that one summer, when James was fourteen, her husband went into the shed and found James hanging from a cord, apparently lifeless. He took him down and tried to revive him but was convinced that there was no hope. Then, suddenly, the boy regained consciousness. Forced to admit that an accident of some kind had injured her son, the mother insists that the family doctor revived him, but Mrs. Potter's account leaves the impression that nothing but a miracle could have saved him.

Greene gives a mystical significance to all this by bringing into the story a priest whose prayers may have saved the boy's life. But the play is not about salvation. It is about living with the burdens of the past, the same problem that lies at the heart of "Under the Garden." The distant mother, the kind gardener, the escape to the pond and the island, the taste of freedom and fear in the Dark Walk, the shed and its pile of potato sacks, the dreadful image of the hanging figure—all these things haunted Greene for forty years and more, and they are crucial to an understanding of his life and work.

But is it possible that the hanging was as imaginary as the Russian roulette? All the principal actors in the drama—Ernest Northrop, his wife, Marion Greene, and Graham—are gone, and the only proof is the coded testimony of the crafty writer. The passage of time has not left even a stray rumor drifting in the neighborhood of Harston. At ninety-four, the parlor maid—Mrs. Rivers—could still clearly recall the boy who had stolen the chamber pots, calling him "a little devil," but she did not know anything about his subsequent fate. She lost track of him after he entered his middle teens. "Something happened," she said. "I don't know what, but he stopped coming to the house." When she was told that he had gone on to become a famous writer, her only response was a hearty laugh of surprise.

If the hanging is merely another fiction, it is an amazingly elaborate one—so elaborate that it would seem beyond even Greene's formidable powers of deception. "The Revolver in the Corner Cupboard" appeared without any hints in the previous novels that Greene had engaged in such frivolous experimentation with a gun, and the story does nothing to illuminate his work. But *The Potting Shed* and "Under the Garden" mark the culmination of a process that goes back to the beginning of Greene's career. Two early short stories— "The Second Death" (1929) and "Proof Positive" (1930)—reveal a preoccupation with the chances of restoring life to the dead. In the better of these, "The Second Death," a dying young man is convinced that he has already lost his life once. His mother found his body and assumed he was beyond hope. Then a passing doctor stopped and was able to revive him. But as death approaches a second time, he does not expect another reprieve and is told by a friend, "Miracles of that sort don't happen nowadays." Fearing that he has wasted his second chance, he surrenders to death without a fight.

It is very unlikely that such clues were planted with an eye toward fooling some critic half a century later. In 1929 Greene had no reason to believe that critics would ever think twice about him. And his personal obsession with the subject of hanging went far beyond the demands of any preconceived literary design. He brought up the subject in the most unusual places. Commenting on secondhand bookshops in an article written for *The Spectator* in 1939, Greene casually mentioned an old tome that had absorbed his interest—*The Uncertainty of the Signs of Death*. According to his brief report, the book was especially useful for the details it provided about a woman whose case he had already studied elsewhere—a convicted murderer named Anne Greene, who had survived an execution in 1650. His article does not bother to explain why he had acquainted himself with her story, nor how she had managed to cheat death. But, in light of all that has been said here, the reason for his interest should not be surprising. Her "death" offered one of the more intriguing cases on record of someone who had come back to life after being hanged, cut down, and pronounced dead. The common bond of their last names made the case all the more fascinating. Only the most dedicated antiquarian would seek out information on such an obscure figure, but, for someone with a passion like Greene's, the slightest detail might set off a full-scale search.

The first word of her entry in the *Dictionary of National Biography* is sufficiently striking: "Greene, Anne, criminal." Wrongly convicted of killing her child, she was hanged at Oxford a few days before Christmas:

> At her own request several of her friends pulled at her swinging body, and struck severe blows, so as to make sure that she was dead, and after the usual interval she was cut down and given over to the doctors for dissection. It was then discovered that Greene was still breathing, and with the help of restoratives she soon regained her health. She was granted a free pardon.

The last sentence in this passage is the most resonant. It was Anne Greene's good fortune not only to be restored to life but also to be cleared of guilt. The tragedy of so many characters in Graham Greene's books is that they must struggle to live with guilt and pain that can never be assuaged. The only escape is death, and even that might not do the trick. As Maurice Bendrix fears in *The End of the Affair,* eternity might simply be "the endless prolongation of the moment of death." Scars form, but the wounds are never forgotten. And the scars are not merely metaphorical. They are painfully visible in the faces of characters such as Raven, with his harelip, and the lieutenant in *The Power and the Glory,* whose jaw is scarred—"the relic of an escape."

In one way or another life has conspired against these characters, driving them into extreme situations where all the choices are wrong ones. They are the misfits whose only glory lies in playing that part to the hilt. So the scars become badges of honor as well as marks of shame, and as soon as one wound heals, they expect another. Some of the injuries are self-inflicted, as in the case of Anthony Farrant in *England Made Me* (1935), whose face is marked by a scar under his left eye. Friends and family assume that the injury was an accident. As a boy, he was skinning a rabbit when his knife flew up and hit him. All his elders reprimanded him for his carelessness, but his private reflection on their advice shows that the injury was no accident. Recalling that he had been told to keep the knife pointed toward the ground, he says to himself, "As if I hadn't known it all the time."

It did not take long for Greene to discover the perfect analogy for his permanently injured characters. He used it for the first time in *England Made Me,* as a way of describing the superficially charming but emotionally crippled Farrant. Farrant's sister has learned to be wary of his ready smile and sees in it a warning of danger, like that signaled by a leper's bell. Tormented by new sores and old scars, the poor leper shares an obvious connection with Greene's tragic cast, and the image of the leper comes up again and again in his books. His interest was so strong that he eventually paid a long visit to a leper colony in the Congo and used it as a setting for his novel *A Burnt-out Case* (1961). He collected books and pamphlets on the subject and found in one expert's work a passage that spoke directly to his personal concerns:

> Within limits of normality, every individual loves himself. In cases where he has a deformity or abnormality or develops it later, his own aesthetic sense revolts, and he develops a sort of disgust towards himself. Though with time he becomes reconciled to his deformities, it is only at the conscious level. His sub-conscious mind, which continues to bear the mark of injury, brings about certain changes in his whole personality, making him suspicious of society.

All this physical pain, self-loathing, and suspicion come from an injury so profound that the victim is helpless to escape the effects. Pure imagination could have led Greene to identify with such suffering, but it is hard to believe that imagination alone would have driven him to spend decades reading and writing about lepers, scarred criminals, suicides, hangings, resurrections, and desperate characters in potting sheds. The only thing that could draw all these elements together is the figure of the novelist revisiting the garden at Harston. This is the writer who specialized in cover stories and coded truths, the writer who made easy boasts about playing Russian roulette but who devoted enormous effort to devising a code about a boy hanging from a cord above a pile of potato sacks. Was that boy Graham Greene? The best way to answer that question is to offer one more story from "Under the Garden," a story taken from a biography.

On his way to revisit his uncle's house, Wilditch recalls reading a biography of a Civil War hero who received a mortal wound on the battlefield but who managed to stay astride his horse long enough to ride back to his village for one last glimpse of home. The biographer took the simple view that the man wanted to bid a final farewell to the place dearest to his heart, but Wilditch has another theory. He thinks that the man's last ride was an effort to banish every illusion from his mind before accepting death, to turn a cold eye on the life that had to be relinquished. In that "absolute moment," Wilditch says, the man was free to think of "nothing but his wound."

Told that he may be dying, Wilditch has undertaken a mission like that of the soldier in the biography. He must get rid of the cover story and go back to confront that small, dark space under the garden—the home of the crippled man named Javitt. Even the name sounds violent. He is the ugly, festering sore that will not heal. And he is also the scar, the proud symbol of survival against all odds. The nature of Wilditch's wound is unclear, but he thinks that he is dying of a lung disease, and his bronchoscopy has filled him with the nightmarish sensation of being choked by an instrument shoved down his throat.

If Greene needed any reminder of the sensation of being slowly choked to death, his own bronchoscopy must have brought back vivid memories. But he did not need reminding. And he did not need to revisit Harston. All the important details were sharply etched in his mind, as was the unremarkable face of Ernest Northrop. It seems fair to suggest that Northrop was the man who cut him free, and thus the man who marked him for life.

CHAPTER FOUR

YES AND NO

Berkhamsted School makes an unconvincing image of hell. The wide quadrangle is bordered by modestly attractive buildings, and the neighborhood is quiet and leafy, with a gently flowing canal and a large castle in a picturesque state of ruin. On a hill overlooking the school is the long stretch of gorse, fern, and woodland that constitutes Berkhamsted Common. From this vantage point on a sunny day, there is no hint of the grim little place portrayed in Greene's memoirs—a town seemingly full of murderers, suicides, and sex-crazed youth. Where others found provincial tranquillity, he found ubiquitous degradation. It was the home of all his troubles.

But why was it bad enough to push him toward suicide? Most of the things that upset him at the school were common to any institution of its type. He complained of the dirt, noise, and lack of privacy in the dormitories, but millions of other young people have endured the same conditions, or worse, without reaching for a gun or a rope. Being the headmaster's son was a trickier problem. With a man such as Charles Greene in charge, the pupils could never feel safe, and they could never completely trust any son of his. When Graham joined the boarders' house called St. John's, he was thirteen and had never lived with anyone except his family. Until his fellow boarders could be sure of his loyalty, they could be expected to bully him ruthlessly, and they did. At one point, things became so unpleasant for Graham that he was given a special exemption to spend every Sunday at home, but that arrangement helped only to reinforce the belief that he was his father's spy and to encourage the pupils to make more trouble for him.

He made an easy victim. Tall and bony, he was acutely shy, spoke with a faint defect (he could never say his *r*'s properly), and showed no aptitude for games. The mere sight of blood would make him faint, he trembled with fear if any bird flew near him, and he was so physically awkward that he could not master the simple skill of fixing a bayonet during the drills of the school training corps. It also did not help that he was susceptible to bad attacks of hay fever. Few boys could resist tormenting a headmaster's son whose many physical weaknesses were compounded by watery eyes and a runny nose. And, to make matters worse, Graham committed the grave error of revealing that he liked to read poetry. There could be no peace for such a boy.

Nothing had prepared him for the communal struggle of dormitory existence. For thirteen years he had enjoyed the material comforts of life in his parents' household, where toys and books had been plentiful, and where a small group of servants had attended to his needs. He was the sheltered child who suddenly had to fight his own battles, but he seemed powerless to stand up to his enemies. They mocked him to his face, played jokes on him, jabbed him with various sharp objects, and twisted his arm. His chief adversary was a boy named Carter, who never seemed to tire of torturing him and derived special pleasure from teasing the headmaster's son about his love of poetry.

According to Greene, this kind of abuse went on for three years, until he was sixteen. It ended only because his parents were forced to accept that he was incapable of overcoming it on his own. After running away to the common and threatening to kill himself, he finally impressed on them that they could no longer ignore his problem or "hush it up." For the strict headmaster and his proud wife, it was painful to admit that one of their own children could not adapt to school life. If Graham had been someone else's child, they might have taken the standard contemporary view that children needed to be forced to adapt, but they could not risk such a thing with a boy who was capable of hanging himself in the lavatory. They had to consider not only his welfare but also their own. A suicide at the school by one of their sons would have been a scandal so terrible that the headmaster might have been forced to resign. How could the parents of his 500 pupils rest easy if they knew he had failed to control his own son?

Any incident at the school would have been difficult to hush up, and there was already the danger that the boys were talking too much about Graham's odd behavior. As he claimed later, he had sat up one night trying to saw open his knee with a dull penknife.

The only solution was to send him away. It is convenient to say that he was sent to London for psychiatric treatment, but that is not strictly true. He was sent to board with a man who practiced his own version of psychoanalysis but who had no medical qualifications for the job. He did not try to hide his lack of experience or his lack of formal training, and the Greene family seemed unconcerned about it. The science was new, and there were still opportunities for inspired amateurs. But the main thing was to keep Graham out of Berkhamsted for a while, and his parents were not too particular about the choice of a minder.

In addition to being unqualified in psychiatry, Kenneth Richmond stood for almost everything that Charles Greene was opposed to. Richmond campaigned for educational reforms that would have put men like Charles out of work. He wanted schools to give pupils the maximum amount of freedom to learn at their own pace and to their own satisfaction. His views on the subject are easy enough to ascertain. In 1919—only two years before Graham was sent to stay with him—Richmond spelled out his radical ideas in his book *The Curriculum,* which begins with the sweeping proposition "There is only one subject—knowledge; and only one object—free and active development." This was strong stuff for 1919, and Richmond might actually have made some progress with it if he had not been such a dilettante. In addition to being an amateur educational theorist and psychoanalyst, he was an occasional book reviewer, an aspiring playwright, the manager of a boardinghouse, and a "psychical researcher" who tried communicating with the dead in his spare time.

Graham played no part in the family's choice of this independent thinker, but he was delighted to find himself in the company of such an unconventional man. He later claimed that the six months spent with Richmond were the most agreeable of his life. And well they should have been, because he was given the freedom to do whatever he liked for much of each day. After breakfast he sat with Richmond and talked about his dreams for an hour, and that was the extent of his treatment. The rest of the day could be spent sitting under a tree with a book in Kensington Gardens—a short walk from Richmond's house—or wandering the streets of London in search of adventure. There was time for visiting music halls and law courts and second-hand bookshops, and for strolling down some odd backstreets. More important, Richmond's circle of friends in the literary and theatrical worlds gave Graham the chance to meet a few famous writers of the day. One evening he was introduced to Walter de la Mare, whose short stories he admired. And on another occasion Richmond gave him an important introduction to Naomi Royde-Smith, the literary editor of the *Weekly Westminster,* who would later become an ally in his efforts to establish a literary career.

Near the end of his six months, the family dispatched Graham's attractive cousin Ave—who was a year older—to Richmond's house for a brief stay. Nothing seems to have been troubling her, and she has never been able to explain why her family wanted her to be psychoanalyzed by Richmond. Perhaps she was merely being used to check up on her cousin's progress. Whatever the reason, she quickly realized that the "treatment" was unusual but harmless and that the casual atmosphere had helped to revive her cousin's spirits. She was soon caught up in Graham's easy way of humoring Richmond:

> Graham and I always met for breakfast before our morning sessions with Mr. Richmond, and [Graham] used to ask, "Do you remember your dream?" and I said, "No, I can't remember," and he said, "Let's make them up." So he made up his dream, and I made up a dream, and then we went in to see Mr. Richmond—not together, but separately— and then Mr. Richmond would take it all down. . . . Whether it did us any good or not, I don't know, but this is what we had every morning, and in the afternoons we were left on our own.

Richmond did not impress Ave, who found him a "strange man, rather quiet, very reserved. He had awful pimples on his face." But she was inclined to take a sympathetic view of Graham's troubles, believing that his parents' expectations had been unreasonable. "I think Uncle Charlie used to be a little more severe with his son. . . . I think he didn't want to pander to his children." Marion was so "prim and proper," and so insistent that "her children had to be correct," that she had little patience for dealing with a son who seemed determined to rebel.

When his six months were up, Graham returned to a changed world in Berkhamsted. Unwilling to risk any problems, his father decided to spare Graham more misery at St. John's and allowed him to live at home as a day boy while finishing his final year at the school. His family and the rest of the staff treated him with the greatest delicacy. He was excused from duty in the Officers' Training Corps and was given more free time for individual study. Best of all, the dreaded Carter had disappeared, apparently a victim of Charles's quiet method of ridding the school of troublemakers. The records show that L. A. Carter left in spring 1921 and that Graham returned to Berkhamsted the following autumn.

The victory over his adversary was complete, and in the process Graham had also won an important battle against his father's rule, acquiring a certain measure of independence within the rigid system. Such a triumph should have encouraged him to forgive and forget, but all his inclinations were against that. Over time his feelings for his father mellowed, but the bitterness toward Carter made a lasting impression. Eighteen years later his anger was still hot as he recalled his school torments in the prologue to *The Lawless Roads*. Referring to Carter by the name of Collifax, he lashes out at him as the embodiment of pure evil, a character who was capable of inflicting "appalling cruelties" on others without any hesitation. Carter cast a hellish glow over Greene's image of Berkhamsted, but this is a remarkable achievement for a villain whose evil deeds seem limited to some harsh words and schoolboy punching. His "cruelties" must surely have been more "appalling" than these paltry crimes.

The dark qualities that Greene ascribes to Berkhamsted in the prologue of *The Lawless Roads* are concerned almost exclusively with sexual violence or sexual corruption of the young. In the little town servant girls race off at night to lie on their backs in ditches, tough young men smoke at street corners and wait to pick up easy women, a wife stabs her husband with a bread knife, a young couple commit suicide by placing their necks on the railway, schoolboys leer at pornographic photos, and a schoolmaster surveys his young pupils with a look of "demoniac sensuality." The pervasive sense of cruel sexuality leads Greene to recall a quotation from Rilke: "All the torments and agonies wrought on scaffolds, in torture chambers, madhouses, operating theatres, underneath vaults of bridges in late autumn."

It does not take a suspicious mind such as Charles Greene's to conclude that Carter's bullying must have taken on a vicious sexual edge. Of course, Charles had been quick to think that his son's problems had arisen from some kind of homosexual involvement, but Graham always denied it. In later years he liked to describe himself as "aggressively heterosexual," and near the end of his life, he stated flatly, "At Berkhamsted I was completely unaware of homosexuality." An interviewer once suggested to him that his interest in "duality" might have led him to take at least some interest in homosexuality, but he disagreed, saying that the subject had failed to engage him either as a man or as a writer. This response brought no argument. He was known as a man who had an eye for interesting women, and he was always finding ways to drop hints about his romances—even to boast about his occasional visits to brothels in exotic places. He was regarded as an old-fashioned man's man.

But this image has nothing in common with the awkward, sniffling boy who lived in constant fear of Carter and who became suicidal as a result of the pressure. He was distressed by something more substantial than nasty remarks or arm-twisting. The truth was not something that Greene could confide to Kenneth Richmond, but thirty years later he did find a physician who could help him deal with his memories. This was Eric Strauss, a prominent psychiatrist at St. Bartholomew's Hospital and the coauthor of a textbook called *Sexual Disorders in the Male*. For most of the 1950s, Greene was one of Dr. Strauss's regular patients, and Strauss is the model for a character in *The Potting Shed*—Dr. Kreuzer—who tries to help James Callifer come to terms with his dark memories of childhood. Strauss became a close friend, and at one point he invited Greene to share a house with him. Greene declined, but he did arrange for his friend to have the use of his villa in Anacapri for a few weeks each year. At one point in their relationship, Greene was suffering from such severe depression that he asked Strauss to give him electric shock treatment. Instead the doctor suggested a more appealing therapy. As Greene remembered it, "He said, 'Start writing something, even if it's only a diary. Anything. And then come back in a fortnight.' I did and then the depression lifted. . . . That was the first of an autobiography I wrote called *A Sort of Life*. I began it then."

One of the things that Greene revealed in his memoir is that his resentment of Carter had a connection to another boy. In the version that he prepared for publication, he included few details, but the basic story is that he was betrayed by a boy named A. H. Wheeler (the published account calls him Watson). They were friends, but at some point the boy "deserted" Greene and joined Carter's gang. Such was Greene's anger over the betrayal that he longed for years to exact some revenge for the deed. He had made the mistake of confiding in the boy, of trusting him with some of his secrets, and his friendship was undermined when Wheeler shared those secrets with Carter. In this published version, the nature of the friendship is not explained, but there is good reason to believe that it is fully detailed in the early draft written for Strauss. Any hidden element of homosexuality in the relationship would have interested the doctor, not only because he was a student of male sexuality but also because he was homosexual— a fact that was known to Greene.

Greene's image as a man's man was simply another cover—perhaps his most convincing one. He could manage the part as well as any other, and enjoy it. There was nothing fake about his interest in women. But the "aggressively heterosexual" image helped to mask fears about his masculinity that had almost overwhelmed him in his teens, and continued to affect him in later years. Anyone could figure that out from Greene's attachment to his toy bear Ted. In the 1950s, and later, Ted went to all kinds of fascinating places with Greene. They were even caught up in some shooting between Israeli and Egyptian troops during a visit to the Sinai desert. To comfort Ted in that frightening incident, Greene held him close. At least one color photograph of Ted has survived. It was taken during a visit to Havana with Greene. Ted is sitting on a window ledge of their hotel room and is wearing a pretty blue ribbon, which Greene had wrapped around his neck. Greene later joked that the title of this shot should be "Our Ted in Havana." (The photograph was published in *The Independent* of London on July 28, 1994, as part of an article about this biography. Copyright problems have prevented its publication here.)

Long after he had left the nursery, Greene still felt the need to carry around a teddy bear. The tough-talking, hard-drinking adventurer, the expert on opium dens and brothels, had a toy animal in his luggage. Greene's attachment to the bear is not a complete surprise. True to form, he left clues in his work, but—as in the Harston references—no one would have known what to make of them when they first appeared in print. An early, obscure story called *The Bear Fell Free* (1935) is about a doomed young man and his good-luck charm, a teddy bear. In *A Burnt-out Case* a priest asks Querry whether he has a favorite prayer, and he replies that all his prayers are "for a brown teddy bear." Understandably, the priest thinks that his leg is being pulled. And if anyone had ever seriously questioned Greene about his strange friend, he could always have explained it by saying it was a gift for someone else or part of some private joke.

As trivial as Ted may seem, Greene regarded him as a symbol of what he had lost in his teens—a sense of innocence, a feeling of security. This weak, sentimental side is embarrassing, and it is no wonder that he tried so hard to cover it up. The only thing that redeems it is his art. In *The Bear Fell Free* the various elements of Greene's private drama are transformed into a poignant story. To prove his bravery, an innocent young man accepts a ridiculously dangerous challenge from someone pretending to be his friend. Farrell, the young man, is drunk when he agrees to fly his small airplane across the Atlantic. A party of mindless revelers watch him take off, and, as a sign of his fearlessness, he tosses his life belt from the cockpit while the plane rises above the crowd. His only companion on the flight is a teddy bear given to him by his faithless girlfriend. Through a series of short scenes, the narrative moves back and forth in time, revealing not only the inevitable crash but also the girlfriend's disloyalty. Farrell is killed, the girlfriend ends up sleeping with the false friend who challenged Farrell, and one of the few things salvaged from the crash is the teddy bear.

Of course, the evil friend's name in the story is Carter. The name Farrell may have been suggested by Sir Arthur Quiller-Couch's novel *Foe-Farrell* (1918), which Greene read several times at St. John's. Its account of a long, drawn-out process of revenge was a satisfying fantasy for him at the time. All the elements of Greene's crisis at school are given a place in *The Bear Fell Free*. As a story about destructive sexual conflict, it involves a vain effort to prove masculinity, an unfaithful companion, a heartless rival, and a symbol of lost innocence. Greene may have given only his heart to Wheeler, but whether his love was physical or spiritual, it was obviously enough to stir up an enormous sense of shame. He had entered the forbidden territory over which his father kept such close watch. If Carter and Wheeler taunted him about his confused feelings—making threats and humiliating him in front of other boys—that would certainly explain why he turned suicidal. It is really the only plausible explanation for such an extreme reaction. It made him aware that cruelty breeds a desire in its victims to be cruel in return—to others as well as to themselves.

II

Understanding this crisis is important not only because it caused Greene so much grief but also because it made him so determined to hide any homosexual feelings. When he denied that his work reflected an interest in homosexuality, he was wrong. Because the evidence to the contrary is so extensive, it deserves to be laid out at some length. At the very time that he was dismissing any link between homosexuality and his love of "duality," he was working on two plays based on that notion. The first is a one-act drama called *Yes and No*. It is a clever verbal duel between a homosexual director and the young actor he is trying to seduce. The director is supposedly preparing him for a small part in a new production, but it is not the sort of part that requires preparation. The young man has been cast as the lover of an older man, and his only lines are "yes" and "no." These are also his only responses to the director, who bombards him with suggestive remarks and questions, hoping that he will say yes to an affair. The director's hopes grow more intense, but he is never able to get anything more definite from the young man than a tantalizing "Yes—and no."

This one-act play was staged in 1980 as a curtain-raiser for Greene's three-act farce, *For Whom the Bell Chimes,* a work that can best be described as one long gay romp. Even the title is a none too subtle dig at the exaggerated masculine pretensions of characters such as Hemingway. The plot reaches a climax of sorts when two long-lost homosexual lovers are reunited at a murder scene. They seem to have a good chance of falling in love all over again, despite the fact that one of them has undergone a dramatic change since their last meeting. He—or rather, she—is now a female police inspector who declares proudly, "As you see I have made up my mind which sex to be."

A slightly earlier play, *The Return of A. J. Raffles,* is much more farcical. Although the Raffles stories give no hint that the "cracksman" is gay, Greene's version presents him as such and puts him in the company of Oscar Wilde's lover Lord Alfred Douglas. When Lord Alfred politely asks the cracksman's partner, Bunny, whether Raffles is bisexual, he is given the indignant reply "He never looked twice at a woman." This is contradicted by Raffles, who tells his companion not to be so contemptuous of the opposite sex: "In the absence of a good chef, Bunny, they serve to warm the soup." Later in the play Bunny is given the opportunity to make a short speech in favor of sodomy. For his part, Raffles has the good luck to be alone in a lady's bedroom with the prince of Wales, who talks to him about sex and praises him for being such a good listener. It is so good to have someone to confide in, the prince says, mentioning the whores he likes to talk to in Paris. Unfortunately, the prince is interested in discussing only women.

From beginning to end the subject of homosexuality is an intrinsic part of Greene's work. His male characters are forever searching for some elusive bond with another male. In *The Man Within,* Andrews cannot stop thinking about how much he loved his friend Carlyon in their early days together. He dreams of sleeping beside him, of listening to "the cool beauty of his voice" as he recites poetry to him. But he is also tortured by such thoughts, and an inner voice delivers the stern reprimand "You are not a man." In "The Basement Room" (1935), the young boy Philip yearns to be alone with the butler Baines—to enjoy the pleasures of a man's world without the interference of Baines's nagging wife. He especially enjoys hearing the butler's stories of life on the West Coast of Africa, where Baines found so much comfort in the company of certain native men. As he explains to the boy, it was bliss just to watch these men walking through their villages holding hands and laughing. They seemed to take such pleasure from touching each other. They were not in love, Baines insists, but he "couldn't help loving them" for their uninhibited display of manly affection.

Similarly, in *Brighton Rock* young Pinkie is devoted to the memory of his dead mentor Kite; in *The Heart of the Matter*, Scobie's closest friend is his "boy" Ali; and in *The Third Man* Martins insists on solving the mystery of Harry Lime's "death" because of the "sentimental" attachment he feels to his old school friend. At the beginning of the novel, Martins weeps uncontrollably at Harry's bogus funeral, and later the "resurrected" Harry makes a mockery—in word and deed—of his friend's devotion. When they go up together in the cable car attached to the old Ferris wheel, Harry gives a tip to the operator so that they can be alone in the car, but he enjoys teasing Martins about it, saying that his tip simply follows the custom of lovers who pay extra to have a car to themselves. The same love-hate relationship exists between Maurice Bendrix and Henry Miles in *The End of the Affair*, and between Fowler and Pyle in *The Quiet American*. Although the first of these two novels is ostensibly about Maurice's love for Henry's wife, she ends up dead, and Maurice moves in with Henry. By the end of the book he is wearing Henry's pajamas to bed, and they are spending their evenings quietly sipping drinks together.

Homosexuality attracted Greene for many reasons, not the least of which were its associations with risk, secrecy, and—especially in Greene's youth—guilt. These aspects are all present in the strange dream that comes to Arthur Rowe in *The Ministry of Fear*. He imagines that he is walking toward a meeting with an innocent girlfriend but finds himself instead meeting a policeman, who speaks to him in a woman's voice and takes him to a dark corner of a urinal. When he protests that he wants to go home, the policeman calls him "dear" and assures him that their "sad world of shared love" is "home." He finds that he cannot run away and imagines that the floor lets out a cry every time he tries to take a step. "He couldn't move an inch without causing pain."

Greene's short story "May We Borrow Your Husband?" (1963) offers the most interesting combination of attraction and revulsion. Two flamboyant homosexuals show up in Antibes looking for fresh faces, and the narrator—a middle-aged English novelist named William Harris—explains how he came to take an interest in their activities despite his firm preference for women. They were so loud and colorful that his attention could not help but be drawn to them, Harris says, and even when he follows them into a gay bar, he assures the reader that it was only his novelist's curiosity that led him to check out the place. Gradually, he becomes a friend and is drawn into their plot to seduce an attractive young man on his honeymoon. The two gay men manage to separate the husband from the wife partly because Harris agrees to keep the wife occupied. He protests to the reader that he was a reluctant player in the gay couple's plot and did not even take advantage of the beautiful wife. Over dinner she tries to seduce him with candid talk about how neglected she feels, and how hot and sensitive her breasts are, but he braves this assault with admirable fortitude, keeping up a good front as the detached novelist whose interest in this sexual comedy is strictly professional.

His explanations are, however, unconvincing. His decision to assist the gay couple's plan is deliberate, and well timed. He cannot hide his pleasure at seeing the enterprising couple overcome the difficult challenge of seducing a man on his honeymoon. And Harris's failure to accept the overtures of the young woman makes the conquest of the husband and wife complete. She is not even allowed the consolation of having her own affair. One detail helps to explain why the supposedly "straight" novelist would join forces with the gay men. The reason that Harris is staying in Antibes is that he has come there to work quietly on his next book—a biography of Lord Rochester. Any true follower of Rochester would be happy to play the kind of sexual prank described in Harris's story. And he would not be the least concerned about switching loyalties from heterosexuals to homosexuals. The nobleman was often at a loss as to whether he should sleep with a woman or a boy:

> Nor shall our love-fits, Chloris, be forgot,
> When each the well-looked linkboy strove t' enjoy,
> And the best kiss was the deciding lot
> Whether the boy fucked you, or I the boy.

In old age Greene finally gave himself a direct part to play in one of his tales about sexual ambivalence. When his *Getting to Know the General* appeared in 1985, it was universally regarded as a straightforward story of Greene's interest in the political struggles of Panama's leader, Gen. Omar Torrijos. The book's true nature would have been more apparent if Greene had called it "Raffles Goes to Panama." The general and his shadowy gang of old cronies and idle thugs—including the singularly nasty Colonel Noriega—serve merely as an exotic backdrop for the campy adventures of Greene and his official guide, Sergeant Chuchu, a loyal member of the Torrijos entourage and a former Marxist professor of philosophy. It is not the general whom the reader comes to know but Chuchu. Torrijos makes infrequent appearances in the book, rarely says anything worth remembering, and, even when he does speak to Greene, Chuchu must do the translating.

The book pays so much attention to the sergeant's words and actions that it sometimes seems as though Greene and Chuchu are the only people in Panama. But it is obvious that Chuchu's combination of bookishness and boyishness makes him a perfect companion for Greene. In no time they become fast friends and relish each other's company during the writer's several visits to Panama. When they are not spending hours together eating and drinking in restaurants, bars, and hotel rooms, they travel around the country paying visits to a haunted house, a mysterious airstrip, and an isolated beach where they play in the surf. While the general is off plotting strategy against the imperialist devils, Greene and Chuchu are reciting poetry to each other. The sergeant shares his favorite verses by Spanish poets, and the novelist replies with Baudelaire's great love poem "L'Invitation au voyage," "To kiss as we choose . . . in that land resembling you!" The bond of friendship is sealed when Chuchu charms Greene with his erratic driving. Dangerously drunk, the sergeant jumps a traffic light and hits a car. "I think my deep affection for him began that day," Greene writes.

On their many excursions together—sometimes by car, sometimes by light aircraft—Chuchu boasts about the secrets of his manly life. No one can count all the children he has fathered or all the prostitutes he has been with. "You are a good lover?" Greene asks. Patiently, the sergeant explains that what women really appreciate is tenderness after intercourse. Such talk gets a little confusing, however, because Greene has—in his words—an "imaginary woman" along with them. She is the foreign journalist who will be taking Greene's part in the novel he wants to write about Chuchu. As Greene explains to his friend, a fictional general will give a fictional sergeant the job of escorting the woman. The two characters will "go off together, just as we have done." Getting caught up in the excitement of the story, Chuchu asks, "We make love together?" The answer is a complicated one, a sort of "yes—and no" problem. "She's not like the other women you have known," Greene says.

Such camp becomes too much in at least a couple of places. When Greene gets extremely drunk and falls fast asleep, he dreams of designing a new coin for Panama. One side will feature pictures of the general, and the other will have the smiling face of Sergeant Chuchu. With a few more remarks of that kind, Greene might have made his ploy obvious to even the most solemn reviewers. For anyone on to the game, things do get a little out of hand in another passage, which sums up various things Chuchu has said about life. Sitting contentedly in the car while his friend drives them to a pretty little hotel at the edge of a mountain, Greene reviews each wonderful memory and then informs the reader, "Impressions were clustering like bees round a queen."

So much talk about homosexuality suggests that, for Greene, talking about it took the place of engaging in it. Stray pieces of evidence indicate that he did have some homosexual experiences as an adult—it would be surprising if he did not—but some of this evidence concerns people who are still alive and prefer not to be questioned about the subject. And some vital witnesses are dead, including—regrettably—the great Chuchu, who was the victim not of a bullet or a car crash but of a weak heart. The crucial thing, however, is not whether Greene said yes or no. What matters most is his constant compulsion to pose the question in his work.

The question was deliberately left unresolved. At first, fear and shame made him retreat from a direct answer, and then—in old age—comedy gave him a pleasing mask to hide behind. The pain of the Carter-Wheeler episode was replaced by the comic flirtation of *Getting to Know the General*. As with so many other things, Greene preferred to make evasive moves in border territory. That meant employing the usual tactics—taking sudden leaps in one direction or the other, dropping hints along the way, covering important tracks, and laying false trails. "Yes—and no" is the only answer he wanted to leave. But a few tracks were left behind on an island in the Mediterranean.

III

If Greene needed an actual place to embody the sexual border zone of his imagination, he made the right decision when he went to the little town of Anacapri in 1948 and purchased the Villa Rosaio. In those days the island of Capri was legendary for its tolerant attitude toward many types of sexual conduct, and it was a relatively easy place to escape to. It was on Capri that Oscar Wilde was reunited with Lord Alfred Douglas after being released from Reading Gaol. And Noël Coward took the title for his song "A Bar on the Piccola Marina" from the island's favorite gathering place for free spirits. Capri was also home to Norman Douglas, who was Greene's closest friend on the island in the late 1940s and early 1950s. He and Greene used to spend hours drinking and talking at various bars and restaurants, and the older man was forever passing along useful advice. Before Greene made his first visit to the Far East, Douglas sent a word of warning, "Look out for syphilis—a friend of mine came back from Malaya in a deplorable condition—I am in a pretty groggy way myself."

Douglas's *South Wind* (1917) captures the mood of open sensuality favored by many of Capri's refugees from the cold north. It was a popular novel of Greene's generation and gave a special allure to the island for anyone wanting to make a real pursuit of pleasure in a warm, invigorating atmosphere. The novel praises the "frolicsome perversity" of the place and condemns countries such as England for showing "the monotony of a nation intent upon respecting laws and customs." *South Wind* helped to foster the prevalent impression that anything was possible on Capri.

Douglas certainly put the impression to a rigorous test. His preferred pleasure was seducing children. This caused him a great deal of trouble over the years. People tended to be extremely difficult when they discovered what he wanted. In the backstreets of Naples one day, he was given a firm blow to the head by the brother of a young girl whose companionship he had recently purchased from the children's mother. When Douglas discovered, however, that the boy was "even prettier" than his sister, he decided to forgive the injury. "Not long afterwards the boy fell in love with me desperately," Douglas claimed, "as only a southern boy of his age can do; so blindly that at a hint from myself he would have abandoned his work and family and everything else."

Douglas was always looking for new young friends, and he was incapable of passing a child in the street without stopping to chat. An English friend, the editor Roger Senhouse, recalled that "Norman used to ask little boys in the street, 'Have you been naughty today?' If they had, he gave them a shilling, but nothing if they hadn't." When Nancy Cunard wrote to him asking whether he could give any help to the Spanish people during the Civil War, he responded that he did not want to take sides but would be "ready to take charge of [a] Spanish child—orphan or otherwise."

One of Douglas's hobbies was collecting limericks, and this was a side of him that Greene particularly enjoyed. If someone craved racy talk about homosexuality, Uncle Norman—as he was often called—was the man to see. One example from his collection testifies to his lingering affection for Spanish youth:

There was an old man of Madrid,
Who cast loving eyes on a kid.
He said: "Oh, my joy!
I'll bugger that boy,
You see if I don't"—and he did.

Drawing on his many years of experience, Douglas was able to provide an extended gloss on this text when it appeared in print. "Some Spanish kids are remarkably pretty. . . . The old man in the poem no doubt gave this particular one a few chocolates or a packet of cigarettes, or even both, and made an appointment for another meeting. Who wouldn't?"

When Douglas died in 1952, Greene had just finished helping him with the Heinemann edition of *Venus in the Kitchen,* the old man's treasured collection of aphrodisiac recipes. In his introduction to the book, Greene made some vague references to the variety of his friend's love affairs, but he was outraged when Douglas's sexual interest in children was openly discussed in Richard Aldington's memoir *Pinorman* (1954). He did everything he could to discredit the book, vehemently attacking it as the work of a coward and a liar. His review of it was so unrelentingly defamatory that no one would take the risk of publishing it. Greene tried to get around this by sending a copy of the review to Aldington with a note saying that it would be cowardly of the writer to sue him for libel. This moral blackmail did not work. Aldington was unwilling to let Greene hurl personal abuse at him in public.

Aldington had struck a raw nerve, but his criticism of Douglas's literary works and general character are too mild to account for the fierceness of Greene's attack. The comments on Douglas's pedophilia made the difference. Greene could not bear to see that part of his friend's life mentioned except in the most innocent form. Never mind that Aldington's discussion of the subject was restrained and that he was simply pointing out obvious truths. Greene wanted to deny it all, or to make Douglas's interest in children look so innocent that no one would dare question it. His review—which was published in 1966, a few years after Aldington's death—goes to great lengths to excuse the old man's constant efforts to pick up children. Aldington had complained in his book that he resented it when Douglas asked to be driven around with one of his slum children at his side. Greene responds by professing amazement at Aldington's lack of generosity, implying that Douglas was just trying to give a poor child of the streets an innocent outing.

The review reaches its lowest point in the final paragraph, when Greene assumes the mantle of the self-righteous Christian and charges that the evil Aldington would have been the first to throw a stone if he "had been present at a certain Gospel scene." Greene laments the injustice of Aldington waiting to publish his book until Douglas was dead, when the old man was no longer able to strike him down or drag him into court. But Greene showed the same discretion by publishing the review after his villain was no longer able to answer him. It was a wise decision. If Aldington had been around to answer Greene, it would have been possible to bring up much more interesting evidence about Douglas than any memoir could have offered in 1954. The following limerick from Douglas's published collection might have made a good response, either on its own or with Douglas's expression of regret that the Turks had changed their ways since the piece was composed:

> There was an old man of Stamboul
> With a varicose vein in his tool.
> In attempting to come
> Up a little boy's bum
> It burst, and he *did* look a fool.

All the emotional energy that went into this dispute—energy so strong that Greene was still holding a grudge after his foe had died— has nothing to do with the facts. Everyone on Capri knew that Douglas was gentle and witty, and an unashamedly dirty old man. The exaggerated tone of Greene's review suggests that he is trying to defend something besides Douglas's reputation. What seems to worry him most is that secrets can be revealed with impunity once a writer is dead. The passion in his review is all on the side of the poor author whose art and good characteristics may be overshadowed by revelations of some private weakness. But Douglas's reputation did not require protection from Aldington any more than Greene's requires protection from other writers. Douglas's worst enemy was his mediocre talent. If he had written better books, his happy readers would keep his name alive. And whatever Greene's pleasures were behind the high walls of his villa, no amount of evidence or speculation can keep people from admiring *Brighton Rock*.

Greene took extraordinary precautions all the same. Even finding the Villa Rosaio is a challenge. It is far removed from the increasingly noisy crowds of tourists in the town of Capri. At the opposite side of the island, spreading along a mountain slope high above the

Bay of Naples, is the more peaceful town of Anacapri. On its out-skirts, at the end of a maze of narrow lanes, is a small iron gate in a corner wall, and beyond it is the paved walk that leads to the villa. Once inside Greene could enjoy complete privacy in a miniature par-adise of his own, with a view of the sea from the upper floor of the villa and a garden below with shade trees, a bougainvillea arbor, and sunny terraces overflowing with flowers. Few sounds interrupt the peace, and the only trespassers are the bright green lizards that crawl among the rocks in the garden.

From very early days a frequent visitor to the villa was Norman Douglas's doctor, an Austrian named Elisabeth Moor, who had a per-manent home in Anacapri. To all her friends and patients she was known as the Dottoressa. She was a stocky, energetic woman who spoke a lyrical form of broken English and who had opinions on everything and a great fund of stories about life on the island. Greene was fond of the Dottoressa, and—as he acknowledged in print—she was the inspiration for Aunt Augusta in *Travels with My Aunt*. She could be immensely amusing, with her quirky ideas about medicine and her outspoken complaints about her busy life. But she could also be overbearing and indiscreet. In 1975, the year of her death, Greene edited her autobiography and published it under the title *An Impossible Woman*.

Over a period of nearly thirty years, the Dottoressa learned a lot about Greene and was aware that he indulged in an occasional homo-sexual adventure at the Villa Rosaio, usually with Italian boys who stayed with him on the island for a day or two. She confided that information to her friend Gitta Bittorf, who used to stay with her during annual summer visits to Anacapri. In Greene's presence the Dottoressa also told one of Greene's English friends—Michael Richey—that it was "assumed in the village that Graham preferred men to women." Richey later called this assumption "ludicrous," but it seems unwise to dismiss the views of the Dottoressa, Greene's clos-est friend on the island.

In her autobiography the Dottoressa makes a suggestive connec-tion between Greene, Norman Douglas, and another man whose interest in boys was as great as Douglas's. His name was Baron Ekkehard von Schack. He was a tall Prussian who had been an officer in the kaiser's army and who always honored his ex-monarch's birth-day by wandering about Capri in full military uniform—complete with shiny breastplate and pointed helmet. He lived above a small restaurant not far from Greene's villa, and he became a good friend of the novelist, who used him as a model for Dr. Hasselbacher in *Our*

Man in Havana. As the Dottoressa explains in her autobiography, the kaiser's birthday was not the only one that the baron liked to honor in a special way. But this other birthday celebration did not require fancy dress. The only requirements were some wild orchids and a boy. After they were in hand, boy and flowers were sent off to the Villa Rosaio: "If Graham was on Capri, always on his birthday in October would come very early a little boy with a great platter of little white flowers. You could say that after food little boys were the baron's great pleasure as they were with Norman." The Dottoressa does not say why such a gift was appropriate for Greene, but any further comment would not have survived the novelist's editorial pencil. The wonder is that he let this much stand.

The people of Anacapri are not overly curious about the ways their foreign guests amuse themselves, but one resident had reason to see a good deal of Greene in the days when the novelist was still new to the island, and when Douglas was still alive. Attilio Scoppa was at that time a young man whose job at the post office required him to deliver all the telegrams in Anacapri. Because Greene frequently received telegrams from his publishers and agents, Scoppa would see him at odd times through the week and was surprised to find that Greene often had Italian boys staying with him, and that the same boy was never there more than once. Most of them appeared to be between the ages of fourteen and sixteen. Not knowing much about Greene, Scoppa could only guess why these young visitors came and went, but other people in the town told him that the boys came for sex. It was an easy way to taste a forbidden pleasure. There were no potentially embarrassing attachments and not much chance of being found out. Just a brief foray across the sexual "border," then back to "normal" again.

Stories of this type were heard less frequently in later years. Old rogues such as Douglas and the baron died off, Anacapri slowly expanded and became less private, and Greene was seen less often in the town. When he first arrived there were far more famous people than he living on the island, but by the 1970s he was one of Anacapri's most distinguished part-time residents, and a local literary journalist proposed that Greene should be made an honorary citizen of Anacapri. The civic authorities agreed, and in 1978 the distinction was granted to him in a public ceremony. Greene was immensely gratified. It was one of the few places where he felt at home. And, as one of the island's honorary citizens, he joined an elite group. As far as anyone could remember, the last literary man to receive such an honor was Norman Douglas.

CHAPTER FIVE

OXFORD: A TOUCH OF THE POET

G reene made his final escape from his father's school in 1922, when he went up to Oxford. It was not an easy getaway. In fact, without his father's help, it would have been impossible. Unlike such famous contemporaries as Cyril Connolly and Evelyn Waugh, Greene did not have the advantage of a scholarship; he failed the scholarship examinations on two occasions. Fortunately, his father was willing to pay all the necessary costs of an Oxford education.

In the first year Charles Greene gave his son an allowance of 250 pounds a year. That may not seem much by today's standards, but in the 1920s it was twice the annual income of the typical working-class family. This kind of munificence would have bankrupted most schoolmasters, especially those with six children, but Charles Greene could count on his rich brother Edward for financial assistance. As a partner of a London company that managed vast coffee plantations in Brazil, Edward had enough money to assist his relatives in many ways, and he was unfailingly generous. Among other things, he helped Sir William buy Harston House and made substantial donations to Berkhamsted School.

With his uncle's money and his father's educational contacts, Greene did not have to worry about finding a place at Oxford, but his father took care to choose the right kind of college—one that would make some allowance for the independent ways of his sensitive son. Of course, it was also important to have a trusted friend around who could watch the young man and keep him from straying too far. Charles found what he was looking for in Balliol College, where one of the dons—Kenneth Bell—was a governor of Berkhamsted School and a former pupil.

A good-natured man in his late thirties, Bell became Graham's tutor and proved to be a good ally. He looked after him in a casual way and did not put undue pressure on him. He took a sympathetic view of undergraduates who were determined to assert their freedom. According to one Balliol man of the time—Anthony Powell—Bell was the "champion of any undergraduate he thought intelligent, especially one in difficulties of some sort with the authorities. . . . He was prepared to stand up for ability concealed by an awkward manner, rackety behaviour." Bell did as much as anyone to preserve Balliol's "tradition of tolerance." As Powell recalled, "No one was expected to live the same sort of life as other members of the College simply because they were members of the College; and many Balliol men, even of the same year, never exchanged a word with each other during their Oxford residence."

Surviving in such a world was certainly manageable for Greene, who was never in danger of becoming embroiled in college life. Powell remembered speaking to him only once and receiving for his trouble a sharp reply. In the memoirs of his contemporaries at Oxford, Greene is rarely more than a vague presence in the background. He does not shout poetry through megaphones with Harold Acton or play the piano with Robert Byron, or dine with Kenneth Clark. And no one ever spotted him carrying his teddy bear through the streets, in the fond manner of John Betjeman. There is a brief glimpse of the young man in A. L. Rowse's *A Cornishman at Oxford,* which describes Greene as having "curly flax-gold hair and the odd strangulated voice . . . those staring, china-blue eyes, wide open to the world." Evelyn Waugh's "impression" at Oxford was "that Graham Greene looked down on us (and perhaps all undergraduates) as childish and ostentatious. He certainly shared in none of our revelry." It was only after they were both established novelists that Waugh and Greene became friends. Cyril Connolly summed up Greene's social life at Balliol by saying, "He was of us, but not with us." Even his school friend Peter Quennell was mystified at how successfully Greene managed to keep his distance from the legendary social life of the "Brideshead Generation": "Why Graham at Oxford should have so carefully avoided notice is a question that I cannot answer."

Greene's low profile had nothing to do with a greater sense of maturity. He was simply enjoying his own semiprivate version of the Brideshead life. Oxford gave overprotected boys from schools such as Berkhamsted the freedom to be left alone, and Greene was happy to spend much of his time enjoying the solitude. Just to have a room of his own was a great relief. As Betjeman pointed out, part of Oxford's appeal for Greene's generation was that it allowed "Privacy after years of public school; / Dignity after years of none at all." In any case, the conspicuous "revelry" of figures such as Acton, Brian Howard, and Waugh held no appeal for Greene, who preferred to have some element of subterfuge in all his pastimes. He may have been tempted to stand below the dean of Balliol's window and sing, as Waugh did one night, "The Dean of Balliol sleeps with men, / Sleeps with men, sleeps with men," but it was not his style to employ such a direct approach. He found more satisfaction from such things as entertaining German spies in his rooms.

Ordinary college pranks could not compare with the thrill of receiving mysterious nighttime visits from a man named Count von Bernstorff—a spy who "loved luxury and boys," as Greene later put it. While the dean was preoccupied with minor troublemakers, Greene was free to indulge in coy games with the count and his henchmen, who liked to show up without warning and talk over drinks in his rooms.

It was Greene who had initiated contact with these spies. In 1924 he got in touch with the German embassy and offered to write some pro-German articles for an Oxford paper. He wanted to investigate conditions in the Rhine—where the French and Germans were at odds over the creation of a separatist Palatine Republic—and he promised the embassy that his findings would support the German side. The first secretary of the embassy, Count von Bernstorff, interviewed him about the offer, and the end result was a trip to the Rhine with all expenses paid by the German government. Greene returned and published his promised piece of propaganda in the *Oxford Chronicle* (May 9, 1924), and the Germans were so pleased that they asked him to go back to the region and spy on the pro-French separatists. He accepted the job and was ready to leave when, much to his disappointment, a peaceful settlement of the conflict made his trip unnecessary.

Although he did not mind acknowledging this episode in later years, he treated it as merely an innocent bit of youthful adventure and joked about the credulity of his German employers. At the time, however, not many young Englishmen would have wanted to be so helpful to Germany. There was not yet a Third Reich to trouble the conscience, but it was rather brazen to serve a foreign land that had so recently slaughtered several hundred thousand British soldiers. Part of Greene's plan may have been to use the episode to hurt his father. His letters home made no secret of his connection with the Germans, and his father—the proud defender of the British war dead—was suitably upset. Charles told Graham that if he really wanted a free trip to the Continent, he could have the money for it from home. But Graham said no.

What his father did not know was that Graham was also using the Germans to enjoy his first adult experience as a double agent. Like his brother Herbert, Graham was prepared to spy for more than one foreign power. While he was waiting to make a return trip for the Germans, he contacted a pro-French paper in England, secured a commission to write propaganda for it, then used this connection to gain the confidence of the French embassy. He was on the verge of becoming an agent for both France and Germany when peace ruined his plans.

Shortly after this episode, Greene experienced a similar disappointment when he tried to do some spying in Ireland. He had made a few interesting contacts in Dublin during a trip there in 1923 and had decided that the new Irish Free State might want to employ a talented Oxford student as a spy in Northern Ireland. He made an offer to the right authorities, but it was turned down—no doubt because he was suspected of already being a double agent for France and Germany. "I believe the Irish were very much more distrustful than the Germans," he told the *Irish Independent* in 1989. "Not one representative of the Free State came to knock on my door." Strangely enough, no one commented on this odd recollection when it appeared in print.

In old age Greene was more willing to speak about his past, but this story is especially worthy of comment because it brings him perilously close to saying that he was prepared to commit treason. It is true that, in 1923, the Irish Free State held dominion status within the British Commonwealth, and was formally subject to the Crown, but the link was an extremely tenuous one. If his offer was not technically treasonous, it was certainly close to the spirit of treason, because British control was the real issue at stake in both parts of Ireland. Maybe Greene's story was more fancy than fact, but there is no evidence to contradict it.

With his love of secrecy, Greene was not one to attract a wide range of friends at Oxford. His small circle tended to be unimpressive characters who were not likely to challenge him or make excessive demands on his time. Peter Quennell tried to fit in with Greene's circle but found them "tedious." Another old acquaintance from Berkhamsted—Claud Cockburn—was more receptive. Cockburn, who later enjoyed some success as a political journalist, was frequently at Greene's side in the Oxford years. Like Graham, he had acquired a taste for the game of espionage from Charles Greene's style of education. He accompanied his friend on the trip to the Rhine that Count von Bernstorff had commissioned, and he joined him in an ambitious plot to enter the Soviet Union as visiting Communists.

In January 1925 Greene and Cockburn became members of the British Communist Party, vaguely hoping that this bold move would eventually bring them invitations to visit the Soviet Union as guests of the Party. They paid their dues for a month, but it soon became apparent that no one was going to send a couple of novices to see the wonders of communism at work, so the green membership cards were put aside as souvenirs.

This episode was more than a prank, however. Greene was no Communist, but he was serious about using his membership card as a passport to adventure, and he certainly would have continued paying dues for much longer if doing so had produced some worthwhile offers to write propaganda, or to spy. Cockburn was just as eager for further experience in foreign intrigue and found more than enough of it a decade later in Spain. During the early days of the Civil War, he served the Republican government as a section leader in the counterespionage department and shortly afterward helped to spread disinformation on behalf of the Comintern propaganda department in Paris. It is hardly surprising that he and Greene spent so much time together at Oxford. As self-taught secret agents, they were natural companions.

On a more innocent level, Greene amused himself at Oxford by trying to stay drunk for long periods of time. Lord Rochester had boasted that for five years he was never sober, but Greene was content to claim that he had remained equally sauced for a single university term. In the pursuit of this goal, he did not meet any resistance from his tutor, who was rather fond of drink himself. Fortified with alcohol Greene could even be persuaded to spend a little time enjoying social life among such eccentric groups as the Hysteron-Proteron Club. According to Waugh, its members liked to "put themselves to great discomfort by living a day in reverse, getting up in evening dress, drinking whisky, smoking cigars and playing cards, then at ten o'clock dining backwards starting with savouries and ending with soup." In a similar spirit of undergraduate frivolity, Greene and his friends liked to travel in disguises, dressing up in Moorish costumes or putting on rags and pushing a barrel organ around the country-side. Like most of his famous Brideshead contemporaries, Greene had lots of time for all kinds of activities except academic work.

But Waugh was right when he sensed that Greene wanted a great deal more from university life than a good time. He emerged from his ordeals at Berkhamsted with an overwhelming desire to prove that he was not an inferior being who could be pushed around, that he could be someone important in the world's eyes. Success would be his revenge for past humiliations, and his best protection against any new enemies. Anxious to avoid being in such a defenseless position again, he was determined to make his sensitivity a source of power instead of weakness. There was never any real doubt that a literary career was his best hope. He loved books, had a natural talent for writing, and knew how to make the right contacts. But to further his ambitions he needed to spend his time doing something more useful than playing masquerades, drinking, or studying for a good degree. He needed to build a solid base for his literary career. And this he did in earnest from the start.

It may have been easy to ignore Greene in the social life of Oxford, but his literary work was hard to miss. It popped up routinely. During his three years at Balliol, he published more than sixty poems, stories, articles, and reviews, the bulk of which appeared in the student magazine *Oxford Outlook* and in the *Weekly Westminster Gazette*. His poetry also appeared in three successive volumes of the prestigious annual *Oxford Poetry,* and a short selection of his poems came out in hardcover from the publisher and bookseller Basil Blackwell. He worked so fast to make a place for himself in the literary scene that within a year of coming up to Oxford he was an editor of the *Oxford Outlook* and was making all kinds of grand plans to expand its circulation and to attract famous contributors. His biggest catch was Edith Sitwell, who was easily seduced into submitting a poem after hearing a few well-chosen words of flattery from the young editor.

Greene was not shy about contacting the most celebrated writers of the day. Immediately after joining the staff of the magazine, he wrote to his boyhood hero, John Buchan, to ask whether he would contribute some piece of work. The audacity of this request is a good illustration of the nineteen-year-old writer's soaring ambition. As the author of *The Thirty-nine Steps* (1915) and *Greenmantle* (1916), Buchan was one of the best-selling novelists of the time and not a likely person to waste a story by giving it away to a student magazine. Buchan was kind enough to write a polite note of refusal, sending it to "H. Graham Greene, Esq." at his Balliol address, and it was probably some comfort to the young man to have at least this signed scrap of paper from his old hero. But he also seems to have gained satisfaction from the fact that Buchan lived close to Oxford. When Greene played his pretend game of Russian roulette—with a blank cartridge safely loaded in the chamber—he chose to do it in the countryside near the village of Elsfield, whose most famous resident, John Buchan, had done as much as anyone to make Greene think such games were romantic.

Greene's most inventive way of advancing his literary career at Oxford was to organize a national broadcast featuring six young poets reading from their works. He was also, of course, one of the participants in the Oxford Poets' Symposium, as it was called. It was all done live in those early days of the BBC, and the poets were understandably nervous about having to address their words to the strange boxlike microphones. Children of the Edwardian age, they approached the new medium with some of the trepidation of a remote tribe examining a fancy mirror. One of the poets—A. L. Rowse—recalled "feeling rather a fool, being emotional into the mouthpiece of a machine." But the event was reasonably successful, and Greene was delighted to have been the mastermind behind this new method of generating publicity. The only sticky moment occurred when the poet Patrick Monkhouse dared to use the word *damned* on the air. A few BBC officials worried that this indiscretion would result in some angry letters from prudish listeners, but Greene enjoyed making a joke of it, telling readers of a local Oxford paper, "Mr Monkhouse voiced the feelings of the whole room towards that confounded box when he swore at it very loudly."

Everything went Greene's way until his last few months at Oxford. His failure to excel in his final examinations was no great surprise—he received a Second Class degree in history—but the poor reception given his first book in spring 1925 was a serious disappointment. Although most poets expect modest sales, the unimpressive figures for Greene's thin volume of poetry were hardly worth recording. A first printing of 500 copies was planned, but this was eventually cut back to 300, and the majority of these went unsold in the first year. This dismal news could be hidden from friends and family, but the bad reviews could not easily be dismissed. The notice in the *Times Literary Supplement* was painfully direct—"full of inconsequences and irrelevancies." Even a poet from his radio symposium—Harold Acton—could not resist ridiculing the book, declaring in *Cherwell* that the poems were nothing more than "the slender banjo-tunes of an adolescent hysteria." With the embarrassing title *Babbling April,* the book was probably doomed from the outset.

Greene tried to forget this mistake as quickly as possible, and crit-

ics were gracious enough to ignore it after the writer went on to produce great books with impressive titles. But what could have made
the young literary lion of Balliol choose such a poor title? One explanation is that he was trying too hard to hide a secret in plain sight. It
was the very first of his many allusions to the experience of death and
rebirth, but in this case the context was too slight to be meaningful.
A biographical critic who pondered the significance of the title found
"little relevance to the contents, except that it probably pleased
Graham to call April names."

Aside from the joy of castigating April, Greene did have a more
substantial point in mind. He took the regrettable phrase from the
poem "Spring" in Edna St. Vincent Millay's book *Second April*
(1921):

> It is not enough that yearly, down this hill,
> April
> Comes like an idiot, babbling and strewing flowers.

It was Millay's subject matter, not her style, that attracted Greene's
interest. She was famous for a poem she had written at the age of
nineteen—"Renascence"—which is about a poet who dies, is buried,
and is then suddenly brought back to life. As the blood stirs in her
body again, the poet stands in an apple orchard with rain streaming
down her face and marvels at the strangeness of her rebirth. Many of
the images are similar to ones that Greene associated with his uncle's
place, Harston House. But in the later poem from which Greene took
his title, Millay's image of rebirth has lost its magic. April's beauty is
no longer "enough" to impress the poet, who cannot forget what she
has seen of death. Her most effective reply to the innocence and optimism of April is the cold declaration "I know what I know."

In an awkward fashion, Greene used his title to establish a sort of
kinship with Millay. Like her, he saw himself as a young person who
knew death too well and was haunted by the notion of suffering a
"second death." The truth of Shakespeare's great line "And Death
once dead, there's no more dying then" does not apply in the world
of Greene's *Babbling April*, where the poet seems to regard dying as
an endless process. When death is not stalking him, he is stalking it.
He is the failed suicide who cannot decide whether he wants one
more chance for life or death. This dilemma dominates the book, but
Greene's rough poetic skills cannot do it justice. The sentiments are
overblown, and much of the language is trite. After such mawkish
poems as "If You Were Dead" and "Death and Cosmetics," the
weary reader may wish to change the book's title to "Babbling Poet."

All the sickly introspection and melodramatic expressions obscure whatever was genuine in Greene's confused feelings about the temptations and terrors of extinction.

The fact that even Harold Acton, the indulgent dandy, found Greene's poems excessively emotional is some indication of how weak they are. What is even more amazing is that the dandy felt compelled to add to his *Cherwell* review the admonishment "For God's sake, be a man!" This was harsh criticism indeed from a fellow poet who lavished praise on young Evelyn Waugh as "a prancing faun. . . . So demure and yet so wild!" Under the circumstances, Greene felt that he had to make some reply to Acton's slur. But all he could manage in his letter to *Cherwell* was a mild joke about "Mr Acton as a professor of Manliness."

In his rush to make a name for himself, Greene had put out a bad book and paid the price. There was not much he could say in its defense. The only excuse is that, at twenty-one, he was too young to know better. The experience did show him, however, that making too great a show of his poetic soul was hardly worth the trouble. He did not bring out another volume of poetry until more than half a century later—in 1983—and even at that late date he was careful to make certain that few people would notice the book except collectors. The manuscript was given to a small press in California called Sylvester & Orphanos, which published it in a limited edition under the title *A Quick Look Behind: Footnotes to an Autobiography.*

From a commercial standpoint, it made sense to treat Greene's poetry like goods that needed to be smuggled in the back way, especially because people tended to laugh at him for fancying himself a poet in the first place. In a way the Balliol poet did suffer a second death. Over the years he sank deeper into the background as Greene worked to establish quite a different identity. It was a lot safer to be the tough novelist who wrote books with aggressive titles such as *Stamboul Train, It's a Battlefield* (1934), and *A Gun for Sale.* But a few critics could not help noticing that the tough novelist had a strange poetic streak. The Balliol poet was not really dead. He had simply found a good way to hide behind the mask of prose.

II

The odd thing is that becoming a tough novelist made Greene a better poet. Within the large framework of a long prose narrative, he could afford to make some poetic experiments, even to the point of slipping in whole passages that could almost stand on their own as separate poems. In time, this technique produced some excellent results. Under the camouflage of chapters and paragraphs, he planted small gems such as the following passage from *England Made Me,* which is presented here as though it had been written in free verse:

> Things one has feared and admired,
> And felt desire for,
> Things abandoned with the sea gently lifting,
> And the lightship dropping behind
> Like a small station on the Underground,
> Bright at night and empty.

This simple touch of beauty is embedded in a long series of random reflections by Anthony Farrant and can easily be overlooked by readers struggling to keep up with all the other aspects of Greene's busy narrative. But when set free from its paragraph in the novel, the lines resemble those of an imagist poem—especially one like Ezra Pound's famous work "In a Station of the Metro" (1916). The resemblance is not coincidental. When Greene was staying with Kenneth Richmond in London, he discovered one of Pound's works at a bookshop and became an instant admirer. As early as age seventeen, he was trying to write an imitation of the poet's imagist verse, and by the time he went up to Balliol he knew some of Pound's early work by heart. He won an academic prize of fifty pounds for an essay in which he quoted from memory Pound's "The White Stag." The dons who awarded him the prize did so largely because they believed that Greene had written the poem.

Unfortunately, the poems that he chose to include in *Babbling April* show few traces of Pound's influence. It was only when he began to write novels that Greene found a way to adapt the poet's techniques. Pound said that imagism should "stand for hard light, clear edges" and that precise efforts to embody "an instant of time" would prevent the "emotional slither" of bad verse. "Emotional slither" was Greene's great enemy in his first book, and imagism showed him a way to avoid it in the descriptive passages of his novels. He was not always successful; his weakness for far-fetched similes detracts from his more effective poetic touches. A typically bad simile is "evil ran like malaria in his veins." Perhaps it was this sort of thing that caused him to retreat further from poetry in his later novels, which are written in a generally flat style, with just an occasional burst of rich figurative language. But one of the pleasures of reading the novels he wrote in the 1930s and 1940s comes from watching an imagist at work in prose.

Nowhere is this more apparent than in *Stamboul Train,* which seems to be as much a long poem as a novel. The reader's attention is absorbed not only by the story and its characters but also by the richly detailed panorama of the train journey itself. A constant procession of sharp images helps to convey the sensation of hurtling across Europe on an old steam express in winter. Sparks "like hordes of scarlet beetles" streak past the icy windows, station lamps glow faintly in the snowy darkness, the lights of distant villages glitter, passengers bundled in thick coats stumble along the corridors, glasses of brandy shake to the rhythm of the speeding train, and new arrivals struggle to get comfortable in the cramped second-class carriages: "Men with their waistcoats off sprawled along seats, blue about the chin; women with hair in dusty nets, like the string bags on the racks, tucked their skirts tightly round them and fell in odd shapes over the seats."

In the first half of his career, Greene played down the importance of creating plausible characters and plots. For him the crucial elements in his novels were the same as those in a dramatic poem. As Arthur Calder-Marshall observed in one of the earliest—and best— critical essays on the novelist: "Greene has the imagination of a poet, but it is directed to smaller things than plot—the image, the setting, the word." Greene provides support for this point in his unjustly neglected study *British Dramatists* (1942), which contains the most revealing insights into his own aesthetic principles of the time. In this book character and plot are overshadowed by theme, ritual, atmosphere, mood, scene, and style. With some reservations, he implies that Shakespeare is the dramatic poet whose work is the best model for the writer of "dramatic prose." What he likes best about Shakespeare's plays is their "verbal power which continually puts a scene before our eyes far more vividly than the later scene-painters could do it. . . . The poetry is rightness . . . the *exact* expression of a mental state, the *exact* description of a scene." As for Shakespeare's great characters, Greene thinks that they are not fully developed creations but "mouthpieces for a mood, an attitude to life." In this respect, they are more elaborate versions of the allegorical figures in Morality plays, with Hamlet in the part of Revenge, Othello as Jealousy, Macbeth as Ambition, and so on.

One can take exception to Greene's interpretation of Shakespeare, but all that matters here is that he thought in such terms. It is his own work, and not so much Shakespeare's, that his comments illuminate. Greene's characters in the novels of this general period are best understood as poetic abstractions whose moods are much more important than their motives. They are defined by atmosphere and attitude, and their power over the reader is drawn from the primitive appeal of allegory. They may walk the streets of Brighton or Vienna, or wander through the interior of Africa or Mexico, but their characters are invariably raised to the universal level of allegory. Pinkie in *Brighton Rock* acts Revenge with terrifying skill; Scobie in *The Heart of the Matter* does credit to Despair; Bendrix in *The End of the Affair* is a modern Othello who plays Jealousy to the fair Sarah; the whiskey priest in *The Power and the Glory* is torn between Faith and Doubt; and Harry Lime in *The Third Man* is the perfect embodiment of Greed who emerges from his underground hideout, ascends the Great Wheel, and looks down on the specks of humanity whose lives he would gladly destroy for the right price.

But imposing the patterns of ancient allegory on modern life was not an end in itself for Greene. It was just a beginning. Because virtue and vice are never pure in his world, he was constantly shifting the allegorical patterns, giving characters additional parts. As cruel as he may be, Pinkie sometimes arouses sympathy and appears at brief moments to assume the part of a tormented Everyman. Scobie tries to excuse his suicide by casting himself as Mercy. And the lieutenant in *The Power and the Glory* is tempted to trade Envy for Pity. Whatever the abstraction, Greene is able to save it from triteness by leaving it open to transformation and by using the right images to give vice and virtue the solid feel of life. Or as Shakespeare put it, "To show virtue her own feature, scorn her own image, and the very age and body of the time his form and pressure."

In Greene's time at Balliol, there was one modern poet whose work could not be ignored. Everyone at Oxford with literary ambitions knew T. S. Eliot's poetry, and some undergraduates followed his career with the kind of enthusiasm that later generations would feel for the careers of rock stars. Forty years after coming down from Balliol, Cyril Connolly was still shaking his head with amazement at Eliot's extraordinary impact on his generation: "What can convey the veritable brain-washing, the total preoccupation, the drugged and haunted condition which this new poet induced in some of us? We were like newborn goslings for ever imprinted with the image of an alien and indifferent foster-parent, infatuated with his erudition, his sophistication." It was natural that Greene's appreciation of Pound would lead him to Eliot and that the latter's influence would eventually show up in Greene's work. Although Greene made little effort to advertise his interest in Pound, he was quick to show the world that Eliot's work had made an impression on him. His second novel—*The*

Name of Action (1930)—used several lines from "The Hollow Men" as its epigraph.

But this ordinary gesture of homage to a famous poet could not indicate how deeply Greene admired Eliot's poems and critical opinions. He was so inspired by the "unreal" modern city of Eliot's poetry that early Greeneland often looks as though it is simply a province of the Waste Land. From "The Love Song of J. Alfred Prufrock" to "The Hollow Men," Eliot's world provided Greene with many of the basic ingredients for the sordid atmosphere that is especially present in his novels of the 1930s.

The mind that created *Stamboul Train* and *Brighton Rock* was teeming with memories of Eliot's yellow fog, the gloomy pubs and cheap hotels, the half-deserted streets, the rats and oily canals, scraps of newspapers swirling in vacant lots, stale smells of food and drink, the lonely typist in her furnished room, the random bits of overheard conversation and popular tunes. One of the characters in *Stamboul Train* seems to have entered the novel straight from a page of *The Waste Land*. Eliot's Mr. Eugenides, the foreign trader who wanders through London with his "pocket full of currants," simply undergoes a change of name before boarding Greene's express as Mr. Myatt, the currant merchant who carries a sample of his goods in a waistcoat pocket.

Eliot himself credited Baudelaire for inspiring him to create such characters and scenes: "It is not merely in the use of imagery of common life, not merely in the use of the sordid life of a great metropolis, but in the elevation of such imagery to the *first intensity* . . . that Baudelaire has created a mode of release and expression for other men." Eliot argued that one way to reach this level of intensity is to establish a "juxtaposition of the matter-of-fact and the fantastic." Of course, this is exactly what he does with great effect in *The Waste Land*, placing sordid realities within a visionary framework dominated by the figures of Tiresias and the Fisher King. It is also similar to an approach that Greene uses in several works. Into the sordid lives of Pinkie, Scobie, Bendrix, and the whiskey priest—or "the hollow man," as he is once described—Greene brings intense visions of heaven and hell.

If only Greene had delayed writing his first book of poems for a few years, he might have produced some reasonably good verse in the style of Eliot. As a title for such a book, "The Cruelest Month" would certainly have conveyed a better impression of Greene's outlook than Millay's phrase, and it might also have given him an excuse to appropriate the Hanged God mentioned in Eliot's notes to *The*

Waste Land. But there was not much point in writing poems like Eliot's when the opportunities were so much greater for fleshing out the Waste Land in poetic prose. If Pound was the poet who gave Greene an appreciation for the power of images, and Shakespeare the one who taught him the importance of attitude and atmosphere, it was Eliot who showed him the literary possibilities of a modern world plagued by disillusion and despair. Like the young Eliot, he set himself the task of exploring that world, turning over its fragments to see what lay underneath. The things he discovered were every bit as terrifying as Eliot's "handful of dust."

It is not idle speculation to say that if the young Eliot had given up poetry for fiction, he might have been tempted to write something like *Brighton Rock*. As Greene well knew, Eliot was passionately addicted to thrillers and murder mysteries of every kind. In 1927, as Greene was struggling to find a direction for his own career, Eliot was entertaining readers of *The Criterion* with his enthusiastic review coverage of the latest detective fiction. He managed to comment on twenty-four such titles in the first half of that year. Eliot had the good sense to see that this kind of popular writing could be adapted to more serious purposes without sacrificing any of the enjoyment that ordinary readers demanded from it. In a world with so many mysteries that seemed to defy solutions, the traditional quest of the detective appealed to the author of *The Waste Land* as a metaphor with endless possibilities.

Eliot's approval of the form might well have been the deciding factor in Greene's decision to experiment with it. His first published detective story appeared in 1929 under the title "Murder for the Wrong Reasons." Two years earlier Eliot had made his most convincing argument for revitalizing the thriller in an essay called "Wilkie Collins and Dickens." Almost alone among the critics of his time, Eliot was willing to declare publicly that thrillers are a respectable form of literature, and to support his case he praised the ways in which Dickens and Collins had managed to combine serious artistic purpose and high melodrama in *Bleak House* and *The Moonstone*. Eliot saw no reason to scoff at melodrama, declaring that "the craving for it is perennial and must be satisfied. If we cannot get this satisfaction out of what the publishers present as 'literature,' then we will read— with less and less pretence of concealment—what we call 'thrillers.' "

Rather than settle for the guilty pleasures of an ordinary thriller, Eliot preferred to see some talented novelist prove once again that the form could be the basis for a great work of literature. He complained that too many of the authors working in the form were content to crank out predictable stories with no literary merit. If anyone wanted to reach the highest level, he said, the lead to follow was that of Dickens in *Bleak House*, who had shown not only that a serious novel could incorporate all the elements of a good thriller but also that it could do so with some of the "intensity" of great poetry. Eliot was not prepared to take up the challenge to create such a work, but Greene was. In *Brighton Rock* (1938) he produced the modern masterpiece that Eliot was trying to imagine.

Thanks to the poet and critic Herbert Read, Greene's contact with Eliot was not limited entirely to books. In 1935 Read arranged a dinner for the three of them, and Greene approached the occasion with all the anxiety of a young acolyte who is finally granted an audience with his master. It is interesting that what most impressed Greene about that evening was Eliot's willingness to talk more openly when the subject turned to something for which he felt unrestrained delight—detective fiction. Although Greene and Eliot never developed what could be called a friendship, they did see each other occasionally in the 1950s, when the poet was living in Chelsea. Greene visited Eliot's flat on several occasions in the company of his friend Jocelyn Rickards, who was always amazed at how serious Greene became in Eliot's presence. Long after he had become a success, Greene retained his admiration for Eliot, but the poet never seemed to realize how much he had influenced Greene. And Greene was not the sort to bring it to his attention.

As for Pound, it appears that he and Greene never met. The poet's influence on Greene quickly waned after the 1920s, and there was little cause to seek him out. Greene did not forget the debt he owed Pound, however, and paid a kind of tribute to him at an event held in the postwar years. It was a rally to support Pound after the American government had indicted him for treason. The Institute of Contemporary Arts opened its premises in London for the occasion, and a large crowd filled the hall. Some of Pound's poems were read, and a few speakers made arguments for his immediate release, but when one speaker seemed to offer lukewarm praise, a pair of voices shouted "Shame!" from the back row, and a "small riot" broke out as other members tried to quiet the indignant Pound supporters. Appearing to be under the influence of something more stimulating than poetry, the two protesters—Greene and his friend John Davenport—were eventually thrown out. Told about the incident later, Pound warmly commended Greene and Davenport for having caused so much trouble on his behalf. "Their asperities diverted me in my green time," he said, employing a suitable image.

CHAPTER SIX

TIES THAT BIND:
VIVIENNE

Perhaps the least successful poem in Greene's *Babbling April* is a lovesick lament called "1930," which gets off to a poor start with the dull phrase "Eating a Lyons' chop" and never recovers. The premise of this little poem is that even after the passage of five years, the poet is suffering from the pains of a broken love affair. As he sits alone in the restaurant trying to finish another bad meal, he stares at the crowds streaming past the window and dreams of better days, when the fires of love seemed to brighten everything. But now, in 1930, nothing goes his way—it rains all the time, and his greasy chop is served on a dirty plate. If such abject misery is all the future holds, what is the use of carrying on?

The inspiration for this work was a woman ten years Greene's senior—the governess to his younger brother and sister. Her name was Gwen Howell, and for a few months in 1924–25 Greene idolized her. They saw each other during his university vacations, and Greene began actively pursuing her after catching a good view of her bare legs at the beach. Bored with the routine of looking after Hugh and Elisabeth, the governess found Greene's attentions a pleasant diversion at first, but she became worried when he kept insisting on being alone with her in the nursery at night. Aside from some quick kissing and fondling in the darkness, his chief pleasure seems to have come from sneaking a few dances with her at the Saturday night "hops" in Berkhamsted.

The romance, such as it was, never had a chance. Gwen Howell was not only a good deal older than Greene but also engaged to another man. Through dreams, letters, and poems, Greene tried to heighten the passion of the affair, and to convince Gwen and himself that he was the best man for her. The idea that she had promised to share her "body's secrecy" with someone else was too much for him to accept. She resisted his pressure to break off her engagement, which is just as well, because he had no intention of making life easy for her. In another poem written with her in mind, he described himself as someone who did not really want to fall in love but who had been tricked into it by a temptress with "witch's eyes." With a little effort he was able to see the governess as the seducer—the older woman whose charms had lured him away from the purity and contentment of serving his art.

"The Godly Distance," as he called the poem, is the work he chose to read for the broadcast of the Oxford Poets' Symposium in 1925. Knowing that Gwen was listening to the radio with his parents in Berkhamsted, he was pleased to use this public occasion for the private purpose of sending her a message. She had bewitched him, and it was up to her to say whether he would have his freedom or her "body's secrecy." While it may have excited him to know that only Gwen would understand his poem, she was probably less than thrilled to hear her employer's son telling the world that she was a temptress. There was always the chance that Charles or Marion Greene might read more into "The Godly Distance" than was good for Gwen. Perhaps not entirely to Graham's surprise, she wasted little time removing herself from danger. A month after the broadcast, she left Berkhamsted and got married.

In the dark nursery Greene was searching for something that his mother, with her "state visits" to that room, had never given him. He was trying to find the same thing that his hero desires in *The Man Within*—"deep-breasted maternal protection." Before Gwen came along, he had found a glimpse of this quality in the person of Kenneth Richmond's attractive wife, Zoë, who was in her early thirties when Greene lived at the couple's house. He had been brave enough to reveal his feelings about her in one of his morning sessions of psychoanalysis. Asked to describe his latest dream, Greene told Richmond that it involved Zoë and proceeded to explain how she had appeared to him. She had knocked at his bedroom door, he said, then entered wearing nothing at all. Without a word, she had gone to his bed and bent down beside him, coming so close that her breasts dangled next to his lips. According to Greene, the liberal-minded Richmond took all this in stride as simply another piece of scientific information to be pondered at a later date.

In all likelihood the dream was one of the many that Greene fabricated to keep Richmond occupied and himself amused, but in his waking hours a version of this "dream" could easily have occupied his thoughts. Living with the Richmonds allowed him the rare opportunity to observe up close a grown woman who was neither a relative nor a servant. For a curious boy of sixteen who had grown up in the closed—and often cold—world of Berkhamsted School, Zoë's bosom was a natural object of study and extended reflection. In six months under the same roof with her, he could do an enormous amount of fantasizing about deep-breasted maternal protection. When he later came to encounter an accessible older woman in the family nursery, the situation was almost too good to be true—like something out of a dream, or a nightmare.

Although it was unfair to Gwen Howell, Greene could hardly resist thinking that she was a witch tempting him to do something that had long been forbidden, something mixed with the guilt of lust and incest. As a young child he had developed a grim fantasy about a witch hiding in a linen cupboard outside the nursery door, and he was never able to forget this symbol of his childhood insecurity. Unfortunately for Gwen, her innocent presence in the nursery was a trigger for all sorts of potent fears and desires in Greene. While she was casually flirting with him, he was furiously debating with himself whether she was a witch sent to torment him, a mother to comfort him, or a woman to please him. The one thing that he could not see was the ordinary governess who was trying her best to survive in a strange household.

Just before Gwen came into his life, he had been giving a lot of thought to his pretty cousin Ave, who had stayed at Richmond's house with him. As a love interest she was a good compromise. He had known and liked her all his life, so she posed no threat. Because she was only a year older, she was not a convincing mother figure, but she did have the advantage of looking like a younger—and better— version of his mother. She had a delicate, graceful figure, and whenever Graham caught sight of her in a white skirt hitting tennis balls on the lawn of Berkhamsted Hall, his interest in marrying her would rise substantially. If his father could play it safe by marrying a Greene, then so could he. Except that Ave, for one, did not welcome the idea of another first-cousin marriage in the family. In any case, she had seen enough of Graham to know that he was not her idea of a good husband. Reluctantly, he accepted that marrying her was out of the question. As she recalled: "Graham wanted to marry me. Then he said no, we're cousins, my father and mother wouldn't have it, and your mother wouldn't like it. . . . I was fond of him, but I wouldn't have married Graham. I wouldn't have known from one day to the next what would happen."

Although she enjoyed being with Graham, Ave did worry that there was a touch of madness in him. Herbert Greene's mad streak also worried her, and she thought later that this mental instability was connected to the fact that the parents were first cousins. There was some mental illness in the family background. A family history reports that Charles's father suffered from bouts of "deep depression." Marion told her children almost nothing about her father, and it was only much later in life that Graham discovered why. Carleton Greene was a Victorian clergyman in Bedfordshire who behaved reasonably well until some crisis of conscience overwhelmed him. He became convinced that he was unworthy of his ministry and demanded that it be taken from him. The authorities would not oblige him, so he went into a field near his church at Great Barford and "defrocked himself." He was later sent to an asylum and spent the rest of his life there. All this was the stuff of vague family rumors. The name Carleton was an old one in the Greene family—Marion gave it as a middle name to her son Hugh—but no one seems to have asked many questions about Grandfather Carleton. This made him all the more interesting to Graham and prompted the novelist to create his own imaginary portrait of a mad defrocked clergyman. Acky, in a *A Gun for Sale,* is a Dickensian degenerate who swears in Latin and raves constantly about the sexual "peccadilloes" that forced him to leave the Church.

Carleton Greene died in the very year that Graham began pursuing Gwen Howell, but his grandson—who never saw him—had been under the impression that he had been dead for years. The information about Carleton's demise came to Graham's attention by sheer chance almost forty years later. It is appropriate that the mystery should have been solved while the obsessive author was scanning footnotes in the six-volume Yale edition of Swinburne's letters. While a student at Trinity College, Cambridge, in the 1860s, his grandfather had reviewed Swinburne's *Poems and Ballads,* and news of the piece had pleased the poet, who wrote to his publisher, "Please send me *at once* the January number of a Cambridge magazine called 'the Light Blue' containing an article on my Poems." For this good notice, Carleton Greene was awarded a footnote by the scrupulous editor of the Yale edition, who also had the courtesy to reveal that the once promising reviewer had died in 1924, aged eighty. This was an eerie discovery—suddenly Graham found out that the dead grandfather of his youth had actually been alive all that time. It was a resurrection of sorts, by footnote.

Greene once said, half in jest, that he had been given "bad genes." It would certainly seem so. But even that handicap could have been eased by parents who were genuinely loving. He may have wanted to believe that his mother really cared for him, but he could never get the love from her that he needed. She did not want to show it, perhaps for fear that once she started to reveal emotion, she would not be able to stop. Her silence about her father speaks volumes about her lack of warmth. It is sad to think that Greene had to learn of his grandfather's death from a footnote, but this is an indication of how remote his mother could be, even with her own children. Such a mother is not uncommon, and such coldness is something many children learn to overcome. Graham was one child, however, who never discovered how to do it.

The witch in the nursery was, of course, his mother. The regal shape who glided through on her way to more important tasks became, in the child's mind at night, a witch lurking in the shadows. As Greene recalled in adulthood, the dreaded linen cupboard was one spot where his mother liked to pause on her nursery visits. Keeping sheets and pillowcases in neat order was more to her liking than playing games with children, and one of Greene's early memories of his mother was of watching her tall figure at the cupboard carefully inspecting its contents. What he adored in the light of day, he abhorred at night, secretly teaching himself to hate what he could not have.

In one form or another the witch turns up in several of Greene's works, but she makes her most frightening appearance in "The Basement Room." In this early story she torments young Philip, a sheltered child who has grown up in the luxurious surroundings of a Belgravia mansion. The boy's mother and father have gone away for a holiday and left him in the care of the butler and housekeeper, Mr. and Mrs. Baines. As soon as the parents are gone, the dark figure of Mrs. Baines can be seen busily covering the furniture in the rooms upstairs with sheets, as though she had emptied a whole cupboard to hide all signs of life under a "shroud." Like Greene's mother, she wants things to be neat, and it is impossible to go anywhere in the house without finding that she has arranged everything in perfect order. Even moving about is difficult because Mrs. Baines has put such a slippery polish on the floors.

Philip and Baines feel trapped in the web that she has woven around them, but they are not allowed to escape. Sneaking into the nursery at night, she frightens Philip when he awakens and sees her leaning over his bed. Instead of the comfort of a mother's bosom pressed against him, he finds a few strands of hair hanging above his lips. It is Greene's dream of Zoë Richmond turned into a nightmare, with love and sex twisted into something foul. Trying to calm the boy's fears, Mrs. Baines says that she has secrets to share with him and asks whether he loves her. She intends to catch Baines in the act of cheating on her and wants the boy to help. Too scared to speak, he turns away from the smell of her "stale" breath, which makes him think of the "witches" that have disturbed his sleep on other nights.

Unfortunately, this is not a nightmare, and the boy is forced to witness the subsequent battle between husband and wife as it moves inexorably toward her death and Baines's arrest for murder. With stunning speed the short story drags the boy from the shelter of the nursery to the dark maze of adult passions. The worst thing is that he must confront the ordeal on his own. There is no mother to protect him. Even after he flees the murder scene and is found by the police, he is given over to the care of a sullen woman constable who resembles not a mother but "a female impersonator." Decades later Philip is still trying to understand the strong emotions that the incident aroused in him—his hatred of Mrs. Baines's cold efficiency, his disgust at her ugly sexuality, his childish affection for her husband, and his resentment at being made to share someone else's dirty secrets.

In the story a green baize door divides the family quarters from the basement where Mr. and Mrs. Baines live. At first the door seems magical to Philip, an entry to the world of his hero Baines. By the end of the story, its importance as a dividing line has been rendered meaningless. Once the adult passions are in full rage, there is no way to contain them, and no place to hide from them. It is the same for that other green baize door, which Greene made famous in his autobiographical works, the one that divided the main schoolroom at Berkhamsted from his father's study. Many readers think the door created a clear divide between the turmoil of the school and the peace of family life. It was sometimes comforting for Greene to see it that way, but he was never safe on either side. He found enemies everywhere. Bullies and informers in the dormitories, spies and witches at home. It was just that the occasional torments of home seemed easier to bear than the constant agony in the dormitories.

How could any individual give Greene the kind of love he was looking for? The situation really was hopeless for a man who was carrying such heavy baggage through life—witches, teddy bears, hanged men, lepers, spies, green baize doors, potting sheds, pistols, linen cupboards, Zoë's breasts, a defrocked clergyman, a faithful gardener, the schoolboy Carter, T. S. Eliot, Raffles, Shakespeare, the earl of Rochester, and much more. The only possible way around the problem of romance was to divide his attentions: a boy here, a prostitute there, a mother substitute by the fireside, a glamorous mistress hidden away. Yet risks attended them all, not the least of which was keeping them in safe compartments so that each one was ignorant of the others. Mastering that art would take time, money, and patience. It was almost enough to make a young man despair.

As Greene saw his years at Oxford coming to an end, his frustration got the better of him, and he made an intemperate attack on sex in general. People spent too much time thinking about sex, he complained in the *Oxford Outlook* of March 1925. With the confidence of a man talking to himself, he declared that it was time for everyone to start thinking more about art and religion. This kind of outburst could be expected to draw a few letters of praise from the usual friends of strict morality, but Greene was pleasantly surprised by one response. It was from a young woman who wanted to correct him on a certain point.

II

Vivienne Dayrell-Browning (who later shortened her first name to Vivien) was nineteen when she wrote to Greene. In his article he had spoken of people worshiping the Virgin Mary, but Vivienne felt compelled to tell him that he had used the wrong word. The proper thing to say, she explained, was that people "venerated" her.

Young ladies did not ordinarily write notes to complete strangers in the early 1920s, especially on a matter that some might consider minor, but Vivienne was a fairly recent convert to Catholicism and was inclined to take religious terminology rather too seriously. A single woman whose mind was less noble might have written such a note in order to create a pretext for meeting a rising young literary man of Balliol. Nothing could have been further from Vivienne's mind, as she explained from the vantage point of the 1990s. "After thinking about it for some time," she said of Greene's article, "I thought I had to make a protest. It was a thing like if you saw someone beating a dog in the street, you might go up to them and say, 'That's wrong. Don't do it. Stop it.' But you wouldn't expect to go on seeing the person or anything like that."

Using a religious term incorrectly is a far cry from beating a dog in the street, but Greene liked the idea of meeting someone who would take him to task over such an error, for whatever reason. He wrote to her immediately, offering profuse apologies for his awful mistake and inviting her to tea. She accepted, and he was attracted to her from the moment they met. She was slender, with long, dark hair, a pleasant face, and a soft manner that could easily turn sharp when the need arose. He could not see enough of her. They met in restaurants, cinemas, and theaters, and went for long walks. They went punting on the river and read poetry together. Within three months he was begging her to marry him.

Part of the attraction was that she shared some of his literary interests. She worked for Basil Blackwell, and, like Greene, she was the author of a small book of verse published by the firm. A precocious poet, she had seen her book come out when she was sixteen. Edna St. Vincent Millay she was not, but her book's title was almost as unfortunate as Greene's. It was called *The Little Wings*. Her verses are quite simple, and the dedication is, as Vivienne herself later admitted, "soppy." It reads, "To Mummydar who has shown me beauty everywhere." The affectionate tone of this line is not surprising; it was the work of Mummydar herself. Although all the poems were written by the daughter, it was the mother who had decided that they should be printed and who had taken the liberty of dedicating the book to herself. Vivienne did not know anything about the publication until after her mother had worked out an acceptable arrangement with the publisher. Moreover, Basil Blackwell was persuaded to make Vivienne an apprentice in his firm with the idea that she would eventually become a regular member of the staff.

Vivienne's mother was obviously an ambitious woman who had a clear idea of how to run her daughter's life. She even liked to pick out her clothes. The mother's maiden name was guaranteed to catch Greene's attention—she was born Muriel Green-Armytage. The family was not related to Greene's, but he was fascinated by any link to his name. Unlike his own mother, Muriel had perhaps too much love to shower on her child. She had left her husband several years earlier and seemed happy to devote much of her time to charting her daughter's future. Her desire to show her feelings was sometimes excessive. A surviving letter to her daughter in 1925 is overflowing with the kind of baby talk that was unimaginable in Greene's home. It is addressed to "precious baby sugar kitten" and is signed "your own whiskerspuss."

Vivienne made a slight show of independence when she decided to become a Catholic. Although Muriel disapproved, she did not force her daughter to comply with her wishes in the matter. The decision to join the Church had come up without warning. As Vivienne recalled, "I just woke up one day and said I must be a Catholic. But nobody encouraged me. My mother was annoyed." She enjoyed the freedom of following her own religion, and the pleasures of worship—or veneration—were soon reflected in her poetry. One poem, called *"Lux Mundi,"* shows that religion gave Vivienne a chance to pour out the kind of emotional energy that her mother had been showering on her for years. Instead of sugar kittens, she had the Body and the Blood.

Whether secular or spiritual, emotional excess intrigued Greene, and his new romance gave him the chance to show what he could do in that line himself. He put aside his reserve—not to mention his literary talent—and sent her long, effusive pleas for her heart, using language that comes dangerously close to the level of her mother's baby talk. He could not praise her too highly and was willing to promise almost anything if she would agree to marry him. Rashly, he pledged to accept a celibate marriage if a pure union of souls was what she desired. They could make each other toast and tea by the hearth in a little cottage and live in bliss ever after, never once descending to the nasty level of sex. There were other things to live for, such as poetry. Losing all sense of perspective, he even went so far as to call her a genius and to urge her to polish her literary skills through constant practice. They could win fame as poets together, collecting their verse in a single volume with their names forever joined on the title page. Hardly a day went by without Greene making some new proposal for their future happiness.

Muriel was not opposed to her daughter's new relationship with the Balliol poet, but she had her doubts about his literary aspirations. "Someone with a name like Graham Greene will never be famous," she said. All the same, he would have seemed, on the surface at least, an excellent catch for a publisher's apprentice. But Vivienne had no intention of rushing into anything. Other men had shown an interest in her, and she was young enough to take her time making a decision. Greene kept up the pressure, however, and, when it became too great, Vivienne threatened to break things off. Greene raised the stakes by starting to talk about suicide. He told her about his revolver trick and implied that he might rig some future game of Russian roulette so that he would be killed for certain.

Some women might have concluded that an affair with such a fellow was well worth ending as soon as possible. If they were not frightened away by his talk of revolvers, his friend Hilary might have convinced them to flee. Hilary Trench was not a teddy bear but an imaginary companion who conveniently embodied for Greene all his dark moods. He sometimes used the name as a pseudonym—his poem "If You Were Dead" first appeared under the name. Vivienne was one of the few people to whom he admitted that Hilary was like a second self. Whenever he went into a dark mood, it was Hilary who did the thinking for him. If he pushed things too far with Vivienne, he liked to blame it on Hilary. It was wicked Hilary who planted terrible ideas in his head and made him want to hurt other people. Hilary was his personal devil.

Oddly enough, the devil was not able to get rid of Vivienne. In fact, by September 1925 she had agreed to enter into a secret engagement with Graham. A speculative person might say that Greene had made clever use of his devil, talking him up in order to win the sympathy of an impressionable young Catholic. Whether that was his intention or not, his talk achieved the desired result. Young men in love have always acted strangely, but this particular young man often had a method to his madness. He made impossible promises and extravagant declarations of love because he enjoyed the excess, and because he thought it was what the author of *The Little Wings* wanted to hear. During his years at Oxford, he had spent a lot of time telling people what they wanted to hear, whether they were German spies, officials of the Irish Free State, or secretaries of the local branch of the British Communist Party. He was good at it.

Vivienne's interest in physical purity appears to have weakened considerably under Greene's sustained assault. Their engagement lasted two years, and in a letter written about halfway through that period, she sounds very much like a woman who has finally come to a full appreciation of Greene's merits. Talk of a celibate marriage has given way to a detailed discussion of how a certain amorous feline will welcome her favorite friend on his next visit. Using her considerable resources of kitten talk, Vivienne promised to comfort her friend with generous kisses, affectionate bites, and warm sounds. Muriel's little girl was getting ready to make the leap into marriage. To reach this point, however, Greene had felt it necessary to make one more suggestion. He dangled before her the idea that he might join the Catholic Church. The poets could be one in body and soul.

At the time Greene could not have explained to anyone why he was going to so much trouble for his "girl." He could have found any number of women who would have settled for much less, as long as he did not mention Hilary. The decision to pursue Vivienne was so complicated that he did not bother to say anything about it when, forty years later, he wrote his autobiography of those years. Instead of analyzing his courtship, he preferred to detail his early adventures among prostitutes in London. According to his own reckoning, he developed some sort of relationship with no fewer than forty-seven prostitutes during the 1920s and 1930s. Some he saw repeatedly, some were nothing more than brief encounters. Some he could remember by name, others were simply half-remembered faces or were associated with certain areas, such as Piccadilly or Islington. And no doubt many more slipped from his memory altogether. An early draft of *A Sort of Life* contained a long summary of these adventures, but apparently there was simply too much of it for comfort, and the whole section was finally dropped from the published work.

The problem was that any extended discussion of Greene's sex life raised personal questions that he could never bring himself to answer directly. It was one thing to drop hints or to boast about visiting some notorious brothel, but he could not reveal why he needed prostitutes or even why he needed a wife. Putting some veiled explanations into a novel was another matter. That was safer. And so, in November 1926, while he was still polishing the act that would win him a wife, he began work on a novel that addressed his sexual problems indirectly. For a time he wanted to call it "Dear Sanity"—but that would have said too plainly what he was in need of. So he found a better title—*The Man Within*.

At first glance nothing would seem to be further from Greene's personal experience in the 1920s than the characters and action described in his first novel. The plot does not sound promising. Smugglers in the early 1800s bring a shipload of spirits from France to the Sussex coast and are ambushed by customs officers who have been informed of the exact place and time of their landing. The informer is the hero of the novel, Francis Andrews, who has sailed with the smugglers for three years but who wants desperately to escape them. He slips away during the ambush, is given shelter by a saintly young woman of eighteen named Elizabeth, and falls in love with her. Inspired by her admirable character, he summons the courage to testify against the six captured smugglers, but when they are acquitted he loses all his courage, abandoning Elizabeth to the mercy of the smugglers when they come seeking revenge.

This predictable story seems to have been pulled straight from a back issue of a boys' weekly. There are obvious traces of Joseph Conrad's influence, but so much attention is focused on the action that no subtleties seem possible. And that is the way most critics have looked at the book. It is seen as the apprentice work of a novelist in his twenties, who knows how to handle a rousing tale but whose art touches no depths. Everything that is worth knowing in the book is on the surface.

But that kind of literal thinking has always been a smuggler's best protection, whether he is trading in spirits from France or contraband from elsewhere. The glossy surface is the work of a young and inexperienced novelist who cannot resist playing with superficial effects—elaborate imagery, exaggerated suspense, breathless dialogue—but it is also the work of a writer who wants to bury part of his story under a thick protective layer.

It would not do much credit to Greene's smuggling skills if the only thing slipping past the reader was an idealized portrait of his Vivienne. To be sure, the portrait is there in the character of the warmhearted Elizabeth, whose simple love gives Andrews his only hope of stability in a troubled life. Her little cottage is the island of peace that he has been searching for—the sweet maternal atmosphere that will help him forget three difficult years at sea. The issue worth pursuing, however, is not the comfort provided by Elizabeth but the pain caused by his time onboard the *Good Chance,* as the smugglers' ship is called. What was so bad about this "good" ship?

The ready answer to that question is that the smugglers are a bad lot of fellows engaged in a nasty business, and our hero deserves better. Except that a certain kind of fellow might say that Andrews did not know a good thing when he had it. Under the protection of his close friend, the chief smuggler Carlyon, Andrews is allowed ample leisure to watch pretty sunsets, read Robert Herrick's love lyrics, and share with Carlyon his secret love for soft music, nice colors, special scents, and misty mornings in bed. It was a beautiful sunset that first brought Andrews and Carlyon together. They stood on a hill and watched the red flames of light die out until all that was left on the horizon was a pale blue haze. For three years after, they were inseparable as they went about the business of smuggling things; then Andrews spoiled it all by deciding that so much smuggling was driving him mad. Carlyon is one of the six men against whom Andrews testifies.

The story of this ruined friendship is not just a general reference to Greene's homosexual inclinations, nor is it an effort to dredge up something more specific about his troubled times at Berkhamsted, although that period is alluded to here. The real subject would appear to be Greene's guilty feelings of affection for a particular person in his recent past. It was someone he knew during his three years at

Oxford—a young man who was one of the hearty crew of six poets participating in his radio broadcast. In addition to Greene, Harold Acton, Brian Howard, A. L. Rowse, and Patrick Monkhouse, there was Joseph Macleod—the only one in the group who was a close friend of Greene. Not much is known about his relationship with Greene at Oxford, but Macleod did give away some vital clues when he was interviewed in 1977, not long before his death.

Although he seems to have been a reasonably discreet man, Macleod could not resist mentioning an old disappointment. In 1924 Greene published a little poem called "The Coming—To J.G.W." The poem's reference to a sunset upset Macleod, because he and Greene had enjoyed watching a special sunset together and he assumed that the initials appended to the title were those of an unknown rival: "I told Graham of my jealousy, wishing the initials had been mine." Greene did not try to explain who the rival was, leaving Macleod to imagine the worst rather than telling him the unexciting truth—the initials belonged to an infant nephew. Instead of being honest about the true extent of his feelings for Macleod, Greene played a coy game with words that left his friend puzzled for half a century. Only in *The Man Within* could Greene feel free to reveal the depth of both his attraction to Macleod and his fear of homosexual attachment.

Macleod may not have understood the emotional turmoil that he had aroused in his fellow poet, but Greene never forgot it. Although they went their separate ways after Oxford, the novelist found an occasion to include a direct reference to his friend in a book written many years later. Following graduation Macleod became a successful radio announcer, and in 1943 he achieved a rare distinction among Greene's friends and acquaintances when his full name was dropped into the text of a novel. In the early pages of *The Ministry of Fear*, a radio is playing in Arthur Rowe's flat: "The news began—'and this is Joseph Macleod reading it.' The stranger crouched back in his chair and listened."

It is significant that the reference to Macleod's name is linked in this novel with an act of smuggling. On the pretext of wanting to hear the news, the stranger in question has come to Rowe's flat to steal a document that is to be smuggled out of the country.

As does Andrews in *The Man Within*, Greene forced himself to choose between continuing a romantic voyage with a good friend and jumping ship. When Vivienne came along, he headed for the shore. There was nothing unusual about the undergraduates of his time having their "romantic friendships" and later pursuing wives and mistresses with great determination. But as *The Man Within* suggests, shaking himself free from his attachment to Macleod was not easy for Greene. What stands out in the novel is Andrews's recognition that—when all is said and done—he really belongs with Carlyon. He chooses Elizabeth, who is trustworthy and practical, and who will protect and comfort him, but "romance" lies with Carlyon. Elizabeth is sanity, Carlyon is the madness of a forbidden love. Still, it is Carlyon who finally escapes from all harm, with Andrews's help. Elizabeth and Andrews end as suicides, achieving the hollow victory of being united in death.

Greene seemed to think that, for better or worse, Vivienne was his only choice. That is debatable, of course, and *The Man Within* is the debate. The voice that sways the decision in Elizabeth/Vivienne's favor is that of Andrews's "man within." That inner voice—which he associates with his demanding father—scorns him with the words "You are not a man." The point is that any real man would see Elizabeth as the sane choice. Andrews feels he must prove his manhood, but after he loses Elizabeth to suicide, and Carlyon to the sea, he decides to kill himself in order to silence the voice. Avidly pursued, "dear sanity" is just as avidly destroyed. Although the "man within" is supposed to be the voice of reason, he can turn just as quickly into a destructive inner figure like Hilary Trench.

A further complication is that Andrews wants to "soil" himself from time to time in the company of easy women. He finds such a person in the character of Lucy, a Sussex townswoman who is not too particular about the company she keeps in bed. Andrews enjoys her hospitality but does not repay her kindly. Pushing his face into her breasts, he pinches her flesh, and, although she seems to like this rough treatment, he is disgusted with himself afterward and tells her that she has made him feel "dirtier." Used to such outbursts of postcoital guilt, she tries to reason with him, explaining that any feeling of shame will pass and that he will be ready to sin again in no time. But reason is not what he wants to hear. Although he will not deny the truth of her words, he wants to feel the full measure of his sin, enjoying the shame much more than the sex.

Ultimately, every problem for Andrews comes back to his love of smuggling. The term is not merely a code for homosexuality. Sneaking things past other people is a joy in itself. One reason that Andrews is drawn to homosexual love and illicit sex with women is that both require some degree of secrecy. But the process is without end. He sneaks things past everyone, outsmuggling the smugglers by arranging their capture and betraying Elizabeth by hiding his true nature from her. Smuggling is a part of his nature, and he regards it as an inheritance from his father, who seemed so strong to the out-side world but whose many weaknesses were all too apparent to the son. Behind his confident assertions of manliness, the father was nothing but a frightened bully trying hard to cover up his ignorance and insecurity. The father was a smuggler by nature as well as by trade. And because he knows his father's secrets, Andrews hates him. Yet he also hates him because they are so much alike.

It is significant that reading *The Man Within* was an unpleasant experience for Charles Greene. The autobiographical points in the novel could be smuggled past most people but not past Charles, who knew his son's problems well enough to recognize that there was something too close to home in the portrait of Andrews's relationship with his father. After *The Man Within,* Charles vowed that he would not read another one of his son's novels. One member of the family thought that Charles had been offended by sexual references in the novel, but these pale in comparison with the sharp attacks on the hero's father—a man in whose shadow the son labors without ever feeling sufficient approval from either the father or the father's many admirers. Spying, disloyalty, smuggling—whatever name Greene chose to call his compulsion, it is something that he could always trace back to Berkhamsted. His fate was to be an expert smuggler, and to hate his father for teaching him the trade. But once he had the knack of it, he was unstoppable. In just the one occasion of his Oxford broadcast, he found incentives for smuggling a poetic mes-sage over the air to Gwen Howell and for smuggling a message to posterity through *The Man Within.*

Contemporary reviewers of Greene's first novel may not have wanted to see its homosexual theme, but in more liberal times read-ers must have sensed its presence. Yet nothing was ever said publicly, perhaps because Greene had done such a good job of persuading his audience that the theme held no interest for him. Nevertheless, an overdramatized film version of the book, which came out in 1947, almost unmasked the novelist. In an effort to play up the emotional tension between Carlyon and Andrews, the filmmakers treated the relationship in such a forceful way that some viewers could not help speculating about homosexual motives. It also helped to have a hand-some young Michael Redgrave playing Carlyon and a boyish Richard Attenborough playing Andrews. Greene was annoyed and tried to undermine any speculation by joking that one film viewer in Istanbul had asked whether he had written other books that treated homosex-uality as openly as *The Man Within.* Greene's implication was that only some lonely soul in an exotic backwater would dare to see a homosexual theme in his work. Predictably, he accused the filmmakers of abusing his novel and refused them the right to adapt any more of his books for the screen. All the same, their intentions may have been entirely innocent—as much so as those of the contemporary film critic who called their production "a starry Technicolor costume drama with queer bits."

CHAPTER SEVEN

HEAVEN CAN WAIT

Despite his urgent proposals to Vivienne in 1925, Greene knew that he was in no position to marry. His only means of support was the allowance from his father. After coming down from Oxford in June, he continued to rely on his father's money while he spent the next eight months looking for a regular job. At the beginning of this period, he had a lucky escape from the long bureaucratic claws of the British-American Tobacco Company, which wanted to stick him out in China for four years. Before he knew it his application was accepted, his name was on the payroll, and his passage to Shanghai was booked. His Balliol education had impressed the company, which was making an effort to employ more university men, and his letters of recommendation were full of praise. His tutor, Kenneth Bell, was kind enough to lie a little for him, calling him "a good mixer." Fortunately, at the last minute Greene realized that his future was not in cigarettes. Unable to face the bureaucrat who had hired him, he sent a telegram informing the company of his resignation. Greene's career with British-American Tobacco lasted ten days.

The prospect of working in China had appealed to his sense of adventure, but it was all wrong for one whose real ambitions were literary. Journalism made much more sense, and Greene turned to it with enthusiasm after his abrupt flight from the tobacco trade. The only problem was that the major newspapers would not consider him until he had gained some practical experience. In an admirable display of common sense, he resolved to learn the business by starting out as an unpaid pupil at a provincial paper. After an extensive search, he found a spot at the *Nottingham Journal,* which was more than happy to let him work six hours a night in the office for nothing. He came to the paper in November 1925, and for the next four months he assisted the subeditors, who graciously allowed him to do a lot of their work without burdening him with much instruction.

Forced to labor in the obscurity of the provinces, Greene found it easy to see the worst in Nottingham. To his eyes, it was a place of perpetual gloom and grime. Heavy fog darkened the skies, rain dripped from sooty buildings, the streets were crowded with grim faces, his room was unpleasant, and amusements were few. Even the prostitutes in town were old and ugly. His only close companion was a new pet, a dog named Paddy, who had the unfortunate habit of being sick on his floor. Taking the dog for long walks was Greene's chief recreation. His only contact with the literary world came during a brief visit to the home of the popular novelist Cecil Roberts, who was a native of the town. Greene brought along a gift—a copy of *Babbling April*—and Roberts tried to give his visitor some encouraging advice about the writing game. But Roberts was not impressed by the "tall, gangling youth." His comment almost fifty years later was "He looked undernourished."

On one of his walks with his dog, Greene was drawn to Nottingham Cathedral, where he made contact with Father George Trollope. Having told Vivienne that he would like to become a Catholic, Greene decided that the time for action had arrived, and by the end of the year he was receiving instruction from Father Trollope. He gave Vivienne earnest reports of his progress, presenting himself as undergoing a genuine struggle to understand and to accept Catholic doctrine. But he was never one to put his faith in other people's doctrines. The main thing was to make Vivienne think that he was becoming a convert for her sake. And there were other incentives as well, some of which were related to the character and personal history of Father Trollope himself.

It was no accident that Greene came to be instructed by this particular priest. In many ways he was the perfect choice for someone with Greene's love of mischief. When he met Greene, Trollope was a stout, middle-aged former actor who had played a variety of small parts before assuming a permanent place in the cast of the Church. In his youth he had joined a large touring company and had quickly mastered the art of repertory theater, slipping in and out of various parts as the need arose. In *The Sign of the Cross* he played both a pagan and a Christian, which meant that he "had to roar like a lion one day, be eaten by one the next." During a brief career on the West End stage, his big roles included Tweedledee in *Alice* and Roderigo in *Othello*.

Greene was delighted by the priest's recollections of life in the theater, and the more he knew of him, the more he liked him. If Greene wanted to play a Catholic convert in a convincing fashion, it made sense to learn the part from an experienced actor. It also made the whole experience more fun for a devious young man eager to find some amusement in a dull provincial town. And the old actor was a wonderfully innocent accomplice, adding a nice touch of farce to the process of instruction by analyzing the fine points of religious dogma in the most unusual places. The busy priest would take his young convert with him as he traveled around the town, and Greene never forgot the day they rode along on the upper deck of a tram solemnly working out the exact date of the Gospels.

But the best thing about Father Trollope was that he enabled Greene to strike a small blow against an old enemy. When George Trollope had decided to convert to Catholicism in 1905, his parents had opposed the idea, and their opposition had been fueled by a close family friend who also happened to be Charles Greene's predecessor as headmaster of Berkhamsted, Dr. Thomas Fry. Greene may have known this connection when he first contacted Father Trollope. It would be rather too coincidental if he had met the priest purely by chance. In any case, a bond of sympathy was formed between priest and convert. The Dr. Fry who had tried to keep George Trollope from becoming a Catholic was the same man who had pressured the Board of Governors to make Charles Greene headmaster, thus inadvertently setting Graham on his long trail of sorrows. What sweet revenge it would be for Graham to announce to his parents, who still revered Dr. Fry, that he was leaving the Church of England and joining the Papists through the ministrations of George Trollope. And, as Greene later noted, the chance to get back at Dr. Fry was not lost on the priest: "It amused Father Trollope to think he was having his revenge by baptising me into the Church."

Greene's parents did not try to stop him from becoming a Catholic. If they could not keep him out of the hands of German spies at Balliol, they could hardly prevent him from consorting with priests in Nottingham. They probably also suspected that he was no more attached to Catholicism than he was to Germany. But religion did have its appeal, especially as a system of thought teeming with powerful images, symbols, and immutable laws. For someone devoted to disloyalty, Catholicism offered endless ways to make trouble without risking any great punishment—at least not on this side of the grave. It was a target too tempting to resist, and one that could serve well a writer who was obsessed with the darker secrets of the heart. It provided specific names for vague hurts and desires, and it made good and evil so easy to personify in the eminently dramatic characters of an invincible deity and a relentlessly cunning devil. There was also something to be said for the thrill of being known as a Catholic in a Protestant country.

In the 1950s one of Greene's friends asked why he had become a Catholic, and the novelist answered, "I had to find a religion . . . to measure my evil against." He may have been joking, but there is some truth in his remark, especially if he meant to say "my sense of evil." Greene never made a secret of his fascination for the way that religion can create a heightened awareness of evil. He emphasized this factor repeatedly in his early comments on the appeal of Catholicism. Damnation and hate—not God and love—are the things that aroused his interest and defined his sense of religious intensity. Everything that conventional believers claim for God and love, he claims for damnation and hate. In the prologue to *The Lawless Roads,* he writes of the deep pull that hate exerts on the spirit, a pull every bit as strong as that of love and one that "demands allegiance." In three separate essays on the false priest Frederick Rolfe (otherwise known as Baron Corvo), Greene never mentions God but cannot say enough about the "spiritual" appeal of evil. Rolfe is the only modern English Catholic who receives any substantial attention in Greene's *Collected Essays.* As Greene makes clear, his own interest in Rolfe's published works is based largely on the writer's ability to capture the "devil's point of view."

This was a quality that Greene also admired in Henry James, and he attributed it to the novelist's admiration for certain aspects of Catholicism. According to Greene, James was a Catholic in spirit if not in fact, and the spirit that touched him was that of "supernatural evil." The tame, unimaginative Anglican Church had made evil seem too weak, but the presence of evil could be felt everywhere in Catholic churches, where the "savage" force of religious feeling was still potent. As far as Greene was concerned, all of James's evil characters reflect this force. They are consumed by something larger than themselves, an omnipresent evil that fills them with passions equal in strength to those engendered by love and goodness. In an essay called "Henry James: The Religious Aspect" (1933), the only religious aspects that Greene discusses are hell, the devil, damnation, and evil.

Henry James emerges from Greene's treatment as some sort of devil's apprentice, stirring up a cauldron of evil in story after story. Moreover, the Catholic Church is made to seem more like a satanic cult than a religion devoted to Christian principles. Greene almost says as much a year later, in a review of T. S. Eliot's *After Strange Gods*. "To be a Catholic . . . is to believe in the Devil," he declares. Whatever truth there may be in this statement is undercut by Greene's failure to say anything at all about the fact that Catholics also think of God from time to time. At every point in his review, he is intent on portraying religion as a way of reaching a deeper awareness of evil. He was especially impressed by Eliot's statement "Most people are only a very little alive; and to awaken them to the spiritual is a very great responsibility: it is only when they are so awakened that they are capable of real Good, but at the same time they become first capable of evil." The implication is that evil has a spiritual quality that can be cultivated in the same way one might cultivate good spiritual qualities. And to be worthy of true evil one must be fully "alive." Or, as Eliot put it in his essay on Baudelaire, "It is better, in a paradoxical way, to do evil than to do nothing: at least, we exist."

Dozens of critics have made wonderfully complicated efforts to explain the Catholic significance of Greene's work. They can even explain how a Catholic can learn to love sin. And Greene himself could easily muster support for the idea that Christianity is really about sinning. For the epigraph to *The Heart of the Matter*, he quoted Charles Péguy: "The sinner is at the heart of Christianity." Greene had a point, of course. One could almost say that the religion needs sin as much as it needs virtue, although the point of Christianity is lost when so much emphasis is placed on the former.

It is a mistake to assume, however, that Greene was trying to be true to any Christian ideas. His concept of spiritual life was essentially personal and would have found a place in his work without the influence of the Church. What one finds in his work is an eccentric mixture of simple but powerful assumptions: God is tyrannical, the soul must assert its independence, sin can have its charms, easy virtue can corrupt, evil can be overwhelming, and damnation can be a noble act of defiance. What Catholicism gave to all this was the right background. It gave him rules to break and props to knock over. And that was a lot. The Catholic Church was an enormous edifice that could sustain heavy assaults without collapsing. He could subject it to one indignity after another, turning its good points into bad ones, making its God a devil and Lucifer a saint. He could ridicule its priests and parody its rituals. Best of all, it was possible to do this from within, to pose as a friend in the day and to chip away at the foundations at night. And in the end the Church would have to forgive him, because that is what the religion is all about.

The props are unbeatable, and a novelist needs his props. In an essay on François Mauriac, Greene says nothing about the Catholic ideas that he supposedly shared with the French author, but he speaks at considerable length about a novelist's need for vivid backgrounds. He praises novelists such as Mauriac for portraying the struggle between good and evil as a solid, inescapable reality. The struggle is not abstract but tangible, and the props of the Catholic Church help to put it before the reader's eyes. They make the spiritual visible in ways that are evocative and easily recognizable. Greene could dispense with the theology, but he could not do without the plaster statues, the candle flames, the Communion wafers, the wine in the chalice, the rosary beads, the Latin phrases, the stuffy confessionals, the figure of Christ hanging above the altar with his painted wounds.

For Greene's purposes, such things must be held sacred by true believers. They must be more than mere props in order to be worth subverting. In that sense he took Catholicism seriously. It was something real to fight against. In any case, he had been looking for ways to cross swords with religion long before he joined the Church. At Oxford—when he was keen to advertise himself as an atheist—he had published a story called "The Trial of Pan," which portrays God as a boring tyrant whose mind is falling apart. The old bully can no longer remember why he created the world, and he spends his time mechanically passing judgment on a parade of sad souls. Then the sexy figure of Pan is dragged before him for judgment. Before the lively pagan can be banished to hell, he begins a catchy song, and soon everyone in heaven is seduced by the music except God, who loses all his followers to Pan. In another story from the same period, "The Improbable Tale of the Archbishop of Canterbridge," God and Satan are revealed to be the same entity. After God admits the awful truth at the end of the story, he dies "in a bubble of bloodstained laughter."

Greene's basic view of religion never changed. He simply expanded his opportunities for subversion by presenting himself as a member of the largest—and most complex—Christian denomination. It took a while before he was confident enough to promote himself as a

Catholic writer, and bold enough to take full advantage of the possibilities of this role. But when critics began paying too much attention to the "religious aspects" of his work, he staged a strategic retreat, complaining that he hated the term "Catholic novelist." It was always easy for him to twist things whichever way he wanted.

He could even play the self-righteous Catholic when it was convenient. Feeling in the mood to criticize Hilaire Belloc and G. K. Chesterton, he made this extraordinary complaint in 1933: "Both these authors have done a good deal of harm to English Catholicism (I speak as a Catholic) by associating religious faith with beer-drinking, with local patriotism, with sentimental Irishmen." Of course, such things were minor compared with what Greene would later do to "religious faith" in *Brighton Rock, The Power and the Glory, The Heart of the Matter*, and *The End of the Affair*—associating it with adulterers, murderers, suicides, and whiskey priests.

He was adept at escaping from any trap, producing excuses that cut off all chance of debate. In 1951 he dismissed some non-Catholic critics of his work by declaring flatly, "They're so far from Christian thinking that they cannot enter into my world." But when critics in the Catholic press occasionally took him to task for presenting a distorted view of the religion, he had a different response. He was writing fiction, not "a moral treatise," he said, so no one should expect his work to be theologically sound. He also realized that any opposition from Church authorities could be used to his advantage. On the eve of the New York opening of *The Potting Shed*, Greene joked to a reporter, "Wouldn't it be a marvellous thing for *The Potting Shed* if only Cardinal Spellman could be persuaded to ban it?"

By and large, however, Greene did not have to work hard to defend himself in Catholic circles. There always seemed to be more than enough Catholics willing to rush to his defense. One prominent Jesuit in America, Father Harold Gardiner, argued that even though Greene was no theologian, there was still a great deal of theology hovering around the edges of his books: "Mr. Greene . . . is not interested particularly in solving theological questions, but he *is* interested in delineating the terrific impact of theology on human souls." In other words, the priest could not find any evidence to support his case, but he knew it must be hiding there somewhere.

At the height of his career, Greene benefited from the fact that so many Catholics were happy to have someone of his great standing associated with their religion. As David Lodge has pointed out, Greene "made Catholicism, from a literary point of view, interesting, glamorous and prestigious. There were no Anglican novelists, or

Methodist novelists . . . but there was, it seemed, such a creature as a Catholic novelist." As long as Greene was willing to be identified as a Catholic, there were good reasons for others in the Church to view him in the most sympathetic light and to stretch the limits of doctrine to accommodate his ideas. Everything could be explained away, although Greene did make the job increasingly difficult for his Catholic friends in later years. It was awkward having to defend a "Catholic atheist" who liked to refer to the Vatican as the "politburo" of the Church.

It would have been even more awkward if those friends had known of Greene's secret passion for causing trouble in the confessional. The screenwriter Guy Elmes, who was an occasional companion in the 1950s, remembered how much pleasure Greene took from trying to shock priests with outrageous confessions. One day when the two men had been working hard on a script of Greene's story "The Stranger's Hand," the novelist suddenly proposed that they take a break. "Let's find a little church with some awful little priest," he said. "I'll go in and confess some ghastly crime. Let's cheer ourselves up." Elmes went first and made a fairly mild confession. Then it was Greene's turn: "Father, I've fucked an Alsatian this afternoon. How many Hail Marys?"

And to think it all started in Nottingham with a little instruction from an ex-actor who had once played Iago's right-hand man. It may have been that Greene never intended to do more than have some fun at Father Trollope's expense, but with so many reasons tempting him to become a Catholic, how could he not see the game through to the end? In the last week of February 1926, Father Trollope baptized Greene. It was a simple ceremony with no friends or family present. But the young convert gleefully informed Vivienne of every detail and made it very clear that he was expecting a reward for his exemplary action. As a new Catholic, he would be needing a great deal of guidance and encouragement. It was almost a matter of religious duty for her to marry him. She owed it to God to keep this strange lamb in the fold.

For one thing, it was now more important than ever that Vivienne keep him from entertaining further thoughts of suicide. She would not want a fellow Catholic to put his soul in danger. As he warned her in a letter written in January, suicidal thoughts were still disturbing his peace. He dreamed that he had shot himself, he told her, and she had been the cause. In the dream she was flirting with another man, and in a frenzy of hate he decided that the best revenge was to make her think that she had driven another Catholic to commit the terrible sin of self-annihilation. That would cause her lasting pain, he felt sure. But, of course, he was not talking about real actions. It had been only a dream. A harmless dream.

II

A few months of journalistic experience in Nottingham proved sufficient to win Greene a spot on a London newspaper. And not just one. The *Daily Telegraph,* the *Daily News,* and *The Times* all offered him employment as a subeditor. He chose *The Times* and began work in March 1926 at a salary that just managed to equal his allowance from his father—250 pounds a year. At last Greene was able to support himself, although neither he nor Vivienne thought it was enough to support both of them. But more money lay ahead. If he satisfied his new employers, his salary would double in a year. And the work was not onerous. He was required to be in the office for seven hours every weekday evening, but he usually had a couple of hours free to read or write on his own.

He wrote some pieces for the paper, but primarily he spent his time checking other people's work for errors and unnecessary words. Douglas Jay, one of Greene's fellow subeditors on *The Times,* later said that their chief aim was to reduce paragraphs not merely to "the shortest number of words, but [to] the shortest number of letters." To liven up the work, Greene and Jay used to have little competitions to see how many times they would have to cross out certain empty phrases in the copy put before them. "In connection with" and "in regard to" were among the phrases they were eager to spot. In time the job became more of a game than anything else. Jay recalled, "We both prided ourselves that we could reduce any given typescript put between us to one third of the length without any loss of meaning."

In his odd bits of free time on the job, and in the mornings at his new lodgings in London, near Battersea Park, Greene began work on the novel that would become *The Man Within.* This was not his first attempt at writing a novel. Two dismal failures had preceded it. "Prologue to Pilgrimage" (also called "Anthony Sant") had been completed while he was still at Oxford and was rejected by at least three publishers before Greene gave up on it. This unusual tale never had a chance of appearing in print. It is the story of a black child whose parents—by some strange quirk of nature—are white. The child, Anthony Sant, attends a school very much like Berkhamsted and suffers many of the torments that Greene experienced. By making his hero black, Greene is able to provide an obvious motive for the school bullies who make Anthony miserable, a motive far removed from the one that inspired Greene's persecutors. But this awkward effort to disguise his own story prompts the novelist to add offensive details, such as the "darkie songs" that Anthony's enemies use to mock him.

The next attempt was, in Greene's words, a "historical novel under the influence of Conrad's *Arrow of Gold,* about Spanish exiles— Carlists—conspiring in Leicester Square." Almost everything Greene knew about these Spanish rebels and their cause was taken from Thomas Carlyle's *The Life of John Sterling.* It would have been under- standable if Greene had abandoned this obscure story after a chapter or two, but whatever else can be said for the young novelist, he was a man of extraordinary energy and determination. He began "The Episode," as the novel was called, shortly before he joined the *Not- tingham Journal,* and he finished it shortly after joining *The Times.* But energy and determination were not enough. The first publisher who received the manuscript kept it for several months, then turned it down. Greene was so disappointed that he did not bother to send it elsewhere. The only positive thing was that the rejection had come in a personal note from the managing director of the firm—Charles Evans of Heinemann—who encouraged Greene to send him the next novel. That was enough to make the young writer undertake a third book and resolve that he would send it to Evans as soon as it was fin- ished.

Writing "The Episode" also taught Greene a valuable lesson about the dangers of dropping big chunks of autobiography into his fiction. He had made the mistake of giving a copy of his manuscript to Vivienne, who was shocked by a scene in which a male character named Hilary is rejected by a young woman to whom he has pro- posed. Vivienne believed that all the basic details of the scene had been taken directly from an early time in their relationship when she had turned down one of Greene's proposals. She let him know how much she was hurt by this exploitation of their personal experience, and Greene tried to put her mind at ease. The similarities were mostly coincidental, he said. He had outlined the scene in his imagination long ago and had simply borrowed a few details from life when he wrote it up later on.

He was very convincing, but the more he denied her point, the less convincing he became. Finally, he broke down and admitted that he was lying. She was right. The whole scene was drawn from their expe- rience, and he was ashamed of himself for using it in his novel. He threw himself at her mercy, and she forgave him. But, of course, his repentance was only temporary. It was hardly the last time that he would bring Vivienne into his fiction. And it was certainly not the last time that he would strenuously deny an obvious connection between his life and art. He came to understand, however, that there was rarely any need to break down and tell the truth. The better thing was to brazen it out. As a novelist, he always had a good excuse: "I made it up." There was no reason to surrender the excellent cover provided by the Power of the Imagination.

Greene was ruthless in his willingness to use friends and family for "copy." Nothing was too private—even the intimate pains of strangers glimpsed in passing. No wonder he was often tempted to write biography, an art that must subject private lives to intense scrutiny. While he struggled to finish "The Episode," he considered at least three possibilities for a biography—the Elizabethan poet Robert Southwell, who was hanged for his Catholic beliefs (a nice combination of themes for Greene); the Irish poet George Darley; and the Scottish poet John Davidson, who committed suicide in 1909. They were not promising subjects from a commercial stand-point, and Greene soon gave them up in favor of a character closer to his heart, Lord Rochester. But there was a special reason for dropping Davidson. Before killing himself the poet had done something much worse—he had forbidden anyone to write his biography.

It is a "splinter of ice" in the novelist's—or biographer's—heart that enables him to plunder other lives for material. Or so Greene dis-covered one day in 1926, when his career at *The Times* was briefly interrupted by a personal crisis. He suffered an attack of appendicitis six months after joining the paper and was forced to undergo an operation at Westminster Hospital. The operation went well, but what remained most vivid in Greene's mind afterward was not his pain but the pain of a mother who had visited his ward. Her young boy had died suddenly, and she had come to weep over his body. The scene was agonizing. The mother's cries filled the ward. All the patients put on their radio headsets to block out the sound—but not Greene. He was busy gathering material, carefully observing the drama on the chance that the details might prove useful one day in a novel or story. He was aware that his action seemed cruel, but he also appreciated the nature of his calling. It was his job to listen—to intrude on this private grief—because, even though the child was dead, there was a story to tell.

The story was eventually transformed into something quite differ-ent—the description of an adult dying in a ward full of indifferent faces, each patient lost in his own world, each protected from the suffering of others by a headset. This is Conrad Drover's last vision in *It's a Battlefield*, and his sad end is a perfect one for a character who always considered himself an outsider. But the most interesting thing about this scene is that Greene managed to transfer the splinter of ice to the other patients. Now they are the ones who seem most cruel. They have taken refuge in their headsets, cutting themselves off from life, because they lack the heart to face its more painful moments.

Greene knew that the rigorous demands of his literary ambition—not to mention his many psychological fears and compulsions—would be difficult for Vivienne to bear, and he had the good sense to wonder whether their marriage would be the biggest mistake of their lives. He dropped a few warnings to her in letters, and Vivienne knew enough of his odd behavior to sense that trouble might be in store for her. But he had done so much to win her over—becoming a Catholic, promising her an idyllic life of poetry and religion, and landing a well-paid job on the staff of a great national newspaper. Surely he would continue to work for her happiness. He was young and full of plans. Everything would work out.

He had also honored her with a special place in his private world, confiding secrets to her about his ambitions, his weaknesses, his needs. He even taught her a secret code, one that would allow them to be fearlessly intimate in their letters. His ultimate aim was to develop such an intricate code for them that they could carry on secret conversations in public. While outsiders listened to them make innocent small talk about the weather or travel plans, they could actually be saying something quite different, entertaining each other with outrageous comments that they would never express openly before strangers. Vivienne seems to have enjoyed this kind of innocent fun. At the time she could not have anticipated how pervasive the codes would become in Greene's life, nor how other codes in the future could be used to deceive and hurt her.

Whatever reservations the couple may have had about each other, they agreed to marry in 1927, and early in the year Greene acquired a flat in Golders Green, where they would live after the marriage. Its chief merit seems to have been the spacious bathroom and an ample supply of hot water. In July he placed a short notice in *The Times* saying that he and Vivienne would marry in the autumn. From that point there was really no chance that either of them could back out. On October 15 the big event took place in a small Catholic church in Hampstead, St. Mary's. The groom was twenty-three, the bride twenty-two. Immediately afterward they headed for the South of

France for a short honeymoon, assisted on their way by the ever generous Uncle Edward Greene, who provided a tidy sum of cash and a car to take them from the church to Victoria Station.

Liberated from her job at Blackwell's, Vivienne looked forward to a long and happy existence as a housewife. Despite Greene's praise for her poetry, she had no literary ambitions. "My job," she said later, "was to make our money go as far as it could and to make a good life at home." A young wife's expectations were simpler then: "In those days when you married, your husband kept you for the rest of your life." But unlike so many other couples, they were not anxious to have children. Greene was especially opposed to the idea, feeling that a child in the house would be too much of a burden, emotionally and financially.

The couple seemed content to live in their own cozy world, and, in the early days of the marriage, they were extremely close. Ave Greene saw them frequently during those days and was taken aback by the intensity of the relationship. "When they were first married, they were always together. You couldn't part them, it was almost too much. . . . They were always holding hands, and wherever one went, the other went. . . . They were too sweet." Interestingly, one member of the Greene family who was not especially pleased with Graham's constant companion was his mother. As Vivienne recalled, "My mother-in-law used to say, 'And this is my other daughter-in-law. She's very artistic, you know.' It wasn't a compliment. It meant one was dreamy and liable to forget things."

Three months before Greene's marriage, his father had relinquished his position as headmaster of Berkhamsted School. Charles Greene's health was not good, and he had reluctantly decided to retire at sixty-two. He was suffering from diabetes, and his illness led to a long, slow decline in the once mighty figure who had reigned supreme over so many boys. He moved to Crowborough, East Sussex, and settled into a life of quiet obscurity. Marion Greene became the dominant power in the house, striving to keep up appearances and to care for her weakened husband. She kept him on a strict diet and gave him his injections of insulin. In Vivienne's young eyes, her mother-in-law was a daunting character, and Charles was a gentle but rather sad and lonely old fellow: "Marion was the driving force. I think she was fonder of [Charles], and of her two daughters, than of anybody. It was everything for Charlie. He smoked very much, and everything smelt very strongly of pipe tobacco. He played chess by himself or by correspondence. He sort of mumbled about. He was a sweet old thing, but I don't think he had much to say for himself."

As is so often the case, the end of the father's career came just as the son's was beginning to take off. Greene was doing well at his job, and there was practically no chance of losing it. In those enlightened days of English journalism, a job at *The Times* was a job for life. With such security, and with a devoted wife at home, he was able to concentrate most of his energy on his third—and possibly last—chance for placing a novel with one of the great London publishers. He was coming tantalizingly close to success. If the third time proved to be the charm, he would be on his way. And then he could "keep" his new wife in style. Maybe even for the rest of her life.

CHAPTER EIGHT

THE MAN WITHIN

G reene made speedy progress on *The Man Within*. At the end of 1928, the typescript was in the hands of Charles Evans at Heinemann, and Greene was anxiously wondering whether another rejection letter would soon be on its way. An acceptance seemed too much to hope for. Why should he deserve a place on Heinemann's distinguished list, which included works by Joseph Conrad, John Galsworthy, D. H. Lawrence, Somerset Maugham, J. B. Priestley, and H. G. Wells? No one at the firm had ever heard of him, except for Evans, whose earlier words of encouragement may have been—for all Greene knew—merely a polite gesture. Days passed and no letter arrived; then early one morning he received a telephone call from Evans himself. A restless man, the publisher liked to work quickly once his mind was made up. And he had no doubts about wanting *The Man Within*. Announcing his favorable decision, he asked Greene to come immediately to his office, where they could work out the details of a contract. With dizzying speed Greene was swept into the Heinemann ranks, and there he would remain for more than thirty years.

Evans was enthusiastic about his new author but not to the point of risking much money on him. He offered a small advance of 50 pounds, which Greene was glad to accept, and arranged for a first

printing of only 2,000 copies. Given the difficult market for new novelists, the publisher had good reason to be cautious. But Evans—and
everyone else—underestimated the appeal of Greene's tale of the
smuggling trade.

When the book came out in June 1929, the first printing quickly
disappeared from the shops, and sales continued to boom until
13,000 copies were in print. All but a few hundred of these were sold.
It was a stunning success, especially for a relatively unknown writer
who was only twenty-five. Suddenly, Greene was not just a promising
discovery but one of Heinemann's brightest stars. Even the critics
were impressed. The *Guardian* praised the "great power and beauty"
of the prose; *The Spectator* found the story "exceptionally fresh"; the
Daily Telegraph thought it was a "perfect" first novel; and *The Times*
was fully appreciative of the subeditor's "sensitive style."

After the American edition also did well, Greene decided that he
was no longer obliged to take small advances. Evans soon discovered
that his star had a sharp interest in financial matters. Instead of
increasing his price by a few hundred pounds for the next book,
Greene devised a more ambitious plan. He let Evans know that working for *The Times* was too much of a burden and that it jeopardized
his ability to turn out another best-seller. Eager to please his star, the
publisher agreed to pay him 650 pounds for each of the next three
years, in return for three more novels. At a time when most novelists—even well-established ones—were lucky to get an advance of
200 pounds, this offer was incredibly generous. It meant that Greene
could leave the newspaper and still live very well while he concentrated on writing fiction. It was also an extremely risky deal. For the
publisher to make money, each of the future books would need to
match the popularity of *The Man Within*. The chances of a young
novelist sustaining such a level of success were not good. He was sure
to make mistakes, but there was no room for mistakes in this deal.

Although he realized the danger, Greene found the offer irresistible. In late 1929 he had the pleasure of astounding his superiors
at *The Times* by giving them a most extraordinary document—his letter of resignation. They could not believe that anyone would volun-
tarily give up a place at their august institution. Efforts were made to
talk him out of it, but nothing could sway him from the prospect of
becoming a full-time writer. Not even Vivienne could change his
mind. She did not like taking risks, and now he was throwing away all
the security that he had promised her before they married. One major
reason for delaying their marriage had been to make certain that he
could adequately support them, yet he was determined to abandon

his job for life in exchange for only three years of income, at the end of which they might well be left with nothing.

But, besides security, *The Times* had nothing to offer him. After writing a best-seller, he could hardly be content to sit in an office editing the copy of less accomplished writers. Despite his new fame, he was still a minor functionary on the staff, and promotions came along rarely. Whatever the risks, it was time to move on. He had experienced only one period of real drama at the paper. During the General Strike of 1926, the editorial staff had supported management against the rest of its workers, and Greene had been happy to help break the strike. He was caught up in all the excitement of putting out a limited edition each day and did not hesitate to do such common tasks as packing and loading the papers for distribution. It was the first time that he had engaged in daily physical labor.

He was even more excited by his brief experience as a special constable during the strike, although this job involved nothing more challenging than patrolling Vauxhall Bridge in the company of a regular policeman. Still, he was proud to have a place in the front lines of the battle and confided to Vivienne that he was hoping for civil war to break out. The actual grievances of the poor held little interest for him. He could not understand why people making a hundred pounds or less a year were desperate to change a system in which a young subeditor like himself could be paid a salary of several hundred pounds. The thrill of witnessing a revolt mattered more than any vague notions of social justice. Or rather it is better to say that art mattered more than anything else—more than his newspaper, the government, the poor, the threat of an uprising. Greene was always thinking of how life could be put to use in art, and a good civil war was sure to yield enough material for at least a couple of novels. He would never have any trouble finding that sort of material abroad, but he began by looking for it at home, his cherished splinter of ice firmly lodged in his heart.

There can be no question that rebellions appealed to Greene as subject matter for his fiction. They are featured in each of the three novels written to fulfill his new contract with Heinemann. In *The Name of Action* the dictator of a Rhineland state is overthrown. *Rumour at Nightfall* resurrects an old idea from Greene's rejected novel "The Episode," using the Carlist uprising in Spain as its background. And in *Stamboul Train* the most dramatic moments are occasioned by Dr. Czinner's doomed plot to start a revolution in Belgrade. The deep social causes of the strife are unimportant. What Greene cared about was the moral and social confusion created by such events. It was the ideal atmosphere for his explorations of individual crimes and fears. Although the foreign settings can be tied to real places and events, they are treated almost as mythical backgrounds—dark landscapes of modern chaos and destruction. The individual characters stumble across these landscapes like tormented figures lost in the shadows of a surrealistic painting.

The Name of Action does draw on Greene's memories of his 1924 visit to the Rhine as a secret German propagandist, but the visit remained a vivid memory partly because it provided him with his first real images of a modern world plagued by disorder. In fact, according to Greene's published account of his visit, some German areas under French occupation seemed in danger of reverting to primitive lawlessness. Although his intentions were propagandistic, the vision he created had its literary uses. He spoke of soldiers raping and stealing at will, families forcibly relocated, people imprisoned for the slightest offenses, schools shut down, mounted soldiers attacking citizens in the streets without warning.

The worst conditions were in the town of Trier, where—Greene claimed—common soldiers were allowed to run loose and had raped hundreds of women and boys. On this subject the writer obviously allowed his imagination to run wild. And—most irresponsibly—in his eagerness to see civilization on the verge of ruin, he also tried to aggravate racial tensions. The French had used a large contingent of colonial soldiers from West Africa to help enforce their occupation of Trier, and Greene charged that these black troops, with "their lack of discipline and restraint," were responsible for most of the rapes and that their mere presence was "a deliberate insult against a defenceless people." Greene's evidence was slight, however, and he later admitted that his atrocity stories had been based mostly on rumors. But he and his friend Claud Cockburn did make a determined effort to witness a rape in progress. They spent a night following a group of Senegalese soldiers in the expectation that something might happen. Nothing did.

Whether real or imaginary, Greene's unpleasant tales made Trier a natural choice as the capital of the despotic state in *The Name of Action*. There are no black soldiers deflowering Rhineland maidens in the novel, but the story does depend on a question of sexual freedom. Paul Demassener, the supreme ruler of the land, fears the savage beast lurking in the hearts of his people and has taken vigorous measures to suppress it. A self-professed puritan, he boasts that his strict rule has put an end to his country's "sexual debauch." Before he came to power, Trier was "the brothel of Europe," but now the people live "in clean chains." Although his entire political philosophy is based on keeping sensual appetites under control, Demassener is blissfully ignorant of the sexual connotations of his repressive system. With disdain he dismisses the loss of civil liberties as a small price to pay for purity. If he has a slogan, it is "Freedom means freedom for the animal in man." One can easily imagine Charles Greene saying such a thing, and perhaps Graham was thinking of his father when he created the character of Demassener.

True to his beliefs, the dictator refuses to soil himself in the dirty practice of sex. This decision is particularly unfortunate in his case, because his wife—Anne-Marie—is the most beautiful, and most sensual, woman in the country. Her husband's devotion to his cause drives her straight into the arms of a handsome young English visitor named Oliver Chant, who is rich, adventuresome, and ripe for an affair with a frustrated woman. He also happens to be a secret financial supporter of Demassener's chief political rival, and thus the affair with Anne-Marie allows him to undermine the dictator's rule on two fronts, so to speak.

And the dual assault works. The wife confides that her husband is impotent, and Oliver shares the news with the opposition leader, who uses it as the centerpiece of a propaganda war that ultimately destroys the dictator's rule by making him a laughingstock. But, as Demassener falls in a rebellion, a strange thing happens to Oliver. He discovers sympathy for the dictator, who becomes human in his disgrace. By contrast, the wife and the opposition leader turn inhumanly cruel, showing no pity for the fallen puritan. Angry with his friends, the young Englishman decides to join his "enemy," helping Demassener escape from the rebels—who have added a bullet wound to the dictator's pains. Oliver takes him to the railway station and is last seen escorting his new "friend" to a safe retreat. Back in the capital, prostitutes slowly reappear in the streets, ready to do business again.

This tale transfers the elements of an ancient drama to the modern Waste Land of Trier. Part Fisher King, part Hollow Man, the impotent dictator vainly tries to impose order on an undisciplined populace, but the greatest disorder lies in his own house. He is unable to live at peace with either himself or his wife. His impossible ideal of sexual purity is simply a form of slow sexual torture and is more corrupting than the debauchery he denounces. Oliver Chant enters the drama with equally impossible notions of love and justice. Like some medieval knight who has wandered into a land of misrule, he tries to set things right. He helps the rebels and frees the fair lady from her chains. But in the modern world such actions cannot guarantee anything. The rebels may turn out to be worse than the despot, and the lady's heart may be as cold as her jailer's. Disenchanted, Oliver Chant flees the stricken land with the deposed ruler—one man wounded physically, both wounded spiritually.

Quite a few false notes are struck in this novel, but its ambitious aims raise it above the level of *The Man Within*. At least two scenes can be called masterly, which is saying a lot for a novelist still in his twenties. The first takes place at night in Trier when the opposition leader shoots a policeman in a deserted street and Oliver is forced to help dispose of the body. The struggle to haul the sagging body to the riverside is described in excruciating detail. As he carries the corpse, Oliver is overwhelmed by the full horror of the violence done to the man—the warm bloodstains, the smell of the blood itself, the frozen look of pain on the face. And pushing the "dark burden" into the river seems to take forever, as Oliver tries to prop up the "dangling comedian's head." When the deed is finally done, the splash sounds like an "explosion." To finish the cover-up, another accomplice drops raw meat on the spot where the murder took place so that passersby will think the blood came from someone who slipped on the way home from the butcher.

The other great scene takes place in a Catholic church. Anne-Marie has arranged to meet her lover secretly in the dark recesses of the church, among the candles and old women fingering their rosary beads. The sights and smells prompt Oliver to make an effort at prayer. Then the seductive figure of Anne-Marie approaches, her expensive fur collar in sharp contrast to the poor worshipers shuffling past her. In answer to her idealistic lover's pleas for a promise to marry him, she says that marriage is not necessary. He demands to know her feelings for him. He expects to hear something about "love," but she gives an honest reply that shatters all his illusions. It is only one word: "Lust."

Hopelessly trapped between their ideals and their passions, Oliver and the dictator make a natural pair after all. When they board their train for a quick escape from hellish Trier, they are joined by the kind of character Greene never tired of ridiculing—the pushy American journalist. In this case the villain is said to represent the *Chicago Tribune*. What he wants is a "scoop," the inside story of the rise and fall of Paul Demassener, and, as the novel ends, he is trying to get it. But the reader knows that the real story can never be told by someone looking for simple explanations in 750 words. How can the significance of the dictator's impotence be explained to the folks back in

Chicago? Even if it could be reported in simple terms, they would have a hard time understanding why his wife's lover would surrender her for him.

The true reporter in that railway carriage is the novelist himself, whose "scoop" is 70,000 words long. It is Greene's story in more ways than one. Trier is his world. He is the debauched connoisseur of brothels, the impassioned adulterer, the spy, the deceiver, the enemy of order. He is also the puritan, the self-righteous critic, the disciplined worker, the masochist, the sadist, the confused romantic. He loves lust, and he hates it. And there is no solution, only periodic escapes. He flees Trier with Oliver and Demassener, and he shares their wounds, but, unlike them, he will go back. The only thing that will change—from novel to novel—is the name of the place.

II

In addition to showing off his improving literary skills, *The Name of Action* reveals Greene's highly developed talent for undermining a good thing. His vision of Trier would work perfectly well without the addition of a certain detail to the character of his chief villain, Joseph Kapper. He is the opposition leader who engineers the rebellion against Demassener and the one who shoots the policeman. As the novelist repeatedly tells us, Kapper is also a Jew. The bad thing is that his Jewishness is portrayed as an integral part of his villainy.

He is a caricature of the worst kind—devious, moneygrubbing, and inherently unclean. Oliver is aghast when Kapper shows him a new weapon in the propaganda war—a poster featuring a painting of the dictator's scantily clad wife propositioning an enemy soldier. The Englishman is not so much bothered by the poster as he is by the idea of a Jew entertaining dirty thoughts about the beautiful lady. It is "hateful," the narrative explains, for Oliver to realize that Anne-Marie is "a woman in the eyes of the German Jew, a woman to be examined by those dark, desecrating eyes." Earlier the narrative describes the Jew's eyes as a "black, shifting curtain" that hides visions of "dark halls and clammy mysteries and perpetual night." These comments are meant to represent Oliver's point of view, but there is no hint anywhere that the author disapproves. In fact, the novel creates the impression that Demassener's fall is pitiable partly because it is the result of a Jew's scheme. Bitterly, the defeated ruler asks "the Jew": "Can you imagine anything more laughable than me beaten by you?"

There are a great many reasons why Greene would use such a

stereotype in his novel. In 1930, when his book came out, anti-Semitic remarks were not only commonly voiced in public but also regarded—in some circles—as fashionable. For literary inspiration, he could look to Eliot, who used Jews as symbols of modern degradation in "Gerontion" and "Burbank with a Baedeker: Bleistein with a Cigar." One could also say that Greene was young and impressionable, and that his treatment of Kapper is simply an isolated instance of literary excess. And it could be argued that the Jews were just another irresistible target for him, that he was an equal opportunity subversive who liked bashing all sorts of people—Jews as well as Catholics.

But there is no point in trying to minimize Greene's contempt for Jews, which is reflected in several works—not merely in *The Name of Action*—and which provoked his worst insults. It would seem, on the surface, that he had no motive except a desire to lash out at a vulnerable and, to his mind, unsympathetic group. Moreover, as life became increasingly perilous for so many Jews in the 1930s, the virulence of his attacks increased. It was not from any lack of appreciation for the danger confronting European Jewry. During the early days of the Third Reich, Greene was able to learn a great deal about events in Germany. From 1934 to 1939 his brother Hugh was a *Daily Telegraph* correspondent in Berlin and routinely wrote home with news about the "gangsters" running Germany. Hugh visited the concentration camp at Dachau at the beginning of his stay and wrote to his mother of how "brutal" the SS guards looked. Something else stuck in his mind: "The eyes of the prisoners were horrible."

It is difficult to believe that a man in Graham Greene's position would deliberately stir up hatred for people who had done him no harm but who were in harm's way themselves. Yet the poison of hate is undeniably present in his work of the 1930s. *Brighton Rock* is the best-known example, although it is not the worst. The rich gangster who controls most of the criminal action in Brighton has an Italian name—Colleoni—but for no obvious reason Greene makes him Jewish and does his best to imply that Jews have a natural talent for shady dealing. As he did with Joseph Kapper, Greene plays up a sinister quality in the Jew's appearance. Colleoni is said to have "raisin eyes" and an "old Semitic face" that gives nothing away. When the Jew talks on the telephone, Greene draws attention to the deceptive smoothness of his "low Semitic voice."

Colleoni delights in his domination of the English town, where his influence extends to the police and other officials. His headquarters—the Cosmopolitan hotel—looks like the outpost of a foreign conqueror. There is an "alien" feel to the place—all the furnishings are exotic, and the main rooms have foreign names: the Louis Seize writing room, the Pompadour Boudoir, the American Bar. The idea that Colleoni is a generalissimo of crime who has successfully taken over Brighton is reinforced by his name, which is taken from the unscrupulous mercenary leader Bartolomeo Colleoni, who profited from the wars between Venice and Milan in the fifteenth century. Corrupt and complacent, the master of Brighton's underworld is surrounded by his own little contingent of idle Jews. When Pinkie visits the hotel, he is regarded disdainfully by two "Jewesses," who are also identified in the narrative as "little bitches." Seeing Pinkie, one "Jewess sniffed at him bitchily." A male friend of Colleoni is an equally unattractive Jew, although Greene tries to turn the fellow's superficially slick appearance into a joke. Crab, as he is called, is someone who was "a Jew once, but a hairdresser and a surgeon had altered that."

There may always be people who will laugh at such a vulgar "joke," but at the time of *Brighton Rock*'s publication, in 1938, Greene's mockery was especially cruel. The long Nazi campaign against the Jews was gathering speed in early 1938 and reached a gruesome climax in the November violence of *Kristallnacht*. It was vital for writers such as Greene to speak out against the persecution, but instead he simply added fuel to the fire by showing the readers of *Brighton Rock* that Jews were unworthy of sympathy. Why would England want more Jewish refugees, when the "dark" aliens would simply swell the ranks of parasites such as Colleoni and Crab? It was a dreadful message to send into a world threatened by the growing evil of Adolf Hitler. Significantly, in his 1934 review of Eliot's *After Strange Gods*, Greene found no reason to contradict the book's infamous statement "Reasons of race and religion combine to make any large number of free-thinking Jews undesirable."

In September 1939, the very month that Hitler invaded Poland, Greene used his novel *The Confidential Agent* to launch his strongest piece of anti-Semitism, depicting a rich Jew as a mysterious figure intent on destroying traditional English culture from within. At first glance Forbes seems to be a perfectly typical English businessman of the period. He is fond of wearing tweeds, smoking a pipe, spending weekends at country houses, and making influential friends among the upper classes. He has done everything he can to hide his real background. Even his name is not his own. "Only the shape of the skull," the narrator says, "disclosed the Furtstein past." Like those of Greene's other Jews, the appearance of Forbes/Furtstein is seen as a reflection of his twisted nature. Again, the "raisin eyes" create a menacing appearance. Above them is the "domed Semitic forehead."

Although his English girlfriend likes to call him by the unappealing nickname Furt, he cannot resist the attraction of her "Aryan" beauty. To please her, he will try anything—even doing a good deed for a stranger. He has a perverse sort of interest in the features of "little Aryan faces." During a business meeting, Furtstein amuses himself by drawing such faces and giving them "goo-goo eyes" with "long lashes." He fills out the rest of the bodies and puts bathing shorts on them. As his girlfriend discovers, he is a weepy and dishonest lover. The main rival for her affection is the hero of the novel, and he is disgusted by her relationship with the Jew, especially after he learns that Furtstein keeps another woman on the side. He says to himself, "She deserved something better than a man named Furtstein who kept a girl in Shepherd Market."

Greene's use of the word *Aryan* is especially disturbing. Until the Nazis achieved prominence, the term was primarily used by philologists as a way of referring to the language family now commonly known as Indo-European. The Nazis gave the word its ugly racial overtones by defining it as any non-Jewish Caucasian. Greene clearly uses it in this second sense, which creates the impression that Furtstein craves women who are in some way forbidden or superior. The scene in which the Jew is admiring his slightly erotic drawings of Aryan beauties is very much like a scene from *The Name of Action*— the one in which Joseph Kapper is admiring his poster of a scantily clad Anne-Marie. In both the point is that the Jew has cast his "desecrating eyes"—to use the phrase from the earlier novel—on the fair form of the Aryan woman. It conjures up the same kind of rape images that Greene had used in his article on the threat of black troops in Trier. Obviously, it appeals to the worst instincts of the racist—the fear that a supposedly inferior race cannot resist raping women of a superior breed. (There is another hint of this thinking in Greene's story "A Little Place off the Edgware Road," which was written in the same year as *The Confidential Agent*. In the story, Jews with "acquisitive" faces stand near Marble Arch trying to pick up any girl who looks available. The reference was later eliminated from the version in Greene's *Collected Stories*.)

To make matters worse, Furtstein is also the owner of a supermodern seaside hell called the Lido. Despite Furtstein's accomplished efforts to appear English, the Lido resort is further evidence of his vulgar foreign streak. Unlike the cozy traditional English inn, his enormous resort is an impersonal construction of steel and glass with neon lights, rubber steps, and an ugly clock tower that glows in the dark. The entire complex is described as looking more like an airport than like a resort. Everything is cheap and artificial, and every day is full of mindless group activities in the big gymnasium, in the heated swimming pools, or on the vast playing fields. The implied danger is that rich Jews such as Furtstein are helping to turn England into a soulless commercial empire, paving over the beautiful countryside and pandering to the lowest desires of an increasingly subservient populace. If the Lido represents the future, Greene does not want any part of it—including, of course, the Jewish influence. The irony in this case is that he based the description of the Lido on Billy Butlin's holiday camp at Clacton, which was not exactly a hotbed of Semitic intrigue. A further irony is that when the artist Paul Hogarth visited the camp in the 1980s for his book *Graham Greene Country*, he found it "lying derelict like some forgotten concentration camp of the Hitler years."

The notion that Jews are constantly looking for a way to make quick money comes up often in Greene's work. The Semitic features always give the game away. In *Journey Without Maps* the author refers to "that Semitic expression . . . above the hooked nose of being open to the commercial chance." Similarly, in *A Gun for Sale*, Sir Marcus—the villainous Jewish industrialist who wants to sacrifice English lives for war profits—is described as having a "crooked nose and a tuft of beard." Before the old man is murdered, his killer taunts him for being a Jew and implies that the man's religion will do him no good in his final moments. "Better people than you . . . believe in a God," the doomed Sir Marcus is warned.

There is also the rich Jew in *Stamboul Train,* whose thick fur coat, Savile Row suit, and first-class compartment help to insulate him from the pains suffered by ordinary people. Perhaps as a joke, Greene gives him the first name of his lunatic grandfather. His full name, Carleton Myatt, helps to disguise his Jewish background, but his appearance—"short and stout and nasal"—brings him frequent anti-Semitic insults. Customers criticize him for cheating in business, but he prides himself on knowing many ways to outwit suspicious "Gentiles." And he cannot stand dealing with "disguised" Jews—those who have had operations to fix their noses. Such hostility does not stop him from seducing a Gentile. He takes advantage of a chorus girl who is down on her luck, and although his conscience prompts him to try rescuing her when she is in trouble, he turns his back on her eventually and marries for money. Or, as the narrative puts it, he decides to "set up his tent and increase his tribe."

In 1936 Greene had the opportunity to meet a man who had survived six months of imprisonment in Hitler's Germany. He was Stefan Lorant, a Hungarian-born editor who had been in charge of a picture magazine in Munich when the Nazis arrested him "on suspicion of Bolshevist intrigue." Pressure from Hungarian authorities helped to win his release, and, after fleeing to England, he wrote a frightening account of his ordeal, which was published in 1935 under the title *I Was Hitler's Prisoner*. It was one of the earliest books to sound the alarm about the Nazi campaign of terror against innocent citizens, and its preface closes with a blunt appeal for the victims who were not as lucky as Lorant: "DO NOT FORGET THEM!" But, after meeting the author at a literary party in London, Greene wrote in his private diary that Lorant was nothing but an overweight Jew who enjoyed recounting his troubles and was uncommonly pleased with himself. He thought that Lorant derived some sort of sexual thrill from all the attention he was getting. Whatever the man's personal manner may have been, Greene's reaction to him is notable for its lack of compassion or concern. It did not seem to cross his mind that anyone who had managed to escape from the Nazis might be entitled to make a fuss about it, if only to warn others of the dangers ahead.

After the war started Greene had the good sense to back away from anti-Semitism, but a couple of stray remarks did appear in the postwar years. In 1952 he published "Notes from a Journal of the Blitz, 1940–41," which included a paragraph about "a large fat foreign Jew" whom Greene had encountered one night while serving as an air-raid warden in Bloomsbury. According to the journal entry, the man made a nuisance of himself after being wounded by a bomb blast. The Jew's foot was "crushed and bloody," but Greene was annoyed by his "whimpering" and disliked having to bear the burden of the man's considerable weight as he helped carry him to a first-aid station. In his journal Greene makes a point of saying that the Jew was the only person who behaved in a cowardly fashion during that night's raid.

In *The End of the Affair*, the heroine's mother remarks in passing that she was once married to a Jew and adds that if people think Jews are "generous," they are very much mistaken. Her husband, she says, "was a mean man." Although this sort of insult can be attributed to the prejudice of the character, it does seem gratuitous within the context of the story. But Greene eventually realized the need not only to avoid all such future comments but to eliminate some old ones. In the 1960s—when sensitivity to racial insults increased dramatically—the novelist became uneasy about the more direct anti-Semitic slurs in his work, particularly those in *Brighton Rock*. He decided to clean up the text of the novel, removing most of the offensive comments from future editions. (He missed the one about the cosmetic work on Crab.) There was no apology for the insults and no effort to draw attention to the cuts. All the surgery was performed in perfect silence.

This cover-up was largely successful. A few critics complained about the anti-Semitism in the old edition of *Brighton Rock*, but many either overlooked it or chose to ignore it. And no one questioned the ethics of quietly altering a published text to eliminate unpleasant facts. Every author has the right to revise his work, but Greene was trying to revise literary history, not art. It is perhaps even more significant that Greene did not bother to doctor the text of *The Confidential Agent*. Because that novel has never received the kind of critical attention given to *Brighton Rock*, he was not asked to defend its use of anti-Semitic ideas and language. If no one dared to press the issue, he was willing to pretend that it did not exist.

One of the few people who directly confronted Greene about the basic issue of anti-Semitism was the literary scholar Maria Couto, who interviewed him in the late 1980s. The novelist's response was expertly disingenuous. Commenting only on Colleoni's identification as a Jew, Greene said: "During those years we did not think in those terms, and I meant the term 'Jew' to be descriptive. When I reread it later because the anti-Semitic idea was pointed out to me, I could see that it could be regarded as anti-Semitic, and I replaced it by 'tycoon.' But it was not meant to be anti-Semitic."

This defense would be funny if it did not concern such a serious subject. Greene pretends that the only real problem in the book was the use of the word *Jew* and suggests that everything could be set right simply by calling Colleoni a "tycoon." The greatest absurdity is that someone needed to point out the problem to him, as though his talk of Jewish "bitches" and "raisin" eyes had innocently popped into his head by chance and had just as easily been forgotten. Unfortunately, Couto did not seize the opportunity to challenge his statement.

Greene's case was helped by the facts that the books were old ones and that many of his ardent fans in later years were familiar only with *The Power and the Glory, The Heart of the Matter*, and major works published after the 1940s. History is easily ignored, but it is shocking that the creator of Colleoni, Furtstein, Kapper, Sir Marcus, and Myatt eventually received a major award from the Jewish homeland. In 1981 Greene was invited to Israel as a guest of honor at the Jerusalem International Book Fair. The mayor of the city gave him the Jerusalem Prize, which included a cash award of $5,000. According to its sponsors, the honor is meant "to recognise an author who has contributed to the world's understanding of the freedom of the individual in society." One cannot help wondering whether the judges of the prize had ever heard of *The Name of Action* or *The Confidential Agent*. Certainly they cannot have read the books. But Greene was delighted to have the award and was quick to use it as the ultimate defense against charges of anti-Semitism. How could he be anti-Semitic when he was the proud recipient of the Jerusalem Prize?

His evasive tactics would not have done him any good, however, if someone had developed the full case against him in a prominent forum. That case is more extensive than this chapter has shown— further examples from his film criticism will be taken up in another chapter—but, aside from the passages in *Brighton Rock,* very little of the evidence was openly discussed during his lifetime. (In the introduction to the Everyman edition of *Brighton Rock,* which appeared two years after Greene's death, John Carey makes a brief but perceptive appraisal of the evidence in that novel.) Reviewers in the 1930s stayed away from the subject, perhaps because Greene was then widely regarded as a thriller writer and thus did not merit serious attention. It was also hard for overworked literary journalists to keep track of the emerging pattern of anti-Semitism in his novels. Another reason may be that some reviewers simply failed to see the importance of the subject in those pre-Holocaust days. And some may have sympathized with Greene's treatment of it. In any case, his treatment would have seemed more subtle in the 1930s than it does now, and subtlety was a great weapon in his hands. But why was there not an uproar over it after the 1940s, in the years when Greene's reputation and readership figures soared?

Several major studies of his work say nothing about the pervasive anti-Semitism of Greene's early career. Such obvious silence on a crucial topic does not do justice to anyone, but there seems to be a feeling among some students of literature that certain unpleasant facts are better left alone. There is also the sticky question of self-interest among any group of biographers and critics. If you admire Greene's work enough to study all his books carefully, you will naturally be eager to discuss the good things you find and to touch lightly on the bad, or to find good excuses for overlooking them. It is painful to say negative things about a body of work to which you have devoted many hours of close attention.

The unspoken fear behind this attitude is that Greene's anti-Semitism somehow negates his literary talent. The treatment of Colleoni and company is indeed a terrible stain on a great novel, but it does not ruin the book. The inescapable fact is that Greene's genius is marred by a wide streak of malice. Nothing can wish that away or excuse it. But it is not a valid reason for dismissing his novels as works of art. Nor can the art excuse, in any way, the malice. In an essay on Salvador Dalí, George Orwell struggled with this conflict between art and life, and decided that it ought to be possible to condemn the actions and views of the man and still respect the art. Reaching that conclusion was not easy for him, because he objected to almost everything that Dalí glorified. He called him a "disgusting human being" and raised specific objections to the artist's obsessions with excrement, necrophilia, and violence—especially violence against women. "But against this has to be set the fact that Dalí is a draughtsman of very exceptional gifts," Orwell admitted. "He has fifty times more talent than most of the people who would denounce his morals and jeer at his paintings."

Orwell was responding to Dalí's boastful confessions of misconduct in the autobiography *The Secret Life of Salvador Dalí,* but the issue is trickier when the artist in question is highly accomplished at evading the truth and at suppressing it—indeed, when evasion and suppression are part of his art. As usual with Greene, boundaries are never easy to map. We may admire the art, and may want to separate it from the message it serves, but sometimes he makes that almost impossible to do. In the case of his anti-Semitism, he did his job too well, burying the hate deep within the narrative structures of his novels. Colleoni can be called a "tycoon" instead of a Jew, but this simple change of terms cannot reduce his importance in the book as a dark alien sowing corruption in society. He is an integral part of *Brighton Rock,* and that is why Greene's later alterations are so difficult to accept. The awful stereotype has merely been disguised, not revised. The hate lingers on under the protection of another name. It would have been better for Greene to acknowledge the injustice of the original version and then to let it stand as an accurate reflection of his tarnished talent. But coming clean was not in his nature.

The wonder is that he got away with so much for so long. In that respect he is a bit like the criminal Grünlich, in *Stamboul Train,* who prides himself on taking great risks and never getting caught. Grünlich will try anything and will somehow find a way to get what he wants. If things go wrong, he can slip out of the tightest trap. One of his great advantages is that he is a brilliant liar. He is such a thorough scoundrel that the reader is tempted to feel a little admiration for his audacity while at the same time being appalled by his misdeeds. It is even possible that Greene identified with him. He gave him a name that would suggest as much. In German, Grünlich means "greenish."

III

There is a very good reason why the anti-Semitism in *The Name of Action* has not been more widely noted. For the past sixty years, the book has been a collector's item, available only in secondhand bookshops or large libraries. Greene forbade any reprinting of the novel after the first edition sold out, and he continued to enforce the ban for the rest of his life. In this case, however, he does not seem to have been concerned that anyone would object to the treatment of Joseph Kapper. No protest was ever raised. What bothered him was the artistic quality of the book. He regarded it as an embarrassing failure and did not want its imperfections to cast a shadow over his more mature work. But it is really not a bad book at all—in many ways it is far superior to *The Man Within*. Greene was proud of it at first, but his view was soured by its failure to match the success of his first novel. Many of the reviews were bad, and the sales were far below those of *The Man Within*. Given the large size of his advance, the poor sales were a great blow. They threatened to put him deeply in debt to Heinemann.

But if he had not tied himself to the unrealistic terms of his contract, he would have been able to take a more objective view of his second novel, which could not be regarded as a failure in ordinary circumstances. He later exaggerated the commercial disaster, claiming that it sold little more than 2,000 copies. In fact, it sold nearly 5,000, a figure that would have thrilled most young novelists of the day. But it was a great setback for Greene, who had been hoping to sell at least twice that number. Although the reviews were rather depressing, there were a few bright spots. The *Observer* praised his "slow, careful sensuous prose," and *The New York Times* called the novel "brilliant." Some reviewers clearly failed to give the complex story the attention it deserved—a common fate. Evelyn Waugh was one such offender. In his short, and generally unfavorable, review for the *Graphic*, he failed even to get the title right. He called it *The Name of Reason*.

His third published novel is another Greene rarity. It, too, was suppressed after it proved a commercial disappointment, but the reading public is probably better off without it. Unlike his previous two novels, *Rumour at Nightfall* is practically unreadable. It is a dreary effort with bland characters, fuzzy scenery, and no lively action. One might assume that the setting in Spain during the Carlist wars would provide at least some drama, but everything in this book is muted. Even the occasional play of gunfire seems to take place in slow motion without any sense of excitement or immediate danger. The main characters talk in circles and look at each other with dark expressions. Descriptions seem to go on forever, and there are few of the sharp images that enliven so much of Greene's work elsewhere.

Greene had only a vague knowledge of the historical background and the scene of the action, but his greatest problem was the simple one of not having a clear focus. The novel is ostensibly concerned with the efforts of an English journalist to cover a late stage of the Carlist wars, in the 1870s. His great ambition is to write an exclusive story about the rebel leader who is struggling to keep the lost cause of the Carlists alive. Helping the journalist with his mission is a close friend from London—together, their names sound like those of a bad comedy team: Chase and Crane. The tough, ambitious journalist is Chase. His overly sensitive, dreamy companion is Crane. Inevitably, a pretty Spanish woman comes between the two friends, undermining their strong feelings for each other and threatening to destroy their plans for a good war story.

But war and women are just diversions. Once again Greene's mind is preoccupied with men loving men. The smuggling motif in *The Man Within* gave him a creative way of approaching the subject without getting himself into trouble, but in *Rumour at Nightfall* his only way of disguising his intentions is to lay down a weak smoke screen of sentimental language. When the novel appeared in 1931, its average reader could only have been bewildered by the spectacle of Chase and Crane engaging in long, mysterious discussions on the future of their "friendship" and the danger presented to it by the intrusion of a woman. The action is repeatedly put on hold while the two men give each other moody looks and exchange vague comments. Without knowing something about Greene's personal interests, the innocent contemporary reader might have assumed that all this talk was merely the novelist's way of stretching out a thin story. In fact, the strange tension between the two men is the only part of the book that matters.

It takes some work to disentangle their love story from the turgid dialogue and from the rambling narrative about devious rebels and passive peasants. After spending ten years in a close relationship, neither man is happy with the prospect that a woman might break them apart. Fearing that Crane is falling for the woman, Chase demands to know "which of us you prefer." Crane refuses to give a straight answer but worries that he is in danger of destroying "something precious," by which he means their relationship. "And am I to lose you?" Crane asks, with all the trembling anxiety of a conventional lover torn between two hearts. Chase plays the part of the spurned lover, throwing a photograph of the dreaded female at his friend and telling him, "in a high voice," to go to her if he must: "Go back then. Can't you keep off a woman for an hour?" This last remark has a rather hollow ring, because neither man seems to have made a habit of spending much time with the opposite sex.

But, alas, the seductive charms of the Spanish beauty finally overwhelm poor Crane, and, when he decides to marry her, his friend is furious, denouncing the proposed union with the bitter words "Another good man for her lust." Chase cannot bear the thought of being abandoned and bemoans his loss as the destruction of "everything" worth having in life. Reluctantly, he concludes that one day he may have to break down and take a bride of his own—perhaps even start a family. But that will be no consolation for losing his man. "There is no woman or child who will take his place," he laments. Naturally, the wayward Crane must die for the crime of breaking his friend's heart, and Chase puts the deed in motion by telling the rebels that Crane is their enemy. The unfortunate fellow is murdered on the night of his wedding, no less, and his friend is instantly consumed by guilt. Just as Francis Andrews betrays Carlyon and then regrets it in *The Man Within*, Chase cannot believe that he has set up the murder of "the friend he had loved." And it was all "because he was going to marry."

Unable to be more direct about his homosexual theme, Greene succeeded in leaving his readers more confused than ever. His audience declined dramatically. Sales of the Heinemann edition failed to rise above 3,000, and the American edition sold a mere 1,018 copies. Reviewers struggled to find words for a story that seemed pointless. One sad critic in New York vainly tried to explain why Chase and Crane were a mystery to him: "Mr. Greene avoids giving us direct accounts of what manner of men his characters are, and we get to know them, in so far as we know them at all, through their reactions to the situations in which they are placed." The experience of reading Greene's tortuous novel had obviously affected the critic's own style.

The failure of *Rumour at Nightfall* threatened to put an end to Greene's career. He was costing Heinemann large amounts of money, and Charles Evans could not afford to waste much more on his faded star. Greene was still obliged to produce another novel, but if the work lacked the potential for big sales, Evans might choose to pass it up and cut his losses. The pressure on Greene was tremendous, and he began to worry that he might soon be forced back into the lowly life of a subeditor. Even before *Rumour at Nightfall* was finished, his fear of another failure had encouraged him to reduce his expenses. The greatest savings came from his decision to abandon hectic London life for a quiet, inexpensive existence in the country.

In early 1931 he and Vivienne moved to a thatched cottage in the Cotswolds, on the outskirts of Chipping Campden. Greene was able to give more attention to his work in the relative peace of their new home, but he was not exactly the type to mix well in village life. Walking was his great diversion, and he liked to go far beyond the boundaries of his village. The surrounding countryside was ideal for sightseeing, and he would sometimes cover fifteen miles in a day. The villagers did not learn much about him, but he paid careful attention to them, storing up memories of faces and words for possible use in the future. Some of these surfaced a few years later in the seemingly odd context of his travel book on Liberia, *Journey Without Maps*. But his point in the book was that England had its share of primitive types. There was Buckland the gypsy gardener, who seemed to thrive on a diet of snails dug from Greene's garden; and the local madman Charlie Sykes, who wore rags and a long beard and who shouted nonsense to strangers in the marketplace; and Miss Kilvane, whose great mission was to keep alive the memory of a nineteenth-century prophetess and who confidently informed Greene that the millennium would arrive in fifty years.

Recording details about the local people was one thing, but getting to know them well was less appealing. A glimpse of Greene's attitude can be gauged in his response to an accident suffered by the servant who helped Vivienne in the cottage. Despite the fact that the woman had the perfect name for the job—Greenall—she seems to have been on distant terms with the master of the house. One day she gave her finger a good whack while chopping wood in the garden, and, instead of seeking help from Greene, who was working in his study, she ran to a local shop, where she found someone to bandage her deep cut. When Greene learned later what she had done, he was greatly relieved, but not because he was glad to hear that she was recovering. He was simply pleased that she had spared him the sight of her blood and tears. Presumably she went back to chopping wood for the cottage in a week or two.

Vivienne had an easier time adapting to village life. She took part in some local activities and kept busy at home trying to improve conditions in the old cottage. Her ambition was to make it the kind of snug hideaway that she and Greene had dreamed of acquiring before their marriage. She also found it easy to occupy herself with a few hobbies. She began collecting various Victorian objects and developed a curious passion for pictures of tigers. Whenever she found an illustration of a tiger in a newspaper or magazine, she would cut it out and paste it in a scrapbook. Meanwhile, her husband was secretly cultivating one of his favorite hobbies, and it was not something that could be done at home with scissors and paste.

While he was working on *Rumour at Nightfall,* Greene began slipping away to London more often. His primary excuse was that he needed to start gathering material for his proposed life of Lord Rochester. Considering his financial difficulties with Heinemann, this uncommercial project was the last thing he should have been thinking about, but he obviously felt the need for an escape—not only from the relentless demands of his fiction but also from the rather too snug arrangement at his cottage. As he had realized long before he married Vivienne, she could not hope to satisfy all his needs. But on his own in London he quickly learned to find whatever he wanted.

There were ample opportunities for encounters in the street with willing women or men, or for an occasional visit to a brothel, but Greene's interests were also expanding in new directions. Close study of Swinburne's life and times raised his curiosity about the Victorian fondness for underground literature on flagellation. Greene decided to seek out some of these classics, especially *The Whippingham Papers,* which was available to "serious" students at the British Library. There was also a whipping establishment in London that Swinburne used to visit, and Greene was eager to know whether it was still in business. It is uncertain whether he was able to avail himself of its services, but searching for the place was probably a pleasure in itself. For a man who was so fascinated by wounds of one kind or another, whipping and bondage were natural attractions.

In the opening pages of his first novel, an allusion to the pleasures of pain occurs in a suitably strange metaphor. While Francis Andrews is racing to escape his fellow smugglers, he runs straight into a thick hedge and is momentarily bound by its dense pattern of twigs. Scratched and bleeding, he imagines that the thorns are like the nails of "a harlot" cutting into his flesh. The experience has its sensual appeal—the pulls at his clothing from the twigs are described as "small endearments," and the thorns create a "restraint" that resembles "a caress." It is instructive to see how much fun one can have from just a few minutes inside a hedge.

Given the nature of Greene's interest in Swinburne's life, it is not surprising that he spotted his Grandfather Carleton's name in one of the many small footnotes to the Yale edition of Swinburne's letters. He was clearly paying close attention to every detail. And such vigilance would have been amply repaid in ways that went beyond the mild satisfactions of genealogical research. Thanks to Yale University Press, Greene could savor letters such as the following, in which Swinburne requests help from a friend with a talent for handling a delicate tale:

> I want you to compose for me a little dialogue (imaginary) between schoolmaster and boy—from the first summons "Now Arthur (or Frank—or Harry) what does *this* mean, sir? Come here"—to the last *cut* and painful buttoning up—a rebuke or threat at every lash (and *plenty* of them) and a shriek of agonized appeal from the boy in reply. (Describe also the effect of each stripe on the boy's flesh—its appearance between the cuts.) I want to see how like real life you will make it.

Apparently, Greene never lost his fascination for such things. As later chapters will show, at least two of his women friends were able to please him by inflicting a cigarette burn on his body. And then there were always the professionals who offered specialized services. In later years he had no trouble affording such services. Whenever he felt the need to explore the limits of discipline, his favorite brothel in Paris was able to supply him with the right woman for the job. He often boasted of the wide variety of women available at the brothel and was happy to introduce a few select friends to the madam.

CHAPTER NINE

MAKING ENDS MEET:
STAMBOUL TRAIN

While Greene amused himself with researching and writing *Lord Rochester's Monkey*, the day was fast approaching when his payments from Heinemann would run out. If he wanted to remain a commercial author, he needed to produce a novel that would make money, and lots of it. And he needed to do it soon. In 1931 an idea came to him for a novel set on the Orient Express, a narrative that would weave together the fates of several characters making the long journey from Ostend to Constantinople. In the back of his mind was the hope that a big film company would adapt it for the screen, and that the extra cash from the box office would help to replenish his dwindling bank account. After the disaster of *Rumour at Nightfall*, he was determined to avoid another unfocused, slow-motion tour of his subconscious. The "train" novel would allow him to bring to life a vivid, self-contained world in which everything was constantly in motion. And by periodically shifting the focus from one character to another, he could keep the reader's attention engaged from beginning to end.

Greene had briefly visited Constantinople in 1930, when he was still enjoying the new riches from his Heinemann deal. He had sailed there after a long cruise among the Greek islands. But his only experience of the Orient Express was limited to its run from Ostend to

Cologne, so there was a great deal of scenery his imagination would have to supply. In January 1932 he began writing the book—using a recording of Arthur Honegger's "Pacific 231" as a daily source of inspiration—and eight months later he submitted the finished manuscript to Charles Evans, whose experience with the previous novel had given him every reason to dread reading this one. It was hard to imagine that the new novel could dramatically reverse the decline in Greene's career. But, as Evans quickly discovered, his erratic author had finally settled down and produced the necessary goods. *Stamboul Train* looked like a winner.

In fact, Evans was so pleased by the new book that he failed to notice a potentially damaging piece of mischief on Greene's part. Although his financial difficulties were his own fault, Greene found a way to get back at Heinemann for pressuring him into writing a highly commercial novel. Slyly, he included a character in *Stamboul Train* who is a parody not only of best-selling authors in general but also of one Heinemann star in particular. Greene's creation—Quin Savory—boards the Orient Express on a fact-finding mission for his next novel, a sentimental tale about the exotic travels of a Cockney tobacconist. Savory specializes in writing fictional tributes to the resilient Cockney spirit and has won great fame and fortune for his epic *The Great Gay Round,* which is half a million words long and features a cast of two hundred characters. Other details—including his pipe smoking and his reputation as a modern Dickens—suggest that Savory is a slightly disguised portrait of J. B. Priestley, who was Heinemann's most popular novelist in the early 1930s. His long novel *The Good Companions,* which came out in the same year as *The Man Within,* was such a success that Heinemann's new Windmill Press was kept busy throughout the year turning out one new printing after another. The novel has a huge cast of characters and lots of Cockney dialogue, and it earned widespread praise as a book worthy of Dickens's talent.

When Priestley read Greene's novel in a proof copy, he had no trouble identifying the object of the author's ridicule. He demanded changes from Evans and threatened a libel suit if they were not made. Greene pretended to be shocked by the threat, claiming that he had never intended to parody a fellow Heinemann author, but he made the changes anyway and had to pay the cost of altering a large number of copies that had been printed and bound. In some accounts of this affair, Priestley has been made to seem pompous and unreasonable, but he was right to be outraged. It was not the trivial details that made the portrait so damaging but the suggestion that the good-hearted champion of the common man was actually a potential sex offender. Mabel Warren—the tough journalist who interviews Savory on the train—notices how excited he becomes as his eyes follow a bouncing skirt down the corridor, and she detects signs of an uncontrollable sexual energy in his words and manner, especially when he talks about his crusade to bring a healthy outlook to modern literature. In her cynical eyes he looks like someone who is sure to be arrested one day in Hyde Park for an act of indecency. In fact, Savory is glimpsed at the end of the novel in a suggestive scene. He is surrounded by a large crowd of Turkish children and is absorbed in shooting photographs of them as fast as he can.

Considering the nature of Greene's attack, he is extremely fortunate that Priestley refrained from carrying out his legal threats. But it was clever of him to have chosen his victim so carefully. If he had done this sort of thing to a powerful author from another firm, he might well have lost everything in court. But it was not in Priestley's interests to destroy a young author whose future success was so important to Charles Evans. And no doubt Evans himself made that point to Priestley when the trouble surfaced. All the same, Greene was playing quite a dangerous game. If the parody had not been noticed until after all the books were in the shops, Priestley might have been less forgiving. And if the sales of *Stamboul Train* had been disappointing, Evans might well have decided to rid the firm of a brilliant but unreliable novelist.

As it turned out, Greene emerged from the affair relatively unscathed. He was required to cut only a few things, and they were all minor, such as the reference to Dickens. More important, the novel's commercial appeal proved greater than anyone had hoped. Heinemann sold 21,000 copies, and another 5,000 were sold in America. By the end of the novel's first year in print, Greene received the best reward of all. As he had hoped, the book's cinematic qualities were not ignored. Twentieth Century–Fox paid the equivalent of 1,500 pounds for the film rights, and there were no strings attached to this deal. Unlike Heinemann, Hollywood put the money in the author's pocket and walked away. It gave Greene his first taste of real wealth, and this was only the beginning of a long and highly lucrative association with the film world. Looking back on this early triumph, Greene found just the right cliché to sum it up: "The devil looks after his own."

Judging by the literary quality of *Stamboul Train*, the devil must also know something about writing. Perhaps the price Greene thought he had to pay for the extra assistance was to criticize Jews and J. B. Priestley. It is tempting to believe that the novel would have worked just as well if Quin Savory had stayed home, and if Carleton Myatt had become a Methodist preacher before the train pulled out of the station. But Greene would not have been Greene if he did not have characters to stick pins into. Of course, at least one sharp pin is always reserved for the average reader, who yearns for pleasures that Greene has no intention of providing. Naturally, happy endings are out—unless they are used for comic effect—but, most of all, Greene wanted to violate our easy assumptions about life. We are too predictable, too idealistic, too trusting, too fond of tidy explanations. We put our thoughts on a single track and speed confidently ahead to a certain destination. But Greene was the saboteur on the line, showing us all the places where bridges can be blown, tracks pulled up, tunnels blocked, wires cut.

The easy assumption to make at the beginning of *Stamboul Train* is that Carleton Myatt will be the main character. His point of view is the dominant one in the opening section of the novel, but just when we are beginning to see the journey through his eyes, the focus abruptly shifts to the journalist Mabel Warren and then keeps shifting. The initial expectations of Myatt linger, however, and the subtle effect is that we tend to retain a hopeful view of him long after Greene has begun undercutting his character. Some readers even finish the book thinking that Myatt is a good character and that the narrative uses the man's Jewishness to draw out sympathy for him. It is certainly possible to like Myatt, but to do so you must ignore a great deal of what the narrative reveals about him. He is coarse and selfish, and the "help" he gives to the chorus girl Coral Musker is nothing but a convenient way of seducing her. As soon as she is out of the way, she disappears from his mind as quickly as she entered it.

If anyone in the novel can be called the main character, it is the political leader Dr. Czinner, whose great purpose is to reach Belgrade in time to start a revolution. Or is that really his purpose? Mabel Warren thinks it is, at least at first, and is desperate to interview him for a "scoop" about the rebellion. But she is a much more intelligent journalist than the man from the *Chicago Tribune* who appears in *The Name of Action*. The more Warren thinks about Czinner's motives, the more she doubts that the real story lies in his plans for Belgrade. She gives her newspaper the "scoop" it wants, but she suspects that a better story may lie back in England, where Czinner lived in lonely exile for five years. He had found work as a schoolteacher and was firmly established in his job. Then something happened to make him give it up and return to a country where he was a wanted man.

Warren is never able to make sense of his actions. All his talk about the oppressed and the corrupt ruling class would lead one to think that his motives are entirely political, but there are many suggestions in the novel that he is running not *to* something but *from* something. There are hints of a troubling life at the school, and Warren clearly suspects that Czinner was involved in some scandal. A better explanation is that life as an exile had become a living death for the proud doctor, who had gone from being a hero of the Belgrade working class to being a minor figure at a third-rate school in Great Birchington-on-Sea. Memories of his years at the school keep breaking into his thoughts, and all the images are bad. His "malicious" pupils taunted him with half-suppressed laughter, impudent gestures, and defiant looks. They had no respect for his political wisdom. He was merely a funny foreigner who could not keep order in his classroom.

As the train races toward the Yugoslav border, Czinner feels that he is finally alive again, but that feeling comes entirely from the knowledge that his return home is almost certain to result in his death. One way or another, the government will stop him from spreading his message of revolution. The thrill for him is that he will go out in a blaze of glory, valiantly standing up to defend socialist ideals before a packed courtroom. But this is only a fantasy. He is chasing death for his own satisfaction. His trip to Belgrade will make no difference in the lives of his countrymen, and he knows it. He is not a revolutionary hero but a sad failure whose suicidal mission is nothing but an escape from the slow death of Great Birchington. It offers a respectable way to end his misery. When he is captured shortly after crossing his country's border, he is relieved to know that his fate is sealed. "He was at peace," the narrative tells us. The one disappointment is that his noble speech is wasted. Denied a public trial, he addresses his pleas for social justice to a couple of bored guards.

Like Quin Savory, Dr. Czinner has a weakness for grand but empty sagas. The legend that he creates for himself is as sentimental, and as predictable, as anything created by the Cockney novelist. But it comforts him to think that he is sacrificing himself for others, in the same way that Savory's readers are comforted by the bad storyteller's simplistic notions of life. They want fearless heroes who die for great causes, lovers who live happily ever after, rich men who give their gold to the poor, and ordinary people who triumph over adversity.

This is Savory's "healthy" tradition of fiction, but he does not need to promote it to his fellow passengers on the Orient Express. They are all suckers for it. Czinner dies for it, lying about his motives right to the end. Coral Musker tells herself the comforting lie that Myatt will take care of her, but the only thing he takes is her virginity. When she is detained by Yugoslav soldiers, Myatt pretends that he will be the hero who saves her, but he quickly disappears after gunfire erupts and never returns. Mabel Warren is proud of being a ruthless career woman, but she is easily fooled in matters of love. The one character who might seem immune to seductive stories is the criminal Grünlich, who is so good at making other people fall for his lies. But he cannot resist the fable of the perfect crime, a flaw that he shares with his creator.

All the same, Grünlich suffers no disillusionment in this novel, although he walks into the same trap laid for Dr. Czinner at the Yugoslav frontier. The soldiers arrest him for carrying a gun and may soon discover that he is wanted for murder in Vienna. Coral Musker is also held, on the suspicion that she has helped Dr. Czinner. While the doctor smiles contentedly in the face of death, Musker tries to comfort herself with the thought that Myatt will be her salvation. The train has moved on, but she feels certain that he will come back for her and use his money to win her release. By contrast, Grünlich neither bemoans his fate nor hopes for a sudden show of clemency. His response is to begin plotting his escape with cool precision, using a brain that works like the "wheels of a watch." He calculates the odds of getting hit by a bullet if he makes a run for it and persuades the chorus girl and the doctor to escape with him, thinking that their slow-moving figures will shield him from fire as he heads for cover. He is right. When Czinner is mortally wounded, Musker stops to help, and Grünlich races ahead. He finds Myatt, who has hired a car to search for Musker, and makes his getaway in the vehicle as more gunfire erupts.

This is exciting stuff, but it all depends on Grünlich's ability to manipulate the expectations of others. They are easy to mislead. Having been denied the chance to play the martyr in public, the doctor is ready to die in a desperate escape attempt. The chorus girl takes the bait because she believes that Myatt is waiting nearby to help her. And after rescuing Grünlich, Myatt finds it convenient to believe the criminal's story that "no girl" was being held by the soldiers. The shots and Grünlich's lie give Myatt the only excuses he needs to abandon Musker. In all the excitement, the criminal makes a clean escape and lives to fight another day, just like the hero in a "healthy" novel.

It is fun to read a best-seller that revels in its assaults on the conventions of popular fiction. Greene craved commercial success, but he wanted it on his own terms, and, like Grünlich, he was good at calculating the best way to win. In those days the quickest way to boost sales was to gain the approval of the Book Society, which could guarantee that 10,000 copies would be sold to its membership. Greene's publisher enjoyed a certain amount of goodwill among the selection committee. One of the directors of Heinemann—A. S. Frere—had helped to start the society in the 1920s. But, more important, Greene had two valuable allies on the five-member committee. One was an old acquaintance, the novelist Clemence Dane, whom he had first met at Oxford; and the other was a recent friend—and a recent addition to the committee—the poet Edmund Blunden. In addition, Greene knew the secretary of the society, Rupert Hart-Davis, and dedicated the manuscript of *Stamboul Train* to him.

Visiting Greene in June 1932—a few weeks before the book was finished—Blunden realized that the novelist was in a difficult position financially and said, "I must see whether the Book Society can help you." In October the committee met to choose the December selection, and, as soon as the decision was reached, Hart-Davis sent a wire to Greene with the not altogether unexpected news that *Stamboul Train* had won. Although the publicity and sales from this honor played a crucial part in reviving Greene's career, the novelist did not allow the generous assistance of his friends to corrupt his values. Within a couple of years he was cheerfully criticizing the Book Society for having standards that were "easy"—so easy that a great novelist such as Henry James would not have stooped low enough to meet them.

II

In early 1932, while he was working on *Stamboul Train,* Greene increased his literary burdens by taking up the onerous task of regular reviewing. It added a little extra money to his yearly income, and it kept his name before the public, but it also meant reading a steady stream of mostly inferior books and trying to say something witty or perceptive about them. Many of the writers of Greene's generation devoted too much time to reviewing and could never stop complaining about its bad effects on their lives and their careers. In general, Greene approached reviewing with amazing discipline and efficiency. He rarely complained about the burden, read the books carefully but quickly, wrote highly polished reviews, turned them in promptly, then went straight back to the business of writing novels. The burden was not light. In 1932–33 he reviewed 142 titles, most of which were novels. After performing a similar feat in the 1920s, Cyril Connolly was so exhausted that he felt certain those two years had actually been ninety. He joked that reviewing so many novels was like "building bridges in some impossible tropical climate. . . . For each scant clearing made wearily among the springing vegetation the jungle overnight encroaches twice as far."

Greene wrote most of his early pieces for *The Spectator,* which rewarded his diligence by keeping him steadily supplied with books to review until wartime duties called him away from England in 1942. As did many laborers in the review jungle, he occasionally lightened his load by indulging in personal reflections. One of the most revealing passages occurs in an early review from June 1933. It is not a passing comment but a deeply passionate outburst of almost 200 words, and it is solely concerned with the tyranny that adults exercise over children. Nothing that Greene wrote about childhood in his fiction or formal essays is as vehement and direct as this passage from *The Spectator,* and it is impossible not to think that Greene was speaking from his own experience.

The opening sentence sets the tone: "Childhood is life under a dictatorship, a condition of perpetual ignominy, irresponsibility and injustice." His main complaint is that the child is powerless to break the code of the adult world. Its terrors are constantly before the child, but they appear without warning and seem to have no cause. The child strives to understand what the adults will do next, but they keep hatching new plots and designing new traps. Protected by a thick covering of lies, they remain an unfathomable mystery to even the most curious child, and thus their commands and punishments always seem arbitrary.

These are familiar complaints, but Greene speaks of them with a clear note of rage, as though the injustices of childhood were still fresh. This is the voice of someone with a sharp grievance who is looking for ways to get even and who cannot wait to draw blood. The passage also suggests that the only way to fight the tyrants is to confuse them with more lies, to create more complicated plots, and to stay low. The adult Greene is obviously ready to fight the young Greene's battles, and he does not seem to mind that the original villains have faded away. Any enemy will do. He just wants to hit someone or something now that he is big enough to swing hard and run fast.

Greene's instinct for making hit-and-run attacks found an easy outlet in occasional journalism. It presented temptations that would eventually lead him to criticize Shirley Temple for pandering to male lust in her film *Wee Willie Winkie.* One of his earliest victims was another sacred figure of innocence, Beatrix Potter. In January 1933 he published a very amusing article called "Beatrix Potter: A Critical Estimate," in which he applies the most pompous kind of literary criticism to the Potter canon. Maintaining a solemn tone throughout the piece, he conducts a detailed discussion of her talents and is soon comparing her with E. M. Forster. He scrutinizes her adherence to empiricism, criticizes her unsympathetic portrait of Mr. McGregor, praises the epic characteristics of Peter Rabbit, and hails the publication of the *Tale of Little Pig Robinson* as her glorious last statement, her *Tempest*. He finds a dark period earlier in her career, however, and traces its beginning to the moment when Mr. Drake Puddle-duck enters the canon. He speculates that Potter must have undergone some terrible crisis in her personal life at that time. In this respect she reminds him of Henry James struggling to articulate the bleak vision of *The Wings of the Dove*. He hears Potter's voice of despair most clearly in Mr. Jackson's stark statement "No teeth. No teeth. No teeth."

Greene was so good at keeping a straight face in this article that many people took it seriously. It prompted one critic to pontificate on the ethics of "biocriticism": "Should it be applied to living writers? It is a tasteless practice, to say the least. To hint at emotional disturbances may be justifiable, but it may also reopen old wounds. The question is, where will it stop?" The best response came from the great Beatrix Potter herself. After reading the piece, she wrote Greene an indignant letter taking him to task for his interpretations. She was especially unhappy with his suggestion that emotional problems had plagued her during the Puddle-duck period. Nothing of that sort had bothered her, she protested. It was only a case of the flu. The article itself is funny enough, but Potter's earnest reply is even funnier. The strange thing is that Greene's wild parody turned out to have an edge of truth to it. V. S. Pritchett later observed, "As we know now, from Margaret Lane's *Life* and the published *Journals*, there had been two extreme crises in [Potter's] life and an extraordinary change of personality. Graham Greene had been an expert detective."

Undeterred by the author's objections, Greene wrote one more exercise in Potter criticism, explicating her subtle understanding of pig romance. In "Pigs, Be British" he praises Potter for capturing the feminine mystique of Pig-wig and says that the account of Pigling Bland's relationship with Pig-wig reminds him of Jane Austen's work at its best. His essay quickly turns into a sweeping commentary on literary pigs, from the one who cried "wee wee wee all the way home" to the epic drama of *The Three Little Pigs*. One thing that disturbs him about the typical literary pig is that the reader is allowed no insight into the pig's sex life. Greene is also unhappy with the inconsistencies in Walt Disney's film adaptation of *The Three Little Pigs*, noting that the wolf is excessively violent but that each of the pigs escapes being eaten. Surely, he argues, the two irresponsible pigs should have suffered the ultimate penalty for their conduct.

This kind of satire was a good diversion for Greene, but it was a little too obvious and tame for his tastes. Portraying J. B. Priestley as a sex offender was a more satisfying challenge. Fiction offered the best opportunities for hit-and-run attacks, simply because it was so easy to plead ignorance if the victim started making accusations. In articles and reviews Greene had to know his limits and stay within them, doing nothing worse than tweaking his victim's nose. In his review of Shirley Temple's film, he went wrong by trying to tweak too much. A more typical example of his tactics can be seen in a *Spectator* review entitled "Portrait of a Lady." Asked to consider the merits of *No Place Like Home,* by Mr. Beverley Nichols—a former editor of the *Oxford Outlook*—Greene feigned ignorance of the author's sex and referred throughout his review to the various ladylike qualities of Nichols's work. Sometimes Greene made it impossible for his contemporaries to know whether he was joking or being serious. A good case in point is his review of Erskine Caldwell's *Tobacco Road*. He has only praise for the author and congratulates him "for opening a new field of cruel humour, in which physical ugliness, sexual promiscuity, and even the most painful of deaths are made to cause laughter." These sound like Greene's true sentiments, but his readers at the time must have assumed that he was trying to be ironic.

With his career on the rise again, there was no reason for Greene to be saving pennies in a rustic cottage. In June 1933—a month after the big payment from Twentieth Century–Fox arrived—he and Vivienne moved to a large, modern flat in Oxford. Their new prosperity was not the only incentive for making the move. Two months earlier Vivienne had discovered that she was pregnant. Greene was dismayed at the thought of becoming a father and strongly considered giving the child up for adoption. Still nursing grievances from his own childhood, he was not ready to be the authority figure in a child's life. It might cause him merely to duplicate old wounds. But Vivienne was prepared for motherhood, and Greene gradually became reconciled to the idea of keeping the baby.

He was strangely overprotective of his pregnant wife. In May her mother died, and Greene insisted that she not strain herself by going to the funeral in London. A rail journey does not seem unreasonable for a young woman in the early stage of pregnancy, especially when the purpose was to pay her last respects to her mother. But Greene was successful in persuading Vivienne to stay away while he went to the funeral in her place. The service at the Golders Green crematorium was short, and the novelist later made careful notes of the event in his diary, describing every detail of the coffin's slow progress through the open door that led to the furnace. This sad but brief occasion left Greene some time before he was due back home, so he was able to spend the late afternoon doing something more enjoyable. He went to Piccadilly and met one of his favourite prostitutes, a woman whom he called simply O.

Besides O, Greene was also very attached to a woman in London named Annette, and he was most anxious to find excuses for visiting her. As his bank account grew, he was able to pursue his secret life in London with greater dedication. One reason for his strong interest in Annette was that she did not mind satisfying his passion for anal sex, a fact that he acknowledges in his diary of 1932. As he told another lover in later years, he liked to "make love to every orifice." In fact, according to the woman, "It was difficult to brush my teeth in the morning without having Graham come up behind me." Apparently, his fondness for anal sex was so great that he could become rather too exuberant, as one maid discovered after cleaning the room he had shared with a woman in Jamaica. According to Alan Ross, the editor of the *London Magazine,* the maid bitterly complained to her employer. "Such disgusting beds," she cried. As a small token of gratitude to Annette, Greene gave her a bit part in *England Made Me,* where she is mentioned as Anthony Farrant's favourite prostitute. An inscribed photograph of her graces Farrant's flat in London.

In view of her husband's varied interests, Vivienne had no hope of turning him into a devoted family man. He became a father in December 1933, when Vivienne gave birth to a daughter—Lucy Caroline—but he did not show much interest in the baby. In the first year after Lucy's birth, he began roaming farther from home and stayed away for longer periods. While Vivienne was caught up in the hard work of caring for an infant, Greene found excuses to make trips that took him hundreds, even thousands, of miles from home. "Money gave him some sense that he could do anything," Vivienne recalled. "He realized that there were more things than domestic life."

It took a long time for her to discover the truth about his relationships with other women, and when she did, it was hard for her to understand the extent of his promiscuity: "He was not at all a good judge of character. Some of the people he picked up were quite frightful. Not all the women he picked up were decent sort of people. I think all his judgment of character went into his novels. He told me, 'All that is good in me, all that's anything worth having in me, is in the books. What's life is just what's left over.' " One might answer that he was an excellent judge of character. He knew exactly what his character required, and he found the right people to satisfy his needs. Vivienne satisfied some of those needs for a while. Even after he was aggressively "soiling" himself with illicit love, it was still nice to go home to a "pure" woman. He would see Annette in London, buy Vivienne a charming present—such as a new kitten—then race home to her maternal bosom. But the more "domestic" she became, the less interest he showed in her. To use her blunt explanation of the problem, "I was a homemaker, but he didn't want a homemaker." He was straight with her about one thing. The books always came first. "What's life is just what's left over."

III

In his periodic moments of guilt, Greene was tormented by fearful nightmares. While he was writing *Stamboul Train,* he dreamed that he had been arrested for some crime and was imprisoned for five years. At the beginning of 1933 he had a dream in which he murdered someone, stuffed the body in a suitcase, and left it in a train station. In addition to this dream, his diary includes a thoroughly creepy poem about a murder victim's body after the police have discovered it lying next to a chair in a park. It is the body of a young woman whose cheap beret is stained with blood and whose underclothes have been torn to reveal one of her breasts. The underlying question is whether the alert police detective sifting through the evidence will find the right clue to solve the case.

This seems an odd subject for poetry. Furthermore, the poem and the dream are only a few pages apart. Given Greene's love-hate attitude toward prostitutes, it is perhaps just as well for him that he did not lose his diary in a taxi. If the police had found it, they might not have understood how active a novelist's imagination can be.

Greene did find a way to work this gruesome subject into his next novel, but it seems out of place there. Written primarily in 1933—and published in early 1934—*It's a Battlefield* is about an emotional campaign to win a reprieve for a bus driver convicted of murdering a policeman. In the excitement of a political demonstration, Jim Drover killed a constable who had been on the verge of striking Drover's wife, Milly. The injustice of the case against Drover attracts national attention, especially among Communist activists, who want to stir up agitation against the government. Impassioned speeches are given, and petitions are circulated. A hypocritical Communist leader, Mr. Surrogate, would love nothing better than to see Jim hang, so that the bus driver's name could become a rallying cry for the oppressed masses. Meanwhile, Milly and her husband's brother, Conrad, give each other support during the long ordeal, and, as events draw them closer together, they fall in love.

As these political and personal dramas are played out, Greene keeps bringing up details about two fictional murder cases that share the headlines with the Drover campaign. One case is similar to Greene's dream, the other to his poem. In the Paddington trunk murder case, the dismembered body of a woman has been found inside a trunk at the station, and in the Streatham Common case a woman named Flossie Matthews has been raped and murdered. Her body is found near a park chair with her bloodstained beret beside her. The murderer of the Paddington victim is quickly tracked down, but Greene never mentions whether there are any suspects in the second case. As the novel closes the police are still working on it.

So what is the purpose of having this loose thread floating through the narrative? It does allow Greene to show his assistant commissioner of police engaged in activities beyond the Drover affair, but he could easily have substituted cases that were less specific and could have referred to them less frequently. There must be a better explanation. Greene was not one to give so much space to something of this kind unless he considered it important. Only one obvious suggestion is provided in the novel. The assistant commissioner is intrigued by the victim's woolen beret and seems to think that it may hide some key to the murder mystery. The pattern of the crochet especially attracts his attention. Much later in the novel, Conrad Drover shows unusual interest in a beret that Milly is trying to crochet, and he takes time to help her understand the complicated pattern. Milly thinks it strange that her brother-in-law knows anything at all about the subject and innocently raises the question that torments other male characters in Greene's work: "Are you a man?"

Conrad is definitely a suspicious character. He appears to have no friends outside his family, he wanders the streets of London at all hours, and he is full of hate for people in general. He is also not put off by the prospect of killing someone. The unfair treatment suffered by his brother has convinced him that crime and punishment are meaningless terms. The rich and powerful get away with major crimes, he tells himself, while ordinary citizens are severely punished for minor misdeeds. If the law can brand his good-hearted brother a murderer, then Conrad is willing to test the definition of the term. "Why shouldn't I be a murderer myself?" he asks. As his first name suggests, there are parallels between his story and that of Joseph Conrad's "Secret Sharer," in which one character closely identifies with another who may have been unjustly accused of murder.

Conrad Drover also has troubling thoughts about women. He despises Milly's sister for being too forward with men and considers her little better than a common prostitute. Yet he has a deep need to be with prostitutes, and they seem to have been his only sexual partners until he falls in love with Milly, whom he cherishes as a spiritually higher form of womanhood. And as soon as he sleeps with Milly, he is attacked by guilt. Of course, these problems can all be traced to his insecurity about his masculinity. He is a timid insurance clerk who has brains but no great physical strength, and his vulnerability makes him worry that he is in constant danger of being humiliated. Milly's sister lands a solid blow when she sees him making a bed and says, "What a housewife."

It seems only natural that his difficulties go back to his school days, when he was ridiculed for being weak and for having such a strange name. His stronger brother always managed to stand up to the world, and Conrad developed both admiration and resentment for Jim's physical power. The ultimate display of that power came when Jim killed the constable in Milly's defense. The incident stands as one more reminder to Conrad that Jim is the real man in the family, and, for that reason, he is tempted to commit a murder simply to show that he is not his brother's inferior. When he sleeps with Milly, Conrad proves that he can take his brother's place in bed, but he sees murder as the final proof of his manhood.

He has so much hate in his heart that picking a victim is easy. They are everywhere around him. Walking through town one day, he imagines that a pistol is in his hand and raises it briefly to take aim against some imaginary enemy. Several faces flash across his mind—the faces of people who have done him some injury—but he is not looking for a specific target. He is ready to shoot anyone, including the face he suddenly glimpses in a plate-glass window, which turns out to be his own. When he finally obtains a real revolver, he does not go after another Flossie Matthews. Instead Conrad tracks down the assistant commissioner, whose duties have placed him at the center of both the Streatham Common and Jim Drover cases.

There is no hard evidence to indicate that Conrad had anything to do with Matthews's murder, but Greene tries to show a similar instinct at work in the attack on the Streatham woman and the attack on the assistant commissioner. As Conrad heads for his man, he speculates that murder will ease the burden of his hatred in the same way that sex with prostitutes has relieved physical pressure. Just before he raises the revolver to shoot the policeman, he thinks of all "the dark steep stairs he had trodden at prostitutes' heels." As far as his imagination is concerned, he might as well be trying to kill someone like Flossie Matthews. Luckily for the assistant commissioner, Conrad is a better killer in his imagination than in reality. As it turns out, he has been so preoccupied with thinking about the deed that he has failed to notice two crucial problems. The little revolver he has acquired has a rusty trigger, and it is loaded with blanks. Blinded by rage, he destroys only himself. As he backs away from his victim in a panic, he walks straight into the path of a fast car.

It should be obvious that Greene and Conrad Drover have a great deal in common. They are especially alike in their passion for hating indiscriminately. Conrad thinks that people are constantly staring at him and are afraid to come near him. The suspicious looks irritate him so much that he likes the idea of getting back at people by staring at them first. If he stares hard enough, they will begin to think there is something wrong with them. The pleasure for him comes when they start checking their clothing to see if something is undone or feeling for dirt on their faces. He calls it a "devilishly clever method." In private life Greene called the game by a more direct name: "Hating People." At first, he played it by himself, but later he shared it with a few friends. Guy Elmes remembered the game from the days that he and Greene spent together in Italy during the 1950s:

What you do is you sit at a café table. See the chairs opposite? The eighth person along, [you pretend] that you hate him. In a moment he's going to pick his nose, and he's going to lick the finger that he's picked his nose with. . . . Now, eventually you hate the person. He's made you really hate him. . . . He's going to get up, I bet you, and just leave the exact money for his coffee and no tip for the waiter. Sure enough . . . you shit. And you really loved to hate the person. And he did that in Capri, Rome, Venice. It was a real game for his hating, and he used to do it with women as well. The bodice string. I'll bet you that top—she's eating so much—it will burst open. . . . She's fat, eats too much, too much ice cream. And sure enough, after a while the woman starts fiddling, trying to get it all together, and there we are. Not you, your highness. . . . Don't you hate her? It's a wonderful game. I've played it since with a number of other people.

Some people might prefer a friendly game of bridge, but if Greene played Hating People with so much zeal, it is easy to see why his work created a long trail of victims, from J. B. Priestley and Shirley Temple to Mother and Dad. *It's a Battlefield* adds another family member to the list—Graham's older brother Raymond. Unlike Herbert—the oldest brother in the family—Raymond was blessed with a remarkable degree of self-discipline and courage. At his father's school Raymond was always the model pupil. He worked hard and played even harder, establishing a reputation as an outstanding athlete. He was an avid mountain climber and won fame in his thirties as a member of the 1931 Kamet Expedition and the 1933 Everest Expedition. Graham admired Raymond's ability to handle physical challenges with ease, but he also felt considerable envy. He was so physically awkward that he would not even try to master the simple skill of driving a car. Climbing a mountain was unimaginable. In the year that Graham was writing *It's a Battlefield,* Raymond's name was in the news for his brave exploits on the slopes of Everest, and he was featured in a film about his previous climb, *Kamet Conquered.* It is clear that Graham's ambivalence toward his brother's masculine superiority is reflected in Conrad Drover's feelings toward Jim, whose case is closely followed by the newspapers during most of the narrative.

The novel even includes a subtle attack on Raymond's friend Hugh Ruttledge, who was the leader of the Everest climb. In the early stages of the investigation of the Paddington trunk murder case, the chief suspect is a man known simply as Ruttledge. There is also an allusion to a night from Greene's days as an apprentice in Nottingham, when he had traveled to London and stayed overnight with Raymond and his wife, Charlotte. The one spare bed was taken by Charlotte's sister, so Greene had made a bed for himself between two armchairs. In the novel Conrad Drover sleeps in the same way when he spends a night in Jim's house with Milly and her sister Kay. The most interesting connection to Raymond is Conrad's pitiful little revolver. Like the one that young Graham had found in Raymond's cupboard, it shoots only blanks.

Writing books and articles is another way of shooting blanks. You can scare the hell out of people, work them into a frenzy of outrage, puncture their pride, call them unpleasant names, and, if it is all done cleverly, you can get away with it. In most cases, the verbal bullets wound without drawing blood, and no one ends up in a grave or criminal court. Among Greene's dreams was one in which he killed Priestley, but he did not have to go to that much trouble in his waking hours—not as long as he could take his revenge through a character such as Quin Savory. The disturbing thing is that, as does Conrad Drover, Greene aimed his weapon with the intense concentration of someone who means to do real harm. Greene's mood was murderous even if his deeds were not. His willingness to spread anti-Semitic ideas in 1938–39 shows the extreme to which his hate could take him, and it is difficult to say that he was shooting only blanks in that case. The situation was too dangerous for anyone to be aiming anything in the direction of Jews.

Likewise, his treatment of the rape and murder case in his novel makes the crime feel uncomfortably close to the real thing, as though he and his protagonist were accomplices in the act. Greene's thoughts are too entangled in the crochet pattern of that bloodstained beret. And the significance of the pattern is never explained. "Oh, the pattern," Milly says of the beret she is trying to make. "No one can understand the pattern." No one, that is, except Conrad. "It's easier than book-keeping," he confidently tells her as he begins to crochet. The larger pattern of Greene's book keeps several odd things nicely hidden—such as the significance of the coy reference to Hugh Ruttledge—and the reader may have to conclude that the relevance of the beret is something no one can understand.

CHAPTER TEN

JOURNEY WITHOUT MAPS

On a Monday morning in December 1934, Graham Greene traveled from Oxford to London for an interview with a Mr. Thompson in the Egyptian Department of the Foreign Office. For reasons known to only a handful of bureaucrats, the Egyptian Department was responsible for British relations with the small West African state of Liberia, a mere 3,000 miles from Cairo. For reasons of similar obscurity, the novelist wanted to visit Liberia in the company of Barbara Greene, a pretty cousin in her twenties. The pair of aspiring explorers had never made any previous visits to Africa and were not entirely certain of the conditions they would find in mysterious Liberia, the lone republic on the continent. They knew no one in the country. So Greene went to the Foreign Office in search of guidance and contacts.

Mr. Thompson provided a little of both. He notified the British consul in Liberia that Graham and Barbara Greene were coming and requested that they be given "all possible assistance." He gave Greene a rough idea of what to expect in Monrovia, the capital, but he was taken aback when he learned that his visitor intended to spend most of his time in the hinterland, a largely unexplored area covered with rugged hills and dense forests. He tried to warn Greene of the dangers. The few existing maps of the area were hopelessly vague.

Disease—especially malaria—was rampant, and there were only five or six doctors in the entire country. But Greene seemed unperturbed. Summarizing the interview for his superiors a few days later, Thompson was incredulous:

> Mr. Greene called on me the other day and I undertook that we would do everything possible to ease his path. He is a young man and unfortunately does not give the appearance of being of particularly robust health. Quite frankly, I think he is running a considerable risk in making this journey, on which he is apparently being accompanied by a lady cousin. I rather deprecated the proposal that this lady should also trek through the interior. . . . I don't imagine that Mr. Greene has any experience whatsoever of the tropics. There is, however, nothing we can do to prevent him going on this journey if he is determined to do so.

In the polite language of the diplomat, Mr. Thompson was trying to say that Greene was crazy. Without any training or experience, the novelist planned to become an explorer overnight. He was going to sail to the British colony of Sierra Leone, take a train to a point near the Liberian border, then make a 300-mile journey on foot to the coast without any clear notion of his route. The chance that he would make it was remote. As Mr. Thompson noted, the young man did not have the look of an explorer. He had lost a little weight since his days at Oxford and seemed wretchedly thin. Without a veteran guide to lead the way, he would surely get lost and fall victim to any number of dangers waiting in the bush. It was the sort of journey that even rugged Raymond Greene might have dismissed as impossible, and perhaps that was one reason Graham wanted to make it. After using *It's a Battlefield* to confront the question of Raymond's superiority, he was suddenly ready to prove that he could compete with his brother in the manly business of exploration. Climbing Everest was beyond his powers, but anyone with more imagination than sense could try walking across Liberia. Living to tell about it was another matter.

As Greene explained it to Thompson, the main purpose of the journey was "to collect material for articles in *The Times,* & eventually a book." The detail about working for his old newspaper was spurious, but he had indeed persuaded Charles Evans to commission a travel book on Liberia—although the publisher must have regarded the idea as only marginally better than a biography of Lord Rochester. Of course, travel books were very much in fashion in the 1930s, but Liberia was not exactly a fashionable destination, and Evans could not be confident that his author would return. As possible subjects for a travel narrative set in Africa, the Gold Coast or the Sudan would have held more appeal for readers back at home. Not many would have been familiar with Liberia—a land settled by former American slaves in the 1820s and a nation determined to resist the pressures of European imperialism.

It was the lack of European control over Liberia that aroused Greene's interest. He wanted to go where other Europeans had not left their mark. It was an older, simpler Africa that he was searching for, one in which the inhabitants were still close to their ancient past. In his view Liberia offered perhaps the last chance to see the real Africa, the one that had existed long before the colonial powers had divided the continent into spheres of influence. He was going to be like Marlow in Conrad's *Heart of Darkness,* an intrepid adventurer seeking some primal truth in the wild interior of Africa. No map was useful for that sort of thing.

But Greene had another, less personal, reason for his trip. It was connected to a recent outbreak of violence in Liberia, one that had attracted international attention. The ex-slaves from America who ruled the country were far outnumbered by native tribes and were willing to impose their authority with brutal force when signs of unrest appeared. In 1931 the Kru tribe had tried to resist the government and had paid a heavy price. Forty-one villages were burned down, and many people were trapped in the flames. The "charred remains of six children" were discovered in one village after the government forces retreated, and some soldiers later boasted that they had attacked children with swords and then thrown the bodies into burning huts. One wounded Kru rebel who tried to surrender peacefully was "shot down in cold blood."

The ruthless commander of the government forces was a recent black immigrant—a former American soldier who had fought with General Pershing's Tenth Cavalry in Mexico. T. Elwood Davis's heart of darkness was not in Africa but in Indianapolis. He grew up there around the turn of the century and had settled in Liberia after he left the U.S. Army at the end of the First World War. Capitalizing on his military experience, he quickly won a place for himself as a trusted officer in the Liberian Frontier Force and was a colonel at the time that he led the assault on the Kru rebels. Word spread that Colonel Davis had specifically ordered his men to kill women and children, and that he was urging a campaign of total war against the tribe.

Greene knew all about these internal troubles. The atrocities had alarmed the League of Nations, and threats of intervention were raised. There were also reports of natives being sold into slavery by the Liberian authorities, and this news angered the Anti-Slavery Society in London. The two most important leaders of the society, Lady Simon and Sir John Harris, fervently campaigned for a British or international effort to restrain the Liberian government. What the Liberians needed, Lady Simon announced, was a new administration reinforced by "strong high-minded white men." Lady Simon and Sir John soon found a promising volunteer who wanted to help them win their propaganda war. His name was Graham Greene.

As the records of the Anti-Slavery Society show, Greene first approached the group in September 1934. He was given a copy of an official British report on the misdeeds of Colonel Davis's Frontier Force and was later invited to tea at Lady Simon's home—which also happened to be the foreign secretary's house. Lady Simon was the wife of Sir John Simon, the foreign secretary since 1931. Several years earlier he had won a lasting place in literary history as the home secretary who defended the confiscation of D. H. Lawrence's *The Rainbow,* copies of which were subsequently burned by the public hangman. In the matter of Liberia, it would appear that he shared his wife's desire to see more high-minded white men supervising the country, but for obvious political reasons he was content to let her carry that particular banner in public. Behind the scenes, however, he waged a campaign of intimidation against the Liberian leaders.

He began by demanding that they admit their mistreatment of the Krus and that they issue a promise to protect the tribe from further reprisals. "His Majesty's Government will not content themselves with an empty denial," he told the British consul in Monrovia. When the Liberian reply proved unsatisfactory, he suggested that stronger action was necessary and asked the American government to help. "It would be a dereliction of duty to civilisation," he told officials in Washington, "if the misgovernment of the native tribes of Liberia were to be allowed to continue." From a purely selfish point of view, it made sense for Britain and America to move into Liberia and divide the country between them. That would give America more control over the huge Firestone rubber plantation outside Monrovia, and it would give Britain the chance to expand the colonial borders of neighboring Sierra Leone.

But no one in Washington wanted to go to any trouble over little Liberia, and not enough people in Britain cared about the issue to make direct intervention a real option. There was also some suspicion that the Krus had exaggerated their accounts of persecution. More tales of atrocities were needed to incite the British public against the rulers in Monrovia, but the reports needed to look impartial. The foreign secretary could not appear to be manipulating the situation. Accordingly, on the day after Greene's meeting with Lady Simon, her friend and colleague Sir John Harris wrote a letter to Mr. Thompson at the Foreign Office asking that "all reasonable assistance" be given to the novelist for his Liberian visit. To maintain the appearance of impartiality, everything went through normal channels. Thus Mr. Thompson was led to believe that he was merely helping out some poor deranged writer who had been befriended by the influential Sir John Harris. Like a good civil servant, Thompson was careful to remind Greene that his trip had no official sanction: "I feel I must record that while we are delighted to help you in so far as we can, His Majesty's Government can, of course, accept no responsibility whatever in regard to your trip."

If all went well, Greene would enter the country in the clever disguise of a harmless, independent novelist in search of new subjects, then quietly dig up more damaging material for Lady Simon's campaign. To help with that effort, Sir John Harris gave Greene a letter of introduction to Juah Nimley, chief of the Kru tribe and the most wanted man in Liberia. "I feel sure you will render him all the assistance that may be possible to you," Sir John wrote to the chief. Greene was also advised to begin his investigations in Sierra Leone, so that he could see how well an African country could be governed in the "right hands." As Sir John explained in a letter to the Colonial Office: "I have strongly advised [Greene] to see a properly governed colony before he goes to Liberia, and he is now making arrangements, at my suggestion, to visit first Sierra Leone, travel through the interior, witness the well-ordered and progressive administration on the British side of the border, then enter Liberia."

Sir John Harris or Lady Simon may have given Greene some money for his travel expenses, but it is more likely that he took up this mission for the fun of it, and for the inside information that would help him with his book. But the trip was still absurd—even more so with the letter to Chief Nimley in his pocket. If Col. Elwood Davis and his friends discovered that he was carrying such a letter, they might want to arrange an unfortunate accident for their visiting novelist. Nimley was eager to tell the world of the injustice his people had suffered, and Colonel Davis was just as eager to silence him. Getting involved in the battle between these formidable adversaries was a good way to end up in an unmarked grave.

To avoid attracting the attention of Colonel Davis, Greene notified the Liberian government that he was going to limit his travel to the western part of the country. In fact, his ultimate destination was the Kru Coast, in the southeast. The whole reason for walking hundreds of miles through the interior was that doing so would allow him to sneak into the Kru Coast from the rear. If he had landed first in Monrovia—the logical starting point for any visitor—his movements could have been easily followed. The plan was to meet Chief Nimley in secret, gather evidence from the tribe, then take a boat up the coast to Monrovia. Once he was in the capital, he could count on the protection of the British consul. It was then simply a matter of waiting for a ship to take him back to England, where Lady Simon and Sir John Harris would be eagerly awaiting his news.

Earlier in 1934 Greene had undertaken some sort of spy mission to the Baltic states. His trip had begun with a Lufthansa flight to Nazi Berlin, where he saw his brother Hugh. He then went to Latvia, and later ended up in a small plane bound for Estonia, with the British consul at Tallinn as his traveling companion. No records have survived that might indicate what he and the consul were up to, but it is not inconceivable that Greene himself was working for a foreign power. In his memoirs Greene says that he had been given some information about Estonia from a person identified only as Baroness Budberg. This was Moura Budberg, a Ukrainian who had once been married to an Estonian baron but whose chief claim to fame was her intimate acquaintance with such luminaries as Maxim Gorky and H. G. Wells. She settled in London in 1929 but kept in close contact with the Soviet embassy, and a recent work has claimed that she was "the Soviet Union's most effective agent-of-influence ever to appear on London's political and intellectual stage." How she met Greene is a mystery, as is the purpose of his expensive journey to Berlin and Estonia.

Perhaps this European experience had given him the courage to attempt a much more dangerous mission in Liberia, but there is a strong possibility that Greene never meant to survive his journey without maps. He was half in love with the idea of dying in Africa. For much of his youth he had been fascinated by the "Dark Continent," and his imagination thrived on the romantic images of death that filled many accounts of European adventures in Africa. In a letter written to the *Times Literary Supplement* in 1966, Greene argued that many Victorians who went to the continent—from Dr. Livingstone to General Gordon—were acting out a "death wish," and he noted that it was not uncommon for brokenhearted lovers in Victorian novels to seek death in some remote African colony. Greene's heart may not have been broken in the early 1930s, but the conflicting passions of his sex life were strong enough to drive him to extreme remedies, and his journey to Liberia was certainly extreme.

It would seem that the last thing he needed on such a trip was his cousin Barbara. She was an amiable and energetic companion, but she had led a pampered life and had never been forced to provide for herself. Her father was Edward Greene, Graham's rich uncle. In her youth she had been surrounded by servants at Berkhamsted Hall and had enjoyed such luxuries as playing tennis on her own court and riding her own pony. Every day a maid would have her bath ready for her and her clothes laid out. Her father was so wealthy that the children never had to give a thought to the cost of things. As her sister Ave recalled, "Money was never mentioned in our family. It was just there. . . . Whatever we wanted, we had." According to Barbara, the worst thing about going to Liberia was that she would be deprived of such pleasures as her Elizabeth Arden beauty treatments and her lunches at the Savoy. Speaking to a newspaper reporter before she left, she admitted that she was not at all prepared for the ordeal ahead of her: "I'm ashamed to confess I've never been on so much as a caravan trip before." Her comment was published in the *News Chronicle* below the headline "Beauty of 23 Sets Out for Cannibal Land."

In later years the two cousins always claimed that they had decided to join forces by accident. Both were a little high on champagne at a party when Graham suddenly asked Barbara whether she would go to Africa with him. Although she had no idea where Liberia was, she happily accepted his offer. They both had second thoughts about the idea after the effects of the champagne wore off, but when her father heard about the trip, he encouraged her to go, saying that it would be good for her. He put some money in Graham's hand and bid them a safe journey. According to Barbara, she had no choice but to abide by her father's wish.

This is an interesting story, but it does not sound convincing. If she had really wanted to avoid the trip, Barbara could easily have talked her way out of it. Her indulgent father would not have forced her to go. It is also misleading to see her as a pliant young woman who could be talked into anything. She claimed that she was only twenty-three at the time, but she was not telling the truth about her age. A family document in Ave's possession shows that Barbara was born on September 28, 1907, which means that she was twenty-seven when she set off for Liberia. She was a grown woman who had her own flat in Chelsea and was fully capable of deciding her fate. She also had a taste for romantic adventure—as she proved when she moved to Germany in the late 1930s and became Countess Strachwitz. And a tropical climate was not alien to her. She was born in Brazil, when her father was managing one of his company's large coffee plantations, and she spent the first few years of her life in a big house on the coast, near Santos.

Barbara was not as weak as she pretended to be. She not only completed the Liberian journey but also came through it in much better shape than did Graham. During the course of their march he suffered badly—his hands began shaking, and one eye developed an awful twitch. He may have been flirting with death, but she proved to be a tough survivor and took good care of her cousin when illness threatened him. She faced danger bravely. It is fair to say that, without Barbara along, Graham might well have perished in some desolate part of Liberia.

There are two good reasons Barbara would have wanted to seem a reluctant participant in her cousin's Liberian escapade. First, it is very likely that she was aware of the trip's secret purpose and did not want to admit her part in the plan. She added a perfect touch to Graham's disguise. What could seem more harmless than a mad English novelist wandering through the bush with his flighty female cousin? Barbara may not have been endowed with great intelligence, but it is a bit much to accept her story that she merely did whatever her cousin told her, following him without question for 300 miles across the back end of Liberia. Second, the carefully cultivated appearance of innocence was a good way to deflect curiosity about the nature of her relationship with Graham. We are supposed to see her as a silly young thing who wandered after cousin Graham for three months, beginning with the voyage from Liverpool in January 1935. But matters look somewhat different if we consider that the trip involved a thirty-year-old man leaving behind his wife and infant child so that he could spend three months in close company with an attractive woman of twenty-seven. It is important to remember that Barbara's older sister was the first great love of Graham's life. He was still dreaming about Ave's beauty in the late 1930s, and there is every reason to think that Barbara was just as appealing to him.

Perhaps the hardest thing to accept in Greene's *Journey Without Maps* is the pretense that he abstained from sex during all those weeks with his cousin. In the book he tries to push the question aside by the simple technique of rarely reminding the reader that Barbara was present on the journey. In the account that she later published, *Land Benighted* (1938), Greene is present on almost every page. She is fascinated by him and puts herself in the background so that the reader is constantly being told that "Graham" said this or "Graham" did that. She does give away one element of his interest in her. For most of their trip through the bush, she wore a pair of shorts that were almost like a ballet skirt. With her long legs constantly visible to him, Graham became increasingly unnerved. Ave's tennis skirts had produced a similar effect on him fifteen years earlier. Either he was punishing himself in a most intricate way, or he and Barbara occasionally took emergency measures to alleviate the strain. It was not a question of love. She had no illusions about his character. She thought that most people were "to him a heap of insects that he liked to examine, as a scientist might examine his specimens, coldly and clearly." But this scientist was not so cold that he could avoid sexual contact for weeks at a time. As Otto Preminger once said of Greene, "Sex is on his mind all the time." If Barbara did keep him at bay for three months, she was indeed a woman of admirable fortitude.

One moment in the trip produced the kind of sexual comedy that Graham loved. As Barbara entered a new village one day, she was shocked to see two naked men fondly strolling along with their arms on each other's shoulders. To make matters worse, these "sexual perverts" could not take their eyes off Graham once they had spotted him. Barbara was sure that her cousin shared her outrage at this conduct, but he voices no objection to it when he describes the couple in his book. And a few months later, when he wrote "The Basement Room," he gave Baines a speech in which the servant has nothing but praise for the open display of affection between certain African men.

II

Of course, the cousins were not entirely alone in the bush. They were accompanied by twenty-five carriers, who hauled all the supplies for the long journey. In a social sense, however, the two white explorers were completely isolated, regarding their African servants as little more than overgrown children. Although Greene said that he wanted to see Africa in its purest form, he proved to be a good example of the European who thinks he has a right to exploit ordinary Africans. While he was critical of the economic imperialism represented by such things as the Firestone plantation, he gave his carriers half the weekly wage that Firestone paid its common laborers. For a mere twenty pounds he was able to employ all twenty-five men for a month, and he spent another fifteen pounds on their food. But he found that they worked best when their bellies were empty. In his book he boasts that when the men had to march for two days without food, they seemed "fresher" than ever. Small pleasures such as breakfast just made them sluggish and argumentative.

The actual problems of life in Liberia were of small interest to Greene. He was looking not for the "real" Africa but for the Africa of his imagination—the one that all those Victorian novels and histories had portrayed. He wanted to see savages. He wanted to see animals sacrificed, natives dancing, witch doctors screaming. Most of all, he wanted to meet the devil. The most vivid passages in his book describe his encounters with village devils and their followers. In one village he is delighted to discover that the devil, in off-duty hours, is actually the local blacksmith. When the blacksmith puts on his mask, he is magically transformed into something from another world. Greene watches with enormous interest as a beautiful young girl dances before the devil, thrusting her body toward him in an erotic way as the eyes of the blacksmith stare at her through the slits in his mask. The scene brings together the supernatural and human qualities of the devil's character. He embodies the dark dreams that lie hidden in most people's minds and that occasionally surface with amazing suddenness. In a flash the mask is in place, and the ordinary blacksmith becomes the most dreaded—and the most intriguing—figure in the village.

For Greene, Africa was a storehouse of arresting scenes and suggestive connections, and his visit was a quick raid to replenish his imagination with fresh images. The journey helped him to understand his world more than the Africans'. Periodically, he interrupts the narrative of *Journey Without Maps* to draw some parallel between life back home and life in the bush. As he makes clear, the savage heart beats loudly under the veneer of European civilization. When he leaves England he thinks of the garish lights in Leicester Square, the smell of bad food in a backstreet, the latest headlines about murders and suicides, and the prostitutes prowling Bond Street. The customs, laws, and material wealth of a civilized society help to suppress and disguise the primal urges at work in everyday life, and they lull us into thinking that the local blacksmith—or the plumber or lawyer—cannot suddenly turn on us with the fury of a devil.

The most powerful moment in the book comes near the end, when Greene recalls a stranger he met in the seemingly tranquil setting of Kensington Gardens. At the time Greene was in his teens and was living at Kenneth Richmond's house. The stranger was seated next to him on a bench and looked immensely respectable. He was a retired military officer and an Old Etonian who had a large estate in Scotland. As he calmly watched children playing in the distance, he began to ask Greene questions about being caned at school and about girls' schools where the cane might still be in use. He invited Greene to stay with him in Scotland and then "began to make confidences." The careful composure of the man slowly broke down as forbidden thoughts raced to the surface. He was like the blacksmith staring wildly through the narrow slits of a new mask. Then he tried to regain his control. The devil's mask dropped away to reveal the ordinary features of a distinguished elderly gentleman, a pillar of civilized society. He stood up and walked away with the rigid step of a soldier.

Such a meeting sounds perfectly plausible, but the mild-mannered gentleman with his fantasies about boys and girls and canes could just as well be the adult Graham Greene. He was familiar with the blacksmith's mask long before he knew its exact shape and size. He had been wearing his own version for years—Hilary Trench, his devilish alter ego, was merely one of the names he had given it. The native masks were of such great interest to him that he made a point of interrogating Liberia's foremost authority on the subject, the Methodist missionary Dr. George Harley. The doctor and his wife ran a small clinic in the remote village of Ganta, which was roughly the middle point on Greene's journey. When he was not treating such things as venereal sores and various tropical ailments, Dr. Harley liked to collect devils' masks. During his long stay in Liberia, he found more than 300 masks and eventually donated them to the Peabody Museum at Harvard University. Greene was eager to examine them all, but he was especially attracted to one with European features. He guessed that it had been modeled on some Portuguese sailor who had strayed into the interior after being shipwrecked.

Dr. Harley interested him as much as the mask. Here was a man who had spent several years in the bush surrounded by a tribe that had once practiced cannibalism and child sacrifice. If anyone stood at the heart of darkness Greene was seeking, it was Dr. Harley. He was heroic, but he also looked overworked and extremely agitated. Accordingly, he is portrayed as a man who has a touch of Marlow's Kurtz in him—a wasted, obsessed character who is not sure whether the natives adore him or want to murder him.

Greene's view was influenced by his own ragged state of mind at that point in the journey, and Harley also had good reason to appear upset. Greene arrived in Ganta on the birthday of Harley's second child, but it was not a festive occasion. The little boy had died in 1931, when he was four, and the family was still haunted by the accident that had taken his life. He had found some bright-colored capsules of quinine and had swallowed a fatal overdose. Describing the event many years later, Winifred Harley recalled: "My husband was desolated. I myself was numb. . . . The same little fellow when he was ten days old had turned blue and collapsed one morning as he was being bathed. His father had recognised infantile malaria and a shot of quinine had worked like a miracle. The drug that saved him then, now had killed him. It was a crushing blow."

Greene's Kurtz-like figure was simply a grieving father. Although Dr. Harley was naturally concerned about his safety at his isolated post, he was not a mad doctor ready to succumb to the wilderness but a hardworking scientist who held a Ph.D., as well as a medical degree from Yale University. He was a fellow of the Royal Society of Tropical Medicine, a fellow of the American Geographical Society, and a Harvard associate in anthropology. He and his wife continued their work in Africa until 1960. The only character in *Journey Without Maps* who comes close to resembling Kurtz is the Englishman who seems to think he is Marlow. He drives his carriers through the bush at a furious pace, keeping them on short rations while he wanders from village to village looking for devils and the quickest way to the Kru Coast. At night he reads *The Anatomy of Melancholy* and makes mental notes on the day's events, keeping track of such things as the shape of the female breast among various tribes. (The women of one tribe are described as having "horn-shaped" breasts.) When he becomes exhausted by his long march, he tries his best to stumble ahead, his eye twitching and his hands shaking. And trailing bravely behind him is a pretty cousin dressed in something that looks like a ballet skirt.

Graham moved at such a rapid pace through the hinterland that he almost lost Barbara. At one point they were separated for several hours. Graham had rushed ahead with a few of his carriers, leaving the rest behind with his cousin, but inevitably the two parties strayed in different directions, and for a time Barbara worried that she was hopelessly lost. Fortunately, she managed to catch up with Graham at a river crossing. But even this mad pace was not fast enough. After three weeks of walking, Greene estimated that he was at least another three weeks away from Sinoe, the Kru village where Chief Nimley was supposedly hiding. Despite all his work, he abruptly abandoned his mission. He was so tired and ill that he could not face three more weeks on the march. He decided to head straight for the nearest coastal village and wait for a boat to take him to Monrovia.

This decision probably saved his life, and not only because his health was giving out. As it happened, the dreaded Col. Elwood

Davis was on his trail, or so it seemed. Fifty miles beyond Dr. Harley's village, Greene came to a place called Tapee-Ta (or Tapeta) and discovered that Colonel Davis and a unit of the Frontier Force were staying there. The colonel was not surprised to find Greene in the area. No doubt the old cavalryman had chosen this strategic spot to show the Englishman that his movements were known to the government. At Tapee-Ta it was still possible to veer off in the direction of Chief Nimley's hiding place, but if that remained an option in the back of Greene's mind, Colonel Davis's presence showed him the game was over.

In his book Greene admits that he was worried. His entry papers showed that he had lied about his travel plans, and he was afraid that Davis would regard him as a spy. The colonel did not have to make a fuss about such things. He had accomplished his mission by simply showing his face. If Greene insisted on trying to find Nimley, Davis would know about it. So Greene was cordially invited to meet the infamous colonel, and every effort was made to convince the visitor that Liberia was a peaceful place whose few episodes of civil unrest had been absurdly exaggerated by outsiders. Greene drank whiskey with Davis, who complained that he was terribly misunderstood. He said that he would never have tolerated the killing of Kru children. After all, he was Liberia's national director of Boy Scouts. His sweet temper had its limits, however. He did not like his soldiers belonging to primitive cults, and when he discovered that fifty men had joined the secret Leopard Society, he was forced to take action. Every man was executed, he told Greene.

Using indirect threats—punctuated by broad smiles—Colonel Davis made it clear that Chief Nimley was not worth visiting. As quickly as possible, Greene cleared out of Tapee-Ta and headed for the relative safety of Monrovia, where he and his cousin stayed at the British consulate. The only distraction along the way to the capital was the sight of a young African girl showing off her breasts. Such attractions were small compensation for the total failure of Greene's grand mission. He would have nothing to offer Lady Simon except the hollow denials of wrongdoing from the colonel. Davis was not some cartoon image of the unsophisticated African official. He meant business, and one look at the filthy prison in Tapee-Ta had shown Greene that it was best to avoid becoming a resident in one of its tiny cells. Later Greene wrote that his journey through the hinterland had given him a new appreciation of life. Meeting the ruthless Colonel Davis was a fine tonic indeed for a moody literary fellow.

Among other things, *Journey Without Maps* is about Greene's efforts to outgrow childhood anxieties and grievances. As he confesses, facing the devils of the hinterland was one way of forcing himself to confront his old fear of the witch in the linen closet. Growing up meant banishing the lingering terrors of the nursery and putting to rest his craving for maternal protection. He needed to rearrange the fragmented pieces of his childhood into a pattern that made sense. He would never be able to do that, and would never really "grow up," but his trip does seem to have given him a new sense of toughness and greater self-confidence. It also made him realize that mapping the dark landscape of his mind would be a slow, piecemeal process. In the writings of Oliver Wendell Holmes, he found the right epigraph for his travel book. It reads, in part: "The life of an individual is in many respects like a child's dissected map. If I could live a hundred years, keeping my intelligence to the last, I feel as if I could put the pieces together until they made a properly connected whole."

After spending several days in Monrovia, Graham and Barbara sailed back to England, arriving in early April. Vivienne made an effort to give her wandering husband a special welcome. She wore a blond wig as a homecoming treat.

Wisely, Greene kept his distance from the Anti-Slavery Society and brought his relationship with it to a swift conclusion. In June 1935 he gave an innocuous report to the annual general meeting, flattering Lady Simon and Sir John Harris with a well-chosen compliment but adding nothing of value to their knowledge of the Liberian situation. He had traveled 3,000 miles and back only to announce that he had met Colonel Davis and considered him a murderer. No one needed to be told that. His remarks could not have been more banal: "One was naturally surprised, therefore, to find Colonel Davis still in a position of authority, the facts having been proved to the last degree."

If Sir John Harris and Lady Simon suspected that they had placed too much faith in their literary friend, they were mistaken. They should not have placed the slightest faith in him, as he soon demonstrated in *Journey Without Maps*. Instead of praising white rule in Sierra Leone, Greene attacks it as a sham. He charges that whites merely wanted to get rich off the country and that the British bureaucrats had made it easy to victimize Africans. He takes a glance at the greedy European traders crowding the City bar in Freetown and declares that their corrupt ways are far surpassed by the colonial rulers, who deliberately keep African wages low. (Tactfully, Greene fails to mention that the lowest government wage was equal to the amount his carriers received.) As for the Liberians, they are mostly seen in a comic, patronizing light. Their main problem is that they have tried too hard to mimic the corrupt ways of the white world, and Greene indicates that the introduction of white administrators would make things worse. He even defends the Liberian government's reliance on forced labor, saying that the kind of work done under this system benefits the country as a whole, whereas business concerns such as Firestone give all the benefits to their shareholders.

Of course, the whole idea of white moral excellence is undermined by his general theme that Europeans are no less savage, deep down, than a devil blacksmith in the bush. In Greene's view of the world, Lady Simon's "strong high-minded white men" are likely to be spending their spare hours on park benches trying to seduce little boys. By contrast, Colonel Davis is almost an admirable character, simply because his evil nature is so transparent. He does not need to wear a mask. After dutifully condemning the colonel in his report to the Anti-Slavery Society, Greene treats him with more respect in his book, depicting him as an amusing, fearless buccaneer. Far from strengthening the case against Davis, the book tries to surround it with confusion, playing the image of the killer against the image of the charmer. One is encouraged to think that, even if he is a mass murderer, the colonel has an impressive sense of style. From the safety of England, it was easy for Greene to take such a view. And how could he do otherwise when he knew that Lady Simon would find it a gross outrage?

In her book, Barbara steers clear of political talk and sticks to a conventional narrative, but her hero is a most unconventional traveler. She captures some of Graham's manic quality, and her running account of the emotional tension created by her shorts is wonderful. The last we hear of them, her cousin is "furiously" telling her how much he dislikes the shorts and warning her that she must never think of wearing them in England. In a dubious gesture of goodwill, Barbara gives them to one of their carriers, who must have looked charming in them.

One great flaw in her book is its title. The only excuse for her choice of *Land Benighted* is that she thought it was a phrase the Liberians themselves had created. She quotes a line from their national anthem: "We'll shout the freedom of a land benighted." This does not sound logical. Why would the population celebrate freedom in a benighted land? The explanation is that both she and Graham (who also quotes the line in his book) misunderstood the song. The actual line—"We'll shout the freedom of a *race* benighted"—reflects the happiness of the original settlers, who had been released from the benighted life of black slavery in America and had found freedom in a new land. Although neither cousin acknowledged the error, Barbara eventually realized that her title had to go. When the book was reprinted in 1981, it appeared under a title that might also be suitable for other tales of life with Graham Greene—*Too Late to Turn Back*.

III

If Greene had not made it back from Liberia, his last novel would have been *England Made Me*—a perfect title for a literary farewell. He completed the manuscript shortly before going to Africa, and Heinemann published it a few weeks after his return. Had Barbara known that a relationship bordering on incest is featured in the novel, she might have thought longer before accepting her cousin's invitation.

Baudelaire's "L'Invitation au voyage," which begins with the poet declaring his love for "my child, my sister," was one of Greene's favorite poems. He quotes from it in *Journey Without Maps*, using the couplet "There, all is order and beauty, / Luxury, calm and ecstasy" as a way to express his ideal of an exotic escape. With his thoughts lingering over Baudelaire's sensual phrases, he definitely needed an attractive relative on the voyage, if only to serve as an aid to his imagination. Another quotation from the poem appears in *England Made Me*, helping to highlight the incestuous feelings that Anthony Farrant and his sister Kate have for each other. As Kate twists the dial on a large radio set, she hears a voice reading from Baudelaire's poem, "To love and die / In that land resembling you."

It is the "love and die" line that might have given Barbara second thoughts, although only Anthony suffers such a fate in *England Made Me*. He is killed a few pages after the words of Baudelaire crackle in the air. It is the predictable end for a character who wants more than he can possibly have. He cannot figure out a way to live with his sister or to live without her. All sorts of jobs and people come in and out of his life, but Kate is always at the center, an object of love that can be neither enjoyed nor ignored. She wants him, but there are too many obstacles standing between them, not the least of which is their family blood. Reflecting the frustration—and the excitement—of their repressed passion, Kate suddenly grabs a penknife one day and tries to drive it straight into her brother's hand.

They can do nothing to destroy their passion and nothing to satisfy it. Kate's last words to her brother are meant to wound him for not taking her love more seriously. As he walks away to the death that awaits him, Kate cries out, "Go to hell." And no doubt Greene assumes that her words are prophetic, because Anthony's great crime is that he does take her love seriously—so seriously that he can never bear to acknowledge it. He has always been a man on the run, beginning with an attempt to run away from school and ending in a long succession of abandoned jobs in foreign places. His sister is the only stable point in his life—the one to whom he keeps returning—but even her love is something he tries to escape, because he sees it as nothing more than a dead end. The inescapable reality is that he cannot allow himself to love the one woman who truly loves him. There is no way to make it work in a world where people would be quick to whisper the simple indictment "Brother and sister!" More living would mean only more misery for both of them, so Anthony's life is sacrificed. It is the only way that either of them will find any peace.

England made Anthony Farrant, and what it made is a hopeless mess. Growing up under the fading sun of Britain's imperial glory, he expected an orderly and prosperous future in which good jobs were plentiful and undemanding. He would have his club, a safe income, old boys' dinners, and peaceful holidays abroad. That world was beginning to collapse when he came of age, yet he held on to its unrealistic expectations and grew increasingly bitter as his hopes were frustrated. He is incapable of functioning in a modern competitive world, because his thoughts are bound to an imaginary Victorian paradise, one in which there is always a place for an idle gentleman.

Thanks to his father, Anthony's thoughts are also constrained by rigid Victorian morality. Its standard precepts were championed by his father, who was forever reminding Anthony of his duty to be earnest, honorable, modest, and pure. When Anthony did not take to these virtues easily, they were beaten into him. The harder he tried to please his father, the more he failed. Eventually, he came to expect failure, and to invite it. The moral instruction made him hate himself for his sins, and the greatest of these was loving his sister. Kate is willing to ignore any conventional objections to her love for him, but he cannot put such things aside. His father used to remind him that he must "honour other men's sisters." That is one rule he could not help breaking, but the idea of honor in sexual relations is still part of his thinking, and violating his own sister's honor is something he cannot do.

Kate is not Anthony's only soul mate. She is his untouchable goddess, but he also has a "greenish" devil by the name of Minty. Their ties are almost as thick as blood—they are united by their fear of failure, their loneliness, and their hatred of a world that refuses to accommodate them. At least Anthony has Kate and assorted girl-friends; Minty relies on no one but himself. He is a frustrated homo-sexual who hates women and punishes himself in religious rituals, racing into damp churches at odd hours with the fervor of "a secret debauchee." His miserable little flat is full of meaningless junk, and he seems to live entirely on cold coffee, cigarettes, condensed milk, and an occasional scrap of tasteless food. His eyes are bloodshot, he coughs a lot, and he is forever picking bits of tobacco from his lips and tongue. Like Conrad Drover, he is convinced that strangers hate him and are giving him poisonous looks behind his back.

He shares Anthony's confused sense of morality, obeying and breaking rules without reason. He will denounce women as trivial and cheap but will not use vulgar curses, preferring the ridiculous oath "Holy Cnut" to a more precise expression. His livelihood as a jour-nalist depends on reporting the activities of the fabulously wealthy industrialist Erik Krogh, whose vast business empire has captured the attention and respect of the world. But Minty despises the man and would love to see him ruined. He is motivated by pure envy. The evils of greedy capitalists are of less interest to him than the aggravating fact that Krogh is rich and he is not. If he had the other man's money, Minty would be content to leave the system as it is. The only thing keeping him from becoming rich is his hatred and mistrust of others. People trusted Krogh and helped him to build his empire through generous loans, but no one wants to back Minty. According to his thinking, it is a personal moral failing, not a lack of talent or a loss of ambition, that has made him poor.

As did his creator, Minty fights back against perceived insults and disappointments by turning his weakness into a sign of defiance. If the world will not trust Minty, he will revel in his power to create mistrust. He enjoys finding subtle ways to get under people's skin, being the first to announce bad news or spread a nasty rumor. It is hardly surprising that everyone dislikes him, but dislike becomes his only source of pride. Unable to win the world's approval, he makes a game of arousing ill will, employing his methods on even the most insignificant foes. He delights in keeping a spider trapped under a glass for five days, eagerly testing its endurance and savoring its mis-ery. It is his pathetic revenge against the world—and God. As he sees it, the only difference between him and the spider is the size of the trap.

Then Farrant comes along. The two have so much in common that they might as well be brothers. As they are surprised to discover, they have had similar operations in the same London hospital, and they share an unusual link to the same school. Minty was forced to leave Harrow in disgrace, and Farrant has created the fiction that he also attended the school. Minty responds almost immediately to the young man as a fellow outcast and feels a vague yearning for his friendship. But he has isolated himself for so long that he no longer knows how to make a friend. He thinks back to his school days and remembers that his one friend in that period was a boy named Sparrow, who had no other companions. The only thing they had in common was their loneliness, but that thin bond was enough to inspire a little love in a dark corner of the changing room. Unfortunately for Minty, Farrant seems more interested in women than in men. So even if he knew how to love again, Minty would find disappointment. Like Kate, he cannot have his man.

One critic has speculated that Greene used his brother Herbert as a model for Anthony Farrant's character. There are some superficial similarities. Herbert's inability to keep a job was legendary in the Greene family, and his pursuit of easy pickings had led him to several foreign spots. Everything else about Farrant could have been drawn from the novelist's own feelings and experiences. There is a good deal of Greene in both Farrant and Minty, each one representing certain tendencies in his character. He could be as charming as Farrant and as unpleasant as Minty. He could chase women and want men. The novel itself favors Minty, who comes close to dominating the last half of the book. In its intensity, Minty's isolation is the most convincing, and most painful, aspect of the book.

One problem is that the tale is too slight to make a novel. Greene fills out the narrative with technical experiments—using interior monologues and shifts in point of view—and with long looks at Krogh's dirty empire. Then, for good measure, he throws the whole cast into a foreign setting—Sweden. We never are given anything more than a general picture of the country and its people. All the important characters, including the great Krogh himself, are English, or speak and act as though they were. There is no reason why the novel could not have been set in England. But Greene had visited Sweden in 1933 and was clearly determined to put his sightseeing experiences to use in a novel. The fact that he spent only three weeks in the country is obvious from the novel's lack of detailed exterior scenes and its large number of interior scenes. The best images are of things that have no specific connection to Sweden.

Liberia gave Greene a much better book. With all its flaws, *Journey Without Maps* is a grand tale of misconceived plans and courageous lunacy. It could be called "Mr. Minty Meets Colonel Davis" or

"Anthony and Kate Do Africa." Greene so much enjoyed making fun of others, but nothing could be funnier than the author when he is most absorbed in his outlandish pursuits. The difficulty is that some things are not laughing matters, and often we are left wondering whether we should laugh or cry as he cuts quickly from harmless antics to venomous troublemaking. At his worst he combines the devilish thoughts of a worldly adult with the emotional instability of a lonely teenager—a most dangerous combination. You can hear the voice of this tortured creature as it boasts about underfeeding and underpaying the twenty-five Africans who faithfully followed two strange white people on a dangerous, futile mission. You can see this creature in Minty as he carefully contemplates the spider under the glass and waits for a slow death to take its course.

CHAPTER ELEVEN

THIS GUN FOR HIRE:
MOTION PICTURES

On his way to Liberia, Greene found a surprise waiting for him in the Canary Islands. The big attraction at the cinema in Tenerife was Twentieth Century–Fox's *Orient Express,* starring Heather Angel as Coral Musker and Norman Foster as Carleton Myatt. The studio posters made the film seem like a thrilling love story: "Two Youthful Hearts in the Grip of Intrigue. Fleeing from Life. Cheated? Crashing Across Europe. Wheels of Fate." To simplify matters, Hollywood had cut out Myatt's selfish streak and replaced it with a heart of gold to match Musker's. And in case the title caused any confusion among the locals, Fox's publicity material provided a helpful explanation: "The real Orient Express runs across Europe from Belgium to Constantinople. Therefore, you will go wrong if you interpret the word 'Orient' to indicate something of a Chinese or Japanese nature."

Such words made Greene cringe, as did the film itself. He was appalled to see how much of his novel had been altered by the studio. With most of the flesh stripped away, the skeleton of the story looked ghastly. Still, it was partly his creation, and he felt some pride that its worldwide distribution had brought it to even this tiny island in the Atlantic.

During his long trek through the bush, some of those Hollywood images must have rattled in his brain and aroused a fresh curiosity about the art of the cinema, or lack thereof. At Oxford he had been an avid filmgoer and had contributed to the *Oxford Outlook* a review of several films—including a silent version of *The Call of the Wild*. When he returned from Liberia, he had the urge to become a regular film reviewer and offered his services to his old friends at *The Spectator*. To his surprise his offer was accepted, and, the next thing he knew, he was attending his first preview. It was not an auspicious beginning, but he did manage to work up at least three paragraphs of intelligent commentary on *Bride of Frankenstein,* helpfully pointing out—as only a literary man could—that Elsa Lanchester's face looked like a salamander described in a poem by Walter de la Mare. The review appeared on July 5, 1935. Greene might well have called it quits at this point if he had known how many bad films lay ahead of him. In the next four and a half years, he would sit through 424 films and deliver a verdict on each one. The range of titles is amazing— everything from Garbo's *Anna Karenina* and Olivier's *Wuthering Heights* to *The Lone Ranger* and *Charlie Chan in Shanghai.*

Greene's tastes were unpredictable. It is not surprising to read his praise for such great directors as Fritz Lang, Carol Reed, and Jean Renoir, but he also liked the lowbrow comedy of W. C. Fields and Laurel and Hardy. He rated Stan and Ollie above Charlie Chaplin, whom he greatly admired. What he liked so much about the comedy duo was their complete lack of serious purpose. They did not want to change the world; they simply wanted to make people laugh. During a time when motion pictures were full of social messages, Greene found it refreshing to see nothing but human nature at work in Laurel and Hardy's style of buffoonery. For similar reasons, he was attracted to Garbo's mystery and Gary Cooper's quiet strength.

The films he liked best were those that filled the screen with evocative images. The "poetry" of the cinema spoke to his concerns as a novelist, giving him new ideas for literary imagery. Again and again he praises the directors who knew how to punctuate the action with revealing images. In a review of Fritz Lang's *Fury,* he is enthralled by the director's ability to build up a sense of terror through a carefully selected series of images. As a lynch mob marches to the jail where their victim is being held, Lang's camera focuses on the beaming faces of men and women whose hearty shouts and laughter give such a wicked edge to their lust for blood. A boy sings "I'm Popeye the Sailorman," and a mother holds up her baby to see the first assault on the jail. The innocent victim's face peers from behind the bars of his cell with an awful look of dread. The powerful link between image and feeling prompted Greene to call the film "great," an adjective he used sparingly in his criticism.

He was especially fond of lingering close-ups. The shots that appealed to him in Julien Duvivier's *Un Carnet de Bal* were of a cataracted eye, a dirty hand, and a woman's face behind beaded curtains. In a long digression on Sergei Eisenstein's silent classic *October*, he recalls the images of stout Russian women lying on the billiard table of the royal palace, and of Kerensky fumbling with the czar's decanters. Reviewing *Anna Karenina*, he is excited by the shots of Garbo leaning over a croquet ball and of her face emerging from a cloud of locomotive steam. In every case his admiration is sparked by an awareness of the image's power to convey a wealth of feeling in only a few seconds. What he was learning from such films was a way to make images carry more of the meaning in his work. Imagism had taken him part of the way, but the cinema offered so many new suggestions. Raven's harelip in *A Gun for Sale*, the gulls swooping over the pier in *Brighton Rock*, the yellow-fanged mestizo in *The Power and the Glory*, the misty common dividing Maurice and Sarah in *The End of the Affair*—all these memorable images seem to have sprung from the darkness of the cinema.

To earn Greene's condemnation, a film needed not only to neglect poetic imagery but to fill its story with images that did nothing to illuminate life. He loathed the vulgar spectacle of *The Great Ziegfeld*, with its flashy blondes and gaudy sets. He dismissed Fred Astaire's performance in *Top Hat* as that of a Mickey Mouse figure skipping through a fantasy world. He disliked Hitchcock for relying too much on clever tricks. The heavy-handed moralizing in *The Petrified Forest* bored him. And the only things he liked in *The Wizard of Oz* were the tornado and Dorothy's adolescent figure.

It was daring of Greene to praise the sight of young Judy Garland's "delectable" legs as they dance down the Yellow Brick Road. Only two and a half years earlier, he had lost a lot of money to Shirley Temple for suggesting that she was trying to excite old perverts. But that review had failed to take note of his own interest in the sexual charms of young girls. In an earlier piece on *Captain January*, Greene had found reason to speak favorably of eight-year-old Shirley, remarking that her body looked "voluptuous" in tight pants. Unabashed by his legal troubles with Ms. Temple, he put a seven-year-old sexpot into a novel written not long after the case had been heard. In *The Power and the Glory*, the whiskey priest sees his young daughter after a long absence and discovers that all she wants to talk about is sex. When her father tells her that she does not know anything about the subject, she replies "enticingly," "Tell me," and strikes a pose of "abandonment" on a tree trunk. For a moment she seems like a cross between an ordinary little girl and Marlene Dietrich in *The Blue Angel*. In fact, that is exactly the impression Greene was trying to convey when he wrote about Shirley Temple in *Captain January*. Straining to find the right analogies, he said that she was as big a tease as Claudette Colbert and as stunning in pants as Marlene Dietrich.

Of course, he was trying to be funny, but his recurring interest in the subject suggests that he found more in it than mere humor. He was a great admirer of Vladimir Nabokov's *Lolita* and campaigned vigorously for its publication in Britain when it was available only in a French edition. The book's literary merits do not seem to have interested him as much as its subject matter. Curiously, near the end of Greene's life, an eminent historian—Sir Raymond Carr—publicly accused him of having sex with young girls in Haiti. Writing in *The Spectator,* Sir Raymond charged that "in Haiti I was repeatedly accosted by pimps who claimed Greene had slept with their adolescent sisters." Greene's subsequent denial was mild. He merely dismissed it with the joke that he had managed to avoid all sex in Haiti, even passing up the charms of Papa Doc. After Greene's death, the novelist Francis King wrote in the London *Evening Standard* that Greene used "to pick up teenage girls" on visits to Brighton.

Sexy grown-up girls were not ignored in Greene's film criticism. Besides being attracted to the cool glamour of Garbo, he had a soft spot for the androgynous look. In a review of three films, he said that the only really worthwhile thing in any of them was the sight of Anna Neagle dressed up in the fancy clothes of an eighteenth-century English gentleman, complete with three-cornered hat. Busty starlets did little for him, however. Mae West was too friendly, and Jean Harlow was too intimidating. One of the best lines in his film reviews is his farewell tribute to the recently deceased Jean Harlow: "She toted a breast like a man totes a gun."

Bad American films tended to provoke Greene's worst criticisms. He was especially annoyed by the Hollywood pictures that presented a squeaky clean version of America, with lots of stalwart young men and wide-eyed, wholesome beauties. A war movie featuring a large cast of well-fed midwestern soldiers drove him to distraction. Their breaking voices, smug looks, and easy laughter made him wonder how the Allies ever managed to win the First World War. But Greene was not always listening very closely to the offensive American voices. He began his review of another American film, *Marked Woman,* with a quotation he attributed to one of the characters, "It's feudal." This led him into an intricate explanation of why the American tough guys in the film were like feudal barons. Unfortunately, Humphrey Bogart's accent was a bit hard for him to pick up. What Bogie had actually said was "It's futile."

When the great Louis B. Mayer came to London and spoke at the Savoy, Greene was in the audience, and he later wrote a scathing article on the film mogul, depicting him as a sentimental windbag who could talk of nothing but God, family, and the movies. Mayer wanted to make more films in England, but Greene scoffs at this idea. He takes pains to show that the American knows nothing about England and will only corrupt all who join his enterprise by forcing them to trade artistic integrity for cold cash. Behind all the talk of God and family, Greene hears only the sound of money changing hands. And the speech is delivered in what he describes as a "little level Jewish voice." For a novelist with valuable film rights to unload, Greene was uncommonly eager to spit in Hollywood's face.

But he was even more determined to abuse Britain's most important filmmaker, and his future friend in the spy game, Alexander Korda. In the early days of his film reviewing, readers of *The Spectator* could rely on Greene to heap insults on the latest production from Korda's London Films company. Many of these films are now highly regarded, but Greene's real interest was not in evaluating the work. He wanted to savage Korda.

The idea had entered his mind that Korda was ruining the British film industry by subjecting it to an alien vision. The problem was not just that Korda was Hungarian. What bothered Greene most was the filmmaker's Jewishness. In 1936 he complained that the British film industry was being taken over by foreigners, and he named Korda as the most harmful of the group. His solution was the traditional one of the xenophobe: send them back to where they came from. In this case it was back to the garment trade.

As he told the readers of *The Spectator,* it would not "grieve" him to see Korda in an Eastern land "seated before a cottage loom . . . following an older and better tradition." If the foreigners were not sent packing, the whole film industry would be in their hands, and the "vulgarity" of Korda's work would reign supreme. To frighten his readers, he presented the vision of "the dark alien executive tipping his cigar ash behind the glass partition in Wardour Street." If anyone had doubts about the origin of the "alien" and his "vulgarity," Greene cleared up the question in another article that condemned "the awful un-Aristotelian waste of this Semitic and commercial craft." In April 1939, when Korda's film company was suffering financial difficulties, Greene welcomed the setback, proclaiming that it might signal the end of "tasteless Semitic opulence" in the industry. English films, he declared, might finally have the chance to be truly English. The timing of this attack—a few months before the outbreak of war—was terrible.

Greene was so incensed by Korda's power that he was not content to mock him only in film reviews. There is evidence to suggest that the character of Forbes/Furtstein in *The Confidential Agent* is based on Korda. Like the fictional businessman, Alexander Korda had a more "ethnic" name. He was born Sándor Laszlo Kellner. And, as does Furtstein, Korda tried hard to win acceptance at the highest levels of English society, surrounding himself with the sons and daughters of politicians and the nobility. Just as Furtstein's awful Lido resort is a blot on the English countryside, Greene considered Korda's films a danger to English culture. Greene left behind a clue in *The Confidential Agent* to indicate his intentions. The mission of an odd group featured in the novel is to establish an international language called Entrenationo. They have a word for "heart," and they enjoy using it in a vulgar, sentimental way, repeating it often in their songs. The word, of course, is *korda*.

It is possible, too, that Greene had Korda in mind when he decided to make Colleoni a Jew in *Brighton Rock*. In both cases Greene sees the Jew as someone who has invaded what rightfully belongs to the English people. The image in his film review of "the alien executive tipping his cigar ash" is repeated in *Brighton Rock*. As Colleoni talks to Pinkie in the luxurious office, he seems on the verge of dropping a long ash from his cigar. Presumably, the image is meant to reflect the arrogance and complacency of the alien conqueror.

It is doubtful that Korda was aware of how much Greene resented him, although he was well aware of the drubbing that his films usually received in *The Spectator*. His solution to the problem was to make a handsome peace offering. In 1936 he invited the film critic to his headquarters at Denham and gave him a commission to write an original story for the screen. For a few weeks of work, Greene received about 1,000 pounds—almost twice as much as *The Times* had paid him as an annual salary. But it was not enough to buy Greene's loyalty. In 1937 Korda doled out more money, assigning him the job of writing a screenplay of John Galsworthy's story "The First and the Last." Still, Greene was willing to attack the "Semitic" craft of filmmaking and to poke fun at Korda in *The Confidential Agent*.

Greene's own craft proved inadequate in his first efforts for Korda. The original story that Korda commissioned became *The Green Cockatoo,* a thriller with a strong love interest thrown in. It was a big flop. The Galsworthy project also turned out to be a disaster, despite the fact that its stars were Laurence Olivier and Vivien Leigh. Even Greene was willing to give it a bad review when it was eventually released in 1940 under the title *Twenty-one Days.* As a nice ironic touch, he called the film "sentimental." He also had the grace to admit that he had played a part in its making, and he pledged never to get involved in such a project again.

Korda was not finished with him, however. In 1940 he bought the rights to *The Power and the Glory* for 2,000 pounds, then sold them to John Ford, who eventually made a film version called *The Fugitive,* with Henry Fonda. After the war Korda paid 3,000 pounds for Greene's work on *The Fallen Idol;* 4,000 pounds for the rights to *The Heart of the Matter;* and 9,000 pounds for *The Third Man.* This last figure included the cost of a small yacht—the *Nausikaa*—which Greene used only briefly, and also the cost of buying the Villa Rosaio in Anacapri. Korda used his own large yacht to take Greene on long Mediterranean cruises and occasionally acted as his contact with the Secret Intelligence Service.

Given this massive campaign of kindness and generosity, Greene's attitude toward the "dark alien" could not help but mellow. Colleoni and Furtstein were not such bad fellows after all. In 1955 Greene made gentle fun of Korda in the short novel *Loser Takes All,* portraying him as the rich businessman Dreuther, whose yacht idly wanders from one Mediterranean port to another. Nicknamed Gom—for "grand old man"—he plays a God-like part in the lives of his friends and employees, saving them from ruin but taking his own sweet time about it. Following Korda's death in 1956, Greene wrote that he loved the old man. That may have been, but he certainly had a strange way of working up to it.

II

While Greene was still in his first year of doing film reviews for *The Spectator,* he began writing *A Gun for Sale.* The influence of the cinema is evident throughout the novel. Many of the scenes are placed in short sections that seem ready to go before the camera. The opening is meant to grab an audience right away, with a no-nonsense, almost wordless scene in which two people are swiftly and brutally

murdered by a mysterious gunman. Even the killer looks at the murder scene as though it is something his eyes are filming. When he
enters the house where his victims are working, he looks slowly
around the room like a cameraman executing a careful panning shot,
taking notice of every detail. Once the scene is set, the action
explodes. Only eleven paragraphs are needed for the killer to enter
the house, size up his victims, and take his first shot with an auto-
matic pistol. With such a powerful opening, it is hardly surprising that
the film rights were sold to Paramount studios even before the
novel's official publication date, in June 1936.

Many critics seem to think that anything that can easily be turned
into a film must be weak as a work of literature. But as is the case with
most good novels, *A Gun for Sale* offers much to the reader that no
film could hope to capture. A killer's mentality cannot be adequately
conveyed on the screen, but Greene's novel is able to subject it to
microscopic scrutiny. Unlike Quin Savory, his fictional novelist in
Stamboul Train, Greene had a difficult time dealing with "healthy"
people. What he understood was the "unhealthy" mind, but, until he
wrote *A Gun for Sale,* he did not attempt to place an extreme case at
the center of a novel. The killer Grünlich and the misogynist Minty
are not the main characters in their novels, and Conrad Drover's
sense of evil is restrained by his fears and insecurities. With Raven, a
man of true darkness absorbs Greene's attention. After surviving his
encounter with Colonel Davis, Greene was ready to deal more directly with the questions that had always fascinated him. What is the
attraction of evil? And what price must be paid for surrendering to it?

No attempt is made to soften the brutality of Raven's actions in the
opening scene. He has been hired to assassinate a minister of war in a
small European state, and, when he finds his man, he does his job
with ruthless efficiency. The minister is shot twice in the back; then
another round is fired straight at the base of his skull, breaking it into
pieces. Unfortunately, his secretary is a witness and must be eliminated. Raven's first shot misses, giving the woman time to race into
another room and shut the door behind her. When Raven finds that
he cannot open it, he calmly steps back and fires two shots through
it, at least one of which wounds the woman. Her body falls against
the door, and Raven must push hard to open it. As she lies bleeding
on the floor, he completes his job by placing the pistol to her eyes
and pulling the trigger.

The vague descriptions and uncertain pace that mar some of
Greene's earlier works are absent from this novel. Every move is
described with cool clarity. After the opening burst of action, the nar-

rative begins to unravel not only the purpose of the killing but the real motives of the hired gun. The man who paid for the killing—the steel baron Sir Marcus—is hoping that it will start a war. Raven does not care whether war breaks out or not. As far as he is concerned, he has been at war with the world all his life, and he does not mind if the world gets a taste of what he has suffered. His father was hanged, his mother committed suicide, and he was brought up in an orphanage. Such things could be endured, but not the bright red wound on his face—the harelip that was improperly attended to in his childhood. Ashamed of the deformity—which has wounded his soul as well as his face—Raven wants to punish the world for allowing him to suffer in it.

Like Conrad Drover, he has devised a rationale for murder. The world is evil, the rich and the powerful get away with crimes every day, and protecting others will bring you only more misery. Violence is also Raven's only means of power, his only way of giving himself an identity. He is the gun in the title, the man who will kill for a price. As he walks toward the minister's house, he is described as looking like hundreds of other ordinary people going about their business. He may seem like that from a distance, but at close range his harelip sets him apart, and so does his gun. He is not a part of the crowd. They would not have him, and he is determined not to have them.

He expects to be cheated and is not surprised to discover that Davis—Sir Marcus's agent—has paid him off with marked money. Eventually, he also learns that the minister was not one of the corrupt leaders who deserved to die but a humane man who had worked hard to improve the lives of people like Raven. Davis and Sir Marcus have made it easy for Raven to play the part of a modern Judas, a part for which he has a natural talent and inclination. They go too far, however, when they deny their Judas his pieces of silver by handing him a bogus reward. They must pay for that treachery, and Raven pursues them to Sir Marcus's headquarters in the smoky industrial Waste Land of Nottwich. (The setting is based on Greene's memories of Nottingham.) Like a dark avenging devil, Raven swoops down on the town to hunt his prey.

The action takes place during the Christmas season, allowing Greene to highlight Raven's part as the modern Judas. The killer is scornful of the Christmas displays and the good cheer of the season. Seeing the Christ child in his cradle, Raven turns away with disgust, cursing the "little bastard." Consumed by his mission, he will not allow the purity of his revenge to be diluted by the Christmas spirit. And Greene extends his sympathy to Raven by taking away much of the spirit from the season. Except for a few superficial gestures, no one in the novel seems to be paying much attention to the holiday. It is an empty occasion, a time for putting up a few tawdry decorations or singing a couple of dreary songs. People are much more concerned with the manhunt for Raven or with the news that war might erupt in Europe.

The "little bastard" is insignificant compared with the figure of Raven as he prowls the streets. Raven even makes his bed in the House of God, spending one night in the Catholic cathedral—the fictional counterpart of the Nottingham church in which Greene was baptized. In every way the killer subverts the message of Christ. The modern world has given birth to a predator, not a savior, but there is no longer anything worth saving. In the world of the novel, a Judas makes more sense than a Christ—someone, in other words, who is willing to fight back, to betray others before they can betray him. The Jewish child came with a message of peace, but the ultimate purpose of Raven's mission is to murder the Jewish Sir Marcus.

Raven lives by a bleak code and is prepared to die by it, not expecting mercy from God or man. Although he has good reason to hate the world, he has allowed the hate to twist his flawed human face into an inhuman mask of pain and fury. Somewhere underneath the mask is the face of a young man who might have taught himself to love instead, but he has grown accustomed to his evil mask and has come to regard it, and his gun, as his best protection. It is interesting to note that when he kills Davis and Sir Marcus he is wearing an actual mask. During a gas drill at Sir Marcus's factory, Raven is able to sneak into the old man's office by wearing a gas mask, and he continues to wear it until after he has accomplished his mission.

The only person who comes close to breaking down Raven's cold exterior is the attractive Anne Crowder, who tries to show him some sympathy. But if Raven had followed his initial plan for her, she would not have lived long enough to do anything for him. Having abducted her from the train that brings him to Nottwich, he leads her to a model home in a new housing development and forces her into the small bathroom upstairs. She tries to win him over by speaking kindly to him, and he gives away his reason for coming to Nottwich. But the more she learns about him, the more reason he has to kill her. Doing her best to appear unafraid, Crowder begins to put some makeup on her face. Raven raises his pistol to her back and is about to pull the trigger when voices are heard downstairs. He puts away his gun, and, although Crowder manages to escape, she does not turn him in. Her silence amazes Raven, who cannot believe that anyone would want to give him a break.

The voices downstairs belong to an estate agent and his client, a Mr. Green and a Mr. Graves. It is Greene's coy little reminder that every action is in his hands. Characters live or go to their graves on his whim. The reader is led to believe that Raven will kill Crowder as easily as he killed the government minister and the secretary, but the sudden entrance of Mr. Green with his client—or rather, the sudden intervention of Mr. Greene with his two new characters—is enough to save the day. The novelist cannot avoid teasing his more gullible readers, who may underestimate the ease with which their emotions can be manipulated. But Greene's joke is also a confession of sorts, an admission that his finger is ultimately the one on the trigger. He lets Crowder off this time, but he is not through with her. He has another close call in mind.

In the very next scene Crowder gets involved with Davis, who treats her in a way that parallels Raven's actions. Besides working as one of Sir Marcus's thugs, Davis backs theatrical productions, and he meets Crowder when she takes a part in his Christmas pantomime, *Aladdin*. He asks her out to dinner, then lures her to his hideaway at a cheap boardinghouse. Alone with her in a small bedroom, he tries to seduce her, but his mood changes when he learns that she has talked to Raven. Fearing that she can connect him to the killing of the minister, he tries to smother her with a pillow. Again, the reader is made to think that her death is imminent. Davis's large body has her pinned against the bed, and the pillow is over her mouth. But this time there are no interruptions except the common one of a chapter break. As the scene ends, the reader does not know Crowder's fate but is given every reason to think that she will not survive.

There are obvious sexual overtones in the two attempts on Anne Crowder's life. Both are set in small, intimate rooms, and in both cases the woman appears to be completely at the mercy of the man who has trapped her. There can be no doubt that Davis's effort to smother Crowder is primarily sexual. But, as the reader soon learns, he does not suffocate his victim. Instead he devises a plan more to his liking. She is bound and gagged and shoved inside a fireplace. His interest in this sort of thing is suggested earlier in the novel when he is seen entering a shop that sells "books on flagellation." No Mr. Green follows Davis into the shop, but the novelist does add a personal touch to the boardinghouse in which Crowder is imprisoned. It is run by Acky, the defrocked clergyman whose insanity brings to mind the case of Greene's Grandfather Carleton. Fortunately, Crowder is rescued from this madhouse and is allowed to reach the end of the novel in one piece.

Raven's sexual motives are more obscure than Davis's. Because he does not like to get close to anyone, the best thrill he can manage is

Berkhamsted School, 1914. Graham Greene is seated in the middle of the photo, at his father's feet. His mother and older sister are seated on either side of his father.

Harston House, home of the potting shed.

A fresh face from Oxford: Greene in 1925.

Just married, 1927.

Off to Africa: Barbara Greene and her camera-shy cousin, 1935.

The cover of the first British edition of
Brighton Rock, 1938.

A death in Brighton,
1934.

A scene from the film version of *The Man Within,* 1947, with Richard Attenborough (left center) and Michael Redgrave (right center).

Bill Brandt's vision of the novelist: 5 St. James's Street, 1950.

A new knight: Alexander Korda leaving Buckingham Palace with his wife, Merle Oberon, after receiving his knighthood, 1942.

The new convert: Catherine Walston (seated, far left) at her reception into the Catholic Church, 1946. Father Vincent Turner is at her side, and Vivien Greene is standing behind him.

Trevor Howard and Maria Schell in the film version of *The Heart of the Matter*, 1953.

to attack people with his fist or his gun. When he fires an extra bullet at close range into the minister and the secretary, he seems to be doing it for pleasure as well as for his own safety. And when he points the gun at Crowder's back in the bathroom, he comes as close as he ever will to engaging in something that bears at least a faint resemblance to a sexual act. Later—after she has agreed to help him escape from the police—he spends a night with Crowder in a shed, but in that long night they share no physical closeness. He is afraid of "going soft on a skirt." As befits behavior in any proper shed in Greene's fiction, Raven sits down and thinks of death—the deaths of his parents, the deaths of his previous victims, the anticipated deaths of Davis and Sir Marcus, and his own inevitable demise.

The significance of the gun as a sexual weapon is made more apparent when Raven finally corners Davis and Sir Marcus. Pumping bullets into them is his last orgy of violence, and after the deed is done he feels an enormous wave of relief sweep through his body. When he takes off the gas mask, it is as though he is also removing the mask of rage that he has worn for so long. Just as Conrad Drover sought the sort of physical release from violence that he had experienced earlier with prostitutes, Raven's last murders drain the hate from his body and leave him unable to fire again when the police arrive on the scene. He thinks of Crowder when he kills Davis and even calls her his friend before he shoots the man. So it would seem that, in his own strange way, he does "go soft on a skirt" after all. And he pays for it. A trigger-happy policeman shoots him in the back.

There is nothing redeeming in all this violence. Killing Davis and Sir Marcus will make no difference in the corrupt world of the novel. A character who is said to look and talk exactly like Davis appears at a meeting in Nottwich shortly after the real Davis has been murdered. "They were turned out of a mould," the narrator says, "and you couldn't break the mould." There is no hand of God at work in this novel, only the hand of Greene. And what he sees is a world full of enemies in which a character such as Raven can seem almost noble. You put on your mask and prepare for battle, trusting no one and harboring no illusions. You cannot win, but some ways of failing are better than others. At least Raven is not a hypocrite—like so many other people in the novel. He knows who he is and accepts his fate. There is even a kind of nobility to his hate. Unlike that of Sir Marcus and others, his hatred is not driven by lust or greed. It is pure, fed by a profound disenchantment with life. The irony is that his allegiance to hatred protected Raven until he made a friend. It is Crowder who alerts the police that Raven is on his way to kill Sir Marcus and Davis, thus leaving him no room for an escape. She is kind to him and tries to help, but if he had killed her in the first place, he might have survived his mission. Instead his hatred becomes tainted. In the end he kills for the wrong reason—for some faint notion of friendship. When he allows that unfamiliar emotion to enter his system, he is doomed.

The complexity of Greene's vision was completely ignored when Paramount studios finally decided to film an adaptation of the novel. It was called *This Gun for Hire,* which was also the title of the American edition of the novel. Although the company had been eager to acquire the rights, they did not begin production until 1941, by which time there was no point in having Sir Marcus plotting to start a war. The war in Europe had been raging for two years. Undeterred, the Hollywood screenwriters turned the minister of war into a scientist with a valuable secret formula. Raven's job is to steal it for the evil head of the Nitro Chemical Company, who is selling information to the enemy. With a wave of their pens, the screenwriters also moved the story from Nottwich to Los Angeles. But the greatest travesty is the change in Raven's character. He becomes a halfway decent fellow who does not really want to kill people. All he needs is the love of a good girl and a patriotic cause to fight for. He hates the boss of Nitro for double-crossing him but shoots him down to save America, and to prove himself to the girl who has befriended him.

Alan Ladd was cast as Raven, and, because this was his first big part in a film, he could hardly have been expected to spend eighty minutes on screen with a harelip. It might have been best to forget about the question of a deformity, but the problem was solved by giving Raven a mangled wrist. In an early scene there is a shot of a circular advertising a reward for the capture of the "Broken Wrist Robber" and below the name is an enlarged photo of a broken wrist. If Greene's Raven had been blessed with such a problem, he might have found a big glove and devoted his life to good works.

One good thing in the film is the beautiful Veronica Lake. But the scene in which she is bound and gagged seems to have put curious notions in the minds of the screenwriters. They devised a song-and-dance number for her in which she wears a black rubber outfit. As the music begins, she appears as a singer at a nightclub dressed in the tight outfit, and in one hand she carries a fishing rod. She dances merrily and occasionally tips her rod in the direction of the audience. "I've got you dangling on my line," she sings. It is probably just as well that Greene had given up writing film reviews when this production came out.

CHAPTER TWELVE

BRIGHTON ROCK

D espite the heavy burden of his literary work in the 1930s, Greene found some spare time to plot the downfall of the British government. His cunning plan required no armed resistance or massive public demonstrations. It was so simple that a single madman with an ample supply of postage stamps and pornography could pull it off. First, you selected several good titles from your pornography collection; then you put them in a nice bundle. Second, you attached a typed note announcing that they were a gift from the chancellor of the exchequer. Third, you sent them to the wife of the home secretary. Finally, you repeated the process until everyone in the cabinet appeared to be making regular shipments to the wives of other cabinet members. "A cross-traffic of such parcels," Greene told a friend, "would cause the government to cave in in a matter of days."

Greene had a more complicated backup plan, which involved hiring several expert impersonators of the prime minister, but, fortunately, he never put his ideas into action. He did, however, keep on the alert for items that might be used to implement his first scheme. As he recorded in his diary, the best imported pornographic magazine was called—rather unimaginatively—*Sex Appeal*. He also noted that the trade was now using anything with "Hollywood" in the title as a

code word for flagellation. There were such titles as *Hollywood Revels,*
Hollywood Nights, and so on. If he had implemented his scheme, Lady
Simon would surely have been near the top of his mailing list, and
presumably she would have received a rich assortment of *Hollywood*
This and *Hollywood That.*

Greene found it impossible to take politicians or politics seriously.
While many writers of his generation were eagerly explaining their
positions on a wide variety of issues, he stood to the side and either
said nothing at all or made evasive remarks. Some critics thought that
his negative portraits of characters such as Erik Krogh and Sir Marcus
were an implied criticism of capitalistic society, but Greene was simply attacking convenient figures of authority. He gives the same
rough treatment to Mr. Surrogate, the Communist leader in *It's a*
Battlefield. Greene was not a political animal. Like those of Minty,
Raven, Pinkie, Scobie, and other characters in his fictional world, his
battles are fundamentally private. Political ideas or events may
become involved in the battle, and may even appear important on the
surface, but the heart of the matter is always personal. Taking sides is
not the issue. Betrayal, deception, and evasion are the issues.

When Greene was having fun in the 1980s, posing as a friend of
international socialism, he was sometimes asked why he had avoided
any involvement in the Spanish Civil War. Many of the important
writers of the 1930s had spoken vigorously in favor of the Spanish
Republic and had condemned the fascist opposition of General
Franco and his allies; some writers had even risked their lives in this
cause—most notably Lt. Eric Blair of the POUM militia, who was
also known as George Orwell. But Greene carefully avoided stating a
clear position. In 1966 he explained that his Catholicism had made it
difficult for him to support the Republicans, some of whom had
killed priests and burned churches. But he said that he also disliked
Franco and claimed that the Basques were the only group who had
aroused his interest. In the late spring of 1937, he had tried to visit
Bilbao, the seat of the short-lived Basque Republic, but had given up
when he could not find a plane to take him there. As he recalled:
"There was only one place in Spain where I could go—Bilbao, the
only area that was both Republican and Catholic. I set off—but of
course I never got there. I did get as far as Toulouse, and I was going
to fly on; but the pilot—a tiny little pilot—lost his nerve or something; anyhow he wouldn't go on. Tiny little man."

Writers—such as Orwell—who were really interested in reaching
Spain found ways to get in. But the truth is that Greene saw no compelling reason to become involved. He had nothing to gain from it.

What he was planning to do if he had reached Bilbao is a mystery, but it is doubtful that he had any real sympathy for the Basque Republic, which fell to Franco's forces in June 1937. If the Basques were so important to him, he would not have gone to work for one of Franco's staunchest supporters in England, Victor Cazalet. The same month that the Basques were defeated, Greene began his job as literary editor of the weekly magazine *Night and Day,* whose chairman and principal shareholder was Cazalet. Of course, if the occasion arose he was fully prepared to turn against Cazalet. His damaging review of *Wee Willie Winkie* certainly did nothing to improve the value of Cazalet's 3,500 shares in Night and Day Magazines Limited.

When W. H. Auden and Stephen Spender helped to launch the pamphlet *Authors Take Sides on the Spanish War,* in June 1937, Greene gently mocked it in *The Spectator* by contrasting its serious intentions with the more easygoing attitudes of a nineteenth-century literary group involved in Spanish politics. In 1830 some of the Cambridge Apostles, including Alfred, Lord Tennyson, and his friend Arthur Henry Hallam, had undertaken secret missions to Spain in support of rebel activity. According to Greene, Tennyson and Hallam went primarily for the thrill of it and were incapable of putting too much faith in the political activities of funny-looking foreigners. Greene quotes, with approval, Hallam's frivolous remark on other European revolts: " 'Twas a very pretty revolution in Saxony, and a respectable one at Brunswick." This sort of thing sounded much better to Greene than the earnest tone of his own generation's cry, "I stand with the People and Government of Spain." As a literary subject or as a chance for adventure, the Spanish Civil War made sense to Greene. But he showed no sign of appreciating its importance as a struggle for freedom in a world increasingly threatened by fascist aggression.

The unspoken message of Greene's essay on Tennyson and Hallam is that a writer's first responsibility must be to literature. Politics and other matters are secondary. His work as an editor at *Night and Day* proves his point. At a time when other writers were interested in making literary periodicals more political, Greene helped to start a magazine that was devoted to good writing and entertainment. As long as he put up enough money and did not make a fuss, Victor Cazalet's politics were irrelevant. Likewise, *Night and Day* was no place for articles lamenting the fall of the Basque Republic. François Mauriac issued a pro-Basque manifesto, but Greene stayed clear of such things. *Night and Day* was a magazine for people who wanted an escape from the political unrest at home and abroad. It was intended

to be an English version of *The New Yorker,* and in that sense it
marked a brief revival of the dandyism of Greene's Oxford generation. Evelyn Waugh, Cyril Connolly, John Betjeman, and Anthony
Powell were all contributors. As the magazine's publicity material
informed potential advertisers, *Night and Day* wanted to reach the
sophisticated reader, and anyone else who aspired to that noble status: "By appealing to the ear of the born sophisticate—the man or
woman who sponsors movements, invents fashions, coins the innu-
merable catchwords of modern society . . . you arouse the acquisitive,
imitative instincts of the Ordinary Man."

Thus, one way the magazine could approach the Spanish Civil
War was to discuss its effects on the sophisticated man's supply
of sherry. A.J.A. Symons, of the Wine & Food Society, covered
the subject in his restaurants column. Whatever the topic, the idea
was to keep things light and upbeat. A perfect example was Louis
MacNeice's piece on the Kennel Club, which is distinguished by its
exquisite description of Afghan hounds as "baboons dressed up in
pyjamas." Contributors were expected to do the unexpected. Evelyn
Waugh reviewed *Men of Mathematics;* the Rochester scholar John
Hayward wrote on broadcasting; Cyril Connolly contributed diary
entries from a young middle-class woman named Felicity Arquebus.
The first motoring correspondent was someone named Super-
charger, but he was eventually replaced by Selwyn Powell, who complained to Greene that he lacked the proper qualifications for the
job. To which Greene replied, "No matter. You can drive, can't you?
And write?" Greene also commissioned articles on sports that were
not usually covered in general-interest magazines—croquet, swimming, snooker.

Night and Day began life with great fanfare. On June 30, 1937,
the magazine invited 800 guests to a launch party at the Dorchester,
and a generous portion of the shareholders' money was spent on
drinks and complimentary copies of the first issue. Greene was
allowed a respectable annual salary of 600 pounds, and he appeared
ready to spend at least a few years helping to build up the magazine's
circulation and reputation. The stellar cast of contributors and the
lively tone encouraged everyone to think that the magazine would
succeed, but its sales were modest and each issue lost money. Any
new magazine deserves a trial of a year or two before its chance of
survival can be fairly determined, and the losses at *Night and Day*
were not so bad as to make such a trial impossible. The average loss
was about 200 pounds per issue. But Victor Cazalet and the other
important backers refused to put up more cash, and the enterprise
was allowed to die after only six months.

One reason for this failure of investor confidence was Graham Greene. His editorial work was excellent, but his attack on Shirley Temple was disastrous. With the addition of a few thousand pounds, the magazine could have been kept alive for another six months, but no one knew how many more thousands would be needed to pay off the libel suit against Greene and the magazine. Moreover, Greene's review of *Wee Willie Winkie* damaged the magazine's reputation with the managers of its most important retail outlet, W. H. Smith. The chain refused to carry the issue containing the review. It was not a minor piece buried in an obscure part of the magazine. Greene and his fellow editors were well aware that it would attract attention, and they had invited trouble by advertising its publication with purple posters that carried the blunt announcement "Sex & Shirley Temple." The legal case against Greene was brought before the lord chief justice, and there was the possibility that a charge of criminal libel would be added to the civil suit. In view of these developments, Cazalet must have realized that it was best to accept his losses and get out before something worse happened. Greene's review appeared on October 28, and the last issue of *Night and Day* came out on December 23.

Because of the large financial rewards conferred on him by Hollywood and Alexander Korda, Greene was easily able to pay his share of the libel damages—500 pounds from a total penalty of 3,500 pounds. From Paramount alone he had received the equivalent of 2,500 pounds for the rights to *A Gun for Sale*. If he had been forced to live on his book royalties, the judgment against him would have been devastating. Since the great success of *Stamboul Train*, sales of his work had fallen off considerably. In Britain *It's a Battlefield* sold 7,500 copies; *England Made Me* sold 4,500; and *A Gun for Sale* sold 5,000. American sales were much lower, averaging about 2,000 copies for each title. Greene's deal with Paramount was worth almost twice as much as his combined royalties from three novels. In a way, his payment to Shirley Temple was simply a refund to Hollywood. And, best of all, the money eventually came back to Britain—the child's mother later invested the cash in British War Loan Bonds.

The actress herself was in a forgiving mood when she wrote about the incident in her memoir, *Child Star*. She noted that the original complaint accused Greene of portraying her as an actress whose services had been procured for "immoral purposes." In response, she joked that her share of the settlement—which was worth $7,000 in 1938—seemed "adequate wages for my alleged occupation." She was not even offended when someone drew her attention to an old letter in which Greene had made an ungracious remark about her. In 1938 he had written to Elizabeth Bowen that he was expected to make a formal apology to the little girl, whom he described in a phrase more appropriate to a diminutive female dog. The apology never came, but Shirley Temple Black reflected that, if he had given it, she would have been at a loss to understand what he was apologizing for.

Occasionally, one of Greene's victims had the imagination to devise a quick and efficient form of retribution. A court case was much too messy and expensive. It was better to give him a little surprise that would convey the victim's true opinion of him. In 1936 Greene attacked a film made by an aristocratic foreigner and made a special point of ridiculing the quality of the filmmaker's use of Technicolor. The browns and greens were horrible, Greene complained. Several days later he received an anonymous letter containing a single piece of notepaper. The paper was covered with the vivid browns and greens of human excrement.

During his *Night and Day* period, Greene did try to make himself a more sociable character in the London literary world. He had previously kept that world at a safe distance, making brief appearances when necessary, then disappearing for extended periods. He was on friendly terms with many of the famous writers of the day, but he developed few close ties. Throughout his long career he was careful not to give too much of himself away to his fellow writers. Once, when he was asked about his relations with other literary people, he replied: "They are not one's material. A few of them are very dear friends of mine, but for a writer to spend much of his time in the company of authors is, you know, a form of masturbation."

Perhaps the ideal literary relationship was the one that he enjoyed with R. K. Narayan. In 1935 Greene helped to launch the Indian novelist's career, "discovering" Narayan's first novel when a manuscript copy was shown to him by an Indian student in Oxford. He found a good publisher for the novel and was a strong supporter of the author's work for many years. They established a warm correspondence, and Greene made many helpful comments on Narayan's work. But perhaps the key to this pleasant relationship is that it was confined almost entirely to the safe realm of a long-distance correspondence. Twenty-one years passed before they met, and subsequent meetings were rare and brief.

Greene's work at *Night and Day* gave him reasons to get together with writers more often, and he began giving small parties at home. In 1935 he and Vivienne moved from Oxford to London, and their new address was a fashionable one. The large house is now occupied by five families living in separate flats, but in Greene's time it was still a single-family home. They lived at Number 14 North Side, facing

Clapham Common. A tall, spacious house of red brick, it was built in 1720. Zachary Macaulay, the historian's father, once lived there, and the interior was not much changed from Macaulay's day. There was ample room for entertaining, and Greene made a real effort to play the gracious host. Anthony Powell and Herbert Read were among the select group of authors invited to dine at Number 14.

The best accounts of Greene at this stage in his life come from two minor writers. One is the critic Walter Allen, who met Greene at the offices of *Night and Day*. He had recently read *Journey Without Maps* and could not believe that the literary editor of the magazine was the same man who had walked across Liberia. In Allen's description, Greene is the picture of a soul in torment: "He was very tall and thin; one felt a gust of wind would blow him over. His face was lined, as though he were under strain or perhaps in some pain, and his smile seemed somehow reluctant. . . . His voice, which was lightish tenor, was not so much high-pitched as curiously strangled." Greene reinforced this grim picture by making an unsolicited confession. After taking Allen to lunch at an expensive restaurant, Greene showed disdain for his life of ease in London, declaring that his real ambition was to escape to some South American country "where everyone took bribes and frequented brothels."

A good glimpse of life in Greene's comfortable home can be found in Julian Maclaren-Ross's memoir "Excursions in Greeneland." Eager to create a radio play of *A Gun for Sale,* Maclaren-Ross wrote to Greene about the idea and was asked to discuss it over lunch at Number 14. As a struggling, poorly paid writer, he was impressed by the elegance of the place but was surprised to find that his appearance was not quite good enough to allow an immediate entrance to the heart of Greeneland. An elderly housekeeper inspected him at the door and concluded that he was a common salesman. "We don't want anything today, thank you," he was told. After persuading the woman that he was a legitimate guest, he was told that Greene was "out" and was asked to await the master's return in a well-furnished drawing room at the top of the stairs. He entertained himself by studying the novels of Henry James and Joseph Conrad, which occupied one bookcase. Then suddenly he spotted Greene watching him silently from the doorway. He recalled, "I was startled because not even a creak on the stairs had announced his approach."

Greene quickly put on a smile and tried to appear relaxed, but he was obviously self-conscious and wary. He was careful to reveal that the elegance of the house had not corrupted his soul. Before lunch he took his guest to the local pub, where they bought a jug of beer for their meal, and a little while later Greene made a point of saying "fuck." Maclaren-Ross thought that his host was simply trying to test his reaction to the word, so he quickly replied with a "fuck" of his own, and that was the end of that. As Greene was preparing to shift the conversation to condoms, Vivienne walked into the room, and he fell silent instantly.

He had been trying hard to appear a man's man, but his genteel surroundings did not do justice to the act. In Vivienne's presence there was no funny business. To Maclaren-Ross, she seemed exceedingly modest and proper. She rarely spoke, and after lunch she "busied herself with head bent over some piece of needlework." As soon as she was out of earshot, Greene would turn the conversation back to something more exciting. He recalled a favorite scene from Edgar Wallace's thriller *The Four Just Men*: "D'you remember what they did to the Spanish priest who'd been guilty of Rape? When they condemned him to death he begged them to let him see a priest before the execution, and they showed him—a mirror!" Relishing the wickedness of the scene, Greene gave "full value to the capital *R* in *Rape,* and his eyes swivelled, glinting." Maclaren-Ross was not an easy man to shock, but Greene was almost desperate for someone to whom he could address naughty remarks, as though they had been building up in his mind for days. It was clear that he needed some relief from the respectable domestic life of Number 14 North Side.

Greene's domestic burdens were growing, as Maclaren-Ross discovered when he was shown the nursery on the top floor. Four-year-old Lucy Caroline was there, and so was the newest addition to the family—a son whom Greene had named Francis. The boy had been born in September 1936. He would be the couple's last child, and Greene's relations with his son would often be strained. He rarely made any mention of him in public. As an adult the son has kept out of the spotlight, scrupulously refusing to discuss his father in public. Greene admitted in an interview given late in life that he had not been a good father to his son. Having mentioned Hugh Greene's problems as a parent, Greene told the interviewer, "I'm probably just as bad. . . . With Francis, I don't see very much of him." In Greene's diaries of 1938–39 there is an occasional mention of his children, but he is not much concerned with the joy of parenthood. What distresses him are the inevitable childhood illnesses and accidents. He found it extremely difficult to face such things and was glad to let Vivienne deal with them. But in turning away from pain—the pain of immediate problems as well the pain of his own childhood memories—he found it convenient to retreat from all the responsibilities of fatherhood.

In her old age Vivienne reflected that Greene had never shown much interest in his children until Lucy Caroline became a young woman: "He didn't take any notice until she was about nineteen. [He] gave her a twenty-first birthday party in Albany. But he didn't take any notice when they had measles and mumps and all that sort of thing. It was only when they came to seem interesting. A lot of men are like that. They don't take any interest in small children. But she was very pretty." In his old age Greene had a more convoluted explanation of his shortcomings as a father, placing the blame primarily on external events:

Well, of course at a rather crucial stage, the war came, because when the war came, one of them was three years old and one of them was five years old, and first of all, there was the blitz, and then at the end of 1941, I went off to Sierra Leone, and then I came back in early 1943. In the period before that they had been evacuated, and I was occupied with the blitz. So I didn't see them except for an occasional weekend. But I didn't have any continuity. By the time the war was over, their childhood was really over.

To Maclaren-Ross, Greene was a bit more direct in summing up his attitude toward the little ones in the nursery. When he was safely back in the drawing room, Greene poured his guest a large brandy and asked, "Who was it complained that not enough children get murdered in detective stories?"

II

A simple way to lose the wife and kids for a few days was to travel down to Brighton for a little work and a little pleasure. Greene would take a hotel room with a view of the sea and spend his mornings writing. It was always a good place for curing his periodic attacks of writer's block. Even as late as the 1950s he was making regular retreats to the town, searching for inspiration and amusement. As soon as his morning labors were finished, he would stroll through the streets, observing the crowds and investigating the seamier aspects of life. He liked being in a place where much of the population was transient. It was a pleasure to be surrounded by people who were also escaping the burdens of ordinary home life and regular jobs.

After finishing *A Gun for Sale,* he decided that a similar thriller would work well with Brighton as its setting. The town's criminal element had recently been featured in news headlines. In 1936 one of

Brighton's racecourse gangs staged a bloody attack on a couple of bookmakers, and sixteen men were later implicated in the assault. The gangsters were tried and sentenced to long prison terms. But Greene had taken an interest in this kind of thuggery before the case attracted public attention. *A Gun for Sale* reveals that Raven once belonged to a racecourse gang and was the leader of a mass attack on a rival gangster named Battling Kite. Raven tells Anne Crowder that his boss's life had been threatened by Kite, and that the gang had retaliated by killing the man. They grabbed Kite on a railway platform, and Raven cut his throat with a razor while the rest of the gang blocked the scene from public view.

Although there is nothing in *A Gun for Sale* to indicate that this feud originated in Brighton, Greene brings the story of Kite's murder into *Brighton Rock* and makes it the original cause of all the action. Pinkie Brown is devoted to Kite's memory. He makes a point of continuing to behave in ways that Kite taught him, even to the point of biting his nails in the same manner as his hero. Kite was the only person who had ever given him any attention. He was homeless and ill when the older man found him one night on the Palace Pier. It was cold, and Kite invited the Boy, as Pinkie is often called, to live with him. He became a part of Kite's mediocre little gang and served his leader faithfully. And then Colleoni's gang attacked Kite with razors at St. Pancras Station and killed him. The motive for the attack is obscure, and nothing is said in the novel about Raven. Greene conveniently dropped the character in order to make Colleoni and company an all-Jewish gang. The Jews have not only taken over Brighton but also murdered Pinkie's friend.

The loss is more than Pinkie can stand. Life has taken too much from him, and Kite was the last person who meant anything to him. His bitterness builds through the book, but he can do nothing to strike back at Colleoni, who is protected by great wealth and power. So he turns his anger against vulnerable characters and makes them suffer for his troubles. Even trivial encounters give him the chance to inflict pain. Seeing a crippled child headed toward him, he pushes him away. When he comes across a blind man, he shoves him into the road. But the only person who is made to pay for Kite's murder is Hale, a minor newspaperman. Weak and terrified, Hale is easy to kill. Having provided Colleoni with some incriminating information about Kite, he is the one person outside the gang who can be targeted for revenge. Pinkie takes great pleasure from stalking the helpless man, prolonging the terror by letting his victim make a few desperate efforts to escape. In the end Pinkie and his gang have no difficulty trapping Hale and taking his life with the perfect weapon. By shoving a long stick of "Brighton Rock" down his throat, they are able to kill him and dispose of the weapon at the same time. The hard stick of sugar slowly dissolves in the body, and after the police find Hale, they assume that he died a natural death.

The weapon is also a perfect choice for the seventeen-year-old Boy. All his grievances are those of an abandoned child. Forced to grow up too soon, and denied all the normal satisfactions of childhood, he takes his revenge against innocence by turning a child's sweet into a murder weapon. The sugar becomes a kind of undetectable poison. This seemingly harmless object is far removed from the razor that killed Kite, an item associated entirely with the adult world. Pinkie likes to carry a razor, but he is too inexperienced to use it effectively in a real fight. Although the details of his attack on Hale have to be inferred from a few hints in the text, it seems clear that he chose his weapon carefully, to please his own perverse sense of justice as well as to escape detection. It is the work of a young devil. If ten-year-olds were in the habit of killing each other, no doubt the worst among them would eventually think of pushing something like Brighton Rock down another child's throat.

Hale's death is such a perfect crime that the police close the case after a short investigation. There is no reason for Pinkie to worry that he will be caught, but he takes the precaution of keeping an eye on a potential witness—Rose, a young waitress at a Brighton restaurant. By itself, her evidence is not conclusive. If he had stayed away from her after the murder, it is unlikely that anyone could have proven that he was involved in the crime. Against all reason, he is drawn to her, and what attracts him is her potential as a victim. She seems so young and vulnerable that he cannot pass up the opportunity to hurt her. Rose is almost as poor and ignorant as he was when Kite picked him up. He tells the rest of his gang that she must be silenced to keep the murder a secret, but this reason is only his excuse for engaging in a long process of subtle torture. What he wants to do is make her suffer as he suffered. By seducing her into becoming devoted to him, he will be able to betray that devotion and will thus inflict on her the same kind of pain that he felt when Colleoni robbed him of Kite's companionship.

Despite his young age, Pinkie is masterly at finding ways to enhance his sadistic pleasure. He teases Rose with the idea that he might burn her with a splash from his bottle of vitriol; he pinches her flesh so hard that his fingernails almost meet; he enjoys frightening her with talk about the flames of hell, hoping that his words will increase the torment as he relentlessly tempts her to violate her Catholic faith. His own Catholic background becomes a useful way of establishing a quick bond between them, and it is satisfying to him that they will be damned together. Every step of her seduction is a moment for him to savor. The more she wants him, the more he will enjoy destroying her. Even a simple thing such as treating her to a night at the cinema is a great thrill for him, because it brings him one step closer to breaking her heart. He can inject a sinister air into the most innocent remark. When he talks Rose into marrying him, he sees it as the high point in his life of crime. Having her so completely in his power satisfies his lust for revenge in a way that even the murder of Hale could not match.

But something is not quite right with his plan. Rose likes him too much, and, what is more, she likes receiving pain almost as much as he likes giving it. When he pinches her as hard as he can, tears of pain and pleasure fill her eyes, and she tells him to continue pinching her if he enjoys it. She knows that he is a murderer, yet she wants to be near him, and she is clearly excited by the thought that her dangerous relationship has put her religious faith and her life at risk. After enduring a dreary life of poverty with parents who are quite willing to sell her to Pinkie for a few pounds, she is ready to see his violence and evil as attractive qualities. He is more intense, more daring than anyone she has known, and the risks of loving him make her feel alive for the first time. Pinkie is somewhat disappointed that she likes being hurt. He would feel much better if she occasionally let out a good scream of pain. But there is the satisfaction of knowing that they make such a natural pair. Ruining her life is like ruining his own.

It is also important to Pinkie that his best victim is a woman. He hates women as much as Minty does in *England Made Me,* and he loathes the idea of physical contact with them—unless it involves hurting them. He contrasts his hatred of Rose with his fondness for Kite and recalls how much better his life was when Kite's strength protected him. Although he would never admit it, the Boy's feelings for his mentor indicate a homosexual attachment. Colleoni is the villain who robbed him of his man, but he finds it more appealing to shift the blame to Rose in particular, and women in general. As he sees it, they trap a man and keep him from having what he really wants in life. He also hates the idea that having sex with a woman is a way of proving his manhood. Being Kite's Boy was good enough for him.

Everything in his world seems to reinforce the message that women somehow deserve to be punished. There are many references to inci-

dents in which women have suffered terrible harm. At the door of
Rose's house, there is an old newspaper with a headline about a child
in Brighton who was raped and buried on the beach. Another newspaper headline about a drowned woman is seen in a shop window
crammed with cheap books about sex and sexy film stars. Pinkie
regards the display with disgust, but it brings to mind some other
books that he has seen behind the counter—stories about women
being whipped. Another headline in Pinkie's copy of *News of the
World* describes an attack on a schoolgirl in Epping Forest. Such stories remind Pinkie of a fifteen-year-old girl from his school days who
killed herself because she was pregnant. He gives a vivid description
of the moment she put her head on a railway line. When Pinkie tries
to frighten Rose with his bottle of vitriol, he reminds her of a newspaper story about a girl named Peggy Baron whose face was disfig-
ured by a splash of the substance.

All this violence against women prefigures Pinkie's scheme to kill
Rose by tricking her into joining him in a suicide pact, an idea he
claims to have come across in a newspaper. Of course, he intends to
give her the honor of being the first to shoot herself in the head, leaving him free to go on living. As a cruel joke, it is almost as good as
murdering Hale with a piece of Brighton Rock. And Pinkie sees it as
a chance to pull off another perfect crime. He even arranges for Rose
to leave behind a convincing suicide note. The ghost of Kite appears
to be driving him toward this awful deed. Kite comes to him in a
dream with his mouth bleeding. Handing Pinkie a razor, he says only
two words: "Such tits." The combination of the razor and this general reference to the dreaded sexuality of women creates the most
horrific image in the novel. For Kite's sake, Pinkie is willing to sacrifice a woman's life. He is too cowardly to do it with a razor. He will
not be responsible for the headline "Girl's Mutilated Body Found,"
but in his mind he is no different from the savage murderers whose
crimes are described in the headlines littering the novel.

One particular pair of breasts comes under heavy verbal attack in
the novel, but not from Pinkie. Repeatedly, Greene's narrative makes
scornful comments about the large breasts of Pinkie's nemesis Ida
Arnold. Without Ida's interference, the Boy's plan to kill Rose would
have definitely succeeded. In most novels a woman such as Ida would
be the heroine, but here she is seen as an overbearing busybody
whose views on sex are annoyingly reasonable. She believes in having
a good time, and she loves the warmth and excitement of an old-
fashioned romp in bed. The sadomasochistic games of Pinkie and
Rose go beyond anything she can understand, and she tries vainly to

keep the young woman from playing with fire. She argues in favor of common decency and fair play. Her way is right, and Pinkie's is wrong, and there is no middle ground. But her efforts to assert moral authority are consistently undermined by Greene's efforts to ridicule her simplistic thinking and her vulgar manners. And nothing is more vulgar than her large bosom, which always seems on the verge of exploding. She is portrayed as a gross, cowlike figure who eats and drinks too much, and who pushes herself into places where she does not belong. Her big breasts make her look both intimidating and absurd. Greene stresses her sexual crudity when he describes her taking a bite from an éclair. The cream spurts into her mouth in a way that suggests the climax of fellatio. Naturally, Pinkie detests her at first sight.

Greene takes great pains to suggest that she has strayed into his novel from the pub scene in *The Waste Land*. Like one of the crude figures in that scene, she goes by the name of Lil. When she is not playing amateur detective in Brighton, she works at a pub in the Strand, and near the end of the novel she repeats the phrase "good night" in a way that echoes the final lines of Eliot's scene ("Ta ta. Goonight. Goonight"). She then goes straight to her flat behind Russell Square, where a single letter from her old flame Tom awaits her. It was a good joke, but not many people reading the novel in the 1930s would have understood that Tom Eliot's office at Faber & Faber was in Russell Square. (In some literary circles, Eliot was known as "the Pope of Russell Square.") Perhaps Greene was hoping only to amuse Eliot himself, whose love for detective novels would have made him a likely reader of *Brighton Rock*.

Among contemporary readers only Eliot could have been expected to catch the novel's subtle reference to one of his more obscure poems. As Colleoni walks past Ida in the Cosmopolitan hotel, she overhears him giving an order to his secretary for bananas, oranges, and grapes. He adds that he wants the hothouse variety. "Who's that?" Ida wonders. Besides Greene's Jewish gangster, it is Eliot's "Sweeney Among the Nightingales": "The waiter brings in oranges / Bananas figs and hothouse grapes." The allusion is another way of connecting Ida to the lower-class characters in Eliot's early poetry, but it is also a way of reinforcing the anti-Semitic aspect of the novel. In Eliot's poem the grapes are torn to pieces by an unpleasant Jewish woman named Rabinovitch.

By making Ida look vulgar and insensitive, Greene attempts to shift the reader's sympathy in a direction where most readers would not willingly go—that is, to Pinkie. There are moments in the novel when even the most upright reader may find himself drifting toward Pinkie's side, feeling more sympathy for him than for the colorless Rose or the flamboyant Ida. It is Greene's pleasure to practice the same crafty seduction on the reader that Pinkie practices on Rose. Before we know it we are tempted to sympathize with Pinkie's hatred of Ida and Rose, and to accept his irrational view of the world. This may help to explain why Greene once said that he was Pinkie's "accomplice." The novel encourages us to accept the character's overwhelming appetite for revenge and draws us into following Pinkie's devilish twists of thought until we are in danger of being ensnared by them. In other words, the ultimate aim is to make us accomplices, too, right up to the moment when Pinkie carefully instructs Rose on the best way to position the gun barrel in her ear.

III

Fortunately, Pinkie's plan fails, and it is he who is hounded to death. But this is not portrayed as a triumph of good over evil. Pinkie still emerges as a winner of sorts, for he has the satisfaction of knowing that he has willed his own destruction and damnation. He leaps from a cliff rather than surrender to his pursuers from the ordinary world— the police and big-breasted Ida. That leap into the abyss is also his final flight from God. Earlier in the novel he speculates that even the worst life of crime might be redeemed by a last-minute plea for mercy, but he is too proud and too bitter to seek repentance between "the stirrup and the ground." He goes over the edge with the flames of hell already rising to greet him. His face is literally steaming, the result of an accidental splash from his bottle of vitriol. It is a bold act of defiance and can be seen as a glorious moment if the reader shares Greene's admiration for T. S. Eliot's idea that "damnation itself is an immediate form of salvation—of salvation from the ennui of modern life, because it at last gives some significance to living."

Some critics argue that Pinkie's pursuer—Ida—is likable in spite of Greene's criticism of her, but what they really mean is that they *want* to like her and will not let the evidence of the novel stand in their way. They might point out that there is at least one major piece of evidence in her favor—she helps to save Rose's life. But Greene does not allow her that credit. Near the end of the novel, Ida boasts that not only has she rescued Rose from certain death but she has also returned the girl to the place where all good girls belong—home. Unlike simplistic Ida, the reader should recognize that sending Rose back to her ignorant, avaricious parents is sealing a fate almost as bad as death. Rose certainly recognizes it. After Pinkie's death she confesses to a priest that she regrets not killing herself. She still wants to be with her Boy, among the damned, and therefore refuses absolution and condemns Ida's intervention.

Greene knew how to lay the right traps, and the best one of all was the one he set for the earnest reader who expects every author to articulate some uplifting moral vision. There is nothing uplifting about Pinkie. If he had a bit more courage, he would slash Rose's body to pieces and begin looking for another victim. He never shows remorse, never feels pity for anyone but himself. But give him a few religious phrases to mouth, and place a few religious symbols near him, and certain readers will leap on these things as evidence that Pinkie really wanted to be a good boy all along, and that his story is a Christian tale about God's infinite mercy. One critic says that the Boy "is presented as salvageable human material in his awkward and diffident approach to love." Another claims that Pinkie's "malevolence discloses, in a paradoxical way, the grace for which he hungers." A third discovers a "suggestion that Pinkie could find redemption through human love." But Pinkie is not "diffident," has no desire to "love" Rose, does not "hunger" for "grace," and has no interest in "redemption through human love." His thoughts are firmly concentrated on leading Rose to her death, and he relishes the evil of the plan from start to finish. The only spirit he attends to is the ghost of Kite handing him a razor and saying, "Such tits." The only sign of human feeling in him is his loyalty to Kite's memory, but this is negated by his notion that hurting people is a good way to express that loyalty.

A priest's comment at the end of the novel has given rise to much of the misunderstanding about the "religious dimension" of Pinkie's evil. The priest tells Rose that no one can understand God's mercy, that Pinkie's soul may be saved after all. There is little point in arguing with this notion. Priests say such things, and they may be right. But the novel gives the concept absolutely no support. First of all, the priest's wisdom is called into question when he tells Rose that because Pinkie loved her there must have been some good in the Boy. The priest knows only what Rose has told him about Pinkie and understands their relationship no better than Ida does. More important, there is no indication in the novel that God is, in fact, merciful, or that Pinkie has any intention of seeking his mercy. Passing near an alley one day, Pinkie sees an old woman sitting on the ground absorbed in prayer. He is appalled by her ugliness, but what bothers him even more is the thought that the souls of such people might be saved by their prayers. If the old woman is one of the saved, he prefers to be among the damned. Religion is useful only as a way of making him feel more wicked. When he wins a doll at a shooting booth, he thinks that it resembles the Virgin Mary, so he has a great time dragging the Mother of God along by the hair, then pulling the strands out, one by one.

Hell is at the center of Pinkie's thoughts, and evil dominates his world. It is a world of razors, bullies, poverty, false sentiments, torture, and death. Although Pinkie is not as forceful as Raven—he is, after all, still a boy—his sense of evil is untainted by compassion; there is no danger that he will go "soft on a skirt." In his twisted heart, evil has achieved a kind of sacred purity, making him an excellent illustration of Greene's argument in the review of Eliot's *After Strange Gods*. In that review, the reader will recall, Greene said, "To be a Catholic . . . is to believe in the Devil," and noted with approval Eliot's idea that only the spiritually "awakened" person is capable of real evil.

The "Catholic" Pinkie is certainly attached to Satan's camp. When asked by a fellow gang member if he believes in the Catholic religion, Pinkie replies with a bit of Latin that he knows the man will not understand: *Credo in unum Satanum*. To the ignorant man's ears, Pinkie's creed sounds like something a priest might say. When he was much younger, Pinkie fantasized about becoming a priest—he liked the idea of being forced into celibacy. In a way his fantasy has come true. He serves evil with the enthusiasm of a true believer. Far from objecting to this fate, Greene cannot resist the temptation to make a devilishly bad joke about it. Pinkie's telephone number is the figure traditionally associated with Satan—666.

Brighton Rock is an audacious book. In trying to turn a devil into a heroic spiritual character, it makes a powerful assault on our basic assumptions about art and morality. Like Ida, we want the world to make sense, and we will go to great lengths to create reasonable explanations for things that defy conventional reasoning. As readers we like to think that the author is our friend, and that reading improves the mind by filling it with wise thoughts about the human condition. Most of us do not mind dark portraits of humanity, because we can see them as cautionary tales. Everything can be turned into a reassuring slogan. Even nihilism is fine. We can give it a name and agree with the author that life sometimes looks overwhelmingly bleak. But *Brighton Rock* goes beyond all these acceptable notions. It does not simply tell us that the world is evil. It rubs our noses in the evil and makes fun of us for trying to understand it.

And Greene does all this with such brilliance that we cannot help being amazed. Rarely has sheer nastiness been served so well.

The unpleasant truth is that the author regards us as easy victims. We are the people who sit in restaurants and pick our noses or eat too much or shout in loud voices "Goonight. Goonight" as we get up to leave. Yet we want to be liked, and we want to like others. We want to trust Greene, we want to feel sorry for Pinkie, we want to think the world is not such a bad place after all. And while our smiling faces are busy looking for goodness and wisdom and purpose, Pinkie and Greene are cursing us for being Jews or Catholics, for being fat or crippled, for being old or female.

An excellent example of this situation can be found in the scene that describes Pinkie's visit to a small recording booth. Rose loves him so much that she asks him to make a record of his voice. As she stands outside watching him with admiration, he quietly addresses a message of hate to the microphone, telling the "bitch" how much he despises her. The record is put away, and Rose never has a chance to play it until after Pinkie is dead. When the novel closes, she is preparing to listen to it for the first time, expecting that it will be an eternal reminder of his love for her. We are left to imagine how deeply the truth will hurt her. But we do not need to exercise our imaginations too much. Greene does the same thing to us. Only after a careful reading of his novel can we begin to see how much he has taunted us with words of hate and visions of monstrous cruelty.

IV

There is a real criminal mystery that may have been in Greene's mind when he chose to set Pinkie's story in Brighton. Contrary to the image created by all the gruesome headlines quoted in the novel, Brighton was a relatively peaceful place in the 1930s. The racecourse gangs were tough, but murder was rarely part of their game. They were much more likely to use their razors merely to frighten their rivals. There were, in fact, only two famous murders in Brighton during the 1930s, and both occurred in the spring of 1934—four years before the publication of *Brighton Rock*. A petty thief named Tony Mancini was arrested for killing his girlfriend, whose body was found in a trunk at his flat. Her head was badly bruised, and the authorities felt certain that Mancini would be convicted of murder. To everyone's amazement, he was acquitted in a widely publicized trial, although he admitted his guilt many years later, saying that he had killed her unintentionally during a violent quarrel.

By coincidence, the other murder also involved a trunk, but this crime was a much more grisly affair. On June 17, 1934, the torso of a woman was discovered in a trunk at the left-luggage office of the Brighton railway station. The trunk had been deposited there on June 6—Derby Day—and the stench of the decaying body had finally attracted attention. The torso was wrapped in brown paper and tied with venetian-blind cord. A short time after this discovery, the woman's legs were found in a suitcase at London's King's Cross station. They were wrapped not only in brown paper but also in copies of newspapers dated May 31 and June 2. The head and arms were never recovered, although the police had a reliable report that the head had been spotted along the shore a few miles east of Brighton. The autopsy, which was conducted by the Home Office pathologist Sir Bernard Spilsbury, revealed only that the woman was in her early twenties, was five months pregnant, and had probably died in late May, not long after the Bank Holiday on Whitmonday. It was Spilsbury who confirmed that the legs at King's Cross belonged to the torso.

The murder led to a massive investigation by Scotland Yard, but the biggest obstacle was that no one could identify the body. It could not be linked to a national list of missing person reports, although the police studied cases involving 732 missing women. They were fairly certain that the victim was not from the Brighton area, and there was no evidence of a connection to the Tony Mancini case. A logical theory is that the woman was either a London prostitute whose disappearance would easily have escaped notice or a foreign visitor. Someone could have brought her from London to Brighton, murdered her, then returned with the suitcase to King's Cross. After several months of intensive work, the Scotland Yard detectives were forced to admit defeat. They could not crack the case. The newspapers followed the story avidly, and, when journalists realized that the killer would not be found, they began calling the crime a perfect murder.

The idea of cutting up a body and leaving it in a railway station was a novelty in those days. There was one similar case in London during the 1920s. Police found a murder victim in a trunk at Charing Cross station, and the culprit was quickly tried and executed. There was also a graphic description of such a crime in a book published only three months before the torso was discovered in Brighton. That was Graham Greene's *It's a Battlefield,* with its imaginary account of a Paddington trunk murder. As an earlier chapter explained, the case is linked in the novel with the Streatham Common murder of a prostitute. Details of these fictional crimes were drawn from entries Greene made in his diary in 1932–33. One recalled a dream in which Greene feared that the police would arrest him for murdering someone and leaving the body in a suitcase at the cloakroom of a railway station. The other was a poem about the police searching for clues after a young woman's rape and murder. It is curious, to say the least, that Greene was so preoccupied with these imaginary murders in the year before a young woman's dismembered body was found in the railway station of his favorite resort town.

Even more curious are the connections between Pinkie's story and the torso murder in Brighton. The story begins at the same time of the year the young woman was murdered. The second sentence of the book refers to the Whitsun holiday crowds in Brighton. The awful references to a razor and "Such tits" are made by the ghost of a man who is killed at St. Pancras Station, next door to the station where the severed legs of the Brighton corpse were found. At the time Pinkie tries to cause Rose's death, the two are standing at a cliff a few miles east of Brighton. The suggestion is later made that Rose could be pregnant with Pinkie's child. If Pinkie had succeeded in killing her, his crime would have been as "perfect" as the murder, or as "perfect" as his earlier killing of Hale. And the possibility of escaping detection is raised in the novel's epigraph: "This were a fine reign: / To do ill and not hear of it again" *(The Witch of Edmonton)*.

It is interesting that there is even a connection between the amateur detective who ruins Pinkie's chance for criminal success and one of the policemen involved in the Brighton investigation. When superstitious Ida decides to use her Ouija board in the search for clues to Hale's murder, she pulls the board from a cupboard containing all her prized possessions. There are some pieces of china, a photograph of her mother, a few wooden toys, a picture of good old Tom, and a couple of popular novels, which testify to Ida's bad taste. One is *The Good Companions,* the highly successful novel by J. B. Priestley, which helped to inspire Greene's libelous attack in *Stamboul Train*. The other is Warwick Deeping's *Sorrell and Son*. Greene was not in the habit of throwing in such details at random. The name of the father and son is not a common one, so it may be significant that it is shared by Detective-Sergeant Edward Sorrell, one of two Scotland Yard men whom the newspapers repeatedly identified as the principal investigators in the Brighton case.

When Ida seeks answers from her Ouija board, three strange clues are spelled out—"SUKILL," "FRESUICILLEYE," and "PHIL." In the pink glow of the light she has set up for atmosphere, Ida does her best to decipher these messages from the spirit world. The narrative, however, seems to imply that the really important clue is connected with *Sorrell and Son*. At the end of the scene, Ida is trying to convince herself that she has successfully interpreted the messages, but in the background the "pink light wavered on the Warwick Deeping." It is also worth noting that, at the end of *Brighton Rock*, Greene makes a point of mentioning *Sorrell and Son* again. Having "solved" Pinkie's case, Ida returns to her flat and finds that, in addition to a letter from Tom, there is another surprise. Her copy of *Sorrell and Son* is missing. Priestley's *The Good Companions* is still in the cupboard, but someone has disturbed the novel, and it is lying on its side. In his diary of 1933 Greene connected the dream about leaving a body in a railway station with a previous dream about murdering a real person—J. B. Priestley. Perhaps Ida's charwoman borrowed *Sorrell and Son*, or perhaps her creator simply took it back now that the case was closed. With the excitement of Brighton behind her, Ida is free to go back to her old flame Tom. The last we see of her, she is preparing to ask the Ouija board whether she and Tom should get together again.

If hell is visible anywhere in *Brighton Rock*, it is in the neighborhood of the railway station. Pinkie's lawyer lives on a street parallel to the tracks, and his house seems constantly under assault from the smoke and noise of the trains. Everything in the house vibrates when an engine passes, and the lawyer confides to Pinkie that he feels as though he inhabits a private hell. Like Pinkie's, his hell is full of sexual torment. He stands at his window and watches young typists come and go to their jobs, and he has desires to do something shocking to them. As he tells Pinkie, he wants desperately to expose himself to a woman.

The novelist seems to have taken the Brighton case a little too much to heart. After he finished *Brighton Rock*, he was still haunted by fears that someone would suspect him of committing a murder. In his travel book *The Lawless Roads*, the next book after *Brighton Rock*, he describes a long night in the company of some loose women at a Mexico City nightclub. On his way home at four in the morning, he watches a man walk away to a hotel with one of the women, and he carefully notes her appearance as she lazily moves down the street with her long evening dress dragging behind her. Then, abruptly, he describes a dream in which he and a woman kill someone. They bury the body, but the smell keeps escaping from the ground, and soon the whole world can detect the stench. A similar "dream" is described in the "dream diary" that Greene kept between 1965 and 1989, but in this later version he and the woman have left their murder victim in a railway station and are trying to make their escape before a guard finds the corpse.

In the 1980s Greene authorized a small private printing of his poem on the murdered prostitute whose body is examined by the police. He called it "In the Park." It appears in a book that includes a number of other poems from various periods in his career. On the page facing "In the Park," he placed another poem about a dead body. Called "Finito," the poem describes the speaker's effort to close the eyes and fold the hands of a rigid corpse. Perhaps what is most interesting about this little collection of poetry is its title, which suggests that all the poems have some connection to the author's life. The name of the book is *A Quick Look Behind: Footnotes to an Autobiography.*

In 1965 Greene published a bizarre little story about a man who travels from France to London with a baby's corpse in a large overnight bag. The story is supposed to be funny, and the point of the humor is that no one is willing to believe the killer when he brazenly confides that he is carrying a dead baby with him. He has a long conversation about the corpse with his taxi driver in London, who is delighted to play along with what would seem an obvious joke. When the driver asks how the little creature died, the killer calmly responds, "They die so easily." An occasional reader of true-crime stories, the driver then tries to recall some detail about corpses from his reading of *The Cases of Sir Bernard Spilsbury.* Of course, in one case that completely defeated Dr. Spilsbury and Scotland Yard, a man who murdered a woman and her unborn baby arrived in London with a pair of legs in a suitcase. And probably he took a taxi to King's Cross. If he had been bold enough to joke about having a pair of legs in his suitcase, no one would have believed him either.

Additional references to the murder will be considered in a later chapter. We may never know why Greene's imagination was drawn to the Brighton case; all that matters now is the way his fantasies of violence against women affect his art. The literary versions of his hating game force us to confront a tainted imagination that assaults our deepest values, encouraging us to laugh at snooty Jewish "bitches" and to scorn the good intentions and generous actions of big-breasted Ida. We can resist the evil and see what we want to see in the novel, imagining that Pinkie's death is a sign of divine retribution, or that Greene and God can work in mysterious ways to reveal the healing power of love and mercy in a world torn by hate. But the text will not support such interpretations.

Beginning with *A Gun for Sale,* Greene wrote five consecutive novels in which a female is murdered or barely escapes being murdered. Greene seems to have been playing some sort of game with the last names of a few of the women—Elsie Crole, Violet Crow, Janet Crowle, Anne Crowder. In the last novel of the sequence—*The Ministry of Fear*—the protagonist is guilty of only one crime. Arthur Rowe, a journalist, has poisoned his wife, but he is not sure whether he is guilty of a mercy killing or plain murder. He confides to a private detective that he feels like a "professional" killer because he spent the two years before the killing "dreaming about it nearly every night." Thinking about it was as bad as doing it. Greene is keenly aware of how corrosive such thoughts can be. They create an unreal atmosphere in which the line between fantasizing about violence and committing it becomes blurred. And it is almost impossible for outsiders to understand the mental terror afflicting a "respectable" man who feels that he has crossed the line.

In a dream Rowe tries desperately to make his complacent mother recognize that he is a murderer, but she repeatedly refuses to accept that any child of hers could be capable of such a thing. She grandly dismisses the whole idea with the comment that it is only a "nasty dream." The incident calls to mind an odd comment Greene later made about his own mother. In his autobiography he says that his mother would believe nothing bad about her children. If any of them "had committed murder, she would, I am sure, have blamed the victim."

Some readers seem to share the excessively sympathetic attitude of Greene's mother. They cherish the author's works as noble political and religious statements; they recommend him for Catholic literary awards, the Jerusalem Prize, the Nobel Prize; they eagerly accept his stories of playing Russian roulette or his claim that a long-forgotten novel had suddenly turned up. And all the time they refuse to listen to the record. They do not hear—or do not want to hear—the anti-Semitism, the anti-Catholicism, the misogyny, or the many jokes made at their expense. Perhaps they dismiss some of these things as only fictions—attitudes that apply to characters in the novels but not to their creator. The appearance of these attitudes in novel after novel—and in various nonfiction documents—suggests, however, that they are not merely the vices of certain characters. As the literary record proves, they also reflect something of Greene's thinking. And the record is always there, waiting to be heard, waiting to destroy the fond attachment of Greene's most ardent admirers—just as Pinkie's record waits for Rose.

What will Rose do when she hears the truth? Smash the record? She will have a hard time if she tries. As Greene points out, Pinkie's record is made of hard vulcanized rubber. It may last a long time.

And so may Greene. He had the genius to embed his hate within novels that demand to be read and will go on being read no matter what is said about him in any biography or work of criticism. Some people will always be able to play the record and hear their own song. But even for those who hear the harsh sound of hate loud and clear, the record is worth keeping, and even worth admiring for its art. It makes a remarkable sound. The band plays fast and furiously, and the musical structure is wonderfully complex. The only trouble is that all those high-pitched notes keep bursting through the melody, like something in a very bad dream.

CHAPTER THIRTEEN

ACROSS THE BORDER:
THE POWER AND
THE GLORY

O ne week after the lord chief justice heard the suit of "Temple and Others v. Night and Day Magazines, Limited, and Others," a new case of moral outrage appeared on the literary scene. Under the headline "A Disgraceful Book—It Must Be Stopped," the editor of the *Daily Mail* demanded that the publishing firm of Routledge & Sons withdraw a new book called *To Beg I Am Ashamed,* by a mysterious former prostitute named Sheila Cousins.

Published in early April 1938 with a wrapper declaring it "The Authentic Autobiography of a London Prostitute," the book did not strike the *Daily Mail* as a serious study with socially redeeming value, and the editor was deeply worried that it might find its way into the wrong hands. He warned, "Its effect on the young and impressionable who may read it cannot fail to be debasing and demoralising." After the *Daily Mirror* joined the campaign against the book, Cousins's publisher decided to avoid an embarrassing public fight. Booksellers were asked to return all copies. It was a great victory for the crusading newspaper editor, but in all the excitement no one was ever able to get Cousins's opinion of the case. Perhaps the press did not want to give her "sordid work" any more publicity than was necessary.

But it is difficult to kill off a "debasing and demoralising" book on prostitution. In 1953 a new edition appeared and was quietly accepted by the moral leaders of the popular press. It was even given a good review in the *New Statesman* by a famous Catholic author. Praising its honesty and its insight into human nature, Graham Greene was so taken with the book that he quoted frequently from it in his short review. He especially liked the author's talent for capturing minor characters in a few well-chosen phrases. There was "a canvasser with a pock-marked chin which looked as if it had been nibbled by a rat"; and an old man who "had a red and blotched face and a little paunch that gave the impression less of belonging to him than of going on ahead as he walked." These are indeed excellent examples. They make Sheila Cousins sound almost like a female Graham Greene.

The mysterious author was, in fact, a friend of Greene. As the Routledge files show, *To Beg I Am Ashamed* was submitted to the firm by Greene's agents at the time—Pearn, Pollinger & Higham—and the author's contract was signed by Ronald Matthews. A failed poet, an Oxford graduate, and a Catholic, Matthews worked as a journalist in London and later wrote a book about his friendship with Greene—it was published in France, in 1957, under the title *Mon Ami Graham Greene*. In the mid-1930s Greene and Matthews met at a literary party in London and soon discovered that they shared at least two major interests. One was a curiosity about exotic lands— Matthews was the author of a travel book on Albania—and the other was an unusually strong passion for prostitutes.

Apparently, these two literary "cousins" cooked up the idea of writing Cousins's story, and, although Matthews seems to have done most of the writing, Greene's additions are evident in the quality of the lines quoted in his review. Matthews is such a mediocre writer that the occasional flashes of a real writer's talent cannot help but stand out. The author of *Brighton Rock* can be heard in this description of Cousins's attitude toward another night of work: "The thought that chills me, as I leave my flat at seven, is that once more I must hear tonight, once, twice, three times maybe, the same unending gramophone record of male plaintiveness and pity and boastfulness and desire." In his *New Statesman* review, Greene admitted knowing the "ghost" responsible for *To Beg I Am Ashamed,* and he made a similar confession in the preface he wrote for the German edition of the work. But his connection with the book is also revealed in the story itself. Two of Sheila Cousins's best customers are named Graham and Matthew.

Greene may also have been responsible for the one aspect of the work that the publisher wanted changed in the page proofs. It had nothing to do with sex. Much to their credit, the editorial board of Routledge would not tolerate any unfavorable comments against Jews. In a meeting held one month before publication, the board "agreed that it is absolutely essential to take out the references to Jews in the book. . . . In a book of this kind one has to be particularly careful not to offend any susceptibilities. We therefore propose going to press after making these necessary alterations." The publishing firm might also have saved themselves some trouble if they had decided against advertising the book with the subtitle *The Authentic Auto-biography of a London Prostitute*. With a more modest approach, and without the interference of newspaper editors, the American edition was safely published in May 1938. One female reviewer for *The Nation* was so impressed by the author's mind that she could not understand how Cousins had ever allowed herself to become a prostitute: "The author is obviously a woman of more than average intelligence. She is introspective, she has a keen eye for observation and the ability to translate her observations into terse and graphic phrases. She is imaginative and sophisticated."

Given the book's difficult reception in London, and the lingering threat of criminal prosecution for his comments on Shirley Temple, Greene was wise to leave the country at the beginning of the year, and to stay away until things had calmed down. It was an especially good idea to avoid the lord chief justice, who was not at all amused by the "gross outrage" in Greene's review of *Wee Willie Winkie*. *The Times* printed an interesting exchange between His Lordship and the lawyers for the defendants:

HIS LORDSHIP.—Who is the author of this article?
MR HOLMES.—Mr Graham Greene.
HIS LORDSHIP.—Is he within the jurisdiction?
MR HOLMES.—I am afraid I do not know, my Lord.
HIS LORDSHIP.—Can you tell me where Mr Greene is?
MR MATTHEW.—I have no information on the subject.

At the time these words were spoken, Greene was several thousand miles beyond His Lordship's jurisdiction, somewhere in the rugged countryside of southern Mexico. It was an unusual place for a literary renegade to hide out, but the remote area certainly gave the lawyers good reason to deny any knowledge of Mr. Greene's whereabouts.

Better yet, the writer had a noble excuse for being there. As a

Catholic he could claim that he was investigating the official attacks on his religion in Mexico, especially in the "Godless" state of Tabasco. He had a commission from a publisher to write a book on the subject and thus could say that this pressing duty had caused him to be absent temporarily from His Lordship's jurisdiction. A good lawyer might also argue that Mr. Greene was such a righteous Catholic that he had a compulsive need to condemn immorality, wherever he found it, whether in faraway Mexico or in a seemingly innocent film by a child star. He was not lascivious, simply overzealous.

For part of his long journey, Greene was accompanied by his faithful Catholic wife—who, for reasons of her own, had shortened her name to Vivien. She sailed with him when he left England in late January 1938 and continued to be at his side as he traveled overland from New York to New Orleans. Then he left her behind, sparing her the first great ordeal of his trip—a long and intense inspection of a Mexico City nightclub. While he interviewed a lady of the evening until the early hours of the morning, Vivien waited back in America for a ship to take her home. She stayed at a hotel near the New Orleans airport for a while and occupied herself by counting the different kinds of airplanes that arrived and departed. Although it was understood from the beginning that she would go no farther than New Orleans, Vivien complained later that she had felt neglected. Tabasco may not have appealed to her, but it would have been easy for her to wait for her husband in the relative comfort of a good Mexico City hotel. Instead Greene seemed anxious to get away from her, and to treat her to a more demanding return passage. Of her stay in New Orleans, she recalled, "I was there for several days alone, which was paid for, but there was nothing to read, no books. I had to wait until a Dutch boat came, which was going to take me back to London."

The boat was far different from the attractive ship that had brought her to New York, and she was shocked to find that the accommodations were cramped and drab. Her voyage home was the kind that Greene could suffer through, but he must have known that Vivien would find it a nightmare. She was hurt by the unnecessary hardship he had imposed on her: "Oh, yes, I felt it very much. It was a very bad voyage. It was a small Dutch cargo boat, and there were three other passengers on it. Very, very rough. Ten days or two weeks. And a bad storm. I was lying in the bunk the whole time." The only good thing about the whole experience was her brief stay in New York at the beginning of their trip—it was her first visit to the city. But even then she had felt that Greene was deliberately avoiding her: "I was very much alone in New York. . . . He was seeing publishers, and I would just be left in the hotel. I wandered about Macy's. The shops were so wonderful." All the same, after he left her in New Orleans, she dutifully sent affectionate letters to him in Mexico, signing one particularly loving message "Pussy."

The situation in Mexico did offer a worthy subject for a Catholic writer, although the worst days of religious persecution were over by the time Greene traveled to the country. In the 1920s President Calles had led a campaign to limit the number of priests and to prevent the Catholic Church from owning property. Some recalcitrant clergy were killed or imprisoned. But the campaign was more successful in some states than in others. By far the most enthusiastic enemy of the Church was the governor of Tabasco, Tomás Garrido Canabal. He drove every priest out of the state, demolished the churches, and used their bricks to pave roads. Artists were commissioned to decorate public buildings with murals "lampooning religion and priests." One American magazine informed its readers that Garrido's "favorite outdoor sport is the public burning of altars and images." He was determined to prove that a just and well-run society could exist without allowing any place for religion. To protect the morals of his people, he outlawed alcohol and jazz. The importation of saxophones was "sternly banned." One follower was so devoted to Garrido's grand cause that he carried a business card which helpfully explained that he was the personal enemy of God.

When Greene arrived in Mexico, the restrictions against the Church had been eased in most parts of the country. Only in Tabasco could the visitor find the fires of anti-Catholicism still smoldering, although the great Garrido was no longer there to lead the fight. He was living in exile in Costa Rica, where presumably he continued to harbor resentment against God and saxophones. Unfortunately for Greene, Tabasco was not easy to reach. He had to make a slow rail trip of 200 miles from Mexico City to Veracruz, spend two days sailing down the Gulf coast in a rusty old barge to the port of Frontera, then take a twelve-hour river journey to Villahermosa, the capital of the godless state. The tropical heat made him think that he was back in Liberia, but it was not only the climate of Tabasco that reminded him of West Africa. The rough justice practiced by Garrido's followers against the Church is similar to that which Col. Elwood Davis practiced against the Krus. The zealots of Tabasco burned churches and hunted down priests, whereas Colonel Davis burned native villages and pursued the rebellious Chief Nimley.

Although Greene was supposed to be investigating the persecution of the Church, he found in Tabasco something much more interesting than bigotry. He found his old friend the devil. In the godless state there was no need for the devil to wear a mask. This was hell, and one could proudly advertise that fact on a business card. It was a place where you could actually come face to face with Lucifer—a nephew of Garrido was known by that name. Greene knew what he was looking for when he decided to go to Mexico. At the beginning of *The Lawless Roads,* he describes some hellish scenes in England, then asks himself why he needs to look for hell in Mexico. He quotes the famous lines addressed to Faustus by Mephistopheles: "Why, this is hell, nor am I out of it." These lines are also quoted in *Brighton Rock* by Pinkie's lawyer, and although it is true that Greene never had to look far for images of hell, he could hardly pass up the chance to see the devil's great achievements in Tabasco.

As *The Lawless Roads* clearly shows, Greene did not want to waste time getting to know the concerns of the Catholic Church in Mexico. He spent only a small part of his trip interviewing loyal followers of the faith. He was more eager to see the ruined churches, to hear tales of priests being chased through the swamps or the mountains, to observe the dark rituals of the Indians who practiced their own special brand of religion—which mixed Christianity with paganistic superstitions. He was fascinated by a straw figure of Judas hanging from a cross. The creative Mexicans who constructed this scene also added a straw figure at the base of the cross and called it the brother of Judas. This notion that Judas had a brother was bound to appeal to Greene. Equally appealing was a tour of an anticlerical waxwork display in Mexico City. In little cells monks were shown whipping naked women or questioning them by torchlight.

There are a few muddled passages in *The Lawless Roads* about the need for the Church to become more responsive to the problems of the Mexican people. At one or two points Greene seems to be arguing for the Church to start a social revolution, one that would put an end to the dreadful economic exploitation of the common workers. But his attempt to appear as a true friend of the people is not convincing. Perhaps Greene wanted to make his trip to Mexico sound like a good substitute for visiting Spain. While most writers of his generation were absorbed in the thorny political questions of the Spanish Civil War, Greene was able to have the issue of Mexico almost to himself, sounding wise and suitably radical on a subject that most people in Europe knew nothing about. As his fellow authors argued bitterly over the conflict in Spain, he was free to make all sorts of pronouncements on Mexico without worrying that anyone would question him too closely. It all sounded frightfully interesting but impossibly obscure.

The obscurity of the subject for the general reader in Europe may help to explain why very little was said about Greene's odd way of showing his support for the aspirations of the ordinary Mexican. He sounds friendly enough in the early pages of his book, citing the words of St. James as a reminder that the Catholic Church should oppose the selfish rich and champion the humble poor: "Go to now, ye rich men: weep and howl in your miseries which shall come upon you. Your riches are corrupted, and your garments are moth eaten." But with each passing day in Mexico, the author becomes less charitable. For one thing, he starts to miss the kind of luxury that St. James found so reprehensible. He complains in the book that a glass of beer at a cantina is too warm, that Mexican chocolate is far inferior to the English and Swiss varieties, that Mexican brandy is vile, and that the hotels are uniformly bad. Faced with such miserable conditions, he longs to return to Manhattan and enjoy tea at the Waldorf, where they provide lots of free cinnamon sticks and cherries. Americans are soulless heathens, of course, but Greene has to admit that he enjoys not only tea at the Waldorf but also Coca-Cola highballs.

As Greene sees it, almost everything the Mexicans have to offer is inferior. His cheap sun helmet comes apart, as does his cheap Mexican leather jacket. Again and again Greene finds that *hideous* is the best adjective for things Mexican: a colorful plate of food, the furniture in shop windows, the trinkets sold in the markets, a room in an old convent, a politician's house. And, yes, the people are hideous. A priest's face, the faces of some Indian women, and every pair of brown eyes are hideous. In no time at all the author of *The Lawless Roads* forgets his call for improving economic conditions in Mexico and begins to talk about how much he hates the country and its people. The heat is terrible, the rats and insects are painfully annoying, and the filth is disgusting. The beggars at train stations look like "mangy animals" and are too pushy. Greene hates the guide who takes him on a long journey by mule, and he hates the mule too. He hates a clerk who dines at his hotel, and he hates the noise of the traffic in Mexico City.

Overwhelmed by his hatred, he sits silently in an overcrowded train car and plays the game Hating People. He picks out a large elderly woman dressed in black and watches her every move with a growing sense of hatred, noting the way she blows her nose, the way she removes a tick, the ugliness of her hair and mouth, the slowness of her movements, her vacant stare. He hates her so much that he comes close to wishing for her murder and the murder of everyone like her. "If Spain is like this," he tells the reader, "I can understand the temptation to massacre."

These words sound as though they came from Pinkie, but this book is not a novel. The voice belongs to a real person, albeit one who is always artfully devious. Although *The Lawless Roads* presents itself as a travel book with a moral mission, its author gradually removes the respectable mask of a Catholic novelist investigating persecution and shows us the face of a man consumed by rage. The transformation is so gradual, and is presented in such moderate terms, that we may not fully realize how much hate is packed into this "travel book." In a manner similar to that in *Brighton Rock,* the book tries to smuggle hate under our noses and send it straight to our hearts. The success of this smuggling operation is evident from the fact that so few objections to it have been heard over the years. But there is no mistaking the horror of this message. One cannot fall back on the excuse that the speaker is a fictional character. Graham Greene addresses the reader directly, and his message is clear: Mexicans are less than human, and the urge to hate such people is understandable, even if that urge leads to thoughts of murder. He took the "massacre" remark from his unpublished Mexican travel diary, but the original version is even nastier. Although Greene's estate will not allow the original to be quoted, suffice it to say that the novelist found nothing in the Mexican people that would have caused him to lament their extermination.

There is a fictional parallel for Greene's provocative statement, but it is not to be found in the novelist's own work. In Conrad's *Heart of Darkness* we are told that Kurtz was asked to write a report on Africa for the International Society for the Suppression of Savage Customs. He completed a seventeen-page document full of wonderful comments on the need for the colonial powers to improve native life. "By the simple exercise of our will we can exert a power for good practically unbounded," he wrote. When Marlow reads the document, he is caught up in "the magic current of phrases" and says that its beautiful rhetoric made him "tingle with enthusiasm." The piece was written in the early days of Kurtz's time in Africa, long before his "nerves went wrong, and caused him to preside at certain midnight dances ending with unspeakable rites." But after things began to deteriorate, Kurtz came back to his piece and added a "kind of note at the foot of the last page." Marlow describes it: "At the end of that moving appeal to every altruistic sentiment it blazed at you, luminous and terrifying, like a flash of lightning in a serene sky: 'Exterminate all the brutes!' "

The effect is not so grand in *The Lawless Roads,* but one is reminded of Kurtz when Greene's hate finally causes him to surrender any pretense of goodwill. Placed near the end of his book, Greene's remark about a massacre is so much like Kurtz's that he seems to be imitating him. If he appeared to be acting a bit like Kurtz during his trip to Liberia, it may have been because he was thinking of him from the start. His decision to serve the self-righteous whites running the Anti-Slavery Society is remarkably similar to Kurtz's association with the International Society for the Suppression of Savage Customs. When he is on his best behavior, he can seem like a well-intentioned Marlow leading us on a search for devils like Kurtz, but he can resemble Marlow one minute and Kurtz the next. It is clear from Greene's work that Kurtz fascinated him. Characters who share the name appear in *The Name of Action* and *The Third Man,* and references to *Heart of Darkness* can be found in various books, including *In Search of a Character* (1961), which cites Marlow's words "And this also has been one of the dark places of the earth."

Literature played such an important part in Greene's life that he often appeared to be more at home in books than in the world of his fellow humans. During his journey in Mexico, he spent a lot of time in Victorian England. Readers of *The Lawless Roads* are treated not only to descriptions of all the things that Greene hated but also to discussions of Trollope's *Barchester Towers* and *Dr. Thorne,* which Greene brought with him to Mexico. He became especially attached to the latter novel, regarding it as a refuge from the hateful sights that surrounded him. Unable to speak Spanish, he found companionship in books.

It is not surprising that Greene hated Mexico. Spending so much of his time in an imaginary world of his own, and cut off from ordinary people by the language barrier, he could convince himself that Mexicans deserved to be hated, that they were all sullen, backward, and cruel. Moreover, he was predisposed to think the worst of them. He began by looking for hell, and he found what he wanted to find. The scenery and the atmosphere in *The Lawless Roads* are convincing, but imagination is more important than experience in his portrait of Mexico. He spent only five weeks in the country, and even that short visit was too long. As he admits on the last page of his book, Mexico represented for him a "state of mind." The visit simply allowed him to fill in the background with authentic details.

Spying appears not to have played any part in his visit. There was not much reason for an Englishman to spy on anyone in Mexico. But it may be that certain Catholics in England encouraged him to write something on the subject of persecution. Stories about martyrs are always good for lifting the spirits of the faithful and attracting converts. When *The Lawless Roads* was published, Greene received enthusiastic approval from the Catholic periodical *Blackfriars*. The priest who reviewed the book seems to have overlooked the hate motif. "As a study of Catholicism," he wrote, "it is complete. The Church in *The Lawless Roads* is a living Church, the fulfilment of the purpose of the Incarnation, a linking of the human and of the Divine. . . . Perhaps no other book in English has come so close to the essential spirit of Catholicism." This is extravagant praise indeed for a book in which everyone with brown eyes is damned for looking hideous. But perhaps the priest was influenced by the fact that he was a friend of Graham and Vivien Greene. In any event, Father Gervase Mathew was amply rewarded for his kind words. Greene dedicated the Heinemann edition of *The Power and the Glory* to him.

Such praise from respected Catholic figures helped to make a great many people think that, whatever Greene actually said in his books, he must be a good Catholic in his heart. So the novelist later had no problem convincing innocent interviewers that his trip to Mexico marked a major turning point in the development of his faith. As he said in an interview given in the 1980s, "I had no emotional attachment to Catholicism till I went to Mexico and saw the faith of the peasants during the persecution there." The real importance of the trip is that it provided him with material for one of his most important novels—the story of a priest on the run in a godless Mexican state.

II

Although the setting of *The Power and the Glory* is a place like Tabasco, a major influence on the novel is a poem by a writer who would never have dared to visit the wilds of Mexico. Once again Greene's admiration for T. S. Eliot led him to do some creative borrowing. On one level, *The Power and the Glory* is merely a prose extension of Eliot's "The Hollow Men." Very early in the novel, before the reader has learned the true identity of the whiskey priest, the character is referred to as "the hollow man." His world has much in common with Eliot's vision of a "cactus land" peopled by lost souls who find themselves surrounded by broken images of an abandoned faith. The hollow men wander aimlessly in a landscape of dry grass and ruined buildings, with rats crawling over the rubble. They want to believe in something but have no faith left. All they have is a fragmented language of belief. They struggle with the phrase "For Thine is the Kingdom," not remembering what comes next in the Lord's Prayer. What comes next, of course, is "The Power and the Glory." Eliot also suggests that his living dead have lost even the capacity to feel the horror of their plight, unlike the famous character who surrendered his soul to the heart of darkness. The epigraph to the poem is taken from Conrad's novel: "Mistah Kurtz—he dead."

The Hollow Man in Greene's novel finds that he is the last representative of God in a land that recognizes neither his power nor his glory. Churches have been demolished, and no priest has dared to remain in the area except the Hollow Man, who has lived in isolation for so long that he has created his own version of Catholicism. He was a rather conventional priest before the official campaign of persecution began, but, as soon as he is left on his own, he abandons all the old rules. There are no longer any Church officials who can reprimand him. There is only his will and the threat of death from his enemies. With such freedom, he decides that fasting is unnecessary and that he can give up regular prayers and daily Mass. As he explains near the end of the novel, he is possessed by the same sort of pride that caused Lucifer's fall. He stays in the godless land not because he is brave but because he wants to live by his own rules. It gives him the chance to be the pope in one little corner of the world, to be the sole keeper of all the mysteries of his religion. But this grand ambition turns into nothing more significant than a personal surrender to petty vices. He drinks heavily, plays card tricks, sleeps with a woman and makes her pregnant.

When he is briefly imprisoned for possessing contraband alcohol, he tells a fellow prisoner, "Sins have so much beauty." He praises the beauty of the fallen angels, and his image of God is primarily associated with sin. Religion gives him a way to dignify a meaningless life of dissipation. As the whiskey priest, he can see his weakness as a strength. He may be a drunk, but at least he is God's drunk. Because he is the last priest, God is stuck with him, whether he likes it or not. But as the Hollow Man, he knows that he represents nothing. The old religion has been vanquished, and his whiskey and card tricks are a pitiful substitute for the power and the glory.

Whenever he is required to perform the traditional functions of a priest, he reveals his incompetence. After a long journey he arrives at a village in which an old man asks him to hear the confessions of the villagers. He is so weary from traveling that he cannot face the task and begins to weep. Finally, he agrees to oblige the villagers, but he continues to cry uncontrollably. The old man has to tell everyone that the priest is crying because he is overwhelmed by their sins. On another occasion, he fails to comfort an Indian woman who has lost her baby. After leaving her at a large Indian cross for a short time, he returns to find that she has disappeared. Her dead baby lies at the foot of the cross, and at the child's side is a cube of sugar, which the mother has left behind for the nourishment of its spirit. Tired and hungry, the priest cannot resist the temptation to swallow the child's sugar.

Nothing goes right for the priest. He rushes to the side of a fugitive American gangster who is dying but fails to coax him into confessing his sins. He awakens a spirit of compassion in Coral Fellows, a young English girl who agrees to hide him from the police, but her willingness to help a man on the run gets her into trouble later on. Although the novel is deliberately vague about Coral's death, we are led to believe that she gave some sort of aid to the American gangster and that he repaid her kindness by killing her. The priest can hardly be blamed for her murder, but it does seem that death follows in his footsteps. Three hostages are killed by the police in an effort to force villagers to reveal the priest's whereabouts.

He is such a failure that he cannot face his own death with dignity. He expects that the police will eventually capture him and shoot him—and he takes risks that make this fate inevitable—but, when he is taken into custody, he does not have the will to die a martyr's death. In the last hours before his execution, he confesses his sins aloud, but he does so in a drunken stupor. When the firing squad comes for him, he is in a pathetic condition, suffering from fear and the effects of his hangover. The police have to keep him upright as he is taken to the place of execution. Facing the guns, he is truly the Hollow Man, an empty figure who must die for nothing. As the narrative points out, he is neither bad enough to be "Hell-worthy" nor good enough to be confident of God's mercy. He tries to summon up a little strength at the very end, suddenly raising his arms and attempting to make a last statement. But the only word that comes out before the bullets hit him is "Excuse." Although the moment of his death is filled with the noise of gunfire, it is still more appropriate to say that he died as all Hollow Men must, "Not with a bang but a whimper."

Greene reinforces the ignominy of the priest's death by presenting it from the point of view of the dentist Mr. Tench. Because the chief of police has been suffering from a bad toothache, the dentist comes to police headquarters and is working on the ugly man's tooth when he hears a commotion outside. As he steps to the window, he sees the priest being led to his death. In an ordinary novel such a major event would be seen through the eyes of either the victim or his enemy, but Greene filters every detail through the eyes of a distracted bystander. Mr. Tench is appalled and frightened by the execution, but he is in no position to understand its meaning. He can turn his back and walk away from it. And there is certainly nothing glorious about it. When the shooting is over, the priest is merely a "routine heap" on the ground.

Given his fondness for sin, the priest might have found glory if he had developed a greater passion for sinning. When T. S. Eliot argued that it is better to do evil than to do nothing, he added, "At least, we exist." In other words, whatever else can be said about true disciples of evil, they are not Hollow Men. And it is a mistake to think that the power and the glory are known only to those who serve God's kingdom. According to Eliot, "the glory of man" lies not merely in "his capacity for salvation; it is also true to say that his glory is his capacity for damnation." The priest's great mistake is that, when he decides to start breaking the old rules, he breaks only a few minor ones, and he regrets those. As Pinkie in *Brighton Rock* understands, the only way to make a religion of sin is to serve it with all your heart; then even failure can be glorious. Pinkie would have loved the chance to be God's last priest. It would have given him endless opportunities for madness and mayhem.

There is no doubt that the priest's heart is in the right place. The happiest time of his life occurs on the night he is imprisoned for carrying an illegal bottle of brandy. Sitting in the darkness of a large communal cell, he is delighted by the foul smells, the slimy floor, and the moans from a pair of passionate lovers. "Such a lot of beauty," he remarks of the general scene. The way to enjoy more of this beauty is to abandon the uncertain borderland of good and evil, and to plunge headfirst into the heart of darkness. Instead of Kurtz's magnificent pronouncement on his descent into evil—"The horror! The horror!"—or Pinkie's outburst of hate recorded on vulcanized rubber, the befuddled priest can manage nothing better than "Excuse." It is a hopelessly ambiguous word, but it suits the priest perfectly. *Excuse* is more appropriate for him than a resounding *forgive* or an equally resounding *bloody*, which is one of Pinkie's last words. Part of the problem is that the priest lacks the capacity to hate. He says that hate reveals a "failure of imagination," but *The Lawless Roads* shows that a proud man's imagination can find a great many hideous things to hate.

If evil can be so liberating, one might assume that the priest's chief antagonist—the lieutenant—is the real hero of the novel. With single-minded devotion, he tracks down the priest and summarily executes him, but he is as much a Hollow Man as his victim. Just as the priest dies for nothing, the lieutenant kills for nothing. He begins his pursuit on a promising note of hate, but he lacks enthusiasm. For him, there is neither a heaven nor a hell. There is only the here and now, and a passionless faith in social order. His pride is subordinate to a rigid ideology. He understands power—the mechanical power of the soulless state—but does not appreciate glory. When he finally captures the priest, his victory is an empty one. What matters to him is the pursuit; after that is done, his small supply of emotion is spent. With smooth precision, he goes through the motions of arranging the priest's execution, but he loses his hatred for the "small hollow man" and breaks the law to give him a last bottle of brandy. He performs this act of mercy without any real sense of compassion. He feels only a "bitter kindness." In the end he is not good enough to spare the priest, or evil enough to enjoy his death. He puts a final bullet in the priest's head simply because he must do his job. All the evil glory of murdering God's last priest is wasted on him.

Like Eliot's poem, the novel evokes the agonizing confusion of life in the twilight region between salvation and damnation. This is the territory that Greene knows best, but *Brighton Rock* and *The Power and the Glory* leave no doubt that one side of the border is better than the other. For real glory nothing can match the beauty of sin. But it is not as easy as some might think to make a home in that forbidden realm. One must be willing to abandon God and humankind—to stand in pure isolation, ready to break all the rules, not just a few. The important thing is not necessarily to do evil deeds but to live on one's own terms, absolutely. Nothing is sacred except the will of the individual. Greene's idea of glory involves a complete surrender to this sacred isolation. It is the primal offense of pride or, as Greene also liked to call it, the "rage of personality." The greater the pride, the greater the glory. Naturally, Lucifer is the ultimate role model.

In an essay on Herbert Read, Greene argues that glory can be gained only by a spontaneous act of daring. One moment you see the border in the distance, and the next moment you rush to cross it, never looking back. To illustrate the point, Greene quotes from Read: "Glory is distinguished from fortune, because fortune exacts care. . . . Glory is gained directly, if one has the genius to deserve it: glory is sudden." Read was thinking primarily of glory for virtue's sake, but Greene saw that the concept could be extended to sin, and he found support for that view in Read's poem "The End of a War." In the poem an English officer has the satisfaction of knowing that he has survived the war, but the price of his survival is mediocrity. Like Greene's lieutenant, the officer has done his job in a mechanical way, dutifully fighting for a victory that inspires no passion. He cannot understand the sacrifice of his dead enemy, who fought with "power and pride" for a place in hell, battling against every obstacle until the last moment of life. The enemy soldier was willing to betray anyone or anything in his lonely fight, and when he was killed at last, his "smile" was "the only comment / on the well-done deed."

No character in Greene's work is able to reach such a moment of pure glory—of absolute pride—but Pinkie comes close. Paraphrasing Wordsworth, Greene says that Pinkie "trailed the clouds of his own glory." (Greene was a great admirer of Herbert Read's early book on Wordsworth.) If there is any glory—in the sense that Greene uses the term—in *The Power and the Glory*, it belongs to the author. As one of the few "Catholic" novelists in a godless modern world, he does a fine job of betraying the religion. Besides making the last priest a drunken failure, he takes every opportunity to place him in debasing circumstances. The best—or worst—example, depending on your point of view, is the humiliation the priest suffers after his night in the communal cell. He is given the job of emptying all the pails of human waste in the prison. Greene is careful to describe the process in detail, taking the priest from cell to cell, noting the stench, the overflowing pails that splash the ground as the priest lugs them to the cesspool, and the flies that swarm above a pile of vomit. After being exposed to so much filth, the priest finds that he has seen a little too much of the beauty in this sinful place and must pause to vomit.

His sacred position is also used to parody various aspects of Christianity. The only photograph of him at the police station shows him seated at a table with a group of females surrounding him. It was taken at his first communion party. To make his face stand out, some-one at the station has used an ink pen to give him what appears to be a halo. Beside the photograph is a picture of the wanted gangster, whose last name—Calver—is similar to the name of the hill where Christ was crucified. The effect of this little display is to make the whiskey priest look like a ludicrous imitation of Christ. The joke is continued throughout the book. The mestizo who betrays the priest is referred to as Judas, and the priest recalls attending a dinner party at which he laughingly compared himself to Christ at the Last Supper. Greene takes this parody to an outrageous extreme when he describes a dream in which the priest imagines Christ dancing to the beat of a marimba band. While the band plays, fireworks go off and Christ does an erotic dance. His face is painted like a whore's, but the makeup is meant to suggest blood.

This kind of thing is not much different from the vandalism of churches sponsored by the godless state. In *The Power and the Glory*, Greene conducts his own anti-Catholic campaign. Just as he liked to subject priests to shocking confessions in private life, the whiskey priest is treated to a wild confession from the mestizo. Sick with fever, the mestizo is so desperate to confess his sins that he seems to be trying to impress the priest with their variety. He boasts that he has given money for sex not only to women but also to boys, and that once he had two women at the same time. Eagerly, he begins describing the various acts he performed with the women. Greene could be sure that the scene would shock many of his contemporary readers, but it produces little effect on the whiskey priest, whose considerable experience of sin has prepared him to take such things in stride.

Some of Greene's efforts at ridicule are a bit too contrived. After helping the priest to escape the lieutenant, Coral Fellows enters the shed where the priest had taken refuge and finds that he has drawn a long row of crosses on the wall in chalk. This might lead to a moment of deep reflection and awe in a conventional religious novel. But Greene uses it to provoke a rather more common response. Instead of holiness, Coral feels her first menstrual pains. Greene strives for a similar note of bathos when he describes a stained glass window the dentist has salvaged from a ruined church. The glass depiction of a Madonna is given a new home in one window of the dentist's office. The tools of his trade are behind the sacred figure, and the view from the window is of a yard inhabited by a few turkeys. Of course, given the tropical climate, it is also necessary to drape a mosquito net across the Virgin's face.

Some critics have imagined that the purpose of *The Power and the Glory* is to show how holiness can emerge from degradation. In a mysterious process the whiskey priest is supposed to find sainthood through the mists of his hangover. Many Catholics have shown some fondness for this interpretation, but a few powerful men in the Vatican were reluctant to see the whiskey priest as a good role model for the clergy. Although the book was published in 1940, the Vatican did not find time to lodge a formal protest until 1953. In November of that year the secretary of the Holy Office, Cardinal Pizzardo, informed the archbishop of Westminster that *The Power and the Glory* had been "denounced to this sacred Congregation" and that the Holy Office had "agreed upon a verdict altogether adverse to it." The cardinal acknowledged that the author was "a convert from Protestantism" but did not consider this fact a cause for leniency. And, as an amateur literary critic, His Eminence thought that he understood how the novelist had gone astray in *The Power and the Glory*. In his letter to the archbishop, he made it clear that Greene needed a good lecture on the proper way to write a Catholic novel:

> The author's aim was to bring out the victory of the power and the glory of the Lord in spite of man's wretchedness, but this aim is not attained, since it is the latter element which appears to carry the day, and in a way which does injury to certain friendly characters, and even to the priesthood itself. The novel, moreover, portrays a state of affairs so paradoxical, so extraordinary, and so erroneous as to disconcert enlightened persons, who form the majority of its readers.
>
> I am therefore writing to beg Your Eminence to inform Mr. Graham Greene with your accustomed tact of the unfavourable verdict of the Holy See on his book, and to exhort him to be more constructive from a Catholic point of view in his writings, as all good people expect him to be. As for the book in question, Your Eminence will not fail to ensure that the author does not allow further reprints or translations of it to be published without his introducing into it the necessary corrections that the foregoing remarks would suggest.

It is a shame that Cardinal Pizzardo did not offer a detailed list of necessary alterations, but presumably Christ's dance with the marimba band would have been banished. A complete revision to satisfy the Vatican might have been difficult to produce. A new story built on the trials of a lemonade priest does not sound appealing. The real problem is that the Vatican could not begin to imagine how much revision was necessary. In any event, Greene had no intention of changing a thing. Evelyn Waugh advised him, "They have taken fourteen years to write their first letter. You should take fourteen years to answer it." He did bide his time, but only for a few months. He evaded a direct meeting with the archbishop of Westminster until April 1954, then he waited another month before giving him a written response.

His letter is a groveling one, which makes him sound contrite, but he offers no concessions. Instead he falls back on the excuse that his publishers control the reprint rights, and he politely provides the archbishop with the names of each publisher, with the suggestion that the Vatican address its demands directly to the individual firms—all seventeen of them, from Tammi in Finland to Shincho-Sha in Japan. He knew this idea was absurd, but he also knew that no one in the Vatican would want to make the dispute public. And to make certain that the archbishop got the message, he offered to go to Rome so that he could address his critics personally. Wisely, the Vatican let the matter drop.

Fighting Greene was not worth the trouble, and he knew exactly how to make that point without seeming to be defiant. As soon as Greene became a famous Catholic novelist, the Church was stuck with him, just as God is stuck with the whiskey priest. But Greene was not quite ready to forgive and forget this episode. He took his revenge in the second volume of his autobiography by explaining his side of the story, and then by distorting the name of his adversary for comic effect. He changed the *Pizz* in Cardinal Pizzardo's name to *Piss.*

The Power and the Glory has outlived Greene and "Pissardo" because its poetic quality rises above the dubious message that sin is beautiful. You do not have to agree with the message to appreciate the great images, atmosphere, and language. The priest and the lieutenant inhabit a landscape that is much more vivid than Eliot's "cactus land," but that is partly because Greene had the genius to see how he could combine the imagination of a poet with the experience of a wandering writer. He may have loathed Mexico, but the Mexico of his novel is a powerful reality for the reader, a perfect background for the cat-and-mouse game between the priest and his enemies. The novel is even more enjoyable, however, when one appreciates the subversive game that Greene is playing with his Hollow Men, and with the religion that afforded him so much pleasure.

Although it has nothing to do with God, one more joke in the novel deserves to be noted. Because she lives on an isolated plantation, thirteen-year-old Coral Fellows receives education from a correspondence school in London. It is a third-rate outfit that makes a virtue of teaching children to give safe, unimaginative answers to standard questions. With a little help from her mother, Coral struggles valiantly with the textbooks and examinations, and manages to improve her mind despite the dull methods of Henry Beckley, B.A., principal of Private Tutorials, Ltd. It is a good thing that Charles Greene had stopped reading his son's novels, because he would have instantly recognized that the school was intended to be a parody of his old school. The novel makes that clear when it identifies the

motto of Private Tutorials, Ltd.: *"Virtus Laudata Crescit."* The same
Latin phrase appears on the coat of arms of Berkhamsted School. But
this obscure piece of information is not essential for a good laugh. In
Greene's case, "Virtue increases with praise" is a funny idea on its
own.

This little reference to Berkhamsted was the last that Greene was
able to make during his father's lifetime. The old headmaster died in
1942. At that time Greene was several thousand miles away from
England, doing what his father's methods had prepared him to do so
well—spying. While he was working at his lonely post in Sierra
Leone, two telegrams arrived with the news about his father. One
told him that his father was ill, the other that he had died. It is typical of Greene's life that the telegrams were received in the wrong
sequence. First, he heard that his father was dead. Then came the
news that the old man was ill.

CHAPTER FOURTEEN

BREAKING UP

When Greene returned from Mexico, the atmosphere at home was not good. It was clear that he wanted to make a permanent escape from family life. No matter how much Vivien tried to make him feel at home, he was too restless to enjoy her idea of peace and comfort. For one thing, he was constantly irritated by the sounds of young children in the house. Whenever he was writing, he demanded as much silence as possible, and it was difficult to keep his children completely quiet in the mornings as he tried to work on *The Lawless Roads* and *The Power and the Glory*. The difficulty became so great that he decided to rent a studio where he could work in isolation during the day. He found what he wanted in Mecklenburgh Square, an elegant spot next to the leafy haven of Coram's Fields, in Bloomsbury. Virginia Woolf moved there in 1939, but Greene seems to have succeeded in avoiding any contact with her.

If they had ever chanced to meet in the square, he would not have been at his best. He was working far too hard and was taking Benzedrine at breakfast to put a good buzz in his central nervous system. When he went home at the end of each day, he was a wreck. His hands would begin to shake uncontrollably, just as they did during the worst days of his trip through Liberia, and he would usually sink into a deep depression for the rest of the evening. He spoke sharply to Vivien without reason and kept up a steady stream of complaints. The next morning he would take his Benzedrine, travel from Clapham Common to Bloomsbury, and start the ordeal all over again. But his crazy pace did bring results. In the space of one year he brought out three books. *The Lawless Roads* appeared in March 1939; *The Power and the Glory* was published in March 1940; and in September 1939 he managed to squeeze in a book that was written in six weeks—*The Confidential Agent*. He also found time for a few articles and a dozen or so reviews.

The Bloomsbury retreat was useful for more than literary purposes. At some point in 1938, Greene began an affair with a woman who lived in the area. Her name was Dorothy Glover. Born in London in 1901, she was part Irish and part Scottish, and had lived for a time in Dublin. When Greene met her she was working as a theater costume designer, but she also had ambitions to illustrate and write children's books. She was a short woman with plain features, unmarried, and only marginally able to support herself as a designer. Greene's interest in her is difficult to explain, because he rarely spoke candidly about her to others. Although he had his lingering romantic interests in his cousins, and his constant fascination with prostitutes, he managed to avoid any deep affairs with women until Dorothy came along. Given his various sexual conflicts, and his passion for independence, he could not find it easy to become seriously involved with any woman. But, apparently, he was able to handle the distinctly unglamorous, thirty-seven-year-old Dorothy.

They were closely involved with each other until the late 1940s and remained friends until her death in 1971. At one point Dorothy also seems to have been Hugh Greene's lover. One thing Graham shared with her was a passion for Victorian detective fiction. They enjoyed searching the shelves of secondhand bookshops for rare first editions of works by such writers as Wilkie Collins and Mary Braddon. Over the years they built up a large and immensely valuable collection. But their love of popular literature was not the primary bond between them. A sexual relationship of a stormy nature seems to have been the key attraction.

Greene managed to hide this relationship from Vivien for quite some time, but, when she learned of it in the 1940s, she was surprised to discover how possessive her rival was: "She was very jealous. He told me—he laughed but I think he was rather flattered—that if I put on a button, she would find it. She would cut it out. If I mended his socks . . . she would cut it all out. And once in some altercation—he showed me his hand—she pressed a cigarette on it." In her innocence Vivien would have had little reason to doubt that the burn was the result of an "altercation." But it was probably connected with a moment of pleasure and pain. In a letter to Catherine Walston—the woman who became Greene's lover after Dorothy was relegated to the level of friend—Greene makes a point of saying that his cigarette burn has disappeared, and that he would like another.

The most intense period of Greene's relationship with Dorothy began in late 1939, after the outbreak of war forced Vivien and the children to be evacuated to Charles Greene's house in Crowborough. Graham moved into Dorothy's flat in Gower Mews and lived with her until he was called away to Sierra Leone on wartime service in 1941. During the blitz of 1940–41, he served in the ARP (Air Raid Precautions) and was assigned to Post No. One in Bloomsbury, under the School of Tropical Medicine. Dorothy was also assigned there as a "shelter warden." Although Greene was involved in some difficult rescue work during some of the worst air attacks on London, he was also able to spend a lot of time enjoying himself with Dorothy in the shelter. A fellow warden—the bookseller David Low—recalled how the couple had been caught in the act one day during an inspection. It seems that some important people from the area headquarters of the ARP had "received complaints about the immorality current in Post No. One's shelters." When the head warden of the post led a man from HQ on an inspection, no immorality was uncovered until they came to a shelter in which Greene and Dorothy were spotted in a corner. Thinking quickly, the head warden told his superior, "That's one of our best wardens, Mr. Greene, just off from duty, and he's with Mrs. Greene."

The couple also found less obvious ways to pass the dreary hours of the blackout. They made up children's stories together. Greene wrote the text, and Dorothy created the illustrations. They produced four small books, and after the war each was published. Originally, the idea was to bring them out under Dorothy's name alone, but someone realized that they would sell much better if Greene's name appeared on the cover, so the couple shared the credit for the books. It is a bit disconcerting to think of Pinkie Brown's creator writing children's stories, but the works are perfectly harmless fantasies with such titles as *The Little Train* and *The Little Fire Engine*. The biggest success of the group was *The Little Horse Bus*, which brought Greene his strangest honor. In recognition of his fine work as the creator of the sturdy little horse bus, he received the Boys' Clubs of America Junior Book Award for 1955.

In the theater, Dorothy had used the name Dorothy Craigie, and it is this professional name that appears on her books. After Greene helped her to launch her career as a book illustrator, she went on to illustrate many more works for other authors, and to write children's books of her own. For a few of these works she decided to be known as David Craigie. One of David's books, *The Voyage of the Luna I,* is dedicated to Graham Greene. Most of Dorothy's work quickly went out of print—a common fate among children's authors—but she was not a bad illustrator or storyteller. It is doubtful, however, that anyone will ever want to reprint two titles that appeared in 1960: *Nicky and Nigger and the Pirate* and *Nicky and Nigger Join the Circus.*

In her last years Dorothy dreamed that she and Greene would live out their old age together. She confided to David Low her "vision": "How, after all the hurly burly, there would you, and she be, two old people in their armchairs on either side of the fireplace." But as Greene became more famous, he lost interest in Dorothy. He became involved with younger, and more attractive, women. One of these— Catherine Walston—unkindly referred to Dorothy as "that ugly dwarf." But Greene tried to remain a helpful friend. When a publisher wanted to reissue their four children's books with new illustrations by someone else, he refused to give his permission. After Dorothy's death, however, this show of loyalty ended. A new edition was soon authorized with illustrations by Edward Ardizzone.

A great deal of Dorothy's life is a mystery. She never made much money from her children's books, and when she died her estate was worth only a few thousand pounds. She never married, and many people who knew Greene in his years of great fame were unaware that she had played a part in his life. Vivien met her only once, in the 1950s. At that time Greene was living in chambers at Albany, and Vivien had a house in Oxford.

It was a very strange encounter, the only time I met her. I had come up to London with Francis for some reason. It was December, and we had some time before our coach returned to Oxford. . . . So I went into Albany—we were not expected—and Graham said, "Oh, I'm going out to dinner," and at that moment a little short figure, a stout short figure with blue glasses—it seemed very strange—came up and started back on seeing us, and said, "Oh, can I use your telephone? I wanted to telephone to my furrier." Such an extraordinary thing, it was seven at night. He said, "Oh, do come in." So I said, "Oh, well," and we went away.

Greene and Dorothy seemed to enjoy this little charade. It reveals their fondness for melodramatic secrecy and subterfuge, which may explain why they were drawn to each other in the first place. They enjoyed using their affair to play childlike games of mystery, hiding their relationship from Greene's family, his literary acquaintances, and the great reading public, then dropping obscure clues in prominent places. For many years curious readers could not understand why the author of *A Gun for Sale* had also written *The Little Horse Bus,* and none of them could identify Dorothy Craigie. They also had no way of knowing that she was the same woman who is listed in a rare publication as Greene's partner in collecting Victorian detective fiction. Using her real name, she edited a catalog of their book collection, which bears the uninspiring title *Victorian Detective Fiction,* and Greene wrote a preface to the book, vaguely referring to the literary interests he shared with "Miss Glover." And no one had noticed that Greene appeared to have a friend named David Craigie, who also wrote children's books.

One clue could not be missed. Greene must have known Dorothy Craigie since the days when he was writing *The Confidential Agent,* because the book is dedicated to her. But the best clue was hidden in the book itself. The hero of the novel—who is known only as D.— hides from the police in a flat belonging to a Miss Glover. She has gone away for the weekend, and, after breaking in, D. is able to use the flat not only as a hiding place but also as a secure spot in which to kill one of his enemies. After the man is killed, D. leaves the body on the premises for the mysterious Miss Glover to discover on her return. Through such references Greene was able to create a private detective mystery, which only he and Dorothy could solve. As avid book collectors, they also had the joy of knowing that their secret was hidden inside a murder mystery.

Because Dorothy's own reputation as a children's author has faded, her only chance for immortality may lie in the pages of *The Confidential Agent.* But Greene was too busy making private jokes to do her character justice. Her flat is described as having a "stuffy female" atmosphere, and the general look of the place makes D. assume that Miss Glover is a dull, "unmarried ageing woman." Although she never appears in the novel, her nosy boyfriend— Fortescue—shows up and reveals that their great passion is attending religious meetings in such places as Crowborough. Fortescue is so full of love for his fellow man, and so absurdly stupid, that he overlooks D.'s illicit entry, as well as the fact that the body lying on the floor is dead. This farce must have given Greene and Dorothy great laughs at the time. They may have only dimly understood that it would be her best chance at a lasting monument.

II

Written in record time, and under the influence of those Benzedrine breakfasts, *The Confidential Agent* offers the first overt evidence of Greene's talent for black humor. On one level this is a very funny book. But Greene does not seem to have started it with the intention of being funny. In fact, he did not even plan to publish it under his own name. The original manuscript identifies the author as Henry Gough. In contrast to the serious story of the whiskey priest's failure to win glory, *The Confidential Agent* was meant to be a popular thriller that would earn some quick cash, and Greene was not sure it was worth calling his own. Wisely, he threw out the pseudonym before the book went to press. It belongs under his name, but the humor in the middle part of the book is unexpected. After starting with the grim mood of a tough thriller, Greene slowly begins to develop a lighter touch, which perhaps owes something to an emotional swing caused by Benzedrine.

The first section could not be much more depressing. The hero D. arrives in England on a mission to arrange secret deliveries of British coal to his beleaguered country, which is caught up in a brutal civil war in a distant part of Europe. He represents a left-wing government that bears some similarity to that of the Spanish Republic, but the connection with Spain is extremely vague. In any event, it does not really matter what side he is fighting on. For various reasons, no one trusts him, and his friends are as dangerous to him as his enemies. He has suffered so much during his country's civil war that he has almost lost the will to fight back. His hopes for his mission are not high, and he is unsure whether its success will make any difference in the outcome of the war.

His lack of vitality makes him a ready victim. Soon after he lands in England, he is severely beaten, shot at, and robbed. Everyone seems to want him dead, and the reader begins expecting him to be killed at any moment. He does not appear to have anything to live for. His wife has been killed in the war, and he seems too old and weak to put up a good struggle. Although he is only forty-five, he looks and feels much older. Before the war broke out, he was a peaceful scholar of the medieval period, and now he has found himself thrown into a barbaric war that has pushed his country into a modern version of the Dark Ages.

But suddenly he comes back to life. The catalyst of his regeneration is the cruel death of a young maid in his London hotel. She has helped to protect him, and her kindness results in her murder by people who are supposed to be on D.'s side. The murder is then made to seem like a suicide, and D. is implicated as the man who drove the poor girl to kill herself. This outrage is finally too much for him to take, and he resolves not to be terrorized anymore. What is extraordinary is that, once he has allowed real rage to enter his heart again, he undergoes a sweeping transformation. He immediately looks younger and stronger. Rage is like a tonic, and under its influence the meek scholar becomes a determined killer.

It is one thing to show young thugs such as Raven and Pinkie in the throes of a murderous rage, but the middle-aged D. does not make a convincing killer. Greene lets him play that part, but at the same time he is given a better function. The rage loosens his stiff personality and allows him to laugh at the anarchy of life. His sharp, unrestrained wit becomes a greater satisfaction to him than his lust for revenge.

His best satire is directed against the pompous fools who run the Entrenationo Language Centre in London. The head of the organization, Dr. Bellows, believes that he is at the forefront of a movement that will revolutionize the world, uniting all people by giving them a common language. None of his followers questions the simplicity of his vision, and he does not realize that one of D.'s enemies is using the center as a hiding place. The funniest scene in the novel takes place when D. abducts his enemy from the center. While he points a concealed pistol at the man and leads him away, he distracts Dr. Bellows and others with extravagant promises to establish an Entrenationo branch in his own country. They are so overjoyed by this news that they do not hear the abducted man's pleas for help, expressed in their own silly terms. *"Mi korda,"* he says, in an effort to indicate that he is begging for help with all his heart.

But the more one knows about Greene's source of humor, the harder it is to laugh along with him. It is easy to forget that D. is using comedy as a smoke screen for a possible murder, but it is not easy to overlook the cruelty of Greene's jokes against Alexander Korda and the Jewish capitalist in the novel, Furtstein. Greene cannot create anything—even good comedy—without finding a way to give it a painful edge. He makes you laugh, then laughs at you for understanding only half the joke. D. is unable to kill his enemy directly, but, during the scene at Miss Glover's in which he tries to kill the man, Greene does his best to twist the reader's pity for the victim into uneasy laughter. In a scene that echoes Raven's attempt to kill Anne Crowder in a bathroom, D. pushes his intended victim into Miss Glover's bathroom and fires a shot at him. He misses and leaves the room, but the man later comes out on his knees following after D. like some comical character in a Marx Brothers film. And then, without warning, the man falls forward and dies of a heart attack. D. jokes that his man is dead but laments that he cannot take proper credit for a real murder. The joke falls flat, and the scene recovers only when Fortescue puts his nose through the door and tries to investigate something he does not understand.

Having teased his readers with an unpredictable mixture of comedy and pathos, Greene sets up his biggest trick—a happy ending. At one point in the novel he makes fun of people who like traditional stories with punishments for the wicked and rewards for the virtuous. As D. is sitting in a cinema watching a big musical film, the narrative is able to comment on the unrealistic elements of the story. All the pretty characters in the film struggle hard to become successful, but no one is allowed to become a loser. By the end, everyone is bathed in the warm glow of happiness. Fortunes are made and careers are launched. It is enough to make Greene sick. It is the same sentimental approach—from the heart—that Greene associated with the "vulgar" productions of Louis B. Mayer and Korda. But it is also the sort of thing that audiences supposedly like, especially the ones who might buy an exciting thriller called *The Confidential Agent,* with an angry hero, lots of action, and a pretty young English girl who falls for the hero.

Rose Cullen is young enough to be the hero's daughter, and she readily admits that her love for him is connected to her need for a father. She is the illegitimate daughter of an English peer who has never paid her much attention, with the result that Rose is so starved for affection that she will throw herself at any older man. Furtstein occupies her attention until D. enters her life. Mysterious and dangerous, he is far more interesting than old "Furt," and Rose eventually decides to run away with him. With people such as Furtstein making a mess of England, even D.'s war-ravaged country seems to offer a worthwhile escape for an English Rose who has never found happiness in her own land.

In the best style of a flashy Hollywood director, Greene makes the reader wait until the very end of the story before revealing that the hero has won the girl. The scene is a perfect parody of the Hollywood ending. The short last section of the novel is even called "The End." D. is shown standing on the deck of the ship that is taking him back home. His mission to secure the crucial supply of coal has failed, and his brief stay in "peaceful" England has turned out to be as violent as anything he experienced in his country's civil war. As he stares out to sea, with the wind blowing and the dark sea churning, he hears a familiar voice at his back. At the last minute Rose boarded the ship, and now she stands beside him, ready to face whatever perils lie ahead. The reader can almost imagine the fade-out, the lush strings, and the words "The End" printed over the romantic figures of our hero and heroine. And all this is made possible by good old Furt, who decided not to marry Rose after all. He let her run after D., Rose says, because he wanted to make a sentimental gesture. Just as the Kordas and Mayers use their films for sentimental gestures, Greene uses Furtstein to introduce the necessary gesture that will give his story its happy ending.

But any reader who recognizes Greene's parody can see that the ending is really not happy at all but painfully sad. Yes, the couple are reunited, but their voyage is a suicidal one, and they both know it. Having discovered in England that his friends are just as likely to kill him as his enemies, D. will most certainly find more "friends" waiting to kill him when he arrives home. After all, he is returning from his mission empty-handed, and someone is sure to explain his failure by accusing him of treachery. The "happy ending" will last only as long as the voyage. Looking closely at Rose in their last scene, D. notices that she seems to have aged suddenly. Her impending death is already reflected in her face.

Greene wanted all the sentimental readers to buy his book and make him lots of money, but he could not take the job seriously, and the public was quick to detect the false note. His parody was not understood, and serious fans of thrillers no doubt disliked the strange comic tone that abruptly entered the novel. Not even his fellow reviewers at *The Spectator* appreciated what he was trying to do. His literary editor at the paper, Derek Verschoyle, condemned it as a "straightforward thriller of slight literary pretension" and accused the author of trying to win favor in Hollywood. The editor was right about the novelist's interest in the movies, but he did not see that Greene wanted to win over the movie moguls by ridiculing them. And the scheme worked. Warner Bros. bought the rights to the film and did all the predictable things with it, casting Charles Boyer as D. and Peter Lorre as the pathetic man who is frightened to death by D.'s gun, and miscasting Lauren Bacall as Rose. Bacall later complained bitterly that she was asked to play a "British broad" who was "totally straight and dreary."

Greene's assumption was that the novel would far outsell *The Power and the Glory,* but on that point he was mistaken. *The Confidential Agent* sold only 5,000 copies in Britain, whereas the complicated, less suspenseful tale of the whiskey priest sold 30,000 copies in 1940–41, a remarkable feat considering the dire conditions during that dark period of the war. Better yet, it won him respect. In 1940 he was given the Hawthornden Prize for *The Power and the Glory*. After writing ten novels in eleven years, this was his first major prize. And he was also the subject of an important critical article in Cyril Connolly's new magazine, *Horizon*. In May 1940 the magazine published Arthur Calder-Marshall's "The Works of Graham Greene," which praised the writer for his poetic techniques but objected to his "Catholic" philosophy and the implausibility of certain scenes and characters.

Critics of the 1940s did not know what to make of a writer whose "Catholic" novel *The Power and the Glory* features a seven-year-old seductress. Calder-Marshall, who knew Mexico, politely pointed out that he had never seen such a thing on his travels: "When the priest, returning to a village, where his daughter by an Indian woman lives, finds the child at the age of seven tittering with precocious sexuality and obscenely exposing herself to her father, my certainty that this is untrue of an Indian village child makes it hard for me to judge the validity of the suspicion that the incident is as wrong aesthetically as it is factually." In the strained syntax of this statement, one can feel poor Calder-Marshall squirming in his chair as he writes, wondering to himself why any serious Catholic writer would think that a young girl would behave in such a way. Of course, her presence in the novel tells us nothing about Mexico. But Calder-Marshall could not dare to think that it might tell us something about Greene's imagination. Still, he must be given proper credit for one major contribution to Greene criticism. He was the first critic to use the convenient term *Greeneland* to describe the world portrayed in the novels. When other critics began using the term, Greene complained that it was a meaningless word. He chose to forget that he had suggested the pun in *A Gun for Sale*, which features the word *Greenland* in a song lyric invented by the novelist.

III

One reason that Greene worked so hard in 1939 is that he wanted to produce as much as possible before the war put an end to his full-time literary career. When he was called before a draft board near the end of the year, he was still trying to finish *The Power and the Glory*. By offering to join the infantry, he was able to postpone his call-up and was thus allowed to complete his novel without further interruption. He continued to avoid military service for the duration of the war.

First, he took a job in the new Ministry of Information, then he served in the ARP, and finally he settled into an organization that seemed right for him—the Secret Intelligence Service.

His position at the Ministry of Information allowed him to use some of his talents. As a "specialist" in the literary division, he was expected to "commission and stimulate the writing of books and pamphlets" for the war effort—in other words, he was a frontline officer in the propaganda war. He joined the ministry in April 1940 and quickly produced a piece of propaganda for the American market. At that period in the war, it was crucial to cultivate support for Britain in an America that was still under the influence of isolationists. Many Americans could not understand why a war in Europe should concern them, and it was the job of the Ministry of Information to make certain that the case for helping Britain was put forcefully to the American public. Greene's contribution to this cause was a short story called "The Lieutenant Died Last." Shrewdly omitting any reference to his job as a government propagandist, Greene submitted the story to the weekly magazine *Collier's,* which in those days enjoyed a large readership in the American heartland. The story was accepted and appeared on June 29, 1940, only a few weeks after the evacuation of the British Expeditionary Force from the beaches of Dunkirk. The time was right for showing America that the brave British people deserved all their support in the war against Nazi aggression.

At first glance Greene's story seems perfect for the job. It concerns a German sabotage mission in the heart of England. Twelve commandos parachute into a small village, lock up all the residents in the pub, and march off to blow up a major railway line. The villagers can do nothing but wait helplessly—all except one elderly fellow whom the Germans overlooked. Old Purves courageously follows the Germans with an ancient rifle and proceeds to gun them down one by one, killing last the officer, the lieutenant of the title. Because of the actions of one valiant Englishman, a daring raid is defeated, and the village can rest easy again, secure in the knowledge that their fellow citizens will fight for freedom with the same determination shown by Old Purves.

War has made men do strange things, but this summary does not sound like the sort of thing Greene would write. An optimistic patriot could be told that the story was meant to flesh out such a summary, but the actual details show Greene twisting everything to England's disadvantage. Although Old Purves does methodically kill off the Germans, his daring deed is fueled not by raw courage but by a bottle of whiskey. He is the village drunk and a notorious poacher.

Because he is hiding in wait for game on the local aristocrat's estate, he is able to escape the notice of the Germans. He possesses his old firearm illegally, and, after he has heroically defeated the Germans, his ungrateful neighbors throw him in jail for a week on a charge of poaching. The village itself is a shabby little place, with none of the traditional charms that might appeal to Americans.

Although the bare plot might have won over a few literal-minded bureaucrats in the Ministry of Information, the details reinforce the kinds of stereotypes that made so many God-fearing, teetotaling Americans reluctant to fight for the Old Country. They saw it as a snobbish place full of lords and ladies, big estates, and poor villages where people spent too much time in pubs and not enough time in church. The *Collier's* illustrator helped to promote these notions by depicting Old Purves sprawled against a wall of the aristocrat's estate. He is sound asleep with a large bottle of whiskey between his legs, and in the distance the German paratroopers are beginning their descent.

If the story arouses sympathy for anyone, it is for the Germans. The villagers are surly and vindictive, whereas the German soldiers are polite, efficient, and humane. When a young villager tries to escape from their custody, they fire at him but deliberately aim at his legs to avoid killing him. He is then carefully carried back to the pub. Greene specifically calls their actions humane, which sets up an interesting contrast with the drunken hero. After Old Purves has conquered the German unit, he finds that the lieutenant is still alive. The soldier is unarmed, and the drunk has run out of ammunition. But the officer begs to be shot, and, when Old Purves spots the lieutenant's revolver lying nearby, he quickly decides to pick it up and finish off the man in cold blood. Greene neatly avoids presenting this scene directly—it is alluded to in a way that might make it difficult for some readers to catch. But this act undercuts any sympathy one might have for the Englishman. If Old Purves had shared the humane attitude of his enemy, he would have tried to save his prisoner. The title, therefore, is not a glorious reference to the brave battle fought by the lone defender of Mother England but a chilling reminder of the lieutenant's murder. If a subtle German propagandist had written the story, he could not have done a better job of making England look bad to the American public.

It should come as no surprise that Greene lasted only six months as a literary "specialist" in the Ministry of Information. But no one ever took him to task for sending his story to *Collier's*. In fact, "The Lieutenant Died Last" became the basis for one of the great classics of wartime British filmmaking, *Went the Day Well?* Greene sold the rights to Ealing Studios, and the film was made in 1942 by Alberto Cavalcanti, a friend of Greene. A team of screenwriters changed almost everything in the original story to make it more patriotic and straightforward. In the film the Germans are nasty fellows who invade an idyllic village. They come not in their own uniforms, as they do in Greene's story, but in British uniforms. And they are assisted by a local quisling. Old Purves is reduced to playing a bit part and dies a hero's death without having to gun down all the Germans by himself. Instead the villagers are able to launch an attack on their captors, and they emerge victorious from the bloody battle. "Went the day well?" a poetic caption asks at the beginning of the film. The question is posed by the valiant dead who did not survive long enough to know the outcome of their battle but who nevertheless went proudly to their graves knowing that they had died for freedom.

Reviewing the film in 1942, Dilys Powell had only praise for its patriotic message: "For once, the English people are shown as capable of individual and concerted resourcefulness in a fight and not merely steady in disaster." The success of the film shifted attention away from the original story, and for many years it was available only in the old bound volumes of the now defunct *Collier's* magazine. But shortly before his death, Greene allowed the story to be reprinted in his final collection of short fiction, *The Last Word*. As he confessed to one interviewer, he never bothered to see the film. "I was in Africa when it came out," he explained. "My sister saw it on television recently and didn't like it at all." He also made it clear that he preferred his own title, but he slyly refrained from explaining why.

After Greene left the Ministry of Information, he took a final shot at his colleagues in the story "Men at Work." At the time he wrote it, he told John Lehmann that every word of it was true except for the change of names. He depicts the ministry as a meaningless organization staffed by idlers and self-important hacks. Endless meetings are conducted, but nothing ever gets accomplished. While people busy themselves in a long series of discussions on the content of a pamphlet about the French war effort, the Germans occupy Paris and France surrenders. While debates rage about distributing pamphlets at the New York World's Fair, the fair closes.

The main character in the story is Richard Skate, who endures the dreary meetings with cool detachment, much as Greene must have done. But, occasionally, Skate allows himself to throw a sharp remark at one of his boring colleagues. After news of another bombing raid is delivered at one of the interminable meetings, an official quickly tries to turn the discussion back to a more pressing subject. How will a pamphlet on the British Empire—written by someone named Bone—be distributed? The absurdity of debating pamphlets while the enemy drops bombs proves to be too much for Skate. When his colleague demands an immediate release of the pamphlet, Skate remarks, "That'll show them." His sarcasm makes little impression, however, and the talk soon shifts to the next pressing subject—preparation of the new meat-marketing leaflet.

Unable to tolerate more meetings of this kind, Greene turned with relief to the real dangers of working as an air-raid warden. He found it enjoyable to live in a city under siege and liked to inspect bomb damage after a raid. "I loved the blitz," he recalled. "It was wonderful to wake up and know you were still alive and hear glass being swept up in the streets." He also had fond memories of walking through town at night. "In the blackout you could see the stars. Something, of course, you can no longer do in any city." The novelist Rose Macaulay, who liked to chat with Greene at literary parties, said of him, "How completely those war years were his milieu. He loved walking the bombed streets, wrapped in a shabby mackintosh, admiring the craters, the fires, and the tumbling buildings."

As a warden Greene had ample opportunities to see horrific damage. One night he watched three fire engines run over a corpse lying in the street, and he saw a thief rummaging through the pockets of a man who was bleeding to death. On other nights he saw body parts strewn among rubble and felt the blasts from bombs falling within yards of him. When one explosion forced him to hit the pavement, his hand was cut by shards of glass. And while he was back at Post No. One getting the wound bandaged, three more bombs went off outside and knocked out all the windows. An enduring image from this time was the sight of scores of people standing outside their damaged homes, each looking ghostly in clothes covered with dust and blood. The novelist in Greene was careful to note such details, storing them in his mind for possible future use, although he was well aware that one night the right bomb might suddenly wipe out his future.

The fury of the blitz did not take him completely by surprise. For several years he had been thinking that another world war was inevitable and had tried to imagine the damage it might cause. In "At Home," an essay written in October 1940, he welcomes the blitz as the necessary means of destroying a corrupt world. After a long delay Britain is finally having to pay the price for its wicked ways. Greene is not quite clear about the nature of those sins, but the main point is that he feels better living in a world where everyone—not just Graham Greene—is surrounded by nightmarish torments. He speaks fondly of the bombs and looks forward to many more nights of fires and broken glass. Hell has moved to London, Liverpool, Bristol, and all the other bombed cities.

In the 1930s Greene had to go all the way to Liberia and Mexico to find suitably realistic patches of hell on earth, but now the flames are right outside his door. Describing his state of mind as he sits in his shelter at night listening to the bombers flying overhead, he says that he feels grateful for having met a devil such as Col. Elwood Davis. Their encounter helped to prepare him for the evils of a European war. After seeing the colonel, he was ready for anything. And now that Hitler is trying to kill him every night, he has a spot of "tenderness" in his heart for Colonel Davis. Thanks to the colonel, he feels perfectly "at home" in his dark shelter as the sirens blare and bombs explode.

Fortunately, Vivien and the children were not required to be with Greene during this time. He was happy to have them out of the way, for their safety as well as for his pleasure. Mysterious Miss Glover was the best companion for him during this period, and the war gave him the perfect excuse for keeping his wife and children at a distance. But Vivien was miserable in Crowborough. Living with Greene's mother was difficult, and Vivien did not find the town a sociable place. One of her friends recalled her "unhappy wartime tale about pushing the pram up and down the main street trying to find someone to talk to, and how it always ended with her having to buy buns from the milk roundsman, and so, some social life!"

After several months of this life, Vivien was able to find a new refuge in Oxford, where she and the children were allowed to stay in rooms at Trinity College. After having enjoyed the luxury of Number 14, North Side, she was slow to adapt to her cramped quarters, and, worst of all, she knew that she could not return to her old house. In October 1940, while Greene was thinking of how much he felt at home in the blitz, a German bomb caused heavy damage to their former home at Number 14, making it uninhabitable. The news was devastating to Vivien. To comfort herself, she bought a small dolls' house and began filling it with furniture, carpets, and curtains that she made by hand. Building a toy home was her escape from the loneliness and destruction of the war. She held fast to her childlike dreams of domestic peace, spending long winter evenings creating new comforts for a miniature home that she could keep safe from misfortune. No one could break it up, nothing could make her leave it behind. And, meanwhile, back in Bloomsbury, her absent husband sat in his shelter with another woman and dreamed of more bombs, more fires, more pain.

CHAPTER FIFTEEN

TOP SECRET:
OFFICER 59200

Greene never wanted to be a full-time spy. There was too much work involved, too much responsibility, and far too much supervision. The ideal thing was to do an odd job, have a bit of fun, then get back to the more important business of writing. As he discovered at the Ministry of Information, he was not cut out for life within a bureaucratic organization. But in the summer of 1941, his sister Elisabeth helped talk him into becoming a regular officer in the Secret Intelligence Service.

She had worked for SIS since 1938 and was well aware that her brother shared the family obsession with spying. For one thing, he had done some "miscellaneous" spying for the service in 1940, although the nature of that work is not spelled out in his file. He was under some pressure to give more of his time to the war effort. Since leaving the Ministry of Information, he had been trying to balance his ARP work at night with a day job at *The Spectator*. He was the magazine's literary editor, but he constantly disagreed with his superior and routinely threatened to resign. If he left the job, he might be forced to undertake some boring, underpaid war work. He feared that he might end up digging latrines with other middle-aged men in the Pioneer Corps.

In July 1941 he was given approval to join SIS, and the next month he resigned from *The Spectator*. On his application he listed his uncle Sir Graham Greene as one of his references. One advantage of the new job was its good pay. He received 700 pounds a year, and, like all officers in the service at that time, he was not required to pay any tax on his income. There was also an extra 100 pounds a year for an overseas allowance. At first the plan was to send Greene to Liberia, but then someone took a look at *Journey Without Maps* and decided that the writer might not be welcome in the country. So his destination was changed to the colonial capital of Freetown, Sierra Leone. The town's large harbor attracted a great many foreign ships that needed watching, and there was some enemy espionage activity in the neighboring Vichy French colonies. As a cover Greene was placed in the service of the Colonial Office, but it took a long time for his superiors to establish what his exact job would be. In the end the choice was a most unlikely one. He was made a colonial policeman, with a vague connection to the CID Special Branch.

To prepare him for his mission, the service sent Greene to a training school in Oxford for a few weeks. He had no trouble learning how to do simple tasks, but, when he was given instruction in how to ride a motorcycle, his efforts resulted only in crashes. Operating any kind of motor vehicle was beyond him, and the instructors finally decided that saving their remaining motorcycles was more important than teaching Greene to stay upright on the machines. He then came down with a bad cold and had to spend several days recuperating at the North Oxford Nursing Home. Trying to put a brave face on his unpromising start as a member of the secret service, he informed his superiors that it was not entirely his fault that he had become ill. He put the blame "chiefly" on having to run back and forth in the cold to the outside lavatories at the training school.

Various problems kept him from sailing to West Africa until early December. When he left Liverpool on a new cargo ship, he and other passengers were assigned to stand watch for submarines and to man machine guns. In the middle of the voyage he made the unsettling discovery that they were carrying a cargo of TNT and depth charges. One good hit from a torpedo, and the ship might have been blown to pieces. To keep up his spirits in the submarine-infested waters, Greene drank heavily. There was no lack of alcohol aboard, and he was soon suffering from the effects of his constant drinking. He woke up with a bad hangover on Christmas morning and promptly began trying to "cure" it by consuming a bottle of champagne. Staying drunk was the best way to forget all the TNT he was sitting on. But, despite the great danger of encountering German U-boats in the

Atlantic, the ship was able to make it safely to Africa, and Greene was spared having to fire a machine gun while suffering from one of his hangovers.

As he soon learned, his work in Freetown was not difficult, but there were periods in which the burdens of the job could suddenly increase and result in some long days. Cable traffic was occasionally heavy, and each message needed to be decoded by a laborious process. Also, when neutral ships sailed into the harbor, he was required to examine their cargo for contraband items and to investigate any suspicious passengers. But on most days he was free to take long naps in the afternoon or to sip drinks at the bar of the City Hotel. To convince people that he was a policeman, he tried to make an appearance at the police station each morning. It was there that he sent and received coded messages to his superiors in Lagos and London. He was friendly toward a few of his colleagues, but the only one who made a lasting impression was the middle-aged commissioner of police—a weary veteran of many years in the colonial service. The drab life of Captain Brodie, as the man was known, helped give Greene the basic idea for his hero in *The Heart of the Matter*. Hardly any effort was made to alter the name. With a promotion and the substitution of three letters, Captain Brodie became Major Scobie.

For the most part, Greene's life as a spy in West Africa was a comedy of errors. A large safe was delivered to him, and he was instructed to keep his code books in it. He dutifully locked up the code books but was then unable to open the safe. Eventually, he had to destroy it in order to rescue his vital codes. As a way of covering up the trouble, he told headquarters that the safe had been damaged on the voyage out and that he would require a replacement. A new one was sent, but other shipments found their way to the bottom of the Atlantic, thanks to the work of the German submarines.

He was given the use of a house situated below the main European enclave of Hill Station, and he soon discovered why few of his fellow countrymen wanted it. Besides the rats in the bathroom, there was a major problem every time it rained. The land surrounding the house turned into a bog. To add to the smells of stagnant water, a strong odor would drift in from a nearby piece of open land, which the local people used as a communal toilet. Greene immediately complained about the place to his superiors in London:

This is not a government house, and there is no larder: there is also a plague of house-flies which come from the African bush lavatories round the house. Meat, too, without a refrigerator has to be eaten as soon as it is bought, which means it is as a rule appallingly tough. Can I have authority to buy a refrigerator? This means an expenditure of about £55 if bought locally. They are very scarce, and like cars, can be sold again for at least the purchase price.

Such was the glamorous world of espionage for Officer 59200. To his relief, his urgent request for a refrigerator was granted, but while he waited patiently for its arrival from England, a torpedo sank the boat carrying it. Meanwhile, conditions at his house continued to irritate him. At night dogs howled in a neighboring slum, and the noise became such a distraction that Greene sometimes dashed out in the dark to throw rocks in the direction of the slum, swearing at the inhabitants while he hurled his missiles. As his houseboy informed him, the poor people were not at all pleased with their new white neighbor's nighttime assaults. With a few improvements, this house later found its way into *The Heart of the Matter* as Scobie's residence.

One problem seemed to follow another. His cook went mad and chased the houseboy with a hatchet. After watching a Ginger Rogers film one night, Greene stumbled home from the cinema in the dark and fell six feet into an open drain. He was covered in excrement. He made plans to take train journeys into the interior; then week after week the trains would not run. A local network of government spies routinely passed information to him, but he quickly found out that almost none of it was reliable. The spies were illiterate and hopelessly corrupt. Numbers meant nothing to them. He would ask a few men to report on the traffic near the border, and one would tell him that 200 vehicles had been spotted, another would say 100, and a third would say 50. "Any number over, say, twenty must be considered highly dubious," Greene concluded. Indulging in some arrogant racial generalizations, he told headquarters: "The African, it should be noted, has no sense of colour, and cannot copy markings, so that he is useless for identifications." He also wrote: "One may note, in passing, that cleverness in an African agent is not altogether desirable as their plain account may then be embellished with one or two picturesque features."

He did not have much luck in his efforts to recruit his own agents. Although there was a large population of Syrians in Freetown, Greene found them "completely unreliable." He tried to create some bold plans for espionage operations in the French colonies, but he could never get approval for his best ideas. One plan was to recruit a woman to manage a "roaming" brothel. The notion was that she and her girls would move from town to town, discover various secrets from the Vichy French colonial officers, and pass the information along to Greene. By searching the police files in Freetown, he found the madam he wanted and sent all the necessary information to head-quarters. Giving her the code name B, Greene said of the woman, "She seems to have many of the qualifications we're looking for." He described her as a mixed race female, aged thirty, who spoke several languages and was able to read and write. "I hear from another source," Greene added, "that she is an admirer of Kipling!" Best of all, he was able to report that "she has earned her living on her back for a good many years."

As far as the operation itself was concerned, he was able to assure headquarters that "the cost would not be very large, as prices in these parts are low, and B. should be able to make a prosperous living quite apart from our payments." It was an invaluable opportunity to oper-ate his own prostitution business, and to make the British taxpayer cover all the costs. Instead of laughing at him, his superiors took the idea seriously and only after "careful consideration" decided not to accept it. Their reason was that the proposed madam would not be able to find reliable recruits. Headquarters had somehow learned that most of the really good prostitutes in the French colonies were already working for the Vichy government, and they were afraid that Greene's madam would inadvertently staff her brothel with double agents.

Another daring but rejected plan involved staging an escape from the Freetown jail. Greene had learned that a very left-wing official of the African Youth League had recently been arrested, and he thought that it would be good to trick the young radical into becoming a spy for imperialist Britain. As he explained the plan to headquarters, he wanted to recruit two agents who would be placed in the man's cell and would then talk him into making an escape with them. After they were allowed to make their getaway, the three would cross the bor-der, and Greene's two agents would involve the man in a Vichy French espionage scheme. He would then be lured back to Sierra Leone, confronted with evidence of his spying, and blackmailed into serving as a double agent under Greene's control. It was the sort of fiendish plot that an older Pinkie might have created, and it was almost put into action. It was turned down partly because the colo-nial governor of Sierra Leone was worried that too many people had already escaped from the jail, and partly because London wanted not an African agent but new European ones. The rejection was a disap-pointment to Greene, who was rather proud of his scheme and clearly relished the chance to blackmail the earnest radical. As he told head-quarters, once the man was brought back to Sierra Leone, it would be "an easy matter to put on the screw."

Greene was doing his best to create intrigue in a relatively quiet part of the world, and, although London seemed to appreciate his show of initiative, his superior in West Africa—the station chief in Lagos—was not impressed. According to Greene, the officer resented him for being amateurish, and gradually they developed an intense dislike for each other. Greene sent him snide telegrams, and he responded by holding back Greene's pay and private correspondence. In July 1942 Greene complained to the officer in Lagos about his lack of funds and spoke of having to borrow money or stall creditors.

The dispute reached a climax in August 1942, when Greene asked for permission to meet a potential new agent—Father Parsell of the Holy Cross Mission in Liberia. Greene had met Father Parsell on his journey through Liberia in the 1930s and was now trying to make him one of his chief agents. He believed that the priest would be able to undertake missions for him in Vichy territory. He arranged to con-tact him at the northeast border of Sierra Leone. In his opinion, this was a vital meeting, but the Lagos officer insisted that Greene stay in Freetown to search a recently arrived ship. Greene fired back an angry response, telling the officer that he had arranged the contact on the Liberian border several weeks previously and that he could not be in two places at once.

Although he obeyed the order to stay in Freetown, Greene was so angry that he sent a letter of resignation to London, complaining that a "possible chance of penetration of French territory has been lost." He told his contact at headquarters, "I am not anxious to embarrass you, but I should be glad if you would relieve me of post when you can find suitable representative." Headquarters refused his resigna-tion, but his complaint against his superior brought results. He was allowed to bypass the Lagos office and to deal directly with head-quarters in all matters. Indeed, his superiors in London wrote that the Lagos chief was "most unreasonable" in his relations with Greene. It was a small triumph, but the real problem was that Greene was tired of trying to find excitement in a minor posting. He wanted to go back to London, and in September he asked headquarters to bring him home, arguing that he was not accomplishing anything of value.

Another six months passed before his request was granted, and, in the meantime, there was talk of sending him to other remote stations. When headquarters suggested Léopoldville, he was able to avoid the transfer by pointing out that his "spoken French almost does not exist." The only place he was willing to go in Africa was Mozambique, and that was because his friend Malcolm Muggeridge was there. Before leaving England, Greene had recruited Muggeridge into the service. He was willing to endure a longer stay in Africa if he could spend time drinking with Muggeridge and cooking up wild plans for serving God and king in East Africa. But in February 1943 he was finally told that he could close his office and come home.

Before he left Freetown, Greene prepared a detailed summary of the characters of his colleagues in the colonial police. It was an official evaluation done without their knowledge. Of all the officers, he was most sympathetic to Captain Brodie: "Brodie has served very hard for nineteen years in this colony, often in the most difficult times with only one white officer on whom to rely. . . . He is now an elderly and very tired man on the verge of a breakdown. He lives alone, goes out practically not at all. When he is not at his desk, he is alone at his house." This short description marked the beginning of the process that would eventually transform Brodie into Scobie, but a great deal of Greene's own personality would also go into the character. In addition, he took one specific detail from a junior officer, of whom he remarked: "His relations with the Syrians are very suspect." In the novel Scobie's relationship with the villainous Syrian trader Yusef creates suspicion in official circles long before any hard evidence justifies it.

When Greene arrived back in England, there was a position waiting for him in Section V, and the new job represented a big step up the chain of command. From a secret location outside London, he would supervise counterintelligence operations in neutral Portugal, a country teeming with enemy agents. It did not seem to matter that he knew practically nothing about the country and could neither read nor speak the language. It was just assumed that he would get by somehow, especially under the expert guidance of his boss—Kim Philby.

II

The secret location of Section V was a large country house in the Hertfordshire town of St. Albans. From this pleasant retreat, Philby's Iberian Department kept track of operations at the SIS stations in Madrid, Lisbon, Gibraltar, and Tangier. Greene was put in charge of a card-index file containing the names of all the known German agents in Portugal. The cast of characters was constantly changing, but one legendary figure stood above the others. His code name was Garbo. In 1941 Garbo had offered his services to German intelligence officers operating in Madrid and had been accepted on the understanding that he would go to England and develop a spy ring. But Juan Pujol García—Garbo's real name—had no intention of going to England. Armed with a good map of Great Britain, a Blue Guide to England, and a couple of standard military reference works, he made his way to Lisbon and began giving the Nazis wonderfully detailed reports on Britain's defenses—making up everything as he went along.

Garbo pretended that his information was gathered from a long list of agents whom he had recruited throughout the country. There was an RAF officer at Fighter Command headquarters, a pretty secretary in a government ministry, a Venezuelan man in Glasgow, a waiter named Fred in Soho, and so on. All of them were fictional characters, but the Germans were so delighted to have such a large collection of spies working for them in Britain that they "became entirely dependent on Garbo, regarding him as a sensitive, quarrelsome genius of priceless value." The Nazis were only too happy to believe his tales of convoy movements, troop exercises, and the weak moral character of the British people. Although he had never been to Liverpool, Garbo vividly described scenes from the city's night life, including an account of "drunken orgies and slack morals at amusement centres."

In early 1942 Garbo finally made his identity known to the SIS man in Lisbon and agreed to continue feeding the Germans false information. He was taken to London, and from there he created new stories with the help of the British intelligence services. His list of fictional agents grew to twenty-seven names, at least one of whom "died" of cancer and was replaced. As a way of adding to Garbo's credibility, the authorities in London pretended that he had been arrested for suspicious conduct. He was "released" a few days later for lack of evidence, and the Germans were so grateful to have him back on the job that he was sent a special message of congratulations. In recognition of his service, Hitler awarded him the Iron Cross Class II.

Although Greene was not directly involved with Garbo, he knew the details of the scheme. The false reports to the Germans were always sent through Lisbon. Garbo told the Nazis that one of his agents worked for an airline and was able to smuggle out the reports on regular flights to Lisbon. In fact, SIS men in Lisbon handled the exchange of communications between Garbo and his German contact, sending the reports to "accommodation addresses" in Lisbon and using a safe deposit box to gather new instructions. The service also collected the generous financial payments that the Germans made to their "trusted" agent.

Garbo was by far the most important agent involved in Greene's area of responsibility, and his importance grew as the date of the Normandy invasion approached. Throughout the early months of 1944, he sent convincing reports telling the Germans that an invasion "would not happen for a long time." In his own way Garbo was a great comedian, a practical joker whose victims included the mighty Hitler and the German High Command. Such a monumental comic exercise was the sort of thing that Greene would have enjoyed creating. Like Greene, Garbo was a fiction maker who loved using his imagination to fool the great and the gullible. You can almost hear the snicker of the merry author in the report Garbo gave the Nazis six weeks before D Day, warning them not to believe rumors that an invasion is imminent:

> I am surprised to hear . . . of the nervousness which exists in official circles with regard to the Allied offensive which has been the subject of so much cackling, and I am very surprised, more so after the continuous reports of my agents which I have for some while past been transmitting, telling you that only preparations but no indicative action of concentration is noted. . . . I recommend therefore once again calm and confidence in our work. The Allies have used tricks to date, and it is deplorable that those in Germany should give credence to the great majority of them.

If Garbo's fantastic operation sounds familiar, it is because Greene adapted much of it for the plot of *Our Man in Havana*. He never mentioned that Garbo had been the inspiration for his novel, but there are obvious similarities between the real story and Wormold's imaginary spy ring in Cuba. Like Garbo, Wormold becomes a great spy simply by making things up. His absurd fabrications are eagerly accepted, and he is encouraged to provide more and more secret information. Using a big map of Cuba, a few books, and a copy of *Time* magazine, Wormold is able to create a world of espionage and to make a tidy profit from the fruits of his imagination, just as novelists do. He develops his own cast of characters, creating a list of informers who have specific jobs and interests. His exotic dancer, Teresa, collects racy gossip; his whiskey pilot provides air reconnaissance; a professor reveals economic secrets; and an engineer spies on military installations. Their information is believed by Wormold's bosses, but they are nothing more than fictions. The interesting twist in Greene's novel is that the British spies are not the expert handlers of the deception but the dupes. They follow the example of Nazi stupidity, even down to the detail of awarding their worthless man in Havana an official honor—an Order of the British Empire instead of an Iron Cross. It was typical of Greene to turn a joke against his own side, but he also knew that some of his colleagues in SIS could be fooled just as easily as Garbo had fooled the Germans.

As the man at the Portugal desk, Greene was able to follow Garbo's antics closely, but his own opportunities for comic exploits were limited. Most of his work was routine. He kept his files in order, sent coded instructions to Lisbon, and discussed strategy with his chief. A chance to create a good practical joke did not arise until Section V moved its offices back to London, in July 1943. The new building was in Ryder Street, between Piccadilly and St. James's Palace, and one floor was occupied by a fresh contingent of American OSS officers who called their office X-2. Greene took an immediate dislike to the American spies, although he was intrigued by the scholarly head of X-2, Norman Holmes Pearson. A professor of literature at Yale University, Pearson recruited several intelligent young men for the OSS and later did the same for the CIA. He was also a friend of W. H. Auden, who helped him edit *Poets of the English Language*. It was for Pearson that Auden wrote the poem "The Platonic Blow," with its memorable line "I rocked at the shock of his cock."

One of Pearson's disciples was James Jesus Angleton, who also served in the Ryder Street office. Angleton eventually became the chief of the CIA counterintelligence division, where he advocated Pearson's theory that literary people often make good spies. According to one source, Angleton "believed that those trained in the New Criticism, with its seven types of ambiguity, were particularly suited to the interpretation of intelligence data."

Although Pearson and Angleton were obviously worth talking to, Greene thought that the Americans were generally much too brash and innocent, and that they needed to be taught a little lesson. There was a strict rule at the Ryder Street office that all important documents had to be locked up at night. If a bomb hit the building, any papers left lying on the desks might be sent flying into Piccadilly, where they could fall into the hands of all sorts of people. So anyone who violated the rule was fined. The officers who were assigned to night duty had the responsibility of checking for violations. When Greene served his turn as a night guard, he noticed that one of the filing cabinets in the OSS office did not lock properly. Instead of notifying his colleagues of the problem, he took a few documents from

the cabinet, put them on a desk, and arranged for the victim to be
fined. According to him, he was able to repeat this sabotage again and
again. Finally, when it seemed that Pearson was on the verge of catching him, he made a full confession to Philby over drinks at their
favorite pub, and the affair was allowed to end quietly. But Greene
had made his point. The Americans were not the only good spies and
saboteurs in the building.

Greene knew that he could count on a sympathetic hearing from
Philby, who shared his contempt for the Americans. Indeed, there
was much that the two men shared, and they were good companions
from the beginning of their time together in SIS. They not only spent
long hours working together but also frequently joined each other for
lunch and for drinks in the evening. Sometimes they were accompanied by Philby's good friend Tim Milne, who was also an officer in
the Iberian Department and who shared an office with Greene in the
Ryder Street building. Tim Milne was a nephew of A. A. Milne and
had known Philby from the time they were school chums at
Westminster.

In the memoir written after his defection to the Soviet Union, *My
Silent War,* Philby speaks warmly of Greene, describing their association as "wholly delightful" and declaring that he "added to the gaiety
of the service." He recalls with amusement Greene's plan to set up a
roaming brothel in West Africa and says that he was happy to have
him posted to the Iberian Department. Philby writes of him, "He had
a good time sniping at OSS, and his tart comments on incoming correspondence were a daily refreshment." In his introduction to
Philby's book, Greene praises his ex-chief's relaxed administrative
style, personal charm, dedication, and professional skill. The only bad
thing about Philby, Greene says, is that he was too anxious to push
others aside for advancement within SIS. Fastidious about such minor
sins, Greene notes that Philby tried to draw him into these unseemly
efforts to win promotion but that he refused to play the game.

They came from similar backgrounds. Born in 1912, Philby was a
King's Scholar at Westminster School, a Cambridge graduate with a
Second Class degree, and a former correspondent for *The Times.* He
was a handsome man with a strong appetite for sex and drink, and he
was good at hiding his intentions behind a smile and a laugh.
Malcolm Muggeridge once remarked that Philby's charm had a
schoolboyish quality to it. He saw him as a case of arrested development, an overgrown boy who was always trying to prove his manliness. Philby had read one too many boys' adventure stories and was
anxious to put his "juvenile romanticism" into action. "Philby's

drinking," Muggeridge wrote, "struck me as one more aspect of his essential romanticism and immaturity; he had a Hemingwayesque tendency to adulate crooks and frauds as long as they spoke the language of defiance and violence."

But there was also a clear strain of weakness in his character, a hint of deep insecurity and fear behind the manly exterior. He suffered from what Muggeridge called a "truly appalling stutter; it was really shattering." Others who knew Philby did not think the problem was so bad, but Muggeridge thought it was the worst case he had encountered: "As he struggled to get the words out, his hand would convulsively clench and unclench." As others have suggested, there is a very good chance that Philby was using such extreme displays as an act. He definitely had a stutter, but, by exaggerating the problem, he always had a way to hide mistakes or to delay difficult responses. He was certainly a polished actor who had a genius for escaping from tight spots and was willing to take terrific risks. Recruited by the Soviets when he was in his early twenties, he had a long time to master the act of a double agent.

Philby was, in short, a man after Greene's own heart. Greene could not help but admire such a character, and the more he knew about his treasonous deeds, the more Philby appealed to him. And Greene had his secrets, too. One afternoon his secretary at the Ryder Street office called to Philby for help. Greene was rolling on the floor in great pain, but when Philby tried to assist him, Greene said that there was no cause for alarm. He explained that he was suffering from an internal hemorrhage and that he was accustomed to such attacks. All he asked was that Philby take him home. A taxi was found, and Philby went with Greene to Dorothy's flat in Bloomsbury. Apparently, Greene had tried to keep his relationship with Dorothy a secret from his boss, so he said nothing about her identity. He turned the short taxi ride into something resembling a spy mission, quietly asking Philby to do him a favor: "If, when we get to my place, you notice anything irregular, please keep it to yourself." Philby agreed, and, when the taxi brought them to their destination, he silently approached the door, rang the bell, and showed no reaction when Dorothy suddenly rushed past him. She quickly pulled Greene from the taxi and took him inside, never saying a word to Philby.

It is true that Greene suffered such attacks from time to time, but this incident seems a bit overdramatic. Greene may have enjoyed giving Philby the idea that his private life was filled with mystery. Whatever the reason, the incident made a great impression on Philby, who seemed to like knowing that his friend had a secret life of his own. Because of their mutual passion for secrecy, they could never allow themselves to become very close friends, but it was obvious that they had great respect for each other. They remained in touch for the rest of Philby's life, regularly corresponding even after Philby's defection to the Soviet Union. Greene sent his friend inscribed copies of his books, and they were prominently displayed in Philby's Moscow apartment. In 1986 the old friends were finally reunited when Greene visited the Soviet Union, and they met again on several occasions when the novelist made three more visits to the country in 1987–88. Of the first meeting, Greene said:

> When I went to meet Kim for the first time after all those years, he said, "No questions, Graham." I said, "I've only one question. How's your Russian?" And we drank and conversed about the past. And then I saw him again with one or two others in the dacha of a painter living outside Moscow, and then a third time I saw him at a dinner with the Union of Writers. Finally we had a private dinner. I went by myself to his flat, but I won't say anything about that.

One would think from Greene's various comments on Philby that his friend was really a rather decent chap who had been unfairly punished for cheating at a game that was rigged in the first place. He went out of his way to make excuses for his old boss. Philby's *My Silent War* was primarily intended as a propaganda attack on SIS, but Greene made a point of praising it for its lack of propaganda. Philby's private papers reveal that he wanted his book to "provide a devastating attack on SIS." As he told the KGB, "The attack will concentrate on such aspects of SIS as social snobbery; internal intrigue; coddling of officers and ruthless handling of agents; breach of diplomatic usage; double-crossing of allies, etc." The chance to defend this attack was an act of disloyalty that Greene could not pass up.

Greene carefully played down the unpleasant subject of Philby's complicity in a great number of political murders. As Phillip Knightley has pointed out, there is evidence that Philby was responsible for the elimination of some prominent Catholics in postwar Germany. According to information supplied by MI-5 officers, Philby obtained a list of Catholic activists who were part of an anti-Communist movement in Germany. The list was supplied by Erich Vermehren, a German intelligence officer who defected to Britain near the end of the war. Vermehren stayed for a time with Philby after he was brought to London from Istanbul. Realizing the importance of the list, Philby gave it to Moscow, and the activists were later shot by the Soviet forces occupying East Germany.

In the early 1950s Philby helped to arrange the deaths of at least thirty rebels who tried to overthrow the Communist dictatorship in Albania. A rebel force was trained and supplied by the CIA and SIS. When the men were sent into Albania secretly, government troops were waiting for them. Philby had let Moscow know that the rebels were on their way. As Philby told Knightley, he was pleased to take the credit for "frustrating" this operation, and he argued that the betrayal was justified, because—as were the rebels who were killed— he was serving "a political ideal." It is debatable whether Philby was serving anything greater than his own ego, but his cool ability to excuse his treachery is worthy of a Greene hero.

In his introduction to Philby's memoirs, Greene uses the same kind of logic to excuse his friend's part in the death of a Soviet defector. One of the chapters in the memoirs details Philby's scheme to thwart the defection of Konstantin Volkov, a KGB man in Istanbul. The scheme required a delicate balancing act. Having learned of Volkov's desire to defect, Philby needed to be seen making all the necessary arrangements to bring the man safely to Britain. At the same time, he was working to make sure that the KGB caught the agent before he could escape their reach. In the end he was able to appear completely surprised when the news came that Volkov had mysteriously disappeared. Greene says that no one should lament Volkov's death. He was just another player in the game who made the wrong move and lost. And his motives, Greene suggests, were probably not as good as Philby's. Unfortunately, Volkov never had the chance to explain his motives, but Greene leaves no doubt that he thought the agent deserved to die anyway.

Being so much in tune with Philby's thinking, Greene was naturally suspected of involvement in his friend's work as a Soviet mole. Everyone in SIS knew that the two men were close, but it is also true that there was a sudden split between them in 1944. On May 9, 1944, Greene resigned as an SIS officer. Less than a month later the biggest event of the war, the D Day invasion, took place. Why would Greene want to leave SIS before preparations for this great undertaking were complete? Garbo and other agents were still working hard to confuse the Germans, and Lisbon would remain an important station for many more months. Leaving the service at this vital hour made no sense. In the 1960s Greene said that he left SIS because he wanted to avoid involvement in Philby's power struggle within the service. Philby craved a new job as head of the section for anti-Communist counterespionage, and if he received it, he planned for Greene to take over the Iberian Department. But this cover story does not match the relevant dates. In May 1944 there was no immediate threat to

Greene's office scruples. At that point Philby's plan was just getting off the ground. He did not secure the new job until six months later, and, up until that moment, he had no way of knowing whether his plan would succeed. If Greene liked Philby so much, it is strange that he would suddenly abandon him because of some vague game of office politics.

His decision to leave the service merely led him to take a job in another secret organization, which was neither nearly as interesting nor as congenial as SIS. In fact, the job was not much better than his old position at the dull Ministry of Information. His new job was in something called the Political Warfare Executive, and Greene's mission was to use art as propaganda, editing a literary magazine for distribution in France. While his old colleagues in SIS were plotting ways to undermine the Third Reich, he was gathering contributions for *Choix: Les Ecrits du mois à travers le monde*. It did not matter that his French was bad. Most of the selections were reprints from English and American magazines, and French translators were easy enough to come by.

Despite all his praise of Philby, it is clear that something made Greene determined to drop their working relationship and find a safe, obscure job as quickly as possible. Others may have been fooled by Philby's tricks, but Greene was too sharp to be completely misled. If anyone could spot the truth about Philby, it was Greene, whose eye for deception was unequaled. But in their close relationship he did not need to be a genius to see that his friend was a highly suspicious character. The evidence was all too plain, in his personal as well as his professional life. Sooner or later someone else would spot the clues, and Greene was not one to be caught waiting for a trap to close. To follow the trail of evidence, it is necessary to go back to Philby's early days and forward to Greene's short novel *The Third Man*.

CHAPTER SIXTEEN

ODD MAN OUT: KIM PHILBY AND *THE THIRD MAN*

Some of the senior officers in the secret service wanted to think the best of Kim Philby. They found him charming and efficient, and there was talk that he might one day become the head of SIS. He was, in the words of one former SIS man, "the blue-eyed boy of the establishment." Greene also thought that his friend was headed to the top and reflected—after Philby had fled to Moscow—that it would have been a great joke for the world to learn that the British secret service had been led by a Soviet spy. In the introduction to *My Silent War,* he argues that even if Philby had reached the top, he probably would not have caused much damage. In other words, only undeserving people such as Konstantin Volkov would have suffered.

When Philby entered the service in 1941, his Soviet contact could not believe how simple it was for his agent to win admission. Philby could not believe it either. "It appeared later," he wrote in his memoirs, "that the only enquiry made into my past was a routine reference to MI5, who passed my name through their records and came back with the laconic statement: Nothing Recorded Against." If the security service had studied Philby's past carefully, they might have been surprised by the young man's apparently confused political views. At the end of 1934 he was an ardent defender of socialism who had helped various Austrian Communists to flee right-wing persecution in Vienna. Among this group was a young Jewish woman—Litzi Friedman—who married him partly because she wanted the protection of his British passport. But by the end of 1935 he was a friend of fascism, an active member of the Anglo-German Fellowship. The change could be attributed to a young man's impetuousness, but such an extreme and sudden shift is worth questioning. No one, however, thought to check such things until it was too late.

Of course, it was in response to instructions from Soviet intelligence that Philby tried to hide his early socialist activity and to create a new identity for himself as a right-wing activist. He parted ways with Litzi—who was later to emerge as a Soviet agent in Berlin—and spied on his new friends in the Anglo-German Fellowship, joining them for dinner at tables decorated with swastikas. In 1936 he made several visits to Berlin "for talks with the German Propaganda Ministry and Von Ribbentrop's Foreign Office." He became *The Times* correspondent with Franco's forces in Spain and was wounded by Republican artillery fire. To reward Philby's bravery during the attack, and to recognize his value as a sympathetic correspondent, Franco gave him the Red Cross of Military Merit. When Hitler invaded Poland, Philby cut his ties to fascism and assumed the part of a loyal British subject eager to fight for God and Country. In that disguise he was welcomed into the ranks of SIS.

During their months together at St. Albans and Ryder Street, Greene was able to learn many details about Philby's past. It was common knowledge that Philby had been decorated by Franco. In fact, his Spanish experience worked to his advantage in SIS, helping him to gain acceptance as head of the Iberian Department. But, understandably, he was not forthcoming on the subject of his marriage to Litzi. Greene knew a little about her, however, and was aware that Philby had met her in Vienna. For someone with Greene's powers of observation, it was not difficult to guess that Philby's involvement with the woman had been the result of a romantic adventure among Communist intellectuals. Like most English intellectuals, Greene was well aware of the right-wing effort, in 1934, to crush the Communist movement in Vienna. The persecution was not only closely followed by the press but was also the subject of a well-known work by Stephen Spender—the long poem *Vienna*. Philby's sudden shift from a friend of communism to a friend of fascism was sure to catch Greene's interest. If nothing else, it was a sign that his friend might share his faith in the virtue of disloyalty.

But in the course of their work together, Greene had the chance to see that Philby's "old" romantic attachment to communism was not dead. As the internal SIS investigation later established, Philby's number-one concern during the war was keeping track of peace overtures from Hitler's opponents within the German military. A group of high-ranking officers wanted to overthrow Hitler, set up a new government, and end the war, but they were anxious to know how the Allies would respond to their actions. The policy of the British government was to insist on an unconditional surrender, but, with Hitler gone, anything might be possible, and the German conspirators hoped that they could save their country from total defeat by offering to make peace immediately. It was not, however, in the Soviet Union's interest to see a strong Germany intact after the war. Stalin wanted to occupy Eastern Europe, and his best chance of doing that was to keep Germany fighting on two fronts until the Reich's forces were completely destroyed. Philby's instructions were to frustrate the peace efforts by ignoring any offers that came from representatives of the conspirators in Lisbon and Madrid.

There was a Greene connection to this complicated matter. Throughout the war Barbara Greene, the cousin who had accompanied Graham to Liberia, lived in Germany and was married to Count Rudolf Strachwitz, an opponent of Hitler who was involved in the conspiracy against him. This connection may have helped to inspire an action undertaken by Hugh Greene. In July 1944 Hugh was working for the BBC German Service and was able to use his position for the benefit of the conspirators. On July 20, Hitler survived the explosion of a bomb planted by Colonel von Stauffenberg during a meeting in East Prussia. The next morning Hugh Greene went to his studio at Bush House and broadcast an unauthorized message. The first sentence of his opening news story was "Civil war has broken out in Germany." His official biographer explains: "It was, he says, the only occasion when he knowingly exaggerated because, he thought to himself, there may be people holding out in different places who would be encouraged by the opening phrase 'civil war has broken out.' The Foreign Office next morning was utterly furious." This daring stunt does not sound like something that dull Hugh would have thought up by himself. It is the sort of thing that his older brother might have enjoyed doing, especially since Graham had known for some time about the secret opposition to Hitler. Because of information that had come from Portugal while he was supervising counter-intelligence efforts in the country, Graham was expecting news of an attempt to overthrow Hitler. And he did not have to go out of his way to tell Hugh about it. In July he was working for the Political Warfare Executive in Bush House, not far from Hugh's office.

The advance word about the plot had come from a Lufthansa lawyer named Otto John. He had been involved with the anti-Nazi movement for a long time and had been in touch with the SIS station in Lisbon since late 1942. His work for Lufthansa gave him the opportunity to visit Spain and Portugal, and he used these trips to plead the case of the conspirators, contacting the American embassy in Madrid and the British embassy in Lisbon. But Philby insisted that his SIS people give no credence to John's reports and that they discourage the Americans from dealing with him. In March 1944 John met with Rita Winsor, an SIS officer in Lisbon, and argued that the British should give some support to Stauffenberg's plot, but he was rebuffed. Winsor told him that "strict instructions had been received from London forbidding any further contact with emissaries of the German opposition." Those instructions would have come directly from Graham Greene, acting in accordance with Philby's wishes.

Philby did everything in his power to discredit and discourage John. After the July plot failed, John was able to escape Germany and reach Lisbon. He planned to travel to England but was imprisoned in Lisbon. He believed that Philby had arranged for the Portuguese to lock him up, a suspicion that was confirmed after he was released in October: "Rita Winsor confided to me that up to the very last moment someone in London had been resisting my entry into England—it was Philby." Although, by necessity, Graham Greene helped Philby carry out his vendetta against the German, it is interesting to note that one of the first people to give John work in England was Hugh Greene at the BBC.

Otto John was a brave and adventurous character whose talk about the plot to overthrow the Nazis was the most exciting information to cross Graham Greene's "Portugal desk." The author of *A Gun for Sale* and *The Confidential Agent* had a natural interest in conspiracies, and Otto John was at the center of the greatest conspiracy of the war. After those fruitless months of creating wild schemes in Africa, Greene was suddenly confronted with the wildest scheme of all, something worthy of a great thriller—a band of desperate men intent on killing Hitler and bringing an end to the Second World War. Why fantasize about filling a brothel with spies when you can exchange information with a fearless conspirator eager to talk?

Regardless of government policy, a good spy would want to know more about the plot. Allen Dulles, the OSS spymaster in Switzerland, did everything in his power to acquire information about the plot, and he tried to make his superiors in Washington see that it deserved support. As he quite reasonably pointed out, the revolt might have helped "save thousands of lives of Allied soldiers fighting on the various fronts." And, one can now add, thousands of Jews might also have been spared execution. Even the principle of unconditional surrender could have been advanced by killing Hitler. If the conspirators had succeeded and made unreasonable demands, they would still have represented an improvement. A Germany without Hitler would have been much easier to defeat. "If Hitler had been killed," Dulles said in 1948, "German resistance would have collapsed, and the war would have ended in 1944." But political and military arguments did not matter much to Greene. The main thing was that he could have had great fun helping the conspirators, even if it had meant only talking to them. It was tempting to think that the plot to kill Hitler would succeed, but whatever happened this was a golden chance to be involved in something very big and very secret.

Yet his boss wanted nothing to do with it and, moreover, was willing to go out of his way to oppose it. And Greene was not the only SIS officer in England who knew of Philby's strong views on this matter. When the historian Hugh Trevor-Roper was working for SIS during the war, his office prepared a detailed report about the opposition to Hitler within the German General Staff. According to Trevor-Roper, the report "should have been circulated to the very limited world of those on the *Ultra* list, but its circulation was stopped by Philby." He was "baffled" by this decision and sent two officers "to see Philby and discover the reason for his opposition and argue our case." But the officers had no success: "He was quite adamant and refused to argue, declaring the paper 'pure speculation.' I well remember the return of my two officers. They were mystified and angry at Philby's unreasoning attitude. But he had the right of veto (on grounds of 'security,' which hardly applied in this case), and that was that."

Given his responsibility for Portugal, Greene was in an excellent position to observe Philby's attitude toward the German conspirators. The overwhelming question was why an Englishman would want so much to resist any cooperation with the group. It was an intriguing mystery. Perhaps Greene was tempted to think that Philby had some lingering respect for Hitler, dating back to his days in the Anglo-German Fellowship. But it would not have taken many drinking sessions to see that Philby's fascist work was either a prank or a mysterious ploy. It had to be something that went deeper into his past—all the way back to his old love for Litzi and her Communist friends. Everyone knew that the Soviets were the strongest advocates of an unconditional surrender. Although no one was sure of Stalin's future designs on Europe, it was widely known that he feared a new

German government would make peace with the West and then turn on him. Anyone who could keep Otto John from pleading his case to British authorities would be doing the Soviets a great service.

It is possible, but unlikely, that Philby revealed his true motives to Greene. He was not one to confide secrets. Even so, the truth would scarcely have shocked Greene, as his later comments indicate. He did not regard spying for the Soviet Union as a terrible crime—he may have done a bit of it himself during his trip to the Baltic states in 1934. But he liked to operate on his own, and, whatever Philby was up to, it was dangerous to become involved. For one thing Greene knew that Philby was a hard drinker who might possibly get too drunk and say more than was good for him. Keeping him at a distance made sense, especially when he began to talk about taking over the new anti-Communist section in the service. Philby's Communist wife, his determined opposition to Otto John and other conspirators, and his desire to keep anyone else from getting the anti-Communist post—it was all much too suspicious for comfort. And if Philby did prove to be a Soviet mole, it would not be wise to become established in SIS as his protégé, the man he had handpicked to take his old job. The best thing was to keep quiet and get out quickly, far in advance of any promotion for Philby. Greene's later objection to his friend's office politics was correct, but it was only half the story.

II

After Philby defected to Moscow, the SIS investigators were right to think that Greene had known something about his friend's double life. It may have been hard for him to be certain of anything in 1944, but he had ample reason to be suspicious. If he had cared much about loyalty to the service, he would have shared his knowledge with others. But, as Greene argues in his introduction to Philby's book, silence was the best response to the problem. He makes the case that, when the spy was finally exposed, the controversy simply created bad publicity for the Western intelligence services and more suspicion within their ranks. In Greene's case, there were ways to tell the truth without speaking it directly. The professional spies could keep their code books. He knew a better way of conveying hidden messages. He could always write fiction.

In 1963, when Philby defected, Greene wrote a newspaper article about his affectionate relationship with his former boss. He ended the piece by joking that he had created the phrase "the Third Man" before anyone could have imagined that it would apply to his old friend. He wrote the book version of *The Third Man* in March–April 1948, three years before the defections of Guy Burgess and Donald Maclean had caused people to wonder whether a third spy had helped the two escape. The connection is even stranger when one realizes that *The Third Man* is essentially Philby's story, with the real details scrambled to suit Greene's purposes. In 1948 the novelist was in no position to know that Burgess and Maclean would create the necessary circumstances for Philby's designation as the Third Man. Yet, by sheer chance—or possibly by some hidden design—life followed the pattern of fiction.

The first important fact to recognize is that Greene took some of the main incidents for the story from one of Philby's old friends—a journalist from Vienna named Peter Smolka. The story of Smolka's contribution to *The Third Man* is as bizarre as anything in Greene's fictional works and will need to be explained in some detail. During Philby's visit to Vienna in early 1934, Litzi introduced her future husband to her friend Smolka. After Litzi married and was allowed to leave Austria, Smolka and his wife moved to London and were frequent guests at Philby's home. Smolka and Philby became such good friends that they decided to go into business together. At some point in 1934, they started a small press agency called the London Continental News Ltd. The purpose of the agency was to provide items about Central Europe to various papers in London, but the two young men were unable to find enough buyers for their service to make it profitable, and it was soon abandoned. Smolka remained in touch with Philby after their business folded, and some students of Soviet espionage believe that both men were working as spies for Moscow.

Smolka was in a good position to help the Soviets. He changed his name to Peter Smollett and became a successful journalist in London. In the late 1930s he wrote a series of articles about Russia for *The Times*. These pieces were later incorporated into *Forty Thousand Against the Arctic: Russia's Polar Empire,* a highly favorable portrait of the Soviet Union. After the war broke out, Smolka went to work for the Ministry of Information and eventually became the head of the Soviet Relations Division. In that position he made a strong effort to warn his colleagues against the temptation to believe "the German campaign on the bogey of Bolshevism." One expert felt certain that Smolka was in Moscow's employ throughout his stay in England. In 1987 Anthony Glees, of Brunel University, wrote that "there is now overwhelming evidence to suggest that one of [Brendan] Bracken's most trusted advisers [at the Ministry of Information], Peter Smolka-

Smollett, was a Communist mole." In 1961 officers of MI-5 interviewed Smolka for an entire day in London, hoping to find some hard incriminating evidence about him or Philby, but they were unsuccessful. Smolka died in 1980, and in a recent interview his family vigorously denied any suggestion that he was a spy, calling the charge "rubbish."

After the war Smolka returned to Vienna and became *The Times* correspondent for Central Europe. In 1948 Greene came to the city and was taken to see Smolka by Elizabeth Montagu, an employee of Alexander Korda's London Films. Korda wanted to make a film in Vienna, partly because he saw dramatic potential in the four-power occupation of the city and partly because he wanted to spend his company's Austrian cash reserves, which could not be taken out of the country. He commissioned Greene to create a suitable story for the film and chose Carol Reed to direct it. Montagu's job was to act as a guide and assistant. In that capacity she arranged for Greene to see Smolka, believing that *The Times* correspondent would have some good stories about life under the occupation. And indeed he did. He had written some short pieces about Vienna and was anxious to have Greene's opinion of them. They met one afternoon and had dinner a day or two later, spending almost seven hours together.

One of Smolka's stories described in great detail the large and intricate maze of sewers that ran under the city. Another concerned the black market in penicillin, which was controlled by gangs who used the sewers as a hideout. And a third described the practice of having jeeps roam the city with each of the four powers represented in every jeep. The piece brought out the absurdity of organizing a patrol that always had to include one Frenchman, one Englishman, one American, and one Russian. After his long evening with Smolka, Greene took away these stories and others, and three months later they emerged in different form in the first draft of *The Third Man*.

When Elizabeth Montagu saw the draft in London, she was shocked to discover that Greene had used so many details from Smolka's stories without acknowledgment. Worried that London Films might be sued for copyright infringement, she alerted Korda to the problem. He seemed not to realize its importance and gave no response, but his associate producer for the film—Hugh Perceval—was more receptive. In an unpublished memoir Montagu recalled what happened next:

> I was relieved to see that [Hugh Perceval] took it seriously, and delighted when, a few days later, he told me the matter had been satisfactorily settled. However, I was horrified when he explained, "We've

given Smollett a contract, handling the local press and that sort of thing. There's just one condition in it, though. He can never make any claim—no claim whatsoever—against the company or its associates."

I was speechless. "And he signed that?" I asked.

Perceval smiled. "He hasn't read the script."

This story sounds too incredible to be true, but such a contract was offered in July 1948, Smolka signed it, and he was paid 210 pounds. A copy survives in the Korda papers at the British Film Institute, along with another contract for an additional screenwriter on *The Third Man*, a Mrs. Mabbie Poole, who was paid 300 pounds for her "work in the writing of the dialogue and script." It would seem that neither Greene's story nor his script can be called entirely his own. Besides requiring Smolka to give general "advice" and "assistance," the contract also stipulates, "You will render your services hereunder to the best of your skill and ability, and shall collaborate in the writing of the said script with Mr. Carol Reed and such other persons as the Company may require." The crucial "protection" clause says, "You agree that the entire copyright in the products of your services hereunder shall be the absolute property of the Company."

Neither Smolka nor Poole ever received public credit for contributions to the film. According to his family, Smolka was happy to sign the contract with Korda's company. Two hundred pounds could go far in postwar Vienna, where everything was in short supply. But after the production was completed, he decided that the film portrayed Vienna in an unfair light. His disenchantment with the finished product made him less inclined to seek recognition for his contribution. But Greene and the film's director, Carol Reed, seem to have thought that Smolka's influence on the story was worth at least an inside joke. It appears on-screen but not in the published script. Near the beginning of the film, Holly Martins is given a lift in a car belonging to the British officer Calloway. Martins is asked if he would like to have a drink, and, when he answers yes, Calloway says something to his driver that the viewer can only assume is the name of the bar. But the word he utters does not belong to any bar. In a clear voice he calls out to the driver, without any explanation, "Smolka."

Although Montagu believed that she was introducing Greene to Smolka for the first time, it is likely that they had met before. Smolka's wife thought her husband had met Greene earlier in London. Their paths could have crossed at the Ministry of Information, or at some point Philby might have introduced Greene to his friend Peter Smollett. One way or another, Greene seems to have gained more from Smolka than a few stories about postwar Vienna.

Smolka was a crucial link to Philby's early involvement with Litzi and her left-wing friends in Austria. During the street battles that raged in February 1934, Philby helped hide people in the sewers of Vienna and then helped smuggle them out of the country. With his British passport, he was able to come and go as he pleased, and he proved an invaluable courier for a charitable organization known as the Committee for Aiding Refugees from Fascism. When the government forces attacked workers in their housing estates, Philby recklessly faced gunfire to escort them to hiding places in the sewers. Many people witnessed his actions in these operations. Eric Gedye, the *Daily Telegraph* correspondent, remembered Philby confiding to him, "I've got six wounded friends in the sewers in danger of the gallows." And an Austrian journalist recalled, "I greatly admired Kim Philby. . . . He had shown his courage when joining the defenders of the shelled council estates during the February fighting; he had shared their ordeal in the sewers, had rescued several of them." Near the end of February, he wed Litzi and thereby saved her life by providing her the security of marriage to a British subject. She was able to obtain her own British passport two months later, and they left Austria together.

In altered form many aspects of Philby's life appear in *The Third Man*. Capable of great charm and wit, Harry Lime is a natural leader. Martins has idolized him since they were at school together. But no one can trust Lime, whose boyish smiles and adventurous ways hide a ruthless nature. He is supposed to be working for the International Refugee Office in Vienna, but his only real cause is himself. Although he provides information to the Russians, his primary occupation is selling smuggled or stolen penicillin, some of which is dangerously diluted. The thrill of running this racket is so intoxicating that Lime has moved beyond any concern for his victims. He embodies Greene's belief in the glory of pure evil and looks down on the world as a place in which some poor souls simply do not deserve to live. From his various hideouts in the sewer system of Vienna, he fearlessly pursues his racket, ruling his underworld realm like the leader of "a totalitarian party."

Despite his evil, his girlfriend Anna loves him so much that she refuses to turn against him, even after she learns the worst. For one thing, he has given her the protection of some forged identity papers. She is the daughter of a Hungarian Nazi, and the Russians want to send her to a labor camp. Her forged papers are the only things standing between her and an almost certain death. But when it becomes convenient for Lime to drop Anna, he does so without a second thought, alerting the Russians to the fact that her papers are not in order. She manages to escape the trap, but just barely. And she continues to remain loyal to Lime.

The point of the story is to "dig up" the truth about Harry Lime, and that job falls to his old friend Martins, a novelist with a reputation for writing popular stories full of action and adventure. He makes a good living from his work, but he has always admired Lime for being a man of real action. Martins writes about violence and crime in the Old West and has an inherent dislike of the law. Yet, for the most part, he lives a fairly ordinary life. By contrast, Lime is a real outlaw, a modern-day version of the cattle rustler on the run. Until he knows the brutal truth about Lime's crimes, Martins is prepared to continue thinking the best of his old school friend, whose love of danger and secrecy is infectious.

He is warned not to look too far for the truth about Harry Lime. He might find something "discreditable" about his hero. But Martins is a relentless investigator, and his search for the truth takes him all over Vienna, picking up vital clues from, among others, a man called Kurtz. When the truth is finally established, Martins is faced with the problem of having to betray his friend to the authorities. Shall he let him get away or set a trap for him? Lime warns him not to try playing the policeman in this drama, and Martins is naturally reluctant to help the forces of law and order. The greatest difficulty is that Lime is no ordinary friend. Martins's attitude is almost like that of a lover who cannot decide whether to end a bad affair. When he gets a little drunk, he confesses to Calloway that he has never had a better friend than Harry Lime. Later he tells Anna that he loves Lime. And, when he considers making love to her, he thinks of her as "Harry's girl," as though being with her is the next best thing to being with Lime.

Until the last moment of Lime's life, Martins is torn between wanting to spare his hero and wanting to punish him for creating an impossible situation. In the end he goes after him, playing one last schoolboy game of hide-and-seek but in a hellish setting under the streets of Vienna. Although shots are fired in this dangerous chase, Martins still sees the last act of the drama as a replay of a scene from their youth, when Lime stole a gun and tried to teach Martins how to fire it on Brickworth Common. He wounds his friend in the sewers, then decides to go all the way. As Lime cries, his friend finishes him off.

Greene never betrayed his friend Philby, but he spent the rest of his life thinking about the dilemma. He returned to it again in *The Human Factor* and even sent the manuscript to Philby in Moscow, asking his opinion of the novel. The question of protecting Philby gripped his imagination. It contained so many of the elements that had always appealed to him: a dangerous relationship, an enormous secret, a fear of betrayal, a test of loyalty, a lonely act of defiance. Reexamining these elements over the years, he tried out different responses. In 1978 a journalist asked what he would have done if he had known of Philby's treason in the 1940s. He replied, "I think, perhaps, if in a drunken moment he had let slip a hint, I would have given him twenty-four hours to get clear, and then reported it." For his part, Philby said that he had always tried to protect Greene from suspicion. Near the end of his life, he said, "In 1951 I came under very heavy suspicion, and I didn't want to keep up my close relations with Graham, so as not to compromise him. I knew that he wasn't guilty, so to speak, but at the time they suspected everyone."

When *The Human Factor* came out, it was easy for readers to see that the defector in the novel—Maurice Castle—is loosely based on Philby, who had fled long ago to Moscow. But when *The Third Man* appeared, Philby's connections to the story were simply a private joke, like the sudden mention of Smolka in the opening scenes of the film. The connections should, however, be obvious now: the hideouts in the sewers, the refugee agency, the girlfriend in desperate need of safe identity papers, the secrets passed to the Russians, the ruthlessness beneath the charm, the boyish romanticism, the novelist friend in search of clues, the discovery of something discreditable, the difficulty of choosing the right response. There is even a link between names. Philby's real first name was Harold, which can be altered to Harry, as can Greene's first name, Henry. And there is the delightfully bad pun in Lime, a shade of green. Finally, it should be noted that Philby enjoyed referring to SIS as a "racket"—the word most often used to describe Harry Lime's business. When Philby had joined the service, a colleague had told him, "If you have to work for a racket, let it be an old-fashioned racket."

Although Greene was not a school friend of Philby's, such a relationship was easy for him to imagine and was something that he liked thinking about. Philby was the kind of companion he had longed for at Berkhamsted, someone with whom he could share secrets and plot mischief. And he was also the kind of man Greene had always feared, the reckless friend who would hurt him in some way, as Andrews fears that he will be hurt by Carlyon in *The Man Within*. But it was not necessary for Greene to stretch his imagination in order to visualize a school friendship with Philby. He needed only to look at the man who shared his Ryder Street office, Tim Milne. Kim and Tim were best friends at Westminster School, and they remained close until Philby was forced to leave the secret service. They were King's Scholars at Westminster, which meant that they spent most of their time among a very select group of forty boys. Milne was only six months younger than Philby, but his relationship with him was always that of the younger boy looking up to a hero who could do no wrong. Milne may have had trouble imagining a corrupt hero, but Greene would have found it easy.

There are so many odd twists in the story of Greene's relationship with Philby that it is impossible, especially for a mere literary biographer, to sort them all out. As an earlier chapter explained, Greene's 1948 trip to Austria and Czechoslovakia was more than an expedition to find material for a film. Using Korda's company as a cover, Greene was working informally for SIS, keeping an eye on the volatile political situations in both countries. The threat of Soviet domination in the area was the prime concern, and it may well be that Greene was working under some private instructions provided by Philby, who was then still the "blue-eyed boy" of the service. In that case Greene would have been all the more eager to quiz Smolka about the "good old days" of 1934.

It does seem a great coincidence that Elizabeth Montagu would lead Greene straight to Smolka. He was the one man in Vienna who could discuss Philby's past in detail and who could do it in English. The plot becomes even more complicated when one knows more about Montagu. The daughter of the second baron Montagu of Beaulieu, the Hon. Elizabeth Montagu is listed in the film credits of *The Third Man* as "Austrian Adviser." Earlier, during the war, she had worked for the Political Warfare Executive in Switzerland and had eventually been given a job as one of two personal assistants for Allen Dulles in his OSS office in Berne. Her chief responsibility in that position was to look after Hans Gisevius, an important associate of Colonel von Stauffenberg in the conspiracy against Hitler.

After the war Korda gave her a job as a dialogue coach, and in 1948 he dispatched her to reopen some of his old offices in Central and Eastern Europe, offices that had served as covers for secret service men before the war. When she was interviewed in 1993, Montagu said that her work for Korda had nothing to do with his espionage activities but that both Korda and Greene seemed to have turned against her after the Smolka episode. Korda failed to renew her contract in 1949, and Greene makes no mention of her in his published recollections of visiting Vienna. In later years she suspected that his silence reflected a fear that she would reveal Smolka's part in the creation of *The Third Man*. In fact, he acted as though most of his information about the city had come from Colonel Beauclerk, the future duke of St. Albans, who was controller of information services for the Allied Commission in Vienna. Nevertheless, Montagu's version of events is accurate. She was with Greene almost all the time, arranging his stay at Sacher's Hotel—which was normally reserved for military officers—and giving him various tours of the city.

One night Greene insisted on taking Montagu to a rather squalid night spot. The place was built to look like a small theater, with boxes instead of seats, but she quickly realized that it was primarily a brothel. They sat together in one of the boxes and drank bad wine while they watched a performance featuring a small cast of "skinny nudes writhing and cavorting": "I watched his reaction to this awful place and saw that he was clearly fascinated by it all. I remember asking him how he could equate his religious principles with sitting in a brothel getting drunk. And I remember, too, how convincingly he replied, and how brilliantly he equivocated on every point until he nearly succeeded in convincing me. But by that time we were probably both a little tipsy."

Even before their first meeting, she was given a good insight into Greene's love of deception. Three days before his arrival in Vienna, she received a telegram from him in which he asked that she send a telegram to his wife. Montagu was to send it in his name with a brief message announcing that he had arrived safely in Vienna. Meanwhile, he was in Brighton on some private business. Although she did not like being used in this way, Montagu sent the telegram. After he arrived in Vienna, Greene offered no explanation of his request, but the incident demonstrates how simple it was for him to cover his tracks. Finding that telegram many years later, an unsuspecting biographer would naturally assume that on the day it was sent Greene was in Vienna, not Brighton. In his case the paper trail that most biographers follow so faithfully must be approached with caution, especially if the document is not handwritten.

One final loose end remains in the Philby story. In *The Human Factor* the man in SIS who is charged with finding the mole is Colonel Daintry. The sound of the name and his place of residence in St. James's Street—at a flat above Overton's restaurant—suggest that the character is modeled on Colonel Dansey, the deputy director of the service during the war and an occasional resident of the same flat.

One former officer who knew Dansey well believed that "he would have loved nothing better than to find a Communist mole in SIS," and he may have taken it on himself to keep an eye on Philby. He was not among the circle of senior officers who held the young man in high regard. A crusty old spy, he did not think much of anyone who was too clever or too modern. He enjoyed the old-fashioned, cloak-and-dagger methods of espionage, but Philby claims that he managed to stay off Dansey's "list of pet bugbears." *The Human Factor* suggests otherwise. Through Dansey's good friend Alexander Korda, Greene may have learned that the old colonel was more suspicious than he revealed. But Dansey did not live long enough to follow Philby's postwar career in the service. He died on June 11, 1947. The next year Greene moved into the colonel's old hideout at 5 St. James's Street.

III

Perhaps the most extraordinary thing about *The Third Man* is that Greene wrote the book version in less than eight weeks. The original manuscript shows that he began the story on March 2, 1948—one week after leaving Vienna—and finished it on April 24. The writing was done during a long trip through Italy, and his expenses were paid by Korda. Although some basic plot elements were borrowed from Smolka, the story owes all its success to Greene's skillful treatment of structure, character, setting, and theme. The tale unfolds with smooth precision, despite the complexity of the narration, which presents the experiences of Martins and Lime through the eyes of Calloway.

The Third Man is one work that some critics like to cite as evidence of Greene's weakness for lightweight entertainment. It does have all the qualities of an old-fashioned adventure story, but it is also an elaborate parody of such tales. Old Vienna is turned into the Old West by the overactive imagination of Martins, author of *The Lone Rider of Santa Fe* and other action-packed novels, who is determined to find the bad guys responsible for the mysterious death of his pal Harry Lime. He has never set foot in the American West, but he is so fond of the black-and-white world of his fictional work that he is quick to see everything from its distorted perspective. Having decided that the unhelpful local police are nothing but a pack of corrupt lawmen who ought to be run out of town, he swaggers through Vienna on the trail of his own investigation, never suspecting—until it is too late—that Lime's death was staged to protect an evil scheme worse than anything known in Santa Fe.

The story works extremely well as a short novel, but it is even better in its film version. In the space available to the book, Greene could not do justice to the ruins of postwar Vienna, but they are a major part of his theme. In the film the devastation is visible in frame after frame, constantly reminding us of an evil far greater than Lime's little racket. Lime is responsible for the suffering of a relatively small group in the city; the bombers and tanks that invaded Vienna have not only hurt thousands of people but also destroyed large portions of one of the great cultural capitals in the Western world. With their good intentions the Allied armies have helped to reduce a city of splendid beauty to a sad collection of damaged buildings and piles of rubble. Against this background it is easier to make Lime's evil seem more understandable. He is a devil, but he serves his own interests and knows what he is.

When Lime goes up in Vienna's giant Ferris wheel, he looks down at the people far below and asks Martins whether he would really care if any of the "dots" on the ground were destroyed. For 20,000 pounds a dot, Lime thinks that anyone would be willing to eliminate one dot after another. By itself this seems a singularly monstrous comment, but the ruins of Vienna serve to remind us that "good" bombardiers destroy countless dots and get medals for doing so. Because Harry Lime is such a charming villain, we want to like him. When he speaks of killing dots, we see the evil lurking behind his smile. But Greene does not want to allow us the pleasure of feeling morally superior. With the help of Carol Reed's camera, he surrounds Lime with the overwhelming evidence of a far greater evil done in the name of justice—the destruction of Vienna.

In *The Third Man* Greene makes his best case for giving sympathy to the devil. Lime is on-screen for only a small portion of the film, but he is the most engaging character, and we are not tempted to wish for his capture. As we follow the long chase filmed in the sewers of Vienna, the camera does everything to arouse our sympathy. Using quick cuts Reed makes it seem as though an enormous army is pursuing Lime, closing in on him from every direction. Against such odds Lime's desperate escape attempt looks valiant. Suddenly, he is the hero, a man fighting for his life in the underground world that serves as his kingdom. He is doomed to die in the hell to which the world has condemned him, but the irony is that his hellish sewers look tidier and grander than the bombed city overhead. By the end of the film, we cannot admire the forces of law and order that destroy

Lime. Martins and the police become the bullies. The viewer who falls under Greene's spell may feel that, despite Lime's evil, he was one dot worth saving.

It makes a great difference that Harry Lime is played on-screen by Orson Welles. With the obvious exception of *Citizen Kane,* his brief part in *The Third Man* is his best screen performance. Only he could convey the right amount of devilish charm. His delayed appearance in the story gave him the chance to make one of the great entrances in film history, and he played it perfectly. On the surface the scene appears to be a standard one for a thriller. In a dark street Martins hears someone following him and turns to demand that the villain show his face. He can vaguely make out a figure in a doorway. When a light comes on from a window across the street, the figure is illuminated. Dressed all in black, Harry Lime looks like the perfect screen heavy, except for one detail—his winning smile. Whatever the man has done, that smile makes us want to like him, and, from that moment, the film belongs completely to Welles. An added bonus is Welles's brilliant little speech about the contrast between Italy under the violent Borgias and peaceful Switzerland. The former produced the Renaissance. But the Swiss—"They had brotherly love, five hundred years of democracy and peace, and what did that produce? The cuckoo clock." As Greene later acknowledged, this speech was Welles's own creation.

It is hard to believe that Welles almost failed to get the part. When the joint producers of the film—David O. Selznick and Alexander Korda—drew up the original contract for their production, one clause called for Cary Grant to play Martins and Noël Coward to play Lime. Grant might have done a better job than Joseph Cotten, who eventually was cast as Martins, but Coward as Lime would have been a disaster. He could never have captured the true touch of evil in Lime's character, or created the right mood of fear and pride that attends Lime's last stand in the sewers.

From his headquarters in Hollywood, Selznick tried to interfere as much as possible in the production, sending Reed and Korda a total of seventy-two memos. He never had much effect on the film, but he kept heads spinning by making one crazy suggestion after another. When Grant and Coward were unable to appear in the film, Selznick lobbied hard for young Robert Mitchum to play Lime. No one would have looked more out of place in Vienna. It was Reed who first thought of using Welles, and, fortunately, he was able to get him for the part, although the price was high—$100,000. Meanwhile, Selznick continued pushing wild ideas at the production team. Why not call the film *Night in Vienna?* he asked Greene. His overriding concern was to make sure that the film appealed to American audiences, and he was delighted when the casting choices required that Lime and Martins appear as American characters.

After Selznick's death Greene enjoyed telling various stories about his encounters with the producer. At one point he and Reed were flown to Hollywood for a series of conferences. According to Greene, Selznick was not happy with Martins's determination to uncover the truth about Harry Lime. There was no motive for it, Selznick complained, except "buggery." In an interview with the film critic Quentin Falk, Greene recalled his conversation with the Hollywood producer:

"What's all this buggery?"

I said, "Buggery?"

He said, "Look, chap goes out to find his friend. Doesn't find him. He's apparently dead. Why doesn't he go home?"

I said, "Well, look . . . he's got a motive of revenge. He's been assaulted by the British military police. He's fallen in love with a girl."

"Yes, but that's after twenty-four hours. Why didn't he go home before that?"

Greene used this story as an example of Hollywood ignorance, but, in this case, Selznick was close to the truth. As the full version of the story makes abundantly clear, Martins has always loved Lime. And his love shows signs of repressed sexual desire, which is the main reason—in the tradition of other Greene heroes—he must betray Lime. The excuses that Greene offered Selznick only reinforce the point. Martins is assaulted by the police because he is making a nuisance of himself over their handling of Lime's death, and the main reason that he falls in love with Anna is that she is Lime's girl. No doubt to Selznick's relief, the "buggery" failed to come across in the film. Cary Grant and Noël Coward might have found a way to bring it out, but considerable imagination is needed to see Joseph Cotten and Orson Welles as potential boyfriends.

Because Korda made certain that Reed enjoyed great artistic freedom, the director made a film that avoids many of the conventions of screen thrillers. The location shooting, much of it done at night, gives the film an authentic feel that so many other pictures of the period lack. Moreover, Reed was brave enough to give the story a thoroughly unhappy ending. Even Greene was reluctant to endorse this idea. But Reed stuck with his conviction that Lime's "girl" would not have any reason to love the man who had shot him, so the film ends with Anna walking past Martins as he waits for her, not pausing even for a second to acknowledge him. The only false touch is the omnipresent zither music. A great sensation at the time of the film's release, Anton Karas's "Harry Lime Theme" seems too intrusive now. A little of it goes a long way.

In 1949 *The Third Man* won first prize at the Cannes Film Festival and went on to enjoy success at the box office. Selznick was so pleased that he forgot all his objections to the film and began thinking of new projects for Greene. When he gave him lunch in New York one day, he announced that he had the perfect story for him to script. It was a movie on the life of St. Mary Magdalene. Greene could have had tremendous fun with this idea, but, unfortunately, he turned it down.

One aspect of *The Third Man* did provide an opportunity for mischief thirty years later. Looking through the British and American editions of the short novel, two distinguished Canadian scholars discovered that the texts were quite a bit different. All negative references to the Russians and Americans in the occupation force are missing from the American edition. In an article for *Encounter,* the scholars analyzed the deletions and castigated the unknown American editor at the publishing firm of Viking for "pulling the political teeth of the story." Although the full version of the story has nothing profound to say about Cold War politics, Greene himself encouraged the scholars to make their case, informing them that he did not know of the changes and was "horrified" to hear of them. The implication was that some self-important American had arrogantly tampered with Greene's work, removing anything that might have stirred up Cold War antagonisms. The changes prompted the scholars to wonder "how many American editors see themselves as a latter-day Maxwell Perkins." More important, they thought the case raised "the larger question of other possible transatlantic tamperings with modern British texts."

In this case, however, there was no American conspiracy to violate truth and justice. Greene was deliberately misleading the scholars, although one was a friend who naturally assumed that the novelist's word could be trusted. The fact is that Greene and Carol Reed had prepared a typescript of the story from which they had eliminated all the potentially offensive references to the United States or the Soviet Union. They used this sanitized version to show the American and

Russian officers whose permission was needed for filming on location. Greene mistakenly sent one of these typescripts to Viking. As he explained in letters to his British publisher, he realized the error too late and decided to make no public comment about it. Heinemann was given the correct text and published it a few months after the American edition appeared.

The Canadian scholars make an elegant and forceful argument for their view, but the great danger of writing about Greene is that one can never be sure whether a cherished theory will be blown sky high by hidden evidence. The scholars were right to take the risk, and they cannot be blamed for wanting to trust Greene. Their experience is a reminder that his world is full of traps, and that nothing can be taken entirely on trust. An unauthorized biographer is especially vulnerable, but part of the fun of the chase is discovering all the false leads. Greene's trail is superbly difficult to follow. He was the Harry Lime of the literary racket.

CHAPTER SEVENTEEN

THE UNDISCOVERED COUNTRY:
THE HEART OF THE MATTER

During the period in which he defended the British Empire against spies in tiny Sierra Leone, Greene found enough time to write his eleventh novel, *The Ministry of Fear*. As a piece of wartime literature, it does not inspire confidence in the forces of democracy and freedom. The Nazis in the story are unquestionably a bad lot, but British justice is shown operating at a level not far above the Gestapo's. The British spy catcher, Prentice, will go to great extremes to trap a Nazi, and his determination leaves him with little patience for the fine points of law. When he tells a female spy that she may hang for her crime, she protests that Britain does not execute women for espionage. In response Prentice coolly implies that some women have been executed in secret. As long as the papers do not hear about it, hanging women is something he can accept. It is the price of freedom.

On a personal level, this guardian of justice rather likes making a woman suffer. Before he sends his spy off to prison, he ravages her house, telling his men to "skin" the place. While the woman watches in fear, Prentice makes it his special duty to tear her bedroom to pieces, throwing her cosmetics in all directions, ripping her pillows, smashing her delicate lamp, destroying an erotic book. Normally restrained, he blazes with anger in his savage attack on her house, calling out the word "bitch" as he heads for her bedroom. The excuse for this violence is that Prentice is looking for vital evidence, but his fury goes beyond what the search requires. The whole business is a kind of rape, and the narrative makes a point of saying that Prentice takes "vicious pleasure" from the assault on the bedroom.

Throughout the novel Greene questions the moral authority of the establishment. In the name of law and order, Prentice can behave like a criminal and get away with it. The demands of the war provide easy excuses for everything from imprisonment without trial to murder. The authorities flatter themselves that the killing required by war is different from ordinary killing. But Greene cannot see why an impersonal shooting or hanging in war is so acceptable while an impassioned, personal murder is a tawdry crime.

The hero of *The Ministry of Fear,* Arthur Rowe, is surrounded by murderers—official ones who are engaged in a desperate struggle to defend the country. They shoot at enemy bombers, chase enemy spies, and go off to slaughter the enemy on distant battlefields. Blood is everywhere. But Rowe is amazed at this display of sanctioned killing. He has been away for two years, and, in the England he knew before the war, violence had no place. People were supposed to be civilized. Now he finds himself in a world where killing is encouraged and honored—as long as the victim is a stranger who speaks a different language.

The reason that Rowe is confused by this "normal" state of affairs is that he has been punished for killing someone he loved. A year before the war began, he committed a mercy killing, poisoning his wife. He was put away, and the world that put him away knew exactly what to think of him. He was a criminal, an outcast, someone to be avoided by respectable people, who would never dream of taking a life, no matter how good the reason might be. Then the war came along and gave everyone such a good reason to kill that violence has become a way of life. The whole country is devoted to it. Now, as one character observes, it is "respectable" to kill. You can get ahead by doing it, winning medals, promotions, and even profits.

In such a world Greene's old-fashioned murderer begins to seem almost decent. He has a kind of integrity that the undiscriminating soldiers and sailors and arms manufacturers lack. They deal in mindless massacres, but he spent years planning his murder, knew his victim almost as well as he knew himself, and agonized over the final moments of the deed. He has thought about it so much that he is no longer sure whether he killed his wife to spare his suffering or hers. By contrast, he learns that a friend has been liberated from his difficult wife by the explosion of an enemy bomb. The husband is portrayed as meek but restless, the sort who would want his freedom but would never kill for it. The war has done the job for him, and no one is held accountable. The airman can drop his bombs and fly away from death without a second thought about the individual lives lost. Rowe cannot run away. He is haunted forever by the face and voice of the woman he killed. Although he has been detained a relatively short period for his crime, he feels that he is serving a life sentence, chained to the memories of his crime.

Greene tries hard to make a virtue of the old-fashioned murder. It is easy to make Rowe look good against a background filled with cutthroat spies. When he is drawn, by accident, into the activities of a Nazi spy ring, he becomes the innocent victim, and our sympathy grows for him. We may not like self-appointed mercy killers, but Greene knew that we would identify with Rowe once he became a target of Nazi treachery. And, while we are busy feeling sorry for the hero's spy troubles, Greene develops a subtle argument in favor of Rowe's act of murder. We are led to think that men such as Rowe are not really criminals. The truly bad men are the generals and politicians whose violent ways are crude, insensitive, and dishonest. At least Rowe knows who he is and is willing to live with it. He took a life in a moment of profound passion and agony, driven by a refined mixture of love and despair. Yet the pious will condemn such a man without hesitation, ignoring the complexity of his emotions and motives, and refusing to see that his victim might have sought death or deserved it. At the time of the murder, Rowe had the feeling that his wife wanted to die, if only to give him peace. It was a sort of bargain, the acceptance of death on one side and the willingness to kill on the other.

The point is that outsiders cannot really understand what pushed Rowe into murdering his wife. To appreciate his position we must be shown the world from his point of view; then we might even begin to think that his crime makes sense. After all, Greene's novel implies, Rowe is not so different from the rest of us. Most of a murderer's life is not spent in murdering people. Greene stops the action of the story to show us the ordinary aspects of a killer's life. We are told that he drinks coffee in the morning, reads books, goes to bed early, likes dogs, argues about politics, and gets constipated. In short, he is a part of the world that we all know, and, for most of us, there is no reason to fear him.

When news of Rowe's crime is reported to his friend Wilcox, the man expresses surprise, saying that good old Arthur would not hurt a fly. We forget that even murderers have friends. We may punish them, but their greatest suffering is self-inflicted. Rowe knows the horror of his crime and does not need the world to remind him, especially because our hands are not clean. The passions that raged in him are not as bad as those that rage in the breast of Prentice, the police-man with the heart of a rapist. The representative of the law may not belong to the ranks of real killers and rapists, but, as his name sug-gests, he is a good apprentice.

Greene identifies so much with Rowe that he fills the murderer's world with many details from his own life. "A tall stooping lean man" in middle age, Rowe resembles his creator. Before he is injured in a bombing attack, he listens to the news as it is read by the voice of Greene's old friend from Oxford, Joseph Macleod. And when he is taken to a clinic for shell-shock victims, the grounds of the place are exactly the same as those at Harston House. The brick wall, the orchard, the pond with the small island, the potting shed—they are all there. Moreover, Greene places the green baize door from Berkhamsted in the clinic. After being locked up at the clinic for a while, Rowe begins to feel like a rebellious schoolboy, and he finally asserts his independence by sneaking through the green baize door. On the other side he finds the forbidden secrets of a cruel world.

Rowe's great desire is to start over again, fresh and innocent. He cannot wipe out all the memories of the painful years with his wife, and the world will not let him forget that he is a murderer, but he longs to return to the peaceful world of his boyhood and to believe that the past twenty years of his life have been magically erased. The war gives him some relief. Bit by bit it is destroying reminders of the past, demolishing the streets and houses that formed the background of old humiliations and heartaches. Like Greene, Rowe finds that he cannot return to an earlier innocence but that he can feel more "at home" in a ruined world. The destruction mirrors his broken spirit, and the new legions of official murderers make his unofficial killing look better.

After trying to get his bearings in this new "home," he dreams of sinking further into a life devoted to forbidden pleasures. A male offi-cer of the law motions to him in a dream but speaks in a woman's voice, inviting him to have a sexual encounter in front of a urinal. Rowe asks to be taken home, but the policeman tells him in a reas-suring voice, "This is home." There is a bombing raid, and the ground of the lavatory shakes so much that Rowe can hardly stand in his new "home." He is awakened from this dream by the sound of the all clear siren, but the phrase is heavy with irony. There is no "all clear" for Rowe nor, presumably, for Greene. The past cannot be cleared away. The new home must exist on the rubble of the old world.

Denied a return to the innocence of childhood, Rowe feels cheated by the tranquil Edwardian life that disappeared so quickly. He acquired a set of unrealistic expectations from his mother, who believed that everything could be put right in time and who grandly ignored any problems that upset her. The novel opens with a small fair sponsored by the Mothers of the Free Nations. The atmosphere reminds Rowe of his childhood, but the whole business turns out to be a sham. The organization is a front for the Nazis, and Rowe innocently steps into a trap at the fair. Mothers are seen as betrayers, enemies who plant false hopes of freedom and happiness. From the little we know of Rowe's wife, she seems to have been more of a mother figure than a lover, but killing her did not bring back Rowe's freedom. For Greene's male characters there is no escape from the special tyranny of mothers.

The Ministry of Fear is a war novel only on the surface. The war is the right background for a private conflict, just as Mexico was the right background for the Hollow Men of *The Power and the Glory*. The book is crawling with spies, but they seem to care more about tormenting Rowe than about winning the war. Greene is not interested in the rights or wrongs of the world conflict. He wants to know about the suffering endured in one man's war, and he brings its terrors to life with the same skill that he applies to his portrait of the greater war. The atmosphere of the blitz helps to create the impression that Rowe's life is in complete disarray. To achieve his effects Greene uses all the right images. Barrage balloons hover over the parks, searchlights flash across the sky, blackout curtains hang like shrouds in the windows, antiaircraft guns thump and rumble, and the air is thick with the smell of broken gas mains. He took the images from his own experience, but it is a wonder that he re-created the scene so vividly from his desk in Freetown. Sitting in the African heat, he brought the smoky ruins of wartime London back to life.

The novel was published three months after his return from Sierra Leone. The ominous title attracted no awkward questions from his superiors at SIS, who did not seem to mind that the book contained an account of a spy stealing top-secret documents from a government office, photographing them, then returning them to the office. After all, it was only a novel. No one could take such things seriously.

II

On the strength of nothing more than its title, Greene was able to sell the film rights of *The Ministry of Fear* to Paramount for the equivalent of several thousand pounds. It was a great present to welcome his return from Africa, and there was the chance that this film might finally be an artistic success. The legendary Fritz Lang was chosen to direct the picture, and Greene was hopeful that such a talented man would know how to bring out the best in the story. During his years as a film critic for *The Spectator,* Greene had looked kindly on Lang's efforts, praising *Fury* as an example of truly great filmmaking. *The Ministry of Fear* had the potential to work well on the screen, but it would be difficult for any director to do justice to Rowe's complex psychology.

Unfortunately, Lang never had the chance to create a good script. He was forced to work for the screenwriter and producer Seton Miller, who prepared his own script and insisted that Lang stick to it. Miller's script plays down the unpleasant fact that Rowe is a murderer, emphasizing instead the nefarious deeds of the Nazi spies as they try to keep Rowe from revealing their plans. Soon the viewer forgets that Rowe has ever done anything wrong himself. All that matters is the race to catch the spies before they flee the country. And, once this mission is accomplished, a happy ending is created in which Rowe goes driving off into a beautiful landscape with an adoring girlfriend laughing merrily beside him. When Lang later met Greene in Hollywood, he graciously offered an apology for the film.

Greene enjoyed complaining about the bad adaptations of his books for the screen, but he was always happy to take Hollywood's money. By the end of the war, he was doing well enough to put his family in a house that was almost as elegant as Number 14, North Side. He found a tall house in the center of Oxford, at 15 Beaumont Street, and, although Vivien and the children moved in immediately, he came there only when he could get away from his work in London. The problem was that he could not decide whether to leave Vivien permanently or stay with her until the children were grown. His family was entirely dependent on him for financial support, but the war years had given him independence from family life, and he did not want to be trapped again.

After he came back from Africa, Greene continued to live with Dorothy Glover in London. On some weekends and holidays, he went up to Oxford and endured the pain of playing husband and father. As long as his war work kept him in London, he had a convenient excuse for staying away from Oxford. And when the war ended he had already prepared another excuse. In 1944 he became a part-time editor for the publisher Eyre & Spottiswoode, and he arranged to stay on after the war as the full-time managing director. The firm was second rate, but he thought that anything was better than having to go back to Oxford and stay with his family.

The best thing about working for Eyre & Spottiswoode was that Greene did not have much to do. There was a steady stream of money flowing into the company from its perennial best-seller, the Bible, but the basic list of authors was small and unimpressive. No doubt it pleased Greene to know that his salary was being subsidized by sales of the Good Book, but it was not the sort of firm that he could be proud to serve. During his tenure the annual offering of titles was generally dismal. There were some bad novels by Frances Parkinson Keyes, and an old favorite from Mary O'Hara—*My Friend Flicka*. There were some dull histories, a collection of maxims and reflections from the Rt. Hon. Winston Churchill, a mind-numbing anthology called *Switzerland in English Prose and Poetry*, books on bridge and fishing, and a children's book from Dorothy Craigie, *Summersalt's Circus*. Some of the best titles were American, including Robert Penn Warren's *All the King's Men* and a volume of Allen Tate's poetry.

Greene added books by Mauriac and Narayan to the list and brought out some classic novels in a series of inexpensive reprints. One of these was Henry James's *The Wings of the Dove*, with an introduction by Herbert Read. Although Greene realized that some critics considered his own work nothing more than popular entertainment, his model of excellence in fiction was James. He cared deeply about the art of the novel and profited from studying not only the works of James but also those of the master's great admirers Joseph Conrad and Ford Madox Ford. The section "Novels and Novelists" in Greene's *Collected Essays* is dominated by the lessons of James.

From the early days of his career, Greene was an avid reader of James, and in later years he rarely went on a journey without taking along one of the writer's books. The cherished prize of his personal library was a large collection of James's work, which included many first editions. In the 1930s he wrote two substantial essays on the novelist, and they are full of admiration for his poetic sensibility, his scrupulous attention to point of view, and his perceptive treatment of the battle between innocence and evil. Beneath the charming surfaces of life in James's country houses and hotels, Greene found a sufficient number of devils to stir the imagination, and he liked the highly refined manner in which their treacherous personalities are brought to life. James was able to treat even the most "unspeakable" evil with "the highest kind of justice," which meant—to Greene—"giving the devil his due."

Publishing a new edition of *The Wings of the Dove* with an essay by

Herbert Read was a great pleasure for Greene, but, by and large, he was content to spend a good deal of his time at Eyre & Spottiswoode on less noble activities—taking long lunches on the expense account and traveling on "company" business to the Continent. As a representative of a publisher of the Bible, he had an excellent cover for undertaking occasional missions on behalf of the secret service. And his boss at the firm—Douglas Jerrold—was not one to object to such missions. Jerrold liked intrigue and had been involved in a major secret operation before the war. According to Hugh Thomas's *The Spanish Civil War,* Jerrold—who was a great supporter of Franco—played a small part in the general's plot to start the fascist rebellion in Spain.

Greene worked under Jerrold for four years, and in that time they came to know each other well. Although Jerrold was a Catholic, spiritual matters did not play an important part in their relationship. Indeed, Jerrold soon discovered that Greene's approach to the religion had little to do with conventional notions of faith. He was able to watch Greene carefully and knew him at a time when his novels were beginning to gain a large following. While many readers happily embraced the novelist as a spokesman on religious issues, Jerrold saw a different side of Greene—a more worldly character who knew how to use religion to his advantage. A few years after Greene left his employ, Jerrold wrote a remarkably perceptive profile of the novelist. It is an inside look at Greene from the vantage point of a skeptical friend.

Jerrold believed that Greene's admirers were too much in awe of the religious symbols and themes in the books. He wrote, "In all this chatter about Graham Greene as a religious novelist, there is a confusion between being intensely interested in religion and being religious." Jerrold found an abundance of sin in Greene's work but no evidence of an interest in redemption or good works. The novels do an excellent job of making the reader "an accomplice in the guilt of the protagonists, but not a partner in their salvation." From experience in the office, Jerrold knew how much Greene enjoyed misleading people, especially on subjects that everyone takes too seriously in the first place. He saw Greene as a brilliant child, nursing obscure hurts and ridiculing the adults as they pursue their solemn activities. Nothing is more fun than to trick the old folks into thinking you are a good choirboy and then to make rude gestures behind their backs.

Jerrold recognized the poet in Greene and saw that one of his great themes is hate: "Graham Greene . . . writes with feverish nostalgia of his schooldays, which he hated, and therefore loves to recall. . . . How much is merely emotion recollected in hostility to life in general? For those who have only known him in his later childhood, it is difficult to say." Because he understood the hostile nature of the big child, Jerrold realized that the famous anecdote about young Graham playing Russian roulette was meant as a joke on the reader. While he was working at Eyre & Spottiswoode, Greene published "The Revolver in the Corner Cupboard," and Jerrold was the first person to throw doubt on the story. Noting Greene's comment in the sketch—"I wasn't even excited"—Jerrold made the sarcastic observation, "But everyone else has been."

The best thing in Jerrold's profile is his description of Greene at work in the office. Although he may have been a child emotionally, he was very much a capable adult in matters of business. He always knew how to get what he wanted: "He would settle down to the serious business of the day, telephoning with rapid succession to his bank, to his stockbroker, to his insurance agent, to his literary agent, to a film company or two, and, if it was a really busy morning, to two or three editors. During these conversations the tortured conscience so frequently, and so movingly, on exhibition in his novels was notably absent." Jerrold added, "He is, and does not wish you to know it, an absolutely first-class man of business."

But, once all the necessary business was taken care of, Greene was free to be a child again, hating people, complaining of boredom, looking for pleasure and pain, devising new pranks. At Eyre & Spottiswoode he was able to cause his fellow workers endless trouble by assuming a new identity. As the author Mrs. Montgomery, he wrote letters to the office complaining that his valuable manuscript had been mislaid by someone in the firm. He—or she—demanded immediate action. Creating a convincing imitation of a woman's voice, Greene called various people in the office and tried to arrange urgent meetings in obscure places. In the meantime a man purporting to be her biographer wrote to *The Spectator* asking for information about her. "Mrs. Montgomery" immediately replied with a letter of righteous indignation, objecting to the unauthorized biography and asking that her privacy be respected.

It is amusing to think that, many years later, Greene would make some of the same self-righteous protests on his own behalf, and that the joke would be continued beyond the grave by his literary estate. The charade of Mrs. Montgomery went on for at least three weeks, and, at the end of it all, his fellow workers were not sure whether to laugh or to scream. Jerrold wrote of the episode: "Here for once the whole of Graham Greene was at work in a harmonious universe of his own choosing—the mischievous child, the brilliant man of affairs, the creator of entertainments, the writer of film scripts, and the psychological analyst. Only the power and the glory were ephemeral." When Greene finally left the firm, in 1948, one suspects that he was not sorely missed. It was indeed his last full-time office job. He was made for a great many things, but working in an office was not one of them.

It was the motion picture business that liberated Greene from Eyre & Spottiswoode, once again showering him with so much money that he no longer needed to bother with a regular job. First, the Boulting brothers produced a version of *Brighton Rock,* filming almost all the scenes on location in the town itself. Greene and Terence Rattigan provided the screenplay, and they managed to remain generally faithful to the structure of the original novel. The biggest change came at the end of the film. Instead of having Rose walk away with Pinkie's record, the last scene shows it being played on a phonograph. But the needle sticks, and the scene fades out before Pinkie's terrible outburst of hate can be heard. As endings go it is as bad as anything devised by Hollywood and is the only major flaw in an otherwise superb production. Greene was responsible for the scene. He saw it as a clever compromise: "Anybody who wanted a happy ending would feel that they had had a happy ending. Anybody who had any sense would know that the next time Rose would probably push the needle over the scratch and get the full message."

Nothing mars Carol Reed's production of *The Fallen Idol,* which was released in 1948, shortly after the film *Brighton Rock.* From beginning to end it is a beautifully crafted film. A great deal of the credit belongs to Reed's expert direction, but Greene's script is also first rate. As this film and *The Third Man* amply demonstrate, Greene's literary material could work supremely well on the screen, with the right script and the right director. Reed and Greene worked closely on every detail, spending many hours in hotel rooms pacing the floor as they hammered out each scene together. Greene's short story "The Basement Room," on which the film is based, does not seem, at first glance, to be a promising work for film adaptation. Not only is it very short but it also contains too little visual action to sustain a full-length feature.

In *The Fallen Idol* Greene and Reed solve the problem by placing more emphasis on the world outside the basement room. They move the camera into the streets of London and give a greater sense of the freedom that the boy craves and that his hero Baines represents. The original story has a claustrophobic feel to it, but *The Fallen Idol* places the boy on the exhilarating border between wild freedom in the streets and stifling security in the large house. One way that Reed achieves this effect is to show the boy leaning over the balcony of his house, high above Belgrave Square. The town sparkles in the sunlight, beckoning him to join its dangerous but attractive life. The sense that the boy is standing on the verge of the adult world is reinforced even in the interior shots. Reed uses a set dominated by a grand staircase to create the illusion of great height inside the house. The boy is often shown staring down from those heights, peering at the tragic adult drama that slowly unfolds below him.

Although Greene's literary production slowed down considerably in the 1940s, the motion picture industry made up for his relative inactivity by releasing so many film versions of his work. Admirers of his books could expect a novel from him almost every year in the 1930s, but he brought out only one new novel between 1941 and 1948—*The Ministry of Fear*. That same period, however, saw the release of the films *This Gun for Hire* (based on *A Gun for Sale*), *Ministry of Fear*, *Confidential Agent*, *The Man Within*, *Brighton Rock*, *The Fugitive* (based on *The Power and the Glory*), and *The Fallen Idol*. While these films helped to spread Greene's popularity, they also helped to distort the public image of his work. It was easy for academic critics to ignore him as a popular writer, and it was equally easy for ordinary readers to underestimate the artistic sophistication of his work.

III

Greene's wealth and growing fame gave him all the excuses he needed to stay away from Vivien and the children. He did not need Eyre & Spottiswoode to keep him occupied. Vivien had been functioning more or less as a single parent since 1939, but she was exceptionally patient toward her wandering husband. She did not pry into the details of his life away from home, and she always tried to make him welcome when he returned. Still, the situation was clearly hopeless. He did not love her anymore, and she could not go on thinking that he would eventually settle down in Oxford. There was resentment on both sides. Greene hated the idea of having to choose between ending their relationship and pretending that they were still a family. Vivien felt sorry for the children. As she said later, "I think they felt that their father not seeing them when he was in London, and we were in Oxford, was very sad. He would just come down for the day sometimes." She also resented his absence in times of trouble. When Francis came down with a middle ear infection during the war, he had to be operated on at home because there were not enough hospital beds available. It was a traumatic occasion, but, as Vivien recalled, Greene "was nowhere to be seen. He was back from Africa. You want someone there for support. Someone to be frightened with you."

When he did show up, he was annoyed by the noise of the children and impatient to leave. When visitors came they were struck by the vast difference that had developed between Graham and Vivien. A mutual friend of the couple, the art critic John Rothenstein, visited them at 15 Beaumont Street in 1945. He found it a "very feminine house," full of the dainty objects Vivien liked, including her growing collection of dolls and dolls' houses. Vivien was immersed in the Victorian period and liked to wear "neo-Victorian clothes." As she went through the house "attending to the needs of multifarious tiny fragile objects," Greene looked on "with a detached eye" and amused himself by "discoursing with a fair measure of candour of his visits to nude shows and other places even farther beyond the range of his wife's approval."

Whatever else had happened in their relationship, Greene still regarded Vivien as the mother figure whom he must disobey, trying to shock her with stories of his misbehavior. He was playing a point-less game, but he took it so seriously at times that he would despair of ever being able to end it. In such moments he was driven back to his old infatuation with suicide. The matter was complicated by Dorothy's presence. By the mid-1940s he was tired of her. But end-ing their relationship was no less difficult than cutting his ties to Vivien. Two very different women stood between him and freedom. He felt obligated to help both of them and knew that they depended on his support. If he went his own way, the guilt would be hard to escape.

This situation is reflected in the novel that he began writing in the mid-1940s, *The Heart of the Matter*. Major Scobie, the assistant com-missioner of police in Sierra Leone, is married to a woman he no longer loves. After many years of marriage, he has nothing left to share with her except misery. Louise Scobie wants to believe that their marriage will survive, not because she loves him but because she has no way to survive on her own. She constantly reminds him of how much she depends on him and complains of how lonely she feels. Unwilling to let him go, she tries to keep up appearances, calling him "darling" and using her childish nickname for him, Ticki. But he hates to hear such things and resents all her efforts to be kind. Everything about her annoys him—the way she talks, the odd dresses she wears, the clutter of her collection of little objects in their home. In a moment of candid reflection, Louise admits that she is fighting a losing battle, but she places most of the blame on her husband. Scobie, she says, is incapable of loving anyone, not even himself.

They have had only one child, but the girl died in England when she was three. The news of the girl's death reaches Scobie in a manner that recalls Greene's experience with his father's death. One telegram announces that the girl is ill, the second that she is dead. When the two messages reach Scobie in reverse order, he does not know what to think. Accepting her death is hard enough, but being left in doubt by the second message is the worst part. It seems that his whole life has been dogged by such pointless suffering. As a result he has come to expect the worst, and to be wary of any human ties. If he had his life to live over again, he tells himself, he would live it alone.

The only thing that keeps Scobie from abandoning Louise is his acute sense of guilt. She knows that this is her one source of power over him and does her best to appeal to his notion of right and wrong. She tries to make him go to Mass, although she knows that he has no faith. He jokes that her faith is great enough for both of them, and she says that he became a Catholic only because he wanted to marry her. To give himself and his wife a little relief from such tiresome disputes, he sends her on a long holiday to South Africa. While Louise is away, he falls in love with a young woman who is vulnerable and alone. The affair dooms not only his marriage but also his life. After Louise returns he finds himself trapped between the emotional demands of both women, and his sense of guilt soars out of control, driving him toward death.

Helen Rolt does not fit the stereotype of the other woman. She is neither sexy nor charming, and she is certainly not beautiful; in fact, at one point Scobie admits to himself that she is "ugly." In part, he seems to want an affair simply to make himself more miserable. There is no question that a love of pain attracts him to Helen. He tells himself that her ugliness is more exciting because no one else will give her a second look. If he cannot have beauty and love, he will make a pleasure of ugliness and pain. In no time his "love" for Helen gives rise to a nasty fight. She is deeply jealous of Louise and complains that Scobie will never leave his wife. He falls back on the empty excuse that he is Catholic, and she explodes in anger, pointing out that his scruples keep him from marrying her but not from having sex with her. In time, Scobie thinks, Helen and Louise will be "indistinguish-able" in his mind. He will have two women to dread, two women to keep him trapped. The situation is never as bad as Scobie seems to think. As we later discover, both women *can* live without him. But his passion for overdramatizing his troubles causes him to contemplate suicide, and the more he thinks about it, the more it appeals to him as the perfect escape from a seemingly impossible problem.

There is also the added appeal of defying God, who has failed to rescue him from his plight. As Scobie gets closer to committing sui-cide, he thinks less about the women in his life and more about his confrontation with God. He tells God that he will be doing him a favor by taking his own life. But the pleasure is all Scobie's. At Mass he has a vision of devilish priests celebrating a Black Mass and tells himself that their hatred of God is a kind of "perverse devotion" to him. He regards himself as too weak to reach the level of their power and glory, but his aspirations lie in that direction. Having found so much unhappiness in his life, he wants to wallow in it, making every good thing bad. It is a path of destruction that must lead to the sin of suicide. It is the only way that he can carry pain to the ultimate extreme, and the only way that he can imitate those devilish priests in their proud orgy of hatred.

The Heart of the Matter is the story of a man who seems deter-mined to break the rules. He is a policeman who cannot maintain law and order in his own life, violating the moral prohibitions against adultery and suicide. And, as does *The Ministry of Fear,* the novel makes the emotional turmoil in one man's life the center of attention in a world at war. In Sierra Leone the war is barely felt. There are blackouts but no raids. Wounded people are brought ashore from torpedoed ships, but the actual attacks take place hundreds of miles away. Stuck in an alien land at the margin of an enormous battle-ground, Scobie is free to pursue his lonely duel with God. The rest of the world can take care of itself.

Not long before he died, George Orwell reviewed the novel and harshly condemned it. Honest and straightforward man that he was, Orwell could not find anything in the story to approve. There was no sign of the "ordinary human decency" that he valued so much in life and literature. Indeed, he detected in Greene a certain "snobbish-ness" on the question of sin: "He appears to share the idea, which has been floating around ever since Baudelaire, that there is something rather *distingué* in being damned; Hell is a sort of high-class night club, entry to which is reserved for Catholics only." The wonderful image of hell as a select nightclub is perfect for Greene, but in his goodness Orwell could not see the appeal of hanging out in such a club. "The cult of the sanctified sinner seems to me frivolous," Orwell wrote in his best schoolmaster tone, "and underneath it there probably lies a weakening of belief, for when people really believed in Hell, they were not so fond of striking graceful attitudes on its brink." Of course, an earnest person would not want to strike "graceful attitudes" at hell's gate, but that is the whole point of Greene's work. Unlike Orwell, he was not trying to make the world a better place. He was engaged in a private dance with sin. We may not be invited to join the party, but, as spectators, we are given quite a show. The graceful attitudes are its highlights.

Because Orwell was thinking in social and moral terms, he was outraged by the African setting. As a veteran of five years in the Indian Imperial Police, he knew the world of a colonial policeman much better than Greene did, and he could see that—from the standpoint of realism—Scobie and his surroundings are unconvincing: "Why should the novel have its setting in West Africa? Except that one of the characters is a Syrian trader, the whole thing might as well be happening in a London suburb. The Africans exist only as an occasionally mentioned background." Orwell was right about the action being more appropriate to an English setting, although he could not have realized how right he was, because he knew nothing of Greene's difficulties with Dorothy in London and Vivien in Oxford.

As is the case in most of Greene's work, the setting is realistically described, but one should not be fooled into thinking that it has much importance in its own right. As Orwell correctly understood, the real people and places of Africa are of minor significance. The African characters who drift through the novel are rarely named, are given brief descriptions, and are allowed only short lines of dialogue peppered with expressions such as "Yes, massa" and "Yes, sah." The narrative says that a group of Africans in a crowded street move like insects, and the young black boys who loiter near the wharf are referred to as "human rats" and "flies." Scobie's "boy" Ali does receive a good deal of attention, but he is given no personality. Although Scobie says that he loves him, it is the love of a master for his faithful dog. By contrast, consider this roll call of names from the novel's cast of characters: Colonel Wright, Freddie Bagster, Helen Rolt, H. R. Harris, Wilson, Louise Scobie, Maj. Henry Scobie, Dr. Travis, Mrs. Halifax, Father Clay, Miss Malcott, Mrs. Bowles, Dicky Pemberton. As a group these people would not be the least out of place in a romantic tale of life in an English village during the 1920s.

The evocation of place in *The Heart of the Matter* is not nearly as interesting as its literary evocations. The novel is teeming with books and allusions to books. Literature and language—not religion—are at the heart of the matter. One of the nicknames for Scobie's wife is Literary Louise. Her sentimental personality is reflected in her passion for light poetry, a passion that makes her husband cringe. Throughout the novel books are used as ways of revealing the essence of a character. One of Louise's friends, Mrs. Halifax, is constantly reading novels, but her approach to literature is so shallow that she easily forgets books and mistakenly reads them again. Pemberton, the mysterious young man who commits suicide early in the novel, leaves behind few traces of his life, except his small collection of mystery novels. Robinson, the self-obsessed bank manager, studies *Diseases of the Urinary Tract* as though it were the Bible; and Father Clay will read anything so long as it concerns the saints. It is significant that the hardened villain of the novel, Yusef, is illiterate.

Scobie claims that he does not have much time for reading, but he has a deep imagination and an intense love affair with words. At one point in the story, he makes up his own novel. The priggish missionary's wife, Mrs. Bowles, gives him a book to read to a young boy lying in a hospital bed, but when he sees what a dreary work it is, he changes the story to make it more interesting for the boy. In his hands *A Bishop Among the Bantus* becomes a roaring adventure tale of Arthur Bishop, a courageous spy. Arthur's mission is to track down the Bantus, a band of ferocious pirates led by the great Bantu cutthroat Blackbeard. The missionary's wife returns to find the boy enthralled by the book, but she never learns that Scobie has created a different version of it. She is satisfied that *A Bishop Among the Bantus* is a "safe" book for young minds, something with solid moral value. But, like Greene, Major Scobie subverts the proper religious tale, smuggling an unsafe story to his audience while the guardians of virtue are looking the other way.

In his impromptu creation of Arthur Bishop's story, Scobie shows that he has a lively way with words, but the darker side of this talent lies in his ability to use words against himself. His love of pain and his love of words make a dangerous combination. The narrative says that, like Coriolanus, Scobie longs to show his wounds. He feels that he must "dramatise his pain in words." The words enhance the pain and make him want more of it. It is a pleasure for him to stage an announcement for Helen, declaring, "I've damned myself." The moment loses some of its edge, however, when Helen replies, "Don't be so melodramatic."

The comment about Coriolanus highlights Scobie's fondness for playacting, but it is only one of many references in the novel to a Shakespearean character. Othello, Iago, Hamlet, and Lady Macbeth are also mentioned or alluded to. Yusef claims, for example, to be a great admirer of Shakespeare's *Othello*. He has seen a group of amateur actors from the Royal Ordnance Corps perform the play in Freetown and has fallen in love with it. No doubt the villain is especially drawn to the character of Iago, whose actions and motives resemble his own. However, if we think of Shakespeare and Scobie's story, it is not Othello or Coriolanus who come to mind but Hamlet. Like Greene's hero, the prince wants to playact his way toward self-destruction, using "words, words, words" to mark every stage of his tragic fall.

Hamlet says that he admires a man who is "not passion's slave" and that he would be devoted to such a man: "I will wear him / In my heart's core, ay, in my heart of heart." But there is no room left in his heart for anything other than passion, and it finally undermines him. The same is true of Scobie, who echoes Hamlet's words when he questions the nature of his own passions. Sensing that his love of pain is his driving force, he asks himself whether Louise and Helen really matter at all: "Do I, in my heart of hearts, love either of them?" In his desperation Scobie questions God's right to deny him the comfort of suicide. As Hamlet says, "Or that the Everlasting had not fix'd / His canon 'gainst self-slaughter." Although Hamlet is greatly tempted to take his own life, he backs away from the deed, worried by the thought of that "undiscover'd country, from whose bourn / No traveller returns." But Scobie is undeterred. After many words he crosses that "bourn" and disappears into the "undiscovered country."

Facing death, Scobie gives up on words. He dramatizes his pain for so long that, finally, there is nothing left to say. The words take him to the verge of death, and, having talked himself into that tight spot, he has no choice but to act. His last moments of consciousness are marked by a sudden loss of words: "Dear God, I love . . ." Many readers have debated the meaning of this last statement, some speculating that he is trying to say, "Dear God, I love you." But there is no missing word. The blank space is the answer. It is exactly what Scobie craved, the emptiness of annihilation, the final pain, the end of words. Hamlet says it best, with his last words: "The rest is silence."

With Greene there always has to be an extra turn of the screw. Even in death Scobie is able to use three more words to inflict pain. He cannot go to his death without leaving behind a hidden message, something that will stab another person's heart unexpectedly. His plan is similar to Pinkie's idea of placing a message on a phonograph record, but he uses kind words to hurt his victim. On the day of his death, he sneaks into Helen's house and finds her treasured stamp album. One stamp has a stain on it, and Scobie knows that eventually Helen will want to replace it. Carefully, he lifts the stamp and writes beneath it in ink, "I love you." The act is more important than the sentiment. Just as it was a pleasure to tell Helen that he has damned himself, so there is satisfaction in knowing that the words will wait quietly in the album, then will suddenly scream at her one day when she casually tears out the stamp.

The potent combination of language and pain was something that Greene knew well. Unlike Scobie, he was too attached to words to abandon them willingly. Scobie chose to take his life, Greene chose to write *The Heart of the Matter*. And, although he would go on toying with the notion of suicide, he stayed stubbornly on the side of words, clinging to them for comfort, striking his graceful attitudes at the bourn. Unfortunately, the attitudes grew much less graceful in later years, but the words kept coming, right up to the final year. Published in 1990, its author's eighty-sixth year, the last book is a little collection of stories. Greene gave it the only possible title, *The Last Word*.

Greene's lonely struggle with words in the 1930s and 1940s produced three masterpieces—*Brighton Rock, The Power and the Glory*, and *The Heart of the Matter*. These novels are full of what Douglas Jerrold called "emotion recollected in hostility," and no sensitive reader can get through them without occasionally wincing at the ugliness of the author's sentiments, or resenting a few of his tricks. But they are extraordinary works of art, each packed with sharp insights, poetic images, compelling scenes, subtle messages, and intricate narrative twists. No one else has written anything like them. Among the great unreliable narratives, Greene's must rank high. No author could be more unreliable, more determined to upset the complacent reader. But, like all good writers, he rewards the careful reader, planting surprises on almost every page of his masterpieces. He was not writing for readers like Louise Scobie's friend Mrs. Halifax. Whatever else can be said about his greatest novel, *Brighton Rock,* few of its readers are likely to forget their first encounter with it.

When it was first published, *The Heart of the Matter* attracted the interest of a great many people who seemed to share the general outlook of the missionary wife in the novel. They wanted to debate whether the book was safe to read. It was banned in Ireland, and Bishop Brown of Southwark criticized it for "encouraging" the view that sexual sins are acceptable. Some prominent Catholics tried to defend the book, including a few who knew Greene personally. Evelyn Waugh could not make sense of the novel's "theology" but tried to be supportive anyway, calling the work "profoundly reverent." His serious effort to make Greene sound reverent is hilarious, and finally even Waugh seems to have realized the absurdity of his task. Toward the end of his long review, he suddenly throws up his hands and declares, "To me the idea of willing my own damnation for the love of God is either a very loose poetical expression or a mad blasphemy, for the God who accepted that sacrifice could be neither just nor lovable."

The best response to the novel came from Mother Mary Angelica, a prominent nun in Chicago, who warned the readers of a Catholic newspaper that *The Heart of the Matter* "is definitely a hands-off book for youthful readers. By no means may it be put into any school library." An obvious fan of *A Bishop Among the Bantus*, Mother Angelica condemned Scobie's crimes with the words "What madness of human thinking, what blasphemy of human language." Such words were worth a fortune. People raced out to buy the novel, and the Book-of-the-Month Club chose it as a main selection. In Britain the sales soared to record levels. Greene's previous novel, *The Ministry of Fear*, sold 18,000 copies; *The Heart of the Matter* sold nearly 300,000 in three years. And these figures represent only the British sales. His publishers quickly reissued his earlier novels, giving new life to the unjustly neglected *England Made Me* and *A Gun for Sale*. After nineteen years of hard work, Greene was established for life. From 1948 until his death, he would continue to enjoy large sales and widespread publicity. No doubt he remembered all the Mother Angelicas of the world in his prayers.

CHAPTER EIGHTEEN

THE THIRD WOMAN

In 1946 Vivien was contacted by a beautiful young woman who was planning to become a Catholic. Would it be possible, the woman asked, for Mr. Graham Greene to be her godfather on the great day of her reception into the Church? She admired his novels so much that she wanted to recognize him for helping to bring her into the fold. Vivien consulted her husband and gave a polite reply, telling her that, yes, the author would be happy to accept her request and would send flowers to the ceremony. Vivien volunteered to represent her busy husband on the day of the event. Such requests are the price of fame, and this one might have been easily forgotten if the woman had not been so attractive, persistent, and rich. As Greene later learned from Vivien, the pretty new convert left the reception breakfast in her private plane. Intrigued, he invited her to visit him and his wife at their house in Oxford. When she arrived one look at her was enough to inspire a passion that would not die out for years to come. It was the beginning of the most important affair in his life.

Catherine Crompton Walston was thirty when she met her godfather. She was married to one of the richest men in England and was the mother of five children (a sixth would come a few years later). Although her husband—Henry Walston—was a prominent supporter of the Labour Party, he did not believe in forgoing luxury. He and

Catherine owned a yellow Rolls-Royce convertible, an elegant country house in Cambridgeshire—Newton Hall—a large farmhouse in
the nearby village of Thriplow, a house in St. James's Street, a cottage
on an island off the coast of Ireland, a flat in Dublin, and a banana
plantation on the Caribbean island of St. Lucia. The family farm at
Thriplow covered several thousand acres and employed one hundred
workers in the 1940s. The staff at Newton Hall included four gar-
deners, a chauffeur, a butler, a footman, a cook, an assistant cook,
and various maids. The Walstons shared their wealth with their many
friends by entertaining them frequently and lavishly. Evelyn Waugh's
comment on this hospitality is exquisite. When he proposed dining
with the Walstons on a particular evening, Catherine replied with a
telegram, "Must warn you I have 150 dining that night." Waugh's
response was brief: "Who? How? Why? Particularly, How?"

Catherine was not the typical society hostess. She was lively and
uninhibited, and would often shock her guests with some eccentric
remark or deed. After returning from a dinner at which she had
appeared barefooted, Waugh joked that Catherine was "unaffected to
the verge of insanity." Ian Fleming's wife, Ann, agreed. In a letter to
Waugh, she described a meeting with Catherine in Capri:

> She seized my battered straw hat and declared it a most enviable pos-
> session, she tried it on at various angles and prinked and preened, then
> she displayed the same idiotic enthusiasm for Ian's old walking stick
> and pranced about with the uninteresting object expressing a violent
> desire for it. I suggested a swap for her frock at which she started vio-
> lently undoing the bodice—she's a very maddening woman.

Catherine's friend Frances Donaldson remembered weekend parties at Newton in which the hostess would have great fun violating
the ordinary codes of conduct: "The wives had naturally taken trouble over their clothes and went down to dinner the first night in their
best dresses. Catherine would appear in jeans. Accordingly, the guests
would go down the next night in day clothes to find Catherine in a
long evening dress." After Catherine's wedding her very proper
mother-in-law, Lady Walston, gave a party to welcome her to the
family. In the middle of the event Catherine stunned everyone by
doing cartwheels across the floor. Playful and headstrong, she was
called by one friend "a Marie-Antoinette in elegant jeans."

Her upbringing had not prepared her for life in English high society. She was born in Rye, New York, in 1916, and seems to have been
something of a tomboy from the start—she even had a tomboy's

nickname, Bobs. But, when she became a young woman, the boys had no trouble recognizing the feminine charms of pretty Bobs. "From the age of thirteen," a sister remembered, "she turned heads." She was a nineteen-year-old student at Barnard College when she dropped out to marry Henry Walston. He had come to America for a year to study at Harvard, and they met during a skiing weekend in New Hampshire. Harry—as he was commonly known—was so attracted to her beauty and impulsive behavior that he decided to act impulsively himself. A few days after they were introduced, he telephoned and asked her to be his wife. In typical fashion she said yes before she had a chance to think it over. Although the marriage went ahead, in 1935, she confided to a sister that she did not love him.

In an effort to win her love, Harry gave her whatever she wanted and let her do whatever she wanted. If something made her happy, he was happy. By the early 1940s she had discovered that one thing that made her very happy was to sleep with all manner of men. She had affairs with everyone from an old veteran of the Irish Republican Army to a visiting American general. Yet she always came back to Harry. Eventually he enjoyed a few affairs of his own, but his relationship with Catherine was not destroyed by their extramarital activity. His tolerance and support won her affection, and the couple settled into a comfortable life together. Straightforward and open, they were faithful to each other in their fashion.

Catherine's independent ways did not win her many women friends, especially because she had a habit of showing too much interest in their husbands. But she was sexually free and saw no reason why others should not be. She was happy to make love on floors, in fields, or in forbidden places. During her relationship with Greene, she joined him in a unique endeavor that one friend—Diana Crutchley—later described as "committing adultery behind every high altar in Italy." Always prepared for love, Catherine kept a drawer full of condoms in various sizes. On one occasion she proudly revealed the contents of this drawer to the countess of Huntingdon, an enlightened woman whose only comment on the display was a mild expression of admiration. "So accommodating," the countess remarked.

Somewhere along the exciting path of this sexual odyssey, Catherine found Catholicism to be a particularly potent stimulant. She grew fond of priests and enjoyed trying to seduce them. Some kept her at bay, while others surrendered completely. For many years she maintained an affair with Father Donal O'Sullivan, a Dublin priest who eventually became head of the Irish Arts Council.

O'Sullivan and Catherine often stayed together at her flat in Dublin, and in later years they liked to have an annual holiday in Venice.

Another of her favorite priests was Father Thomas Gilby, a Dominican theologian and a professor of something called Speculative Morals. He was a hearty fellow who wore tweeds, smoked a pipe, and spent a good part of his life drinking in pubs. One of Catherine's children—Bill Walston—was very fond of him. He liked the priest's easy wit and warm manner. For several years Father Gilby seemed almost a part of the family. When Harry was away he sat at the head of the table, and at all times his advice was sought on matters large and small. Harry regarded him as a friend and was content to defer to his judgment. According to Bill Walston, "With the exception of my father and Graham, Father Gilby was the most important man in my mother's life."

Bill Walston did not believe that his mother was sexually involved with the priest, but Catherine's sister Bonté had a different view. She spent two summers at Newton Hall in the early 1950s, and her letters from that period provide an intimate look at the unconventional life of the Walstons. No visitor could fail to notice Catherine's obsession with priests. They were in and out of the house all the time. But Father Gilby dominated the scene, and Bonté slowly developed an intense dislike for him. She could not believe how much power he exercised over her sister. In a letter to her husband, she tried to explain life with Bobs and Gilby:

> I have made several light hints about the character of Thomas Gilby, for I have tried without much success to see him as an intelligent, worldly, well-meaning individual. But his behavior is so extraordinary that it is hard to be neutral & slightly indifferent. Not only does he behave in the most possessive manner with Bobs, but he behaves *sexually* in the most possessive manner, & she is entirely absorbed in him to the exclusion of everything else & everybody else. All morning they remain in her study together writing and reading. At lunch he sits at the head of the table (as Harry is away again) and is deferred to on every question, such as . . . how to bring up children etc. Conversation is quite dead because a series of innuendoes which I don't understand covers most of the talk. Sometimes he makes a remark which hurts her feelings, and then she bows her head & won't say a word for some time, much to everybody's embarrassment. . . . His behavior shows a lack of dignity, coupled with a masked brutality. You feel he owns poor Bobs body & soul, and that he wants you to know it.

However dominant Father Gilby may have been, there was always room for other men in Catherine's life. If she could feel some sort of religious connection to her companion, the pleasure was all the better. One lover—Brian Wormald—was a former Anglican priest. "She certainly had a thing for priests," Wormald recalled, adding that she liked the game of "provoking them into going to bed and then holding off." He thought that she was trying to use her beauty primarily to tease them but that she was also ready for much more. "She would like them to fall in love. That man, Father O'Sullivan—she completely undermined him, I think. I don't know how his reputation survived. She certainly thought that she had captured him." There is no question that she captured Wormald, who found her "staggeringly beautiful" and who regarded her as one of the most important women in his life. He was jealous of her many affairs but realized that he could do nothing to change her compulsion: "She flirted with every man, tried to capture every man." He threw an interesting light on her promiscuity: "Harry didn't appear to object to her carryings on with other men, and I've heard one theory that if she became a Catholic, there would be someone to object to what she did"—that someone being God.

With the right man—one who was willing to push the affair too far—Catherine could succeed in arousing Harry's anger. Everyone who knew of her relationship with Father O'Sullivan was aware that Harry loathed the priest. For one thing, O'Sullivan encouraged Catherine to indulge in long drinking binges. Their affair lasted for many years, and Catherine's alcohol problem became so bad in the final months of her life that Harry decided to take every bottle in the house away from her. Her son Bill thought that, if left alone, his mother would "easily have spent the rest of her life drinking herself to death with Father O'Sullivan." Moreover, the priest was good at talking Catherine into giving him large sums of money. Of course, it was her husband's money that she was giving away, and her "generosity" made Harry furious. When Harry received an insurance settlement for some pearls that had been stolen from Catherine's car, he told her that he would buy her more pearls but would not give her the cash. He was afraid she would simply turn the money over to O'Sullivan.

For a time Greene was also a source of concern to Harry. At the height of his passion for Catherine, he was a great troublemaker who threatened to break up the marriage. He was also something of a bully with Harry, trying to dictate when he could see Catherine at Newton and Thriplow. The impulse to bully the husband may have been intensified by the fact that Harry was Jewish. In some ways Harry could be seen as someone like the Forbes/Furtstein character in *The Confidential Agent*. The family's real name was Waldstein, and the maiden name of Harry's mother was Einstein. To Greene this sort of thing would make a difference, at least at those times when he was looking for more reasons to hate Catherine's husband.

With her unconventional devotion to Catholicism, Catherine had good reason to think that the "Catholic" creator of Pinkie and the whiskey priest would make a great godfather. And, indeed, he relished the sacrilege of having sex with his godchild. A short book of poems privately printed for her included, in one version, a dedication to his "Godchild Catherine Walston." He could always play devilish games with prostitutes, but it was so much more thrilling to play them with a beautiful young wife and mother. This was decadence of the highest order. For her sake he was willing to take a more active part in the Church. Going to Mass, entertaining priests, reading theology, visiting shrines—it was all worth doing because it gave greater substance to their unholy union. The problem was that Greene took the game more seriously than Catherine did. He wanted to play it nonstop, and he wanted to create complications that were far greater than anything Catherine desired.

They became lovers in early 1947, after enjoying a film and a steak dinner at Rules restaurant, in Covent Garden. When they left Rules, they paused in Maiden Lane and kissed beside a doorway. They made love that night and later agreed on a code word for sex—one that recalled an addition to their steak dinners: onions. In a few months he was seeing her regularly and was enjoying lots of onions. He became a frequent guest at her house and was, in the beginning, on friendly terms with Harry, who welcomed his presence so long as he did not make scenes. But it became increasingly difficult for Greene to keep his passions under control. As a houseguest on weekends, he would try to remain polite toward the other guests, but he was always impatiently waiting for moments when he could be alone with Catherine. He began to live for the occasional periods when he could have her to himself for a few days. They would escape to London, to Catherine's cottage in Ireland, to the Continent, or—in later years— to such distant places as Southeast Asia.

For Greene there was a mystical side to the affair. He saw Catherine as someone who was destined to be his lifetime companion, a woman who would be all things to him. With her uninhibited attitudes she was willing to entertain his wildest fantasies and to listen sympathetically to his darkest fears. The fact that Newton Hall was only a mile and a half away from Harston made it easy to connect the beautiful Catherine with the enduring symbols of his childhood—the magical pond and the dreaded potting shed. It was also significant that she was born when he was twelve, when the miseries of his school years began. He could see her as the friend whom time had saved for him, a spiritual sister who would seek him out one day—as indeed she did—and who would help relieve his loneliness. His infatuation led him to attach a special significance to her name. It excited him to find "Catherine" in any book that he was reading, or to fill a page by writing her name over and over, or to fantasize that she was Catherine Greene.

She did what she could to satisfy his expectations. They drank and joked late into the night, shared secrets, talked about literature and art, and even went to a brothel together. In the early 1950s she agreed to dress up like a young man and accompany Greene to an elegant house of prostitution in Venice. He was working in the city as the screenwriter for a bad film called *The Stranger's Hand*. His colleague and friend Guy Elmes remembered the occasion:

> When we finished the movie, the top echelon, whatever you call it . . . we had our farewell to Venice in a whorehouse. All Graham said is, "Could I have the makeup man? Because there is a certain lady I've got in the hotel who I've always wanted to take. Could she come with us dressed as a boy?" And so she was made up as a man with a lovely big cap and all her hair tucked underneath it. And she came in with us and enjoyed it as a man, all our farewell to Venice. . . . She had a whale of a time—roared with laughter—thought it very funny. I can still hear her laughter.

Catherine also served as an audience of one for Greene's short story "Limited Edition," an experiment in pornography. In 1948 he wrote the story during a holiday in Capri, then later tried to destroy it by ripping it into small pieces. Eventually, it was pasted together and a clean copy was made. The story builds slowly to a graphic sexual scene. A young man sits next to a pretty woman in a cinema and decides to put his hand under her dress and stroke her leg. When she does not resist, he slides his hand between her legs and arouses her. She suddenly has second thoughts about this brief encounter and struggles to remove his hand. While she tries to compose herself, the hero stares at the screen and calmly raises his wet finger to his mouth. In the darkness, with the woman still beside him, he licks his finger, savoring the salty taste of her body. To his surprise the woman later indicates that she wants more of his special caresses, and thus a wonderful relationship begins, with lots of excitement for both parties— especially on one occasion when they find themselves alone in a railway carriage. "Limited Edition" will not win any awards, but it is a reasonably good effort for a world-renowned Catholic novelist.

As earlier chapters have indicated, Greene wanted Catherine to indulge his fondness for punishment, asking her to inflict the secret burns he seemed to enjoy. In the figure of Padre Pio, the couple found someone who combined Catherine's interest in charismatic priests and Greene's fascination for mystical pain. It was said that Padre Pio was blessed with a particularly extreme case of the stigmata. He was supposed to have large wounds in both his hands and his feet, as well as a two-inch wound in his side. The wounds bled so extensively that he lost as much as a cup of blood each day, or so the faithful claimed. Yet the cuts never became infected. In fact, some said that they gave "a perfumed odour." After hearing of this miracle, Greene and Catherine decided to visit the little mountain village in Italy where Padre Pio said Mass at five each morning. When Norman Douglas learned of Greene's enthusiasm for this visit, he remarked, "Imagine a great big grown up man going in for that sort of thing." Unfortunately, Greene did not see any bleeding when he attended the Mass, but he did notice some dried blood. Forty years later, when he was interviewed by the Catholic weekly *The Tablet*, he disclosed that he always carried a picture of Padre Pio in his wallet.

With Catherine as his partner, Greene felt free to try all sorts of experiments. After years of writing about lonely characters who seek their own damnation, he was now in a position to enjoy sin in the company of someone who seemed to share his appreciation for such things. To encourage her participation in his little dramas, he quoted Browning's words to her: "Better sin the whole sin sure that God observes." Catherine was simply trying to have a good time, but Greene's overactive imagination created complex parts for them to enact. In particular, he was fond of calling Catherine his Kate Croy. As a great admirer of Henry James's *The Wings of the Dove*, Greene thought that the characters of Kate Croy and her lover Merton Densher were "the most driven and 'damned' of all James's characters." Greene had been rehearsing the part of Merton Densher for most of his adult life. When Catherine came along, he was delighted to think that he had finally discovered the leading lady in his Jamesian fantasy.

A perfect chance to play these parts came during a visit to Oxford in the late 1940s. They had gone to Catherine's cottage on the Irish island of Achill and had decided to stop in Oxford on the way back to London. Apparently on impulse they went to Greene's house at 15 Beaumont Street and presented themselves at the door. By this time Vivien knew that Greene's godchild was his lover, but she invited them in, and, to her surprise, they insisted on spending the night. She made it clear that she disapproved, but she was not able to send them away. For one thing, the children were present, and she wanted to avoid a scene. To her, the humiliating part of this episode was that she had to serve them dinner and make the beds. The pleasure for "Merton" and "Kate" came from seeing the "dove" struggle in the trap.

Students of James might also suggest that Greene and Catherine resemble the strange couple featured in "The Altar of the Dead." It is another of James's works that Greene admired and is concerned with a religious obsession that has strong sexual overtones. James's hero, Stransom, sets up his own private altar in a little Catholic church and uses it solely to worship the dead. Stransom is worried that no one thinks of all the dead and feels that they deserve one devoted servant among the living. But as he is going about his dark business, he finds that a beautiful woman has discovered his altar and is also using it to worship the dead—or so she says. The development of the tale reveals that love and hate and sexual frustration are at the heart of this shared ritual. It is the kind of worship that Greene and Catherine could understand.

What Greene could not have known at the time was that "The Altar of the Dead" was inspired by James's memories of a strained relationship with an American woman. In the early 1960s Leon Edel revealed that James was deeply admired by this woman and that her feelings had caused James considerable confusion. He was drawn to her as a friend but was never able to respond to her romantic interest in him. After her early death he felt guilty about not having shown her more sympathy, and, as a kind of tribute to her memory, he made a point of staying one night in the last house where she had lived in England. The idea for "The Altar of the Dead" came to him that night. The American woman's name—Constance Woolson—sounds remarkably like that of Catherine Walston, but this is worth noting only because of an eerie connection between James's experience and Greene's. The house in which James spent the night—the house where Constance Woolson had once lived—was in Oxford. The address was 15 Beaumont Street. Since 1945 Vivien and the children had been living in the same house where Henry James found the inspiration for "The Altar of the Dead." It was the perfect place for "Kate" Walston and her lover to spend the night.

It is possible that Greene staged his Jamesian drama with some knowledge of the connection between his house and the Master's tale. Although Constance Woolson's influence on "The Altar of the Dead" was not generally known until Edel revealed it, the importance of 15 Beaumont Street came to light in 1947, with the publication of

James's notebooks. Without mentioning Constance, James records that he stayed at the house in September 1894 and that the idea for his story came to him there. If Greene saw the entry, he would surely have been tempted to have his Kate spend the night. The trouble is that the incident cannot be precisely dated. Vivien remembered only that it happened sometime in the late 1940s. And she was never aware of James's experience in the house, or of her husband's desire to play the part of a Jamesian character. Whether Greene understood all the connections or not, the memory of his performance could still bring tears of pain to Vivien's eyes in the 1990s.

Dates can be tricky with Greene. In the whole matter of his affair with Catherine, one has a strange feeling that he may have met her before she first contacted Vivien in 1946. It would not have been beyond their powers to create a pretext for their relationship *after* it had begun—simply for the sake of making Vivien think that she was responsible for bringing the "godchild" into the family. It may seem far-fetched, especially because their early letters show no evidence that they were acquainted before 1946, but the Jamesian episode at 15 Beaumont Street makes one think that anything is possible.

II

The intensity of Greene's attachment to Catherine threatened to end the affair within a few months of its beginning. He was constantly complaining that she did not spend enough time with him, yet, when she was with him, he would often start a quarrel or retreat into the silence of a deep depression. "Graham very depressed" is a typical entry in Catherine's diaries from the early years of their affair. In the summer of 1949 she was writing such things as "Graham unusually gloomy and depressed—even for Graham." She also found that the mood could spread. In one of her letters she speaks of suffering "an almost Greene depression." No matter how much she tried to be with him, it was never enough. He could not understand why she needed her family, her husband, or other men when she could experience endless days of dark passion with him.

Their relationship was always one of extremes. They could be blissfully happy for a time; then Greene would despair because Catherine needed to leave, or he would start a fight because he was afraid of losing her. One moment he would worship her, making extravagant plans for their future—they would each get annulments and marry, then buy an island and hide from the world. The next moment he would bitterly threaten to end the affair, saying that they could never make each other happy. Catherine was amazingly good at riding out these storms. She was genuinely fond of Greene and tried to see the best in him. But she could not give all of herself to him, or to any man. She agonized over their troubles and tried to understand his complicated personality. It was easy to see that his hard exterior protected a fragile ego. In a letter to Bonté, Catherine said that Greene was "very very shy, and cannot conceive of anyone wanting him." In another she wrote:

> How good and dear and kind he has always been to me, and the only thing that I really mind is his own suffering, for which obviously, I am partially responsible, in one way or another. . . . Through cowardice, fear, love, stupidity and selfishness, I have allowed a situation and relationship to grow out of hand, and have never made my position clear enough. Just why one acts and behaves in certain ways is impossible for me to tell about myself. Every answer has its own division—do I remain because I am selfish or unselfish, for good or bad motives? Maybe some of both, I don't know. What a lot of mistakes I have made through fears and bloody-mindedness.

Although she had her own insecurities to confront, Catherine pulled Greene from his shell and encouraged him to think better of himself. Over time she managed to make him a little more outgoing. She introduced him to new people and put him back in touch with old acquaintances. In the early 1950s Waugh said of her relationship with Greene, "She found him very lonely and morose & thought it her duty to enliven him with new acquaintances. Indeed it is thanks to her that I have seen so much more of him during the last three years." She arranged for him to spend weekends at other people's homes, partly to keep him from always wanting to stay with her. At her urging he was a guest at Edward Sackville-West's country house, but Greene's idea of casual conversation was a bit much for his host:

> Graham Greene has been here for the week-end. . . . Odd how every place he talks of seems sinister or squalid. Told me an extraordinary story of equivocal episodes in Lyons, with a *louche* businessman & a mistress & a rich widow. Also—fascinating detail—that the police prison contains a large rosary of leaden beads with which a renegade priest (c. 1890) used to murder people. I fancy that Catherine's insistent favouring of my friendship with G is partly—but only partly—because of a desire to be relieved of some of this burden!

Sometimes Catherine's best efforts were fiercely resisted. As she noted in one diary entry, Greene was not always willing to discuss his shortcomings: "Arguments until midnight over my theories on Graham's general attitude of mistrust of himself and varying aspects." When he lost his temper, he could create frightful scenes, as Bonté discovered one night at Newton Hall. In a letter to her husband, she described how Greene's violent outbursts seemed to be a "normal part" of his relationship with Catherine:

> Graham was in a good mood, considering that the night before the sounds of his irate quarreling that came from Bobs's study made me feel sure that he was about to commit murder. I had gotten in rather late . . . and I shivered in bed a long time, as doors banged & there were shouts & tears. Next morning, however, it was exactly as though nothing at all had happened, so perhaps these storms are the normal part of their odd relationship.

Bonté was right in assuming that these outbursts were not isolated events. In her diary of 1949 Catherine notes that she found Greene in a "very angry" mood one evening. He was staying at her house and had become upset because she had been away for most of the day. There was an argument that ended with Greene "slamming the door to his room." On another occasion "Graham made a scene about my being late; Twinkle [the nanny] telephoned to Graham who swore at her."

Part of the problem was that Greene was drinking heavily. He had an extraordinary tolerance for alcohol, but occasionally he would lose control. When things were not going well with Catherine, or when he was separated from her for long periods, he would drink to great excess. During a trip to America in 1948, he spent so much time drinking that he collapsed and suffered a hemorrhage. He was treated at a New York hospital and was warned by the doctors that his abuse of alcohol had to stop. He managed to stay away from drink for a few days but soon went back to his old habits. Unfortunately, like Father Sullivan, Greene made it easy for Catherine to indulge her weakness for alcohol, although even she complained that his martinis were lethal.

As Greene became more troublesome, Harry turned against him and demanded that he stay away from Catherine. There was a brief separation; then Harry changed his mind. The pattern was repeated a few times—Greene would go too far, Harry would object, Greene would be banished, and Harry would allow him back. It was difficult to keep him away, especially after the summer of 1948, when he moved to St. James's Street. Colonel Dansey's old hideaway at

Number 5 was next door to Harry and Catherine's house. Greene's lease for the first-floor flat at Number 5 was negotiated through a private firm, and Catherine helped to work out some of the details. Naturally, Greene also wanted to be close to Catherine's house in the country, so when his uncle's old place at Harston came up for sale, he thought about buying it. He wanted to do everything in his power to stay near her, but he finally realized that buying Harston House was impractical. The place was much too big for one man to keep up.

Throughout the late 1940s and early 1950s, Greene insisted that his ambition was to marry Catherine. He tried relentlessly to make her leave Harry and claimed that he would have little trouble arranging an annulment of his marriage. But the evidence suggests that he was never serious about breaking all his ties to Vivien. Despite his great obsession with Catherine, he was afraid of becoming trapped by her. With Vivien in the background, he could back away from a serious commitment to anyone else by arguing that his Catholic wife would never give him a divorce. Although he complained about not having full possession of Catherine's love, he clearly enjoyed the complications created by their relationship. As long as there was something forbidden and dangerous about their affair, it was worth sustaining. If they ever married, the joy of sin would be threatened by respectability and routine. And he knew that the chance of Catherine leaving her family was small. Her attitude toward her children was cool and casual, but she did not want to abandon either them or her rich, understanding husband for an uncertain, stressful life with Greene.

In 1948 Vivien and Greene discussed the future of their marriage with a young priest named Vincent Turner. The couple decided to obtain a legal separation, but Father Turner found that Greene was reluctant to accept this arrangement: "Both [Vivien] and Graham had a horror of divorce. He didn't want one. Graham wanted a separation, but didn't even want it formal. Vivien—I think quite rightly—saw that you could never trust the future, and she wanted it formalised." Vivien got what she wanted but worried that outsiders would not understand her reasons for insisting on a legal separation. As Father Turner recalled, "Vivien got very bitter and said, 'Nobody understood because of, you see, Graham's power over words. And he's very persuasive. He can persuade people of anything. I don't have any way with words.'" It was only in Greene's last years that Vivien spoke publicly about their marriage. Although he supported her throughout his life, she felt neglected: "You see, I never had any of the fun—being rich or meeting people or being taken abroad. I had the hard part when we were young and poor. All the mistresses had the good times."

For a time Dorothy Glover was equally bitter about losing her hold on Greene. When she learned of his relationship with Catherine, she lashed out at him for pursuing "an American blonde with a yearning for culture." It made little difference that Catherine was not a blonde. Dorothy knew her appearance could not match Catherine's, so her only hope was to make Greene feel guilty for preferring shallow beauty to a creative mind. Her plan failed, although Greene did take a long time to end their affair and remained a friend of Dorothy until her death. When she finally met Catherine, she discovered that her rival was not so bad after all. It would seem that Padre Pio deserved the credit for this miracle. In 1988 Greene told an interviewer that he had prayed to Padre Pio for one mistress to stop hating another. "Within two weeks they were friends," he said.

To complicate matters even further, there was another American woman seeking Greene's affection in the late 1940s. In late 1947 he met the novelist Jean Stafford, who was separated from the poet Robert Lowell. She decided that Greene was a thoroughly enchanting character. For reasons of her own, she also believed that they looked alike. In a letter to Lowell, she confided: "Greene says he thinks I might be awfully happy in Dublin and he proposes that I come to England next summer and he will take a cottage for me in some romantic sounding place in Ireland where, he says, there will be nothing at all in front of me but America on the other side of the ocean." Stafford later said that she and Greene had been lovers, but he told her biographer that there was no substance to her claim. In this instance, the truth may be on his side. She had only recently been released from a year's stay at the Payne Whitney Clinic, in New York, where she was treated for severe mental problems and alcoholism. In Greene she may have thought that she had found a companion soul, but the affair could easily have been one of her delusions. In any case, she eventually turned against him with a vengeance, condemning him in a review for "his particularly noxious brand of prurience."

Greene's very real affair with Catherine reached an emotional breaking point in 1950. Even though Greene knew that marriage was impossible, he tormented Catherine by talking about it endlessly. On a business trip to New York, he visited Bonté and her husband and begged her to talk Catherine into marrying him. He claimed that she had twice tried to commit suicide and would never be happy until she left Harry. Bonté made no promises to help but tried to appear sympathetic. Several days after his return to England, Greene wrote to

Orson Welles in *The Third Man*, 1950.

The face of treason: Kim Philby, 1953.

A stranger in the theater: Greene talks to Eric Portman, star of *The Living Room,* 1953.

One too many: the
novelist in 1954.

Greene's Italian hideaway: the villa Il Rosaio.

Jocelyn Rickards in Capri.

Laurence Olivier in a television version of *The Power and the Glory*, 1962.

Elizabeth Taylor and Peter Ustinov in the film version of *The Comedians*, 1967.

The wronged woman of *J'Accuse* —
Martine Cloetta.

Greene the bookman, 1982.

A guest of Communist East Germany, Greene inspects the Berlin Wall, 1963.

The farewell at Vevey: Vivien Greene and her daughter at Greene's grave, with Yvonne Cloetta in the background, right.

Greene's last face.

her and explained that he and Catherine had put the question directly to Harry. In a tense scene Harry learned that Catherine was agonizing over whether to stay with him or marry Greene. The discussion continued until late at night, and Harry finally went to bed in tears.

Of course, nothing was decided, and the affair continued to go in circles, but the turmoil caused everyone to suffer, which seems to have been Greene's main objective. Harry's pain interested him as much as Catherine's. For Greene it was not enough to love the wife in secret. He had to bring the husband into the affair as well, making him a vital part of the excitement. It allowed him to have an emotional relationship with two people at once. And as the affair dragged on, he became a sort of second husband who shared more than a wife with Harry. When the Walstons moved from St. James's Street to Albany, in Piccadilly, Greene took a set of chambers near theirs. Harry's secretary, a Mrs. Young, also became Greene's secretary. Greene read Harry's children bedtime stories from Sherlock Holmes and took them on holidays to Capri. But the strangest twist of all is that Harry entered into a long affair with a woman who was one of Greene's intimate friends. The conflict between the two men gradually disappeared, and, at the time of Greene's death, they were on good terms. Given the nature of their relationship, it is perhaps only fitting that they died within a few weeks of each other.

III

The dynamics of this three-way relationship are fully examined in *The End of the Affair*. Harry became Henry Miles, Catherine became Sarah Miles, and Greene became the popular novelist Maurice Bendrix, who narrates the story. Maurice is a lonely man who shares his creator's dedication to writing. Regardless of what is happening in his personal life, he can turn out 500 words a day and finish a novel in a year or two. When he is not writing, he is tortured by emotions that he cannot control and is driven to hurt others for no logical reason. He broods about the past and is amazed at Sarah's ability to live completely in the present. Her beauty and candor fascinate him, but he also feels intimidated by her. As he admits, he is more comfortable with women who are not beautiful. His sexual feelings are usually aroused by the sense that he is somehow superior to their object. With Sarah he can never feel entirely in control. She is too unpredictable.

The affair begins when the couple attend a film and then have a steak dinner, with onions, at Rules. Like Greene and Catherine, Maurice and Sarah have their first kiss at a doorway in Maiden Lane, and they later use the word *onions* as their private code word for sex. People who were familiar with the real-life drama, such as Father Vincent Turner, were amazed to see how much of it went straight into the novel. When he read the book, Father Turner heard not only the voices of Greene and Catherine "but also their very words." Catherine read the book as it was being written, when the working title was "Point of Departure." She appears not to have raised any substantial objections, but the same was not true of her family. When Greene showed a copy of the manuscript to Catherine's younger sister, Belinda, he received a strong rebuke. Belinda told him that it was cruel to use names and events that were so close to the real circumstances. She was particularly offended by his decision to name the husband in the story Henry and to give Catherine's maiden name to the priest, Father Crompton. Saying that his art was above such minor concerns, Greene made it clear that he was greatly offended by the criticism, and Catherine took his side in the matter.

Greene dedicated the book to C. in the British edition and to Catherine in the American. There was surprisingly little speculation in the press about the identity of the mysterious person, but many people in the Walstons' social circle—as well as some on the fringes—were aware of the couple's connection to the book. The Labour politician Richard Crossman had never met Catherine when he visited Newton Hall in 1953, but gossip had already made him familiar with her place in literary history. In his diaries Crossman described his visit:

> Walston's wife, an American, is the heroine of Graham Greene's *The End of the Affair*. No one dares to ask Walston what he feels about this novel, which is all the more embarrassing since Mrs. Walston talks all the time about Graham Greene. During the afternoon, while the others played croquet, she rather ostentatiously immersed herself in reading a translation of St. Thomas Aquinas, which is being produced by her house guest, a Dominican, Father Gilby. Looking up, she said to me, "Strange how 'the heart of the matter' has become a cliché since Graham's novel." I said it was a cliché long before—and then I knew she didn't like me.

In late 1948 Greene began writing *The End of the Affair* during a visit to Capri, and he continued working on it for the next two years.

Throughout the two-year period Greene was expecting the end to come; he had created a situation that was always on the verge of disaster. In fact, the affair lasted until the early 1960s, but the dramatic tension steadily decreased in the 1950s, and other lovers came into their lives. In the complex time scheme of the novel, Maurice's affair with Sarah lasts five years, but most of the action occurs after this period, when the hero is struggling to understand why the affair ended. A novelist with the instincts of a detective, Maurice is able to reconstruct the events and uncover the truth. He begins by suspecting that Sarah left him for another lover but discovers that his only rival is God. When he was injured in a bomb blast during the war, Sarah promised God that she would end the affair if Maurice lived. Her prayer was answered, and she stands by her promise until her sudden death from pneumonia two years later.

Instead of being grateful to Sarah and God for saving his life, Maurice is furious and sees nothing good in the deed. As far as he is concerned, Sarah is still the unfaithful, devious lover who abruptly deserted him, and God is the bully and the cheat who stole her heart in a cruel bargain. He sees God as the ultimate cad, who can do anything to trick his rivals. In an orgy of blasphemy Maurice ridicules Christ and God for resorting to trickery. Staring at a figure of Christ hanging on the cross, he taunts him for not being able to give Sarah's breast a good erotic squeeze. God may have won the woman's heart, Maurice says, but he is a lousy lover: "It was I who penetrated her, not You." Because Maurice is the narrator, his intense hatred of God and Sarah is expressed at great length, and no other voice is allowed to contradict him directly. He does include excerpts from Sarah's diary, but they are chosen by him, and he has the last word. God can play his games in the real world, but Maurice knows that the novelist is the only deity who matters in the fictional world. He cannot undo what God has done to Sarah in real life, but he can tell the story his way. He can say whatever he wants and can even cast God as the villain.

At the beginning of his narrative, Maurice speculates on how writers construct their stories. Confronted with endless ways of beginning and ending each tale, they must make their choices. But Maurice wonders whether, in art as well as life, God is lurking somewhere in the background pushing him toward certain choices. The considerable intricacy of Maurice's narrative shows how much he wants to think that all his choices are entirely his own. As a narrator, he is always doing the unexpected thing—altering the time sequence, devoting a large section to excerpts from Sarah's diary, creating a long anticlimax. He imagines that God is racing to catch up with his every move, but his finished book is the best evidence that God has lost the race. The novel concedes nothing to God. He is the villain of the piece, and the last few paragraphs contain an extraordinary outburst of hatred directed entirely at him. Maurice seems to be looking for the best possible insult to hurl at God, and finally he finds the right words: "I hate you as though You existed." Among blasphemers, Maurice is a pro.

Of course, the real pro is Graham Greene, who found a safe way to convey the sacrilegious nature of his affair with C. At least it was safe from the standpoint of public consumption. No major objections were raised against Maurice's frenzied assault on God. Indeed, a Catholic organization in New York gave Greene a literary award for his work. It is a shame—for truth's sake—that an anti-God organization was not available to present him with an outstanding achievement award. No major novelist has shown as much ingenuity in abusing the God of Christianity. It is a dubious distinction but one that Greene fully deserves. The climax of this effort is not Maurice's well-chosen insult but a two-word challenge that he presents to God. Knowing that Sarah's corpse will be cremated, Maurice sees a wonderful chance to mock God. "Resurrect that," he says. In its simplicity it must certainly stand as one of the gems in the history of blasphemy.

In the 1950s the writer Derek Patmore questioned Greene closely about his commitment to Catholicism and his interest in evil. He tried to get Greene to admit that he was not really a true believer, but the novelist stood his ground firmly: "It's not true. I really am a believer. . . . Don't forget, I always submit my manuscripts, including plays, to Father Philip Caraman, one of the leading Jesuit intellectuals, for guidance." It is indeed true that Greene and Father Caraman were good friends in the late 1940s and early 1950s, but it would be a mistake to hold the priest accountable for the work of the novelist. Father Caraman had great admiration for literary people—he was also a close friend of Edith Sitwell and Evelyn Waugh—and he was happy to publish some of Greene's short pieces in his Catholic literary magazine *The Month*. But Father Caraman's sympathy for Greene, and his broad-minded attitude toward human frailty, did not make him a particularly objective critic. And Greene was delighted to hide behind his friendship with the priest whenever it seemed convenient.

The celebration of hate in *The End of the Affair* is not something that most Catholics would want to endorse. Although Maurice is not directly responsible for Sarah's death, he welcomes it with the kind of glee that would be more appropriate to a murderer. He wants her to suffer for deserting him, but the pain of hate is also more exciting to him than the ordinary satisfactions of love. It is a mistake to call *The End of the Affair* a love story. In the first chapter Maurice says that he will be providing the reader with a record of a hate, and hatred is the predominant emotion from beginning to end. Some form of the word occurs seven times in the opening eight paragraphs of the novel, and eight times in the last eight paragraphs. Maurice is always looking for some way to bring hate or fear into his life. Part of the attraction of an affair with a married woman is that it gives him ample opportunities to experience both emotions. He can fear detection and fear desertion. He can hate the husband for standing in his way and hate the wife for not leaving her husband. God is also good for hating and fearing, because toward him there can be no limits to the emotions. No amount of hatred or fear will ever suffice if it is directed against him.

Maurice's most passionate moment of lovemaking with Sarah involves a strong element of fear. She invites him to her home and prepares sandwiches for them. Henry is in an upstairs bedroom suffering from a bad cold. While Sarah and Maurice listen for any sound of footsteps coming down the stairs, they have sex on the parquet floor of the living room. To stifle the cry of Sarah's orgasm, Maurice must put his hand over her mouth. At every moment of intercourse, their pleasure is heightened by the fear of discovery. And, just when all their energy is spent, they get the extra jolt—the stair squeaks. They must hurry to put their clothing back in order, but, fortunately, Henry takes his time before he enters the room and finds his wife's guest calmly sitting in a chair with a plate of sandwiches in his lap.

An affair built on hate and fear must eventually destroy itself. The end of the affair is inevitable. But in his ecstasy of hate Maurice discovers that Sarah's death will allow him to prolong the "end" forever. When Sarah's spirit defects to God's side, she and God form a couple whose love can cause Maurice endless torment. He can cremate her body and throw curses at heaven, but he knows that he will never win, which is the beauty of the situation. As Maurice points out, it is his professional duty as a writer to develop an overactive imagination, but the same force that fuels his literary creativity sustains his emotional turmoil. Without much effort he can continue the affair by imagining God in Henry's place as the hated rival. And Sarah will always be the impossible lover. In this frame of mind, he finds it easy to dismiss stories from her admirers that they have experienced miracles since her death. He sees these miracles simply as further examples of God's tricks. They are another reminder that God does not play fairly and deserves to be despised.

The only way that Maurice can possess Sarah is to turn her into one of his fictional characters. Within the fixed boundaries of his narrative, she will always be his woman—to love or to hate. God may have the soul, but Maurice has the body, or at least a convincing likeness. Whenever he looks back at his story, he can find Sarah trapped within each page, a prisoner of his imagination. The purpose for his earliest contacts with Sarah is to find material for a story. He is writing about a character whose civil service career is like Henry's, and he asks Sarah to give him details about the daily lives of such men. Gradually this literary exercise is abandoned for the more interesting experience of having sex with the civil servant's wife. But by the end of the novel, Maurice has come full circle. Having won and lost his real woman, he falls back on his old practice of using material from life to make his fictions, "picking the brain" of a friend or acquaintance to create a plausible character. After Sarah's death he has more than enough information to resurrect her as the star attraction of his story. He has picked her brain clean and captured her in his hate-filled image.

The End of the Affair gave Greene the chance to possess a part of Catherine. He took enough from her life to create his own version of the real woman, and he surrounded it with all the confused elements that entered into the real affair—the jealousy, the bitterness, the sacrilege, the mystical attraction. In life he was never sure when the affair would end; in art he could end it at will and imagine all sorts of exciting repercussions. Even the strange bond with Harry is reflected in the novel, but it is given a homosexual slant that was never apparent in the actual relationship, although it may have been part of Greene's fantasy. Just as Greene tried to hurt Harry as well as Catherine, Maurice goes out of his way to taunt Henry until he breaks down and cries. But as Maurice's hatred for the dead Sarah increases, he becomes closer to her husband, finally moving in with him and sharing everything, including Henry's pajamas. The last page of the novel shows him taking Henry out for a drink. With Maurice's hand on Henry's arm, they walk across the misty common at night toward the dark intersection where "lovers" like to meet.

The End of the Affair was published in 1951, and Greene's reward was a cover story in *Time* magazine. "Adultery can lead to sainthood," the cover said. The magazine made other dubious judgments on Greene's work but provided a long description of the middle-aged novelist. It was not a pretty picture: "Frail and lanky, he dresses like a careless undergraduate, walks with a combination roll and lope that emphasizes a slight hump between his shoulders. . . . The face with its wrinkled skin . . . looks as if it had shaken loose from the flesh." The magazine went on to point out that his "washed-out blue eyes" had a "startled . . . slightly bulging" appearance. It would seem that the reporter caught his subject on a bad day. Indeed, the article begins with Greene making small talk as he struggles to overcome the effects of a bad hangover. This was hardly the typical opening for a cover story, but the editors of *Time* could not resist the apparent combination of sin and sanctity, and the reading public showed equal enthusiasm for it. In the 1950s God was good for sales, even if the treatment was less than respectful. *Time* went so far as to wonder whether Greene might be the next Dostoevsky.

Greene did not give himself a chance to bask in this glory. As the *Time* article was going to press, he traveled to a beleaguered French colony on the other side of the world. It was not simply a matter of escaping the publicity. There were many reasons to flee, the most important of which was the latest crisis in his affair with Catherine. Harry was upset again and was demanding that Greene stay away from his wife. After much discussion Catherine and Greene agreed that they should try a six-month separation. He decided to spend most of that time in Indochina. Among other things it was an excellent place for a man who liked to suffer. This was not his first visit to the area, and it would not be his last.

CHAPTER NINETEEN

RED MENACE

One thing that drew Greene to French Indochina was the chance to see medieval Catholic violence and treachery at work. He discovered some of this action during his first trip to the region in early 1951, when he paid a brief visit to the prince bishop of Phat Diem. At the time the bishop ruled over some 2 million people in Vietnam and was the only Catholic leader—with the exception of the pope—who had his own army. Greene liked the ragged look of this army and compared it with the Home Guard at its amateur best. He publicly praised the bishop—Le Huu Tu—as a great man of peace and love. But he knew that was not the truth. The bishop was a sinister character who ruled over his territory with the kind of cruelty that Greene had learned to appreciate in Liberia and Mexico.

The great French journalist Lucien Bodard, who knew Greene in Vietnam, wrote a vivid profile of the bishop under the title "The Ferocious Monsignor Le Huu Tu." He charged that the bishop was so fanatical in his devotion to pain that he had caused the deaths of several monks by ordering them to endure extreme penances. The bishop also liked to torture himself "by flagellation." He taxed the peasants heavily and kept law and order among them through his own courts and executioners. He was a slippery statesman who maintained his power by deceiving both the French colonial government and Ho Chi Minh's Communist forces. From his pulpit he denounced the French, but he relied on their troops for protection. He traded secrets and contraband goods with the Communists but was always ready to betray them to the French. As far as Bodard was concerned, this Catholic domain was full of evil:

> Le Huu Tu was, as it were, the inquisitor of the faith—a faith without love and without charity: nothing but a cruel discipline. The cathedral of Phat Diem was frightening: a huge baroque mass, a forest of superstitions. It was from this place, in the midst of all the incense and all the chanting, that the wrinkled, arrogant Le Huu Tu, reduced to little more than a pair of burning eyes, ruled over his people—people continually on their knees or marching in processions.

Naturally, Greene was attracted to all the things that disgusted Bodard. He loved the awful cathedral and the gloomy processions. In an article written for *Paris Match,* he spoke enthusiastically about the medieval atmosphere of Phat Diem, describing the cathedral in detail and noting the "dirty dungeon" nearby, which was crowded with political prisoners. He also alluded to the bishop's political double-dealing but saw no reason to criticize it. The only thing that caused Greene to lose enthusiasm for the bishop was defeat. First, the French took away his private army; then the Communist victory in the north caused him to make a rather undignified retreat to the south. Although his rule was cruel enough, the grim little bishop was not all that impressive in person, and Greene was never able to see him as a heroic figure of evil. With a distinct lack of racial sensitivity, Greene wrote in *Paris Match* that the bishop had the face of a monkey.

But Vietnam offered Greene other crafty dictators to stimulate his imagination. There was Ho Chi Minh, of course, whom Greene interviewed in Hanoi for the *Sunday Times* of London. He liked the dictator enormously and was especially taken with a phrase applied to Ho Chi Minh by a political rival—"the man as pure as Lucifer." In person, however, the Communist leader seemed a little tame to Greene. There was no fire in his eyes, no devilish laugh. Instead he looked like an Asian Mr. Chips—a friendly but strict schoolmaster. Greene liked this comparison so much that he developed an image of himself as a schoolboy tempted to worship this Mr. Chips. Suddenly he was thinking of Ho on the school quad, with devoted pupils in the background. Thanks to the enduring influence of Berkhamsted, Greene was ready to imagine that any old devil would be at home on the grounds of an English public school. He did admit, however, that he was too old to join Ho's school, confiding to the readers of the *Sunday Times* that he would not be able to follow the rules. Fortunately for Greene, Ho was unaware that he was also working for British intelligence. Any relevant information that Greene gathered on his visit to Ho was promptly presented to the SIS station chief in Singapore. Greene was generously compensated for this work.

He found a more appealing strongman in the southern province of Bentre. Colonel Leroy was the son of a French soldier and a Vietnamese woman, and in the early 1950s he was the military governor of the province. He was autocratic but progressive, and he defended his territory with a well-trained Catholic brigade. Greene was impressed with the colonel's military success against the Communists, but he was even more impressed by the hospitality he extended to European visitors. In the capital of his jungle kingdom, the colonel had created a small amusement park, with a lake, restaurant, bar, cinema, and zoo. When Greene came to visit him, he threw a big party, offering a special entertainment with pretty women dancing to the "Harry Lime Theme." Bottles of brandy were everywhere, and Colonel Leroy graciously poured some down the throats of the dancing girls, just to make sure that the party got off to a roaring start. Full of gratitude, Greene later wrote the introduction to the colonel's autobiography.

In many respects Vietnam was simply a giant playground for Greene, a place where any pleasure was available and where very real dangers added the necessary element of fear to one's enjoyment. Greene spent most of his stay in Saigon, staying at the city's best hotel, the Majestic. He spent some time drinking at the famous terrace café of the Continental Hotel, but he preferred the bar at the Majestic. When he was in the mood, he liked to go somewhere private to smoke opium. He had tried the drug for the first time on a visit to Haiphong in November 1951 and boasted in a letter to Catherine that he managed to smoke five pipes in one night. By the time of his last trip to the country, in 1955, he was devoting a great many hours to smoking the drug. There were also the inevitable trips to prostitutes, but in this respect Saigon offered the ultimate experience. Le Parc aux Buffles was supposed to be the world's largest brothel. With 400 women of many nationalities, it certainly offered enough variety. Besides Vietnamese, Cambodians, and Laotians, there were professional ladies from faraway outposts of the French empire, including North Africa and West Africa. The huge complex was surrounded by a wall and contained separate sections for officers and ordinary soldiers.

Greene did very little work during his visits to Vietnam in the early

1950s. By 1952 he had spent a total of almost three months in the country but had written only one major article about his experiences. While the foreign correspondents in Saigon were constantly facing deadlines, Greene could take his time gathering material and could go off for brief holidays to Hong Kong and Singapore. In 1953 he used a long interval between visits to Vietnam to observe the dangers of the Mau Mau rebellion in Kenya. A few years earlier he had told Catherine that he had an urge to witness a massacre, and Kenya seemed to offer a good opportunity for him. There were stories in the press of wives and children being hacked to death, so he decided to spend a few weeks in search of more atrocities. Nothing very interesting turned up, and Greene later wrote a couple of dull articles on the rebellion for the *Sunday Times*. His articles try to show some sympathy for both the white settlers and the African tribes, but, as was also the case in Malaya, Greene had close ties to the colonial administration. One of his old friends from Balliol, Robert Scott, was the administrator of the East Africa High Commission. In the autobiographical volume *Ways of Escape,* Greene's description of his visit to Scott's "baronial" house in Nairobi is much more lively than anything he has to say about the Mau Mau.

In Indochina he enjoyed the company of a few French colonial officials. His most frequent companions were Réné de Berval, the director of the Revue France-Asie (a literary cultural publication), and de Berval's Vietnamese girlfriend, Phuong. *The Quiet American* is dedicated to the couple. The American writer and foreign service officer Howard Simpson worked in Vietnam while Greene was there and remembered the novelist's close friendship with de Berval and Phuong: "The effete, balding de Berval and the beautiful, lithe Phuong were part of *le tout* Saigon, and Greene went everywhere with them." Simpson and Greene shared a rough plane ride to Laos in 1954, but the American discovered that the famous Englishman was inclined to keep to himself:

> Greene made no secret of his basic anti-American feelings and obviously viewed the increased U.S. presence in Indochina with misgiving. I had been introduced to Greene at the Continental and had expected he might contact me for an interview with [U.S.] Ambassador Heath or General O'Daniel, but it was not to be. Greene remained with his French and Vietnamese friends and contacts, observing the *Amerloques* at a disdainful distance.

Louis Heren, the Southeast Asia correspondent of *The Times,* found that Greene was not much more forthcoming in the presence of a fellow Englishman. On his way to Saigon for the first time, Greene visited Heren and his wife in Singapore, then flew out to Vietnam with the journalist a few days later. As Heren remembered it, Greene showed little interest in anything but drink: "He behaved rather oddly. When my wife asked what he wanted to drink, he said 'Scotch,' and added, 'Lots of it,' as if he was troubled. My wife just put the bottle, water, and ice bucket on the table and let him get on with it."

The heavy drinking and the opium smoking were part of Greene's effort to forget the emotional turmoil with Catherine. Vietnam gave him the chance to punish himself as well as to enjoy himself. In all the free time available to him, he could brood over the past or push it from his mind with drink and drugs. But whatever he did he could not reconcile himself to a permanent break with Catherine. He wrote to her almost every day, and in many of the letters it is not easy to tell that he is thousands of miles away. His thoughts are absorbed with what she is doing, what she is thinking, where she is going, when they will meet again, and what they have done in the past. It must have been marvelous torture. And there was the satisfaction of thinking that he might not make it back. If he died Catherine would have to suffer for the rest of her life with the knowledge that she was at least partly responsible for driving him to such a dangerous place.

Even in the relative comfort of Saigon, there was always the chance that a bullet or bomb would find him. Armed guards were posted throughout the city, and nets protected the sidewalk cafés from grenades. From time to time Greene ventured into the countryside, and he could never be sure that he would return. Tall and unarmed, he was an excellent target. On one trip to Phat Diem he witnessed some especially brutal combat. Following a small contingent of French troops through the town, he came across a canal choked with bodies, including those of a mother and her small boy. Mortar shells exploded in all directions. This should have been enough danger to last him for a lifetime, but it was not the last combat that he would see in Vietnam. Later he accompanied a French pilot on a bombing mission, silently praying that one of two things would happen: either he would survive and marry Catherine or the plane would crash, and he would suffer an immediate death. Looking for more danger, he toured the fortifications at Dien Bien Phu a few months before the outpost fell. If Greene wanted to die in Vietnam, he did a good job of increasing the risk.

But few people knew he was playing with death. Most of the correspondents in Saigon assumed that he was simply searching for good stories. "My main impression," Louis Heren wrote, "was that he was there as a journalist for *Life,* and was gathering material for a book." Although the editors of *Life* magazine never published an article on Vietnam by Greene, they did commission him to go there in November 1951. At the end of the previous year, they had sent him to what was then British Malaya, and from there he had made a quick trip to Vietnam in January 1951. "Malaya, the Forgotten War" was published in *Life,* and at the end of the article Greene managed to squeeze in a short paragraph about Vietnam. On the strength of this piece, *Life* asked him to return to Indochina and do a full-scale article on the French struggle to defend the colony against Communist aggression.

The head of Time-Life, Henry Luce, was keen to warn the world of the Red menace in Southeast Asia. Luce believed that America was destined to lead the world into a new and better day and that it was the nation's "duty . . . to exert upon the world the full impact of our influence, for such purposes as we see fit and by such means as we see fit." In *The Quiet American,* Pyle can be seen as a Luce disciple, an ardent believer in the absolute justice of American power. Greene's commissioning editor at *Life* was an energetic young man whose idealistic outlook was similar to Pyle's. Emmet John Hughes was Luce's wonder boy at the time. He had graduated summa cum laude from Princeton University in 1941, and his senior thesis on the Catholic Church was published three years later as *The Church and Liberal Society.* It was a Catholic Book Club selection. Recognizing a hot new talent, Luce made Hughes the Time-Life bureau chief in Rome, despite the fact that Hughes was still in his twenties and "wet behind the ears," as one correspondent described him. But he did so well in Rome that Luce waited only a year before promoting him to bureau chief in Berlin. Luce treated Hughes like a son, bringing him back to New York to help run *Life* magazine in 1949. When Dwight Eisenhower ran for president, Hughes worked on the campaign and later became a presidential assistant. It was the kind of sudden rise to glory that might have been waiting for Pyle, if he had survived the rigorous test of Indochina.

While he was a bureau chief in Europe, Hughes made a point of contacting prominent Catholic writers and intellectuals, two of whom were Evelyn Waugh and Graham Greene. When he became articles editor for *Life,* he commissioned Greene to write a piece on the veneration of the Virgin Mary. The innocent American could not have known how much this subject appealed to the novelist in the late 1940s. When Greene and Catherine visited Italy, they liked not only

to enjoy themselves behind altars but also to make a game of searching for "breathing Madonnas." One day Greene spotted a particularly promising statue of a Madonna outside a little church and lay
beneath it on his back, carefully watching for any sign of breath. As
Catherine later told Father Turner, Greene stayed in that position for
more than two hours, but he never saw the Virgin's breast move by
even the slightest bit.

He had more luck in Assisi, where whole busloads of tourists came
to see a breathing Madonna at the church of Santa Maria degli
Angeli. In the article that he wrote for Hughes, he reported his success, explaining to the readers of *Life* that he and his "companion" lay
on their backs in the gravel under the statue, closed their eyes, and
when they opened them they "immediately" saw the statue move.
The breast moved, the hands moved, and for a moment Greene
thought that the image would come crashing down. He and
Catherine may well have seen all these things, but, given their fondness for drink, their "vision" should not carry much weight. Of
course, young Hughes took it seriously and published the article with
a glowing comment on "Author-Convert Greene."

Hughes was so happy with the piece that he decided to send
Greene to Malaya for a report on the British campaign against
Communist rebels. Luce and Hughes wanted a good hearty attack on
the nasty Reds who were threatening Western interests in Asia, and
Greene gave them exactly what they were looking for. "Malaya, the
Forgotten War" is pure propaganda, depicting the white planters as a
sympathetic group fighting to save their lands from the ruthless terrorism of the Communists. Greene went on a patrol in search of
rebels, and the article includes a photograph of a British patrol
returning from the jungle with an enemy corpse. Draped over a pole,
the dead rebel is being carried like a dead animal. Greene makes no
attempt to question the savage tactics of the British troops. Instead
he urges the West to pursue a vigorous campaign to suppress
Communist movements throughout Asia. "We have to weaken their
hope," he says of the Communists, and adds that "we" should
"destroy their confidence in each other."

It is a very good thing that schoolmaster Ho Chi Minh did not
know about this article when Greene visited him in Hanoi. Greene's
Mr. Chips might have given him a sound caning. To more objective
critics, Greene could plead that the article was a sort of personal favor
to his younger brother. In September 1950 Hugh Greene became
the head of the British propaganda effort in Malaya. One of his tri-
umphs was a leaflet that contained two scenes. The first showed some

gruesome rebel corpses with the caption "Would you rather be dead like these?" The second showed a tranquil scene of city life with the caption "Or surrender and live like these?" The leaflets were distributed on waterproof paper from airplanes flying over the jungle. Greene speaks admiringly of this propaganda in his piece for *Life* and reports that it is producing encouraging results. He does fail to mention, however, that it was the work of his brother's office.

Greene took almost six months to research and write his article on Malaya. In the meantime Indochina began to assume a more prominent place in the news, and Hughes decided to send his staunchly Catholic, staunchly anti-Communist reporter back to Southeast Asia for another big story on the war against the Reds. But this time earnest Emmet was in for a surprise. Without his brother's job to worry about, Greene decided to take a more tolerant view of the Communist rebels. They were still suspect, but he acknowledged in his report that many of them were idealists who did not belong to a monolithic Stalinist movement. But the most disappointing thing, from Hughes's point of view, was that Greene saw little hope of stopping communism in Indochina. In his article he advises the French to begin preparing for a retreat from the area, and he tells America not to believe that all obstacles can be overcome with force. This was definitely not the message that Luce and Hughes wanted to hear. Unfortunately, many Americans believed that it would be easy to defeat Ho Chi Minh, if only the French would fight harder. Greene stresses, however, that French courage and determination were not the problem. The war simply could not be won.

Hughes rejected Greene's article, and the piece was then accepted by *Paris Match*. Perhaps to soften the gloomy prospect of defeat, Greene loaded the last paragraphs with embarrassingly sentimental tributes to France's gallant fighting forces. He could afford to turn his back on the Time-Life market, but it was an especially lucrative market to lose, and Hughes had done a great deal to help him. The young editor published not only the pieces on Malaya and the Virgin Mary—both of which were given prominent space in the magazine—but also a long article on the pope. More important, Greene's working relationship with Hughes no doubt influenced *Time*'s decision to feature Greene on its cover in October 1951. By that time his three articles had appeared in *Life,* and he was on his way to Saigon with a fourth commission from Hughes. But after he had made the cover of *Time,* there was not much more that Luce's empire could do for Greene. The only remaining task was to mock the attitudes of Hughes and Luce in the pages of *The Quiet American.*

II

On his first trip to Vietnam, Greene met a genuine hero. Gen. Jean de Lattre de Tassigny was one of France's most famous military leaders. At the beginning of the First World War, when he was a young cavalry officer, Lattre was wounded in the chest by a lance yet was able to cut his way through the attacking Germans with a saber. By the end of the war, he had suffered four more wounds and had received thirteen citations for bravery in action. During the Second World War, he commanded an infantry division until the armistice with Germany and was later imprisoned by the Vichy government for insubordination. He escaped by sawing the bars of his cell window and made his way to Algiers, where de Gaulle put him in charge of the Free French forces in North Africa. In 1944 his soldiers landed at Toulon and Marseilles and quickly defeated the German troops occupying the area. After the war, as France tried to rebuild its empire in Indochina, Lattre was asked to lead the fight against the Communists. He was seen as France's best hope for saving its colony.

The general was anxious to win more American support for his war, so when Greene arrived in Saigon as a certified correspondent for *Life,* Lattre made every effort to give the novelist a warm welcome. He invited Greene to an informal dinner and arranged for him to have the use of a military plane. The general and the writer seemed to get along well until Greene made the mistake of flying into Phat Diem for his first look at the bishop's domain. Lattre hated Le Huu Tu's double-dealing and worried that the sly bishop was secretly preparing a trap for French troops in the area. He was suspicious of any outsider who showed too much interest in Phat Diem, and his doubts about Greene's motives began as soon as he learned of the novelist's plane trip.

Lattre also found it significant that Greene's traveling companion was Trevor Wilson, the British consul in Hanoi. As Lattre was well aware, Wilson's real responsibility was managing the Secret Intelligence Service's operations in Hanoi. The general had known the "consul" during the Second World War, when Wilson was the Section V officer in Algiers. Greene had known him since 1943, when they had worked together with Kim Philby at Section V's headquarters in St. Albans. For his distinguished wartime services, Wilson had been decorated by de Gaulle and had also received the Order of the British Empire. His relations with Lattre were good until the news of the visit to Phat Diem reached the general.

Like Greene, Wilson was fond of living by his own rules. He drank hard and liked opium and prostitutes, so he was an easy companion for Greene. He also had a taste for wild stunts. In 1946 he helped the French to land an occupying force at Haiphong, driving General Salan into the city in a jeep flying the British flag. But after giving his assistance to the French landing, Wilson began to turn against colonial rule in Indochina and was looking for ways to help the Vietnamese get rid of their foreign masters. Douglas Bolam, a British diplomat who knew Wilson in Hanoi, wrote of his "quite open espousal of the nationalist cause, comparing unfavourably the French policy in Vietnam with the British withdrawal from India." Apparently acting on his own authority, Wilson devised some sort of secret plan involving the bishop of Phat Diem. In a letter to Catherine, Greene refers to this plan and complains that it had put him in a difficult position. Because Lattre's suspicions had been aroused, both Greene and Wilson were placed under surveillance by officers of the Sûreté.

When Greene came to Vietnam for his second visit, Lattre was openly hostile toward Wilson. A tragic incident had confirmed the general's suspicions. In May 1951 Lt. Bernard de Lattre, the general's only son, was killed in a battle near Phat Diem. The general blamed the bishop for allowing the Communists to sneak up to the position his son was defending, and he considered Wilson an accomplice in the treachery. He made an angry protest to Malcolm MacDonald, the British commissioner-general for Southeast Asia, who informed the Foreign Office that Lattre "criticized Trevor Wilson's activities bitterly." The British Legation in Saigon reported to London that Lattre refused to see the departing British ambassador, Frank Gibbs, because he was so angry at the "unfriendly activities of Mr. Trevor Wilson." The general declared Wilson *"persona non grata,"* and he was given until December 1, 1951, to leave the country.

At a cocktail party in Hanoi, Lattre confronted Greene about his relationship with Wilson. He asked whether it was true that he was working for the British secret service. Greene firmly denied that he had a connection to SIS, apart from his wartime service, and Lattre was never able to get a straight answer from him about anything of substance. The novelist later treated the whole episode as one great comic adventure. The Sûreté men who followed him were funny little fellows, the general was a deluded old fool, and Trevor Wilson was a jolly companion with an admirable knowledge of Chinese massage parlors. In a short sketch called "The General and the Spy," published in the *London Magazine,* Greene makes it seem absurd that Lattre would dare to think of him as a spy. He was working for *Life,* he told the general, and no one else. Lattre wondered why he was spending so much time in Vietnam, especially if the magazine wanted only one article and would pay only $400 for it. Greene smugly corrected the mistake—he was being paid $4,000.

But the general knew his man. Greene was working for *Life* and SIS. He was under the general supervision of his SIS contact in Singapore, Maurice Oldfield. No one, though, seems to know what Trevor Wilson was up to in Phat Diem. Contrary to the comic mood of "The General and the Spy," Greene's letters to Catherine show that he was deeply worried by the trouble that Wilson's activities might cause. It seems likely that Wilson—a Catholic—was trying to assist the bishop, who could have used information about French troop movements as a bargaining chip with the Communists. Whatever was going on, it would be unwise to assume that Lattre was merely imagining a conspiracy. He was a tough realist who knew how Wilson operated, and he was a brilliant soldier who had outwitted more impressive opponents than a minor British spy.

From the beginning of his visit in 1951–52, Greene made it clear to Catherine that he was involved in a secret mission of some sort and would have to watch what he said in his letters. But when he discovered that the police were opening his correspondence, he took the precaution of telling her that it was absurd for the French to suspect him of being a spy. In any case, the problem soon went away, but only because Lattre became ill with cancer and was forced to return to Paris, where he died in 1952. After he was gone the colonial authorities took a slightly more tolerant attitude toward the famous novelist, and he was able to come and go with greater freedom.

But Greene and SIS were well aware that his movements would be watched, and he was advised to confine his activities to "talent spotting." In other words, he was to keep an eye out for any potential recruits whom the service could contact later. The service also worried that the existing espionage network might be compromised if anyone spotted Greene contacting its agents. For his visit in 1954, it was agreed that Greene would give his general views of the situation after he returned, and in due time he presented his findings. He followed the same routine when he went back to Southeast Asia in 1955.

Sadly, the great General Lattre did not live long enough to learn that, in the end, *Life* rejected Greene. Having played out his private drama with Lattre, Greene was ready for a public confrontation with the American officials in Saigon. After Greene accepted his Vietnam assignment from *Life,* he made sure that there would be an embarrassing public incident for Luce and Hughes to confront in the future. When the *Time* reporters interviewed him for their cover story, he "deliberately" let slip that he had joined the Communist party as a "prank" when he was nineteen. *Time* included the apparently harmless fact in its story, but Hughes and others did not stop to think that this prank would put Greene in technical violation of the McCarran Act, which imposed a ban on foreigners who had been Communists at any time in their lives. If Greene chose to make a public issue of the violation, Time-Life would suddenly find its anti-Communist correspondent fighting to overcome his Communist past. One way or another Greene was determined to make a fool of Emmet Hughes.

The public comedy began in February 1952, when Greene applied for a U.S. visa in Saigon. He specifically stated that he wanted to go to New York "to consult with the editors of *Life.*" Noting that he was banned under the McCarran Act, the American authorities dutifully denied his request. Then Greene turned up the heat, reporting the problem to the Reuters correspondent in Saigon. With a nice turn of phrase, he announced that he was unable to break through America's "cellophane curtain." Soon the wire service bulletin was picked up by newspapers throughout the world, and the controversy was in full swing.

One British paper was at a loss to understand what the fuss was about: "The Americans think that he is a Communist. They seem to forget that he is a practicing Catholic—it is impossible to be Communist and Catholic." *The New Republic* rushed to defend Greene, protesting that he was no Red but a trustworthy "Catholic whose long literary career recorded his stand to date against violence and untruth." Arguing that the denial of the visa was a violation of free speech, the magazine raced to take the high ground: "So long as we depend upon the tradition John Milton set down in 'The Areopagitica' perpetuating freedom of the printed word, any action which excludes Graham Greene from entering this country is insidiously tantamount to censorship." For some reason Dr. Lawrence A. Kimpton, chancellor of the University of Chicago, took up Greene's case in a letter to Secretary of State Dean Acheson, asking that the ban be lifted to protect "intellectual freedom." Wanting to avoid any more publicity, the departments of State and Justice quickly issued Greene a special visa.

Greene would continue to have fun with this issue for many years to come. In 1953 one interview reported that "the atmosphere of panic [Greene] found in New York on his last visit recalled to him nothing so strongly as that of England in the late seventeenth century, when the persecution of Catholics was at its height." He liked to give the impression that he was rarely allowed to visit America, but he came and went on many occasions in the 1950s and 1960s. His name did end up on a list of "political undesirables," and each time that he entered the country he had to apply for a special visa. But the State Department wanted to avoid any more trouble from him. In one government memo concerning Greene, an official wrote of him: "He is internationally known as a writer, and from the philosophies expressed in his writings it is evident that he is an anti-Communist. The Department of State is of the opinion that to refuse a visa to this applicant would result in widespread publicity adverse to the interest of the United States."

Occasionally, the FBI took notice of Greene's case and tried to keep track of his movements, on the chance that he might be a real Communist after all. In the 1980s Greene obtained a copy of his FBI file, using the Freedom of Information Act, and promptly sold it at Sotheby's for almost 2,000 pounds. In 1992 the FBI provided a copy to this biographer at the quite reasonable price of twenty-nine cents. The only really interesting thing in it is an FBI agent's account of Greene's effort to create another publicity stunt in August 1954. Without first obtaining a visa, he tried to fly from Haiti to Puerto Rico. In *Ways of Escape* he claimed that he was just passing through on his way back to London and that the American ambassador in Haiti had assured him that he would not need a transit visa. He was probably rather drunk by the time he reached San Juan, and the agents of the Immigration and Naturalization Service were not happy to see him. An "FBI Radiogram," marked "urgent," was sent to Washington with the details of the episode:

INS advised Greene arrived San Juan, PR last night at 8:55 PM via Delta C and S airlines from Haiti. INS advised subject inadmissible to US because of membership in Communist party of England. Was placed under guard by INS and returned to Haiti on Delta C and S airlines departing San Juan 7:30 AM this date. Subject advised INS that he was a novelist and was going to NYC to contact an agent for his books. . . . Subject stated while in custody of INS that he had been a member of the CP of England years ago when he was 19 years old, that he was going to write a book about his experience in San Juan, and that he would make a lot of publicity over his being detained.

True to his word, Greene managed to send a telegram from the airport to the Reuters office in London. Once again the press jumped on the story. Under the headlines "Novelist Sent Back by U.S.— Puerto Rico Bans Graham Greene," the *Daily Telegraph* reported that "Graham Greene, the Roman Catholic novelist, was held overnight by United States immigration officials." According to Greene, his detention was not so bad. "I have not really any complaints to make," he graciously stated, "but it was a very awkward situation." As he explained in *Ways of Escape,* the two agents who were assigned to guard him decided to give him a tour of San Juan's bars. The odd threesome spent most of the night drinking whiskey, and in the morning Greene was sent back to Haiti. He wisely refrained from writing "a book" about his experience in San Juan, but he had another work nearing completion that would expose the folly of America's obsession with the Red menace. A year after his detention he brought out *The Quiet American.*

III

Alden Pyle spends a lot of time thinking about democracy and duty. Along with many other Americans, he has been sent to Indochina to help the French stop communism, but his ultimate goal is to see the entire area enjoying the blessings of liberty, without any colonial ties. He wants a "Third Force" to emerge, one that is free from both the French imperialists and the Communists. Some readers think that Greene invented this phrase to describe his young idealist's philosophy, but it was already in use a few years before the novel appeared. On July 30, 1951, *The New Republic* published an article called "Vietnam *Has* a Third Force." It neatly defined the concept: "Beneath the layers of opportunists, French spies and hangers-on, there is a hard nucleus of patriots who are fighting for a truly independent, libertarian Viet Nam." This was a noble cause, but what is wrong with Pyle's approach is its combination of innocence and brutal efficiency. Confident of his theory, he is willing to do whatever is necessary to support it. If some Vietnamese have to be slaughtered to establish the Third Force, then he is willing to sanction their deaths. Although he supports terrorist activities that have cost many lives, he does not have any of the "virtues" of Greene's favorite villains. Unlike Harry Lime or Pinkie Brown, Pyle thinks his evil acts will bring good results.

Pyle's problem is that he has read too many books with long titles.

Greene's narrator—the English journalist Fowler—imagines Pyle wandering across a big American campus with a stack of books. The young man has immersed himself in a world of "big ideas" and is ready to believe that, with persistence and confidence, any idea can be made to work in the real world. He has all the benefits that an American education can provide, except common sense and hard experience. Fowler associates him with the easy life of materialistic America. His healthy good looks—complete with crew cut—suggest a life filled with big glasses of milk and vigorous outdoor exercise. He expects the world to be like America and assumes that a generous use of money and military force can whip any foreign land into shape.

It was exactly this kind of streamlined thinking that eventually helped to push America into fighting a disastrous war for the "hearts and minds" of the Vietnamese people. From his contacts with Henry Luce and Emmet Hughes, Greene could see the dangerous direction in which America's "best and brightest" were leading the country, but he also met at least two Americans in Saigon who had some of Pyle's characteristics.

The first was Leo Hochstetter, a member of the U.S. economic aid mission in Saigon during the early 1950s. Near the end of his life, Greene said that Pyle "was probably based—not physically, because he was very different physically—on an American I met when I spent the night with a French colonel, Leroy." This American was Hochstetter, whose job with the aid mission was probably a CIA cover. He gave Greene a lift back to Saigon after their night with Leroy, and on the way he talked "about how America should support a Third Force." A few elements of Pyle's personality were borrowed from a young diplomat at the American embassy. The novelist was interested in both the man and his wife:

> There was a rather nice woman at the American embassy who was mar-
> ried to the protocol secretary. I used to take her out for meals some-
> times. She was very sweet and nice. And she was actually fed up with
> him. He was a sort of Pyle. . . . She was bored to death with him
> because he was really a rather feeble type. And what she disliked so
> much was when they were being investigated before he could become
> protocol secretary, he was very Boy Scouty.

Although it has often been suggested that the rough-and-ready Col. Ed Lansdale was the primary model for Pyle, the evidence suggests otherwise. Lansdale was the CIA's counterinsurgency expert in the Far East, but he came to Vietnam two years after Greene had

begun writing *The Quiet American*. He did not suffer from the inex-
perience and bookishness that Pyle exhibits, nor was he as earnest and
idealistic as the fictional character. In the 1960s and 1970s Greene
tried repeatedly to correct reports that Pyle was based on Lansdale,
but no one wanted to believe him, especially because Lansdale was
famous as the model for the protagonist in a book with a similar title,
The Ugly American. People seem to have assumed that Greene denied
the connection because he was guarding the mysterious secrets of
inspiration. It is odd that so much of his misinformation was accepted without question while this effort at truthfulness was ignored.
Greene correctly pointed out that he had never met Lansdale and that
the colonel's activities in Vietnam had no influence on his book. Still
the critics and journalists continued to speak of Lansdale's "influence" on *The Quiet American*.

Greene's portrait of Pyle is the best aspect of *The Quiet American*.
The novelist has no substantial political philosophy to offer, but his
specific analysis of personality is more useful than any philosophy.
The tragedy for Vietnam is not that the French or Americans lacked
policies. The politicians and the intellectuals in their "think tanks"
had all the policies anyone could ask for. What went astray were the
human factors that no policy can control: the lust for empire, the love
of military might, the arrogant faith in "superior culture," and the
sentimentality of political idealism. But few Americans wanted to recognize anything of themselves in Pyle. Many complained that he was
a gross caricature, a villain created by an anti-American writer. It is
true enough that Greene wanted to provoke Americans for personal
reasons, but if there is anything wrong with his portrait of Pyle, it is
that the character should be more despicable. Even with his fiendish
imagination, Greene could not foresee how much damage an army
led by Pyles could do, burning whole villages to "save" them, "carpet
bombing" vast areas, blighting the landscape with chemical sprays,
and—in the worst cases—butchering innocent villagers.

All this does not mean, however, that Greene can be regarded as a
friend of the Vietnamese. He liked to work up his hatred for
Americans—no doubt partly as a way of venting the frustrations of his
affair with Catherine—but he was not overly concerned about the fate
of Vietnam. He was anti-American, not pro-Vietnamese. The country
was simply a place that appealed to his senses. It was pretty, the
opium was good, the brothels were impressive, and the dangers were
exceptionally frightening. The Vietnamese did not disgust him, but
he generally regarded them as little more than colorful children.
Fowler thinks that the Vietnamese peasants want nothing more com-

plicated from life than good work as rice farmers. As does *The Heart of the Matter, The Quiet American* makes no attempt to do justice to the local population. The colonial types are well represented—in this case, they are British, French, and American—but native Vietnamese are limited to minor parts, with the exception of the mistress whom Fowler and Pyle share. Named after the companion of Greene's friend Réné de Berval, the Vietnamese woman Phuong is depicted as an attractive simpleton. In many ways she resembles an affectionate puppy who likes to lick its master's face and do little tricks on command. There is no depth to her character, no sign that she is anything more than a plaything for foreign men.

In fact, the Asian setting has been grafted onto a plot that Greene used before. All the political references and exotic details—such as opium smoking—help to disguise the fact that Greene was basically rewriting *Rumour at Nightfall,* the early novel that he suppressed after its first printing. As the reader may recall, the plot of that novel involved a tough-minded journalist's relationship with his sensitive, idealistic friend. They engage in long, rambling discussions about their strained friendship and about the lovely lady who has come between them. The dreamy character—Crane—gets the girl, and the cynical journalist suddenly decides that his friend deserves to die. The story takes place against the background of the Carlist wars, with ruthless rebels and simple peasants giving a little life to an otherwise plodding tale. The big action comes near the end, when Chase uses the rebels to do his dirty work for him. But after Crane has been killed, Chase instantly regrets it and is doomed to spend the rest of his life trying to atone for arranging his friend's death.

In *The Quiet American* Chase becomes the tough-minded journalist Thomas Fowler, and Crane becomes the dangerous romantic Alden Pyle. Although Fowler dislikes what Pyle stands for, he is at first attracted to his schoolboy innocence. In the early pages of the book, he speaks of his "affection" for Pyle and says that he wants "to protect him." Later they have a long, intimate talk about their love lives, and there is the usual business of having one friend recite poetry to the other, although this seems exceptionally unusual for two adventurous fellows in Saigon. As with Crane and Chase, a woman comes between them and spoils their chance for friendship. Partly from jealousy, Fowler arranges to have Pyle killed by the local rebels. But he has a better motive—he considers it his duty to stop Pyle from sponsoring more terrorist acts. Although this motive may satisfy many readers, it does not ring true. If terrorism really bothers Fowler, he would not want to make any deal with the rebel forces, whose thirst for blood is much greater than Pyle's. And, despite what he may say, Fowler is not "committed" to anything in Vietnam besides his opium pipe. He does not care what happens to the ordinary people of the country. Like Chase, he simply finds it convenient to let the rebels kill the man whom he loves and hates.

Since *The Quiet American* first appeared, its political scene has been the dominant subject of discussion. But except for Greene's insights into the significance of Pyle's character, the book treats political matters in only a superficial way. The wartime atmosphere is brilliantly conveyed, as one would expect from Greene after his long visits to the country, and the accuracy of his experienced eye prevents the book from suffering the fate of *Rumour at Nightfall,* which seems unreal from beginning to end. Many people who knew Saigon in the early 1950s have said that Greene conveyed the look and feel of the place perfectly—at least from the Western viewpoint. Novels, however, are not travelogues. Despite the polished surface of the writing, *The Quiet American* reveals that Greene's genius was beginning to run dry. It is one thing to have variations on a theme, but the Pyle-Fowler conflict is not really a variation. It is nothing but Chase and Crane revisited.

Greene needed three years to write the novel; by the time it was completed, he had passed his fiftieth birthday. Although the political discussions about *The Quiet American* helped to increase his fame, the novel was the work of a tired and distracted writer who had lost his sense of direction. His greatness lay in his ability to create private hells inhabited by such lonely devils as Raven, Pinkie, Scobie, and Lime, but the world is too much with us in *The Quiet American.* Despite its excellence, the descriptions of the war occupy too much space. We see more than enough of the public life of Saigon but very little of Fowler's dark soul. In earlier years Greene spent so many hours alone in his own hell that he had no trouble keeping his focus on private agonies, but fame and money drew him into the larger world after 1950, and he lost that focus. Success set him on his way to becoming "a burnt-out case."

The Quiet American will always be important as a warning against innocence—and not merely the innocence of a certain type of American. There is a bit of Pyle in all of us. We can scoff at Pyle's silly faith in a Third Force, but Greene is also making a joke at our expense, serving us an old plot from a suppressed novel and encouraging us to think that some "commitment" lies behind the political talk that fills the novel. Critics innocently struggled to explain Greene's emergence as a left-wing political novelist. The Soviets were easily misled into thinking that his anti-Americanism meant he was sympathetic to communism. He was invited to visit Moscow, and a play version of the novel was "performed to packed houses on the Moscow stage."

Meanwhile, the American Pyles—Greene intended the name to be associated with hemorrhoids—ignored the warning in *The Quiet American* and continued flooding Southeast Asia with money and arms. Hollywood reflected this happy spirit of innocence when the novel was adapted for the screen. After acquiring the film rights, Joseph L. Mankiewicz changed the story to make Pyle the completely good American, whom Fowler betrays out of ignorance. Played by the all-American war hero Audie Murphy, Pyle is falsely connected to terrorist acts by scheming Communists, and Fowler accepts their lies. The cynical, opium-smoking Fowler—played by Michael Redgrave—represents the corrupt old world of British and French colonialism, while the noble conduct of Pyle points the way forward to a new age of democracy and freedom. As one critic summed up the difference between book and film, "Mr. Mankiewicz has simply turned the issue inside out: the American dies a martyr, the Englishman is exposed as a murderous dupe."

But Mankiewicz's alteration was not entirely wrong. He had glimpsed a dark element in Fowler's character that intrigued him, an element that had nothing to do with politics. After buying the story, he said, "I've often wanted to do a picture about one of those ice-blooded intellectuals whose intellectualism is really just a mask for completely irrational passion. Fowler, I felt, was just such a character." And so was Greene, although Mankiewicz could not have known it. The ending of his film may be politically false, but it hints at something more important. Under the surface details about war and peasants and communism and liberty, an Englishman was alone with his completely irrational passion, hating himself and the world, as he had done for many years, but doing it with less flair.

One American critic was particularly good at noting a striking element of carelessness in Greene's novel. Reviewing the book for *The New Yorker*, A. J. Liebling pointed out that Greene made little effort to provide a convincing American idiom for Pyle's dialogue. Liebling said that Pyle sounded like "a French author's idea of an Englishman." The mistakes in the first British edition are especially funny. Pyle says "shan't" when an American would say "won't"; "did boxing at college" instead of "boxed at college"; "punt" instead of "boat"; "I feel such a heel" instead of "I feel *like* such a heel"; and, best of all, "Got to save our strength," which makes the quiet

American sound like a British actor in a bad film from the 1930s. In later editions Greene worked to make Pyle's speech seem more authentic, but he took an immediate dislike to Liebling and made a point of calling him Mr. Lieberman when he referred to the review in *Ways of Escape*.

According to a friend of Liebling, Greene's anger was all too evident when the critic and the novelist happened to be dining in the same London restaurant a few months after the review appeared. While Nora Sayre was having dinner with the photographer Walker Evans, she saw her friend come through the door: "Greene and his companion had frozen on his entrance; they stared furiously at him while whispering with their heads close together. . . . The charade of deathly enmity persisted through several courses, then Liebling joined our table for raspberries and coffee. Then the lethal glares included all three of us." Sayre did not recognize Greene's companion, but she got a closer look at the "little man in a shiny jacket" when she and Evans left the restaurant and discovered that they were being followed: "Greene and his sinister friend passed us swiftly, then wheeled around to glower at us. All the way up that long street, they followed or flanked us: one would appear scowling in a lighted doorway, then the other would dart ahead of us, then their footsteps would echo loudly at our backs again." This performance seems too good to be true, but it is not wholly implausible, especially if Greene and his accomplice had been drinking heavily. The game ended only when Sayre and Evans managed to escape in a taxi. As they were driven away, they reflected on the incident, "wondering if the great novelist was missing a few marbles—or if it merely tickled him to tease Americans." The answer, of course, was a little of both.

CHAPTER TWENTY

ANTIC DISPOSITION

The interviewers from the *Paris Review* were shocked to find that their subject was living in relative splendor. Having soaked up all the seedy bits in Greene's books, Martin Shuttleworth and Simon Raven seemed to think that the novelist should be living in a dark little basement room at the end of a narrow street. Instead, when they visited him in the early 1950s, they found him in his snug flat overlooking St. James's Street, with the establishment bastion of White's Club nearby and a fashionable oyster bar on the ground floor of his building. It was definitely not a neighborhood for Pinkie and Rose. "It's an area black with smartness," Shuttleworth and Raven observed, "the Rolls-Royces and the bowler hats of the men are black, the court shoes and the correct suits of the women are black, and in the most august flats even the bathing pools set into the floors of the bathrooms are paved with black marble." Greene's own flat was not "august," but its comforts were impressive. There were thick rugs, big armchairs, expensive art work—including some pastel drawings by Henry Moore—and, of course, rows and rows of books lining the walls. It was the perfect place in town for a bachelor of means.

But the comforts bothered the interviewers. They wondered how a man who lived in such bourgeois surroundings could have such a keen appreciation of crime and poverty. "Urbanity, not tragedy, seems to reign in this room," they informed him. Greene smiled and said, "I think you have misjudged me and my consistency. This flat, my way of life—these are simply my hole in the ground." The answer did not satisfy his interviewers, but he was right to imply that his flat reflected only one part of his life. For one thing, Shuttleworth and Raven did not take into account that the red lights of Soho were only a short walk from Greene's respectable neighborhood. And the walk became shorter when Greene moved to his chambers in Albany, in 1953. From the discreet rear entrance, one could slip into Soho in a matter of minutes, and Greene knew the area extremely well.

In this general period, Greene was often unable to enjoy the pleasures of his London life, spending time instead in places far less cozy, such as Saigon or Phat Diem. He was not interested in "consistency." He was always one who liked to mix pleasure and pain. The only thing that changed in the 1950s was that he was finally able to afford a wide variety of pleasures and pains. If he wanted to risk death for a few months in a war-torn country, he needed only to pack a bag and catch a plane. If he wanted to sunbathe in the nude under a warm Mediterranean sun, he could escape behind the high walls of his villa in Anacapri.

Critics who like to think of Greene as a man of danger enjoy drawing attention to his preference for a brief quotation from Robert Browning: "Our interest's on the dangerous edge of things." It is true enough that he wanted to live on the dangerous edge, but it is also a good idea to consider the source of the quotation before making too much of it. The line comes from a poem about a simple-minded literary journalist who wants a convenient phrase to describe an unconventional Catholic author whom he interviews over dinner. This author is also a bishop but one who has used his power in the Church to surround himself with material wealth, and who admits that he enjoys keeping people in the dark about his real character.

In "Bishop Blougram's Apology," the journalist—Mr. Gigadibs—sits quietly while Blougram teases him with a monologue full of indeterminacy. "With me," the bishop says, "faith means perpetual unbelief." Gigadibs wants a straight answer—does the bishop believe in God or not?—but Blougram will not be "classed," will not wear "labels broad" or be weighed by "coarse scales." If he is easily defined, he knows that he will lose the world's interest. So he keeps everyone guessing and boasts to Gigadibs that mystery and confusion are the secrets of his success. His comment on the "dangerous edge" is not about taking risks. It is about building and keeping a reputation:

>Our interest's on the dangerous edge of things.
>The honest thief, the tender murderer,
>The superstitious atheist, demirep
>That loves and saves her soul in new French books—
>We watch while these in equilibrium keep
>The giddy line midway: one step aside,
>They're classed and done with. I, then, keep the line
>Before your sages,—just the men to shrink
>From the gross weights, coarse scales and labels broad
>You offer their refinement. Fool or knave?
>Who needs a bishop be a fool or knave
>When there's a thousand diamond weights between?

Greene always liked to keep everyone guessing about his real nature. With a thousand diamond weights available to him, he could make lots of subtle adjustments to his image. It was also fun to maintain relationships with vastly different friends, and to keep them completely separate. He was never more sociable than in the 1950s, when his friends ranged from the rich and famous—Noël Coward, Margot Fonteyn, Otto Preminger, Evelyn Waugh—to such obscure figures as the writer John Davenport, the sailor Michael Richey, and the Dottoressa Elisabeth Moor. But each friend saw a slightly different shade of Greene, and the more famous ones were barely aware of the existence of such an intimate friend as the Dottoressa.

Although Catherine Walston dominated his love life, there were other lovers as well. He could make Catherine think that she was the center of his universe while at the same time he pursued another woman in secret. In early 1951, when he was putting the finishing touches on *The End of the Affair* and pleading with his dear C. to become Catherine Greene, he began an affair with Jocelyn Rickards, a painter twenty years his junior. An Australian by birth, she was living in London with the philosopher A. J. Ayer when she met Greene and fell instantly in love with him.

While Ayer was away on a long trip to Mexico, Jocelyn and Greene became lovers. In a private memoir she wrote, "We felt no guilt as we climbed into his big bed together—his skin was always faintly sunburned and the texture of fine dry silk. Graham said he felt as though he was holding a boy and a girl in his arms." He found a special pleasure in this androgyny and soon learned that Jocelyn was willing to join him in some interesting experiments. They shared, in her words, "a dazzling sexual recklessness." Outdoor activities were high on their list: "We only had to walk past a flat bed of pansies in a dim corner of the Battersea Pleasure Gardens to want to lie down in it—once comfortably settled the bell rang to say it was closing time in the gardens of the west—the huge gates at the east end clanged shut, and we waited in the dark until everyone had disappeared, and then climbed over the high fence to the safety of the main road beyond." Perhaps their most memorable romantic moments occurred during a brief holiday to Southend:

> Horizontal surfaces were always enticing, the more public, the better. We'd spent two or three days in Southend where I found that curiously far distant horizon, with the sun sinking into it painting a Turneresque pattern in the damp sand, quite bewitching. The trains from Southend to London 40 years ago had no corridors, just a series of enclosed carriages with great brass handles on the doors. A non-stop express train that started its journey at a modest pace, and then speeded up, was made for us, that is, until it started to slow down at passing stations, and eyeball to eyeball, Graham said, "Do you think the police will be waiting at Liverpool Street?" What seemed like seconds later, we arrived and ran like hares to the first taxi where we sat giggling like naughty schoolgirls.

When Greene and Jocelyn were not having fun making love in public, they liked to go to the theater or the cinema, or to Collins Music Hall, where they could watch the singing and dancing from a glass-enclosed bar. Like T. S. Eliot, Greene was fascinated by the old-fashioned world of the English music hall. He and Jocelyn attended the last night of the Granville, Walham Green, and the "potent nostalgia" of the evening left both of them in tears. Greene knew everything there was to know about the night life of London, and he helped to transform Jocelyn's image of city living. And when they went out on the town, they always dined well: "I consumed in our time together more oysters and smoked salmon, champagne, Black Velvet or Pouilly Fumé than I have swallowed in the rest of my life. I indulged his passion for beer and pub sausages in a pub near St. James where the counter was divided by engraved glass screens framed in dark wood, which could be angled for total privacy and secrets."

An occasional companion on their London excursions was John Hayward, the Rochester scholar. Although confined to a wheelchair by multiple sclerosis, Hayward was a lively friend who enjoyed nothing more than exchanging sexual jokes and gossip with anyone who came near him. On his foreign travels Greene tried to remember to send risqué postcards to Hayward for his collection. A typical example features a doctor addressing a nurse who is holding a pair of scissors: "But, nurse, I said remove his spectacles." Greene and Hayward also liked to collect suggestive sentences from serious literature, such as this one from Francis Parkman: "The effort required to keep the irritated organ quiet was so fatiguing that I occasionally rose and spent hours in the open air."

After Hayward's death in the 1960s, Greene fondly recalled his friend's excitement when an attractive woman was taken to visit him. More often than not he would like to entertain a new female visitor by reading to her from Rochester's poem about premature ejaculation, "The Imperfect Enjoyment." What Jocelyn remembered most vividly about her visits to Hayward's home in Chelsea were the occasions when T. S. Eliot, who shared the flat, would make an appearance. He liked to call her Pixie, and she was struck by the way that his "eyes smiled before his lips." Greene, of course, was always in awe of the great man and no doubt valued the friendship with Hayward partly because it brought him into contact with Eliot. An added thrill of any visit to Carlyle Mansions came from the knowledge that Henry James had died in the flat directly above Hayward and Eliot's.

Bright and friendly, Jocelyn did not complicate Greene's life, and he valued her as an antidote to the emotional storms that characterized his relationships with Catherine and Dorothy. He was anxious to keep things uncomplicated. At an early stage in their affair, he said to her, "Promise me you'll never become a Catholic." He felt that he enjoyed thinking of her "as one of Australia's ignoble but engaging savages." Breathing madonnas and priests with the stigmata were part of the darker romantic life that Greene did not want to share with Jocelyn. She had no interest in being a second Catherine, of whom she later remarked: "She was the only one of the women he loved who was cunning. I don't know what Graham really saw in her. . . . I still feel very strongly about her, even forty years after we once met at a dinner party at Freddie Ayer's home. I didn't like her. She didn't like me."

Greene was always kind to Jocelyn and was careful not to create difficulties. She found him to be "a man of irony, wit and gaiety," and rarely did she see him in a depressed state. For a time he talked of marriage, but Jocelyn seemed to realize that he was not completely in earnest. In any case, she felt no desire to pressure him into marrying her. It was easy to maintain a place in his life for Jocelyn; she made so few demands on him. Under such circumstances, they were able to keep their affair alive for a few years, although they saw each other less and less as time went on.

The only time that Greene's behavior "really frightened" Jocelyn was the day that he announced his desire to receive shock treatments from his psychiatrist, Eric Strauss. She could not understand why he would want such drastic therapy. It was another way of hurting himself, but it was also a sign of the desperation that lurked under the "gaiety." After Strauss talked him out of the idea, Jocelyn made him promise "not to think of it again." Although he seemed excessively dependent on Strauss, Greene warned Jocelyn to stay away from all psychiatrists. "Promise me faithfully," he said one day, "that you'll never go near an analyst—you're all right now, but it might change you, and you'll never be all right again!"

His own mood swings in the 1950s were often extreme. For a time he would play the part of the recluse—berating his publisher for giving his telephone number to a journalist or hiding out in remote parts of the world—then he would suddenly appear at a big public event and make a spectacle of himself, or give a revealing interview. In 1954 he allowed *Picture Post* to photograph him while he was pouring a large whiskey for himself. In the picture he looks thoroughly drunk, and the caption reads: "Recreations: Opium smoking, cutting down on whisky, journeying without maps, practical jokes."

Greene's most famous practical jokes took place in the 1950s. Besides the Anglo-Texan Society, there was the John Gordon Society, which was formed in 1956, with Greene as its president. The society was supposed to campaign against pornography, although its real purpose was to deride the guardians of public morality, one of whom was the editor of the *Sunday Express,* John Gordon. In July 1956 the normally shy Greene appeared on a London stage before hundreds of people to debate with Gordon at a meeting of the society.

This wild farce began when Greene recommended Vladimir Nabokov's *Lolita* as his "Book of the Year" in the *Sunday Times.* Taking note of this recommendation, Gordon carefully examined a copy of the novel and was outraged by its contents. "Without doubt it is the filthiest book I have ever read," Gordon told readers of his newspaper, adding that it was "sheer unrestrained pornography." Greene's response was to announce the establishment of a society that would help Gordon stamp out pornography. The society attracted sixty members at its first meeting, all of whom were determined to join Greene in the great sport of satirizing Gordon's views. The editor was invited to give a lecture to the society, a telegraphic address (POGO, LONDON) was established for quick communication with vigilant members in such sinful places as Paris, and a proposal was made to attach the warning "Banned by the John Gordon

Society" to any suspect book. Gordon put up a good fight during his debate with Greene, explaining to the audience that he had probed into the novelist's past and had discovered the details of the Shirley Temple case: "Lord Hewart, the Chief Justice, had described Mr. Greene's reflection on the child as a gross outrage. Was Mr. Greene in court? Not at all. With wisdom and discretion, he had buried himself in Mexico, leaving his publishers to take the rap. If I were Mr. Graham Greene, after that salutary experience I would not get myself mixed up with this sort of thing again."

It was rare for someone to strike back against Greene with such direct criticism, and the novelist wisely refrained from engaging in further public debates with Gordon, although he did continue to make hit-and-run attacks in the press. In 1959 he sent a notice to the *New Statesman* announcing that he intended to write an unauthorized biography called *The Private Life of John Gordon* and asking readers to send him anecdotes and unpublished letters. Gordon may have been a pompous old fool on the question of *Lolita*'s merits, but he knew how to do battle with Greene. He gave a perfect response to the biography proposal:

> I am thrilled that Mr. Graham Greene has decided to become my Boswell. . . . Of course, I realize that such a task involving so much research can be tedious and burdensome. Would it be immodest of me to offer Mr. Graham Greene my help? If he will choose a day convenient to him, I'll be delighted to have him to dinner at which in quietness and comfort we can bare our souls and share our secrets.

Regrettably, Gordon's generous offer was not accepted by his evasive Boswell.

Greene's antics gave him a chance to let off steam, but they could also be tiresome and childish. The John Gordon Society was largely a waste of time, and it simply made Greene look silly in the end. The problem was partly that he was trying to amuse his millionaire friend John Sutro, who helped him launch both the Anglo-Texan Society and the Gordon Society. Wealth and fame had put Greene in the company of rich men who enjoyed idle jests, but it was not the best company for a novelist whose talent was already suffering from a lack of focus. There was so much to divert his attention, and there were so many ways to escape from the burdens of writing. Instead of devoting more effort to his art, he squandered time and energy writing letters to the press about subjects of passing interest and entering contests for the best imitation of his own style. He won a couple of these contests, and his letters to the press involved him in some heated controversies, but none of these things made a positive difference to the only thing that mattered—his art. Even when his public letters address substantial issues, they are often little more than rhetorical exercises, quick ways of striking a provocative pose.

We laugh at the letters containing his mock proposals for the Anglo-Texan Society and the John Gordon Society, but many of his supposedly serious letters are equally absurd. Two years before he died, Greene authorized the publication of *Yours Etc.: Letters to the Press, 1945–89*. There are many funny moments in the book, but overall, reading through this material is depressing. It is unfortunate that the author of *Brighton Rock* and *The Power and the Glory* chose to spend so much time on so many trivial matters. One letter champions the taste of vodka against the complaint that it is the "dullest" drink; another criticizes the typography in a redesign of *The Spectator;* a third speaks up for the coffee houses and ice cream parlors of Moscow; a fourth pleads for the right of prostitutes to solicit customers in the streets; a fifth defends political indoctrination of very young schoolchildren in Nicaragua. A long, rambling letter to *The Spectator* proposes a complex scheme to bankrupt the British postal system, while another urges postal workers to schedule their strikes when income-tax demands are sent out.

In general these letters were taken seriously and prompted solemn responses from various correspondents. After Greene praised the men involved in the Great Train Robbery and protested at the harshness of their sentences, the *Evening Standard* asked several people to comment on the "moral issues" of the case. Stephen Spender helpfully pointed out that "it is not necessary to admire the robbers in order to object to the severity of the sentences." Major G. E. Howard, of Surrey, charged that Greene's "deplorable hero-worship of squalid, cowardly criminals is a major cause of the current appalling level of juvenile delinquency."

People could always be expected to react in the predictable manner, especially on political matters. After *The Quiet American* helped to transform Greene into a political spokesman, he often used letters to the press as a way of creating debates, which he would then undermine by evasive tactics. The passage of time has helped to show how ridiculous his efforts at political punditry could be. In 1959, for example, he told readers of *The Times* that "Dr. Castro" had no ties to communism but was, in fact, a friend of the Catholic Church. Evelyn Waugh was one of the few people who could see that Greene wanted to use such letters as private jokes. He knew him well enough to appreciate that Greene had no taste for serious political activity. He was good at writing letters, but he never took an important part in any significant political movement. After Waugh spent an evening at the theater with him—they saw Olivier in a play by Eugène Ionesco—he teased Greene the next day for writing to the *The Times* about tortures in Algeria: "Why don't you mention the torture inflicted upon us by Laurence Olivier last night?" Similarly, when Greene wrote a pompous "open letter" to the archbishop of Paris protesting the failure to give Colette a Catholic burial, Waugh dismissed the letter as "fatuous," telling Nancy Mitford that Greene dashed it off after having had a little too much alcohol at lunch. (Greene later denied his friend's allegation.)

Whether he was drunk or not, he demonstrated his lack of seriousness again and again by the dilettantish fashion in which he moved quickly from one controversy to the next, rarely bothering to substantiate his charges in extended debates or to follow them up with some sort of constructive action. In 1948, when no one thought of him as a political figure, he wrote an entertaining parody of a literary man who is always sending letters to the press protesting some social problem. He described the man as a loyal member of PEN who races from one international conference to another, speaking out against injustice and gathering signatures in support of his latest letter to *The Times*. The brief parody was part of Greene's contribution to *Why Do I Write?*, a book that also featured essays by Elizabeth Bowen and V. S. Pritchett. The only useful social function for the writer, Greene said, was to be as subversive as possible. He wrote, "We who can be disloyal with impunity should keep that ideal alive." No one can say that he did not give the world fair warning.

The best way to appreciate *Yours Etc.* is to see it as a kind of joke book. Some of the jokes work, some fail embarrassingly, and others are incomprehensible. An excellent example of this last type is a letter to *The Spectator* in which Greene complains about motorcycle helmets. He objects that they are dangerous partly because they can be used by bank robbers, but he then quickly speaks in favor of the bank robbers in the South of France for helping to scare away the tourists. He ends with a brief note of sympathy for the Sikhs in England who had been asked to wear helmets over their turbans. The letter was given the dull headline "Helmets," although it obviously deserved to be called "Mad Hatter."

As a form of therapy such epistolary exercises were at least more enjoyable than electric shock treatments. We can also attach a name to this activity, which is more than can be said for another of Greene's private games. During a stay at Evelyn Waugh's country home in the early 1950s, Greene wandered off to a nearby road, where he spent the day "noting the numbers of motor-cars." Waugh thought that his friend took "omens" from the numbers. In an interview with one of Waugh's biographers, Greene later tried to explain what he was up to: "I was divided in my affections for two people, and I gave one of them one number, and the other, the other number. And I would go in the streets—I had nothing better to do, and it was a nice day—and watch cars go by and see which numbers came up."

But he had another version of this game, which had nothing to do with love or fortune-telling. He explained the rules to Kenneth Tynan, who struggled to make some sense of the "hobby":

> Greene collects car numbers. You must spot first the figure 1 by itself, and then work numerically upward: the first hundred are the hardest. It demands the utmost honesty, this treadmill pastime, since it leads nowhere save toward an ever stronger temptation to cheat. After a few hours in his flat, Greene goes out to stare intently past car headlights. God knows what, if anything, he is expiating.

This obsession with numbers created some real excitement when Greene developed an interest in gambling at the tables in Monte Carlo. The plot for his undistinguished short novel *Loser Takes All* came to him after he experimented with various ways of beating the odds. As the title suggests, the experiments were ultimately unsatisfactory.

Of all his pastimes, sex was always at the top of his list, although it was also the source of much confusion and dissatisfaction. With the money to afford whatever he wanted, he became especially drawn to the attractions of Paris and spent so much time there in the 1950s and early 1960s that he decided to take an apartment in the city. John Sutro recalled that Greene's favorite brothel was in the rue de Douai and that he visited it under an assumed name until the madam discovered his real identity. In one of his antic moments, Greene decided to share a bit of his secret life with his younger sister, Elisabeth, and with John and Gillian Sutro. When his party arrived at the brothel, they were taken to a large bedroom and served champagne. Two women entered, stripped, and began making love on the bed while the Greenes and the Sutros watched the performance from a row of chairs. "I was a bit embarrassed," John Sutro remembered, "the others took it in their stride. More champagne arrived; the girls got down to work with renewed zeal." At some point Gillian Sutro and Greene were invited to join the action. "We could have lots of fun," the French women announced. But, according to Sutro, "the offer was politely declined, and we went home, a rather tipsy quartet."

In the mid-1950s, when Greene was writing a film script for Otto

Preminger's production of Shaw's *Saint Joan,* he often boasted to the director about the glories of his favorite brothel. At last he and Preminger went to Paris, and Greene took him right away to the brothel, still singing its praises as their taxi pulled up outside. "The lady who runs this establishment has amazing resources," Greene told the director. "You can go to any show in Paris, and if there is a girl you fancy, you have only to make a note of her. For instance, you tell the madame that you want the fourth dancer from the left, and she will be delivered to you right after the show." Twenty years earlier Greene had described in *Journey Without Maps* how Major Grant had ordered women over the telephone as though they were pieces of meat. He was now able to follow the major's example and was eager to show off his great power to his famous friend from Hollywood. But his plans went awry. In his autobiography Preminger describes what happened: "We arrived and were admitted to a lavishly furnished anteroom. Graham Greene prepared to introduce me to the madame as she entered, but before he could do so, she rushed past him and embraced me. 'Monsieur Preminger!' she cried. 'How wonderful to see you again!' "

II

With Catherine, Jocelyn, and the rue de Douai to occupy Greene's attention, one might assume that he would not need another major romance in his life, but in 1955 he developed an irresistible attraction to the Swedish actress Anita Bjork. They met in Stockholm while he was visiting his Swedish publisher, Ragnar Svanstrom. As in Jocelyn's case, there was a twenty-year age difference. Exceptionally talented and pretty, Anita had a promising theatrical career in Stockholm, but when she met Greene she was still trying to overcome the effects of a great tragedy in her life. A year earlier her husband, Stig Dagerman, had committed suicide, leaving her to care for two young children on her own. According to a friend, Stig "was a manic depressive, and had several times attempted suicide, but always, except on this occasion, ended by turning off the engine and walking out into the night air." Greene had dinner with Anita on a cold night in November and saw her at Christmas in London. After this second meeting the affair took off, and for the next three years Greene tried to spend as much time as possible in Sweden. He bought a house for Anita near Stockholm and took her on various trips, and they shared some long holidays at his villa in Anacapri.

"He was complicated in a way I was familiar with—and liked," Anita recalled, but she always "had a feeling that [he] didn't like Sweden or Swedes very much." It became a chore for him to fly back and forth to Stockholm, and he complained about the long, dark winters and the difficulty of learning to speak Swedish. He did give some thought to living with her year-round, but he had no friends in Sweden besides Anita and his publisher, and he was never able to learn more than a few words of the language. He suggested that they establish a home elsewhere. "He wanted me to move to France and live there," Anita wrote. "I couldn't leave my children and the theatre." The difficulty was impossible to resolve, and, by the end of the 1950s, the affair was over.

The affair was a pleasant fantasy for Greene, another escape into a different world, but it is doubtful that he ever expected to make it last, in France or elsewhere. For a while he attempted to hide the relationship from Catherine, but she soon found out about it. Then he quickly tried to explain that Anita was only a pale substitute for her. Catherine was special, but, no matter what he promised the women in his life, he never prepared to make a complete commitment to only one of them. Each could absorb his attention for a certain amount of time, and during such a period he could make any number of extravagant plans. But sooner or later he always wanted to change his scenery and shift his attention to a different face. The interesting thing is that he could never bear to break all his ties to the important women in his life. Up until the last months of his life, he was writing letters to Anita and Jocelyn, and, of course, he stayed in touch with Catherine and Dorothy until their deaths. Then there was always Vivien in the distant background, the one and only Mrs. Graham Greene.

As his short story "The Destructors" demonstrates, he still cared enough about Vivien to find some way of hurting her. The tale of a gang of boys breaking into a beautiful old house was inspired largely by Greene's desire to comment on the collapse of his marriage, but he was also aware of a real assault on Vivien. Shortly before Christmas 1951—when Greene was in Vietnam—an unknown man broke into Vivien's house in Oxford. Greene learned about the incident almost a month later and reported the details to Catherine in a letter written from Malaya. The intruder entered the house at night and began attacking Vivien. Their daughter—now a young woman—was asleep at the time but was awakened by the noise and ran to her mother's assistance. Bravely, Lucy struggled with the man and managed to scare him away. Vivien was left with a bruise and a cut on her lip.

Three years later "The Destructors" appeared in *Picture Post* and caused a furor among readers who thought the author took too much pleasure in describing the gang's attack on the fictional house and its owner—a character named Old Misery.

When Greene's affair with Anita was coming to a close, he tried to hurt her in a way that most people would find unforgivable. In 1959 he wrote a mediocre play called *The Complaisant Lover*. In large part it is a satire on his long relationship with Catherine and her husband, but he incorporated one important detail from Anita's life. Near the end of the play, the "complaisant" husband in the story is tempted to commit suicide. He walks out to the garage, starts his car, and leaves the engine running with the garage doors shut. As the exhaust begins to gather, he changes his mind and returns to his house, where he finds that his wife has already figured out what he was trying to do. There is a brief but painful discussion about the pathetic spectacle of death by carbon monoxide.

The writer Michael Meyer, a friend of both Greene and Anita, wrote that *The Complaisant Lover* offended Stockholm's close-knit literary community: "Several Swedish writers who had been friends of Anita's husband . . . were quick to point out that [carbon monoxide poisoning] was how he had died, and suggested that Graham had drawn the parallel deliberately to wound either Anita or Stig's memory or both." Greene asked Meyer to tell Anita that he had not wanted to hurt her, but the parallel with her husband's death was too obvious, and there was no compelling reason to bring the garage scene into the play. The whole episode is typical of the way Greene liked to use literature to strike back at real or imagined enemies, and he may have believed—for a time—that Anita and Stig's ghost were among his enemies. When she was asked about the play after Greene's death, Anita refused to criticize the garage scene, saying only, "It was his work." In other words, she was willing to accept a separation between his life and art.

But others in Sweden were not inclined to forgive and forget. In the 1970s and 1980s, there were frequent complaints in the world press that the Swedish Academy had failed to award Greene the Nobel Prize, and it was known that Dr. Artur Lundkvist, who dominated the Nobel literary committee, strongly disapproved of the novelist. "Greene is too popular," Lundkvist told the journalist Peter Lennon. "He doesn't need the money." He was also reported as saying, "Graham Greene will receive the Nobel Prize over my dead body." Greene acknowledged that Lundkvist was opposed to him, but he dismissed the idea that *The Complaisant Lover* had anything to do with it: "I thought it was because I'd had a friendly relationship with a girl he must have known in Stockholm. Then I came across a review by him of my play *The Living Room,* saying, 'The plague flags should be hung outside the Royal Theatre.' " The performance of the play had been delayed for half an hour because, through no fault of his own, Greene arrived late at the theater. Lundkvist may not have been the most generous of men, but it is unlikely that he would have denied the Nobel Prize to an author because of one bad play or one late performance. Having seen the cruel touch in *The Complaisant Lover,* he could have found other examples of it in Greene's work—such as the anti-Semitic remarks in *Brighton Rock*—and this evidence may have caused him to turn against the author.

In *Not Prince Hamlet: Literary and Theatrical Memoirs,* Michael Meyer defends the novelist against any charge of intentional cruelty, implying that the real blame for the trouble over the garage scene lay with the "petty jealousies" in Stockholm's literary world. During this period Meyer was especially close to Greene, and he was a staunch ally for many years afterward. He was sixteen years younger than Greene and was still vigorously defending the novelist's reputation when this biography was being written. When the affair with Anita came to an end, he helped his friend discover a new escape in faraway Tahiti. In 1959 the two men bought first-class tickets for air flights from London to the South Pacific. They spent Christmas in Fiji, then went to Tahiti, where they spent a month in a small bungalow beside the ocean.

Finding that the "girls were mostly ugly" in this tropical paradise, they enjoyed a quiet life. Greene spent the mornings writing; then the two men amused themselves by swimming among the pretty coral formations or playing Scrabble. They were very competitive players and had some heated arguments about whether certain words were acceptable. Their nerves were a bit strained during the last days of their long stay, but they found some opium before they left Tahiti and were able to relax with a few pipes. Then they flew to San Francisco, where they found a good dictionary to help them settle some of their Scrabble disputes. After six days in San Francisco, they went to Reno, Nevada, where, as Meyer proudly reports in his book, "I won a jackpot and Graham two."

Although they were constant companions for almost two months, they managed to avoid any major quarrels. And, as Meyer points out, Greene did not allow any sexual affairs to disturb their peaceful holiday. One young man in Fiji did make the mistake of assuming that they were "a gay couple," but in *Not Prince Hamlet,* Meyer gives no indication that he was aware of Greene's homosexual interests. Thus one must conclude that their relationship was strictly a friendly one and that for two months the novelist found the strength to behave in a chaste manner.

Another young man with whom Greene enjoyed a tropical holiday in the 1950s was Truman Capote. On a whim Greene decided to go to Haiti in August 1954 with a couple of friends, and after arriving at his hotel in Port-au-Prince, he discovered that Capote was also one of the guests. Apparently, their hotel—the El Rancho—was a bit short on space because, as Greene later reported to Catherine, he and Capote were forced to sleep in the same bedroom one night. Capote spent a lot of time studying his new friend's palm and trying to tell his fortune, but their relationship was platonic, according to Greene. Following this holiday they kept in touch, and in the 1980s Capote gave a warm tribute to his friend during an interview with Lawrence Grobel:

> Graham Greene is a great friend of mine, virtually a lifelong friend. If they wanted to give the [Nobel] prize to an English writer, it certainly should have been given to Graham. . . . Whatever you think of Graham one way or another, Graham at least wrote one *fabulous* book called *Brighton Rock*. . . . It's just an incredibly beautiful, perfect novel. It has the greatest last four paragraphs of any modern novel I can think of.

In the days of *Brighton Rock,* Greene was able to give abundant energy to his work, but in the 1950s much of his time was consumed by traveling. He covered the length of Canada with his daughter, Lucy, who had a passion for horses and wanted a ranch of her own in the rugged landscape of the western provinces. In the mid-1950s, when Lucy was in her early twenties, he found such a ranch and bought it for her, using money from the sale of the film rights to *The Quiet American*. He returned to Canada on several occasions and would sometimes combine these trips with plane connections to the Caribbean. One favorite destination was Jamaica, where he and Catherine spent some time with Noël Coward, who remarked in his diary, "[Greene] has a strange, tortured mind but, like most of God's creatures, aches to be loved."

With the exception of Greene's long excursion in the company of Michael Meyer, his most ambitious journey took him to China by way of the Soviet Union. The trip was made in the spring of 1957 and was organized as a cultural mission. Besides Greene the small delegation included a professor of comparative education, an authority on dance, an official from the British Museum, the Scottish poet Hugh MacDiarmid, Lord Chorley of the British Alpine Club, and Greene's friends the earl and countess of Huntingdon. It was Greene's plan to abandon the group as soon as they reached China, in the hope that he could travel more freely on his own. There were specific things that he wanted see—for literary purposes—and he could go about his business much better if he did not have a crowd following him. At least this was the logic he offered after arriving in the country, but, to his dismay, the other travelers insisted on staying with him.

Writing about the trip for *The Times* in 1985, Greene included the disclaimer "I was innocent of any espionage intentions." The truth, however, is that the tour offered a great opportunity to gather intelligence on all aspects of life in Communist China, and Greene had offered his services to his friends in SIS, who were happy to employ him. A week before he left, an officer of the service prepared a list of items that were of special interest. First on the list was a request for information about naval activity in Hankow Bay. Greene was required to note the identification number painted on any ship or submarine he saw in the bay, and if he managed to get near a specific shipyard elsewhere in the country, he was supposed to look for two large holes hidden by screens on the slipway. No one bothered to tell him what might be in those holes. Apparently, the service could not figure them out and wanted Greene to solve the mystery.

Alas, his mission was a failure. He was unable to get away from his delegation long enough to do proper spying, and he drew too much attention to himself when he began publicly quarreling with Lord Chorley. The real cause of the problem seems to have been his discovery of Mou-Tai, a wine with an alcohol content of 50 percent. Greene developed an instant liking for the wine, and under its influence he made a scene at a hotel banquet, accusing Lord Chorley of encouraging political repression. Relations among the delegates were never quite right after that, and they grew much worse during an overnight river journey. After drinking too much Mou-Tai, Greene picked a fight with the professor of comparative literature, who responded by threatening to throw the distinguished novelist overboard. Somehow they were brought under control and sent to bed, but, when Greene woke up in the middle of the night, he was annoyed by a loud noise that seemed to be coming from the professor's cabin. He got up and shouted, "Stop that fucking noise, you bugger." As it happened, the noise was coming from the chefs in the boat's kitchen, and one member of the delegation later demanded to know why Greene was making so much noise. With the inventiveness of an experienced storyteller, he explained that he had imagined the professor was trying to murder one of their Chinese guides.

The only person whom Greene seems not to have offended was MacDiarmid. When they decided to take different flights home, Greene came to MacDiarmid's hotel room bearing a gift. Opening his door, the poet found the novelist holding something in his hands:

> It was a small stoneware jar of Mou-Tai. . . . He said he daren't take it with him as it was liable to explode and wreck the plane, and he enjoined me to be extremely careful too. "Well," I said, "I can't imagine it can do any harm to a confirmed whisky drinker." So I uncorked it there and then, and drank it. It tasted like a mixture of petrol and vodka, but I suffered no ill-effects beyond the initial "grue" at its taste.

When Greene gave the secret service a report on his trip, he appears to have remained discreetly silent on his discovery of Mou-Tai. But he could not disguise his failure to produce any valuable information. The great mystery of the two big holes remained unsolved. There was clear disappointment with the episode in SIS. The service had hoped, in view of Greene's favorable response to the brief he had been given, that he would acquire at least a few bits of intelligence. With a faint touch of hope, one officer remarked, "I am sure that he must remember something of this trip which is of value." But, thanks to Mou-Tai, Greene was never able to remember anything of great significance.

Appropriately enough, Greene was developing ideas for *Our Man in Havana* at the time that this real-life spy farce took place. His doomed search for the two big holes in China is reflected in James Wormold's vague reports of secret military installations in Cuba. Such is the thirst for intelligence information that even ridiculously impossible constructions can be accepted as genuine, and it may well be that those Chinese holes were as insignificant as the sketches of vacuum-cleaner parts that Wormold identifies as secret weapons. Of course, the main inspiration for the novel came from the work of the double agent Garbo during the Second World War, and for a while Greene intended to set the story in Portugal, where Garbo first began creating his imaginary intelligence reports. As late as 1956 Greene was planning to go to Lisbon, soak up the local atmosphere, then quickly write a screen treatment of the story, in the manner that he had used for *The Third Man*. From the moment that he began to think seriously about the story, he intended it to be the basis of a film.

It was only after he went to China that he decided to change the setting from wartime Lisbon to a contemporary scene with a more exotic flavor. After he had determined that Cuba was the best choice, the project moved ahead smoothly. Because he knew the espionage world so well, and because he had been thinking about the literary potential of Garbo's story for so long, Greene was able to put the story together with great speed. He traveled to Havana in November 1957 and found all the right details to create a convincing background. By the end of 1958 the novel was out, and by April 1959 Carol Reed and his crew were in Havana shooting the picture. In the middle of this swift passage of events, the old, corrupt Batista government was overthrown by Castro's army, giving Greene's story the kind of timely significance that would never have come to "Our Man in Lisbon."

At an early stage of his 1957 visit to Cuba, Greene tried to establish contact with Castro's rebel forces, hoping to win their confidence as a supporter of their struggle against Batista. A Cuban journalist named Lisandro Otero took Greene to a secret meeting with Castro's representatives at a restaurant on the outskirts of Havana. It was decided over dinner that Greene could be of some use to the cause. The rebels in the mountains needed warm clothes, so Greene was asked to smuggle a suitcase full of sweaters and jackets on a flight from Havana to Santiago. His contact, Nydia Sarabia, recalled the mission: "At the time, Batista's police were checking the airport for rebels. Greene was perfect for the job. He was tall, lightskinned, obviously foreign, and he looked like he knew nothing of what was going on." Greene was good at looking innocent, but this was not exactly a death-defying mission. All the same, it won Greene a small place in the rebels' hearts and made it easier for his film project to win approval when Castro came to power.

The great dictator himself visited the crew on location in Havana and gave the film his blessing, although he complained that Greene's story did not do justice to the evil of Batista's rule. He would have done more than complain if he had realized that Greene shared his observations about Cuba with friends in SIS. As it was, Greene could always count on a warm welcome from Castro. During a visit in 1966, Castro put at his disposal a military plane and a Cadillac with a French-speaking chauffeur.

Despite his public statements to the contrary, Greene was never in sympathy with Castro's revolution. He much preferred Batista's Cuba, with its wild abundance of sexual attractions, gambling, and drugs. He was especially drawn to the Shanghai Theater, which featured live sex shows and hard-core films. As Lisandro Otero recalled, the place was always full of "pimps and their prostitutes," and he added the understatement "Greene was interested in sex." On one memorable visit to Havana, Greene watched a character called Superman perform at the Shanghai, visited a casino, ate seafood at the Floridita restaurant, smoked marijuana, watched a lesbian show, and purchased some "cocaine" that turned out to be boracic powder. Under the enlightened revolutionary government, such decadent pleasures were scorned—until financial pressures brought some of the vices back in the 1990s. Just after Castro came to power, Greene urged an English friend in Havana to have a look at the brothels before they were shut down. "When Communism starts, puritanism immediately follows," he said. "You ought to see what is on offer here before it goes."

Batista and his most dreaded henchman, Maj. Esteban Ventura, were the kinds of villains that Greene had always been attracted to. Their influence is felt throughout *Our Man in Havana,* whereas there is no trace to be found of Castro's revolutionary ideals. It is much more interesting to have Greene's version of Ventura—Captain Segura—who tortures and murders people, and who carries a cigarette case made of human skin. His evil is something Greene could understand, but Castro and his friends were right to complain that the novelist failed to give enough attention to Segura's evil. The comic thrust of the story, and its focus on the British secret service, did not leave much room for developing Segura's character. The fact is that the novel creates an uneasy combination of comedy and tragedy, which makes the story more unsatisfactory as it moves along.

Greene's descriptions of the bumbling espionage efforts in the early part of the novel are some of the funniest things he wrote. What he had found so appealing in Garbo's adventures was the way the ostensibly serious business of espionage can be subverted by a talent for creating believable fictions. Like any unreliable narrator, Wormold knows the joy of misleading gullible readers, although in his case the readers—his employers in the secret service—are especially fun to mislead because they are supposed to know better. Imagination liberates Wormold, but it becomes a trap for the unwary reader, who always wants to imagine that the author is a friend or even a hero. The great weakness of the secret service director in the novel is that he creates a false persona for Wormold, imagining that the agent must be some noble merchant king eager to serve God and country. Wormold's humble vacuum-cleaner shop is "drowned beyond recovery in the tide of the Chief's literary imagination." Once that flood has covered up the truth, Wormold can expect that almost anything he says will be accepted. The Chief wants to believe in Wormold because he wants to believe in the image that he has created of him.

The satire would work well if it were milder, but it becomes increasingly savage as Wormold's imaginary games attract the attention of Segura, who is quick to imagine that the Englishman's false agents are real people. Like the Chief, Segura has a potent imagination, but all its energy is directed toward death and pain. Segura likes to think that he hurts only people who, at some level, want to be hurt: "One never tortures except by a kind of mutual agreement." It is a version of the writer-reader arrangement, an intimate affair in which specific readers are attracted to specific writers. Greene could have said that the cruel streak in his work hurt only those who had willingly misjudged him. *Our Man in Havana* illustrates the point by beginning in a light mood, then drawing the reader into a story that turns dark and bitter. The laughter trails off as the reader begins to wonder whether it is worth reading on—that is, whether it is worth submitting to pain by mutual agreement. The game is mild in literature, especially in this novel, but transfer it to Segura's prison and the complete effect becomes terrifying.

Our Man in Havana gives a great deal of attention to the ease with which one can cross the line separating fiction from reality. Wormold's imaginary game produces real casualties, but the power of creating and killing off imaginary agents eventually leads him to kill a real person. The fictional game creates a taste for the real thing. So Wormold finds the right victim, Carter—a nasty little man who is depicted as someone who deserves to die. After he shoots him, Wormold seems surprisingly content. Under the heady influence of fiction making, the mild-mannered salesman is transformed into a self-satisfied killer.

Much of Wormold's satisfaction in killing Carter comes from the knowledge that he is a weak man. Indeed, he is quite a vulnerable fellow, sexually speaking, whose greatest fear is of women. Having killed him, Wormold delivers the ultimate manly insult—"He couldn't undo a girl's corset." The name Carter calls to mind Greene's young torturer at Berkhamsted, the boy who made him feel weak and effeminate. And the name Wormold also had a personal significance for Greene. As he was well aware, Catherine was always mispronouncing the name of one of Greene's rivals for her affection. She called Brian Wormald by the name Wormold. In the Carter-Wormold duel, Greene can identify with both sides. He is the weak one and the strong one, the successful ladies' man and the disappointed lover who is unsure of his sexuality. The only thing for certain is that, throughout his career, sexual insecurity drove Greene to indulge in fantasies of murder. Novel after novel the body count rises.

During the filming of *Our Man in Havana,* Greene met the most famous literary "macho" man of the century. Some of the scenes were shot at Sloppy Joe's bar, and Ernest Hemingway showed up while the cast and crew were working at the location. A local reporter for the *Havana Post,* who was a little mistaken about Greene's proper title, described the event:

> They were shooting scenes in Sloppy Joe's on Tuesday last, and Ernest Hemingway appeared. He said he had come not to witness the filming, but to see his old friend Noel Coward. So he and Coward sat in the back and exchanged intelligence. Hemingway, who is the original "barbudo" of Havana, if the term is taken in its literal meaning, was wearing beard, shorts, and sports shirt. He also said "Howdy" to Sir Graham Greene.

Following that friendly "Howdy," Sir Graham was invited to Hemingway's house for drinks, but he did not stay long. He was intimidated not only by his host but by the trophies of masculine aggression scattered throughout the house. "Taxidermy everywhere," Greene remarked, "buffalo heads, antlers . . . such carnage."

Reed's film is a disappointment, partly because the script is inferior to those of *The Third Man* and *The Fallen Idol,* but also because so many of the actors in the international cast give lackluster performances. As Wormold, Alec Guinness does a good job with the comic side of the character, but he appears awkward in the part when the story grows darker. The American comic Ernie Kovacs is completely unconvincing as Captain Segura. He makes the evil torturer seem like a mildly corrupt traffic cop. The worst mistake was made in the casting of a young, inexperienced American actress as Wormold's daughter. Her accent and manner make it impossible to believe that Alec Guinness could be her father.

The one redeeming aspect of the film is its location shooting, which provides the best look at life in the old Cuba, before Castro turned it into a drab socialist paradise. Although the dictator wanted to be supportive of the film, it was not always easy for Reed to get the look he wanted. When he took his crew to film a scene at the Shanghai Theater, he discovered that the new government had tried to clean up the acts and that many of Greene's favorite performers had been banned from the stage or put in jail. In his pursuit of authenticity, Reed tracked down some of the old "stars" of the Shanghai, but the magic had faded. As one observer remarked, they "were a beat-up vision to behold."

CHAPTER TWENTY-ONE

TO TELL THE TRUTH

While Greene was paying one of his visits to Havana in the bad old Batista days, he received a letter from New York with a tempting invitation to appear on the American game show *To Tell the Truth*. For some reason the producers believed that Greene would make a fascinating contestant. His face was not so well known in America at the time, but, as a celebrated Catholic author, his importance would be easy to explain. Assuming that he would not be familiar with the game, the producers carefully explained that it involved three contestants claiming to be the same person: "In this case, let us say Graham Greene. One of these three is the real Graham Greene, and is sworn to tell the truth. The other two have merely assumed that identity, and they don't have to stick to the truth." For two hours before the show, the impostors were to receive special coaching on Greene's background, then all three were to appear onstage before a panel of four celebrity interrogators. If Greene agreed to participate, the producers promised to pay him $1,000. It was a perfect game for a Greene nightmare. He would have to respond truthfully to any question thrown at him, while two men pretending to be him could make up any lies they wanted. Although it was a chance for him to experience real terror, he decided not to take the challenge. Among other things, he must have felt that his impostors would require much more than two hours of instruction.

The letter was sufficiently intriguing for Greene to send it to Catherine for safekeeping, and perhaps its offer gave him the idea for a major scene in *A Burnt-out Case*—the novel that followed *Our Man in Havana*. The famous architect Querry—the hero of the story—is confronted by a determined journalist who wants an exclusive interview. Querry has quietly abandoned the world of fame and fortune, and has sought obscurity in the gloomy atmosphere of a Congo leper colony. Parkinson, the journalist, wants to know why the great architect, whose face adorned the cover of *Time* only ten years earlier, has turned his back on success. Querry has endured many interview sessions in the past and does not relish answering another set of predictable questions, but something about Parkinson's attitude prompts the architect to take a bold step. For once he decides to speak truthfully. The only question is whether Parkinson will prefer the unpleasant truth to the appealing fiction that has sustained Querry's high reputation.

Acclaimed for designing beautiful Catholic churches, Querry admits that it was "indecent" of him to do such work when he had no faith in God. He tried designing public buildings, but he had no faith in politics, and his work looked "absurd." Whatever he did, he began to repeat himself, so he retired to the Congo, a burnt-out case. Nothing excites him any longer. He was known as a great lover of women, but now he recognizes that he never loved anyone, not even himself. When Parkinson exclaims that the architect is "a cold-blooded bastard," Querry urges him to say as much in print. After years of getting thrills from lies, he finds now that the raw truth is the only thing that can stimulate him.

Parkinson does not know what to make of such candor. But he soon realizes that it will do him no good to tell the truth. The readers of his Sunday newspaper do not want to hear that their hero is a fake, so the journalist resolves to refurbish all the old legends that have attached themselves to Querry. He will portray him as a saint who has surrendered fame and fortune in order to serve the unfortunate lepers of Africa. He can build him up or tear him down, but the truth does not matter either way. What matters is creating the best fiction for his market. Querry the "monster" will not sell. Parkinson, after all, works for a "family newspaper." As his name suggests, Parkinson is suffering from a kind of degenerative disease that is as bad as leprosy: with every story he writes, he moves farther away from the truth.

After Parkinson refuses to accept his confession, Querry tries to explain himself to a local young woman, Marie Rycker, but this time he uses a long allegory about a great jeweler who made exquisite gold and enamel eggs, with crosses on top, for "the King." The jeweler was rewarded for his efforts with great wealth and fame, and his worldly rewards led him to believe that he could get away with anything. He broke all the king's rules, but he continued to prosper, and his prosperity made everyone assume that he was good as well as great. But he grew weary of his work and began making less impressive jewelry to amuse only himself—toad-shaped stones for women's navels and condoms of soft golden mail. He thought these were funny, but everyone else took them seriously, and soon he gave up making anything. Although the public clamored for more eggs with crosses, he had no desire to satisfy the demand, having lost his faith in the king and in his art.

For once Greene told the truth about his career. He was not the great Catholic novelist; he was not the good champion of love, beauty, and liberty; and, worst of all, he was no longer a great artist. But his admirers did not want to hear this. They only wanted more tales from Greeneland, especially ones about God's strange mercy and the triumph of love. And Greene made it easy for them to go on believing in him. Although he told the truth, it is still in a fictional form that leaves room for doubt. He could deny that Querry's truth was his, just as Querry refuses to specify that he is the jeweler. Indeed, the parallels are not exact. Querry has given up architecture, but *A Burnt-out Case* is proof that Greene was not about to walk away from his lucrative profession. The novel is diffuse and uninspired, yet he published it anyway.

In the dedicatory note, Greene quotes a line from John Masefield, "The long despair of doing nothing well." Unfortunately, it was Greene's fate to suffer this despair for many years. Like Querry, he knew that his political structures were shaky and that his great cathedrals were never intended for worshiping God. And he did not know what to do next, except to repeat himself, borrowing the plot for *The Quiet American* from a discarded novel, using Garbo's old story as the basis of *Our Man in Havana,* and going back to Africa for a pale imitation of Conrad in *A Burnt-out Case*. This decline is not the way the story should go. If Parkinson were writing Greene's biography, he would find excuses for the dull writing and the muddled ideas. He would lift the reader into the clouds and show Greene slowly rising to his heavenly reward. Or he would castigate him from beginning to end, digging up all the dirt and burying even his best work under the pile.

Biographies are stories, but they do not have to be fantasies. The challenge flung at Parkinson is to tell the truth without worrying whether it shocks or disappoints. Anxious for him to accept the challenge, Querry says that he has been "waiting" for someone who will accept his confession for what it is. But Parkinson fails him, Rycker fails him, and—after he dies—a priest fails him by trying to think of him as a man of love. No one wants to say that he was selfish, vain, deceptive, coldly irresponsible, and—for a time—a great artist. The tragedy of the burnt-out case, as it is defined in the leper colony, is that the victim survives leprosy but must endure the rest of life with damaged limbs. Until death mercifully removes his suffering, Querry must live as the shadow of a great man. Or, as Matthew Arnold put it in a poem that Greene liked to quote, "To hear the world acclaim the hollow ghost / Which blames the living man."

But was Greene really a burnt-out case? It would make a good story to say that the tormented novelist was driven to the Congo by his despair, and that his book was written in the steamy heat of the bush as he drank bottle after bottle of whiskey and struggled to keep swarms of insects at bay. Although the novelist did spend three weeks researching his story at a leper colony in what was then the Belgian Congo, the fact is that he wrote much of the novel during his visit to Tahiti with Michael Meyer. If one has to suffer from burnout, a beach in the South Pacific is not a bad place to do it. Greene had the luxury of being able to take his misery to the best of places as well as the worst. All the same, the misery was real. He was in a bad way, physically and mentally. A few months after leaving Tahiti, he lay weak and exhausted in a Moscow hotel room, suffering from an illness eventually diagnosed as pneumonia. His constant search for new experiences—for escapes from the novelist's battle with words—took its toll. Recovery from the pneumonia was slow, and a subsequent problem with his lungs only added to his feeling that all the vitality was being drained from his life and art.

By the standards of ordinary novelists, Greene was still able to produce diverting episodes and striking images. But *A Burnt-out Case* offers nothing that he had not done better before. The novel could have been a majestic journey into the shadowy world of the leper colony, with Querry's despair plunging to greater depths as he confronts the suffering of the African outcasts. In 1940 Greene could have done this well, but in 1960 his style had become too flat and restrained to meet the demands of such a subject, and his visions of pain and evil had lost their sharpness. The descriptions of the lepers are given in a clinical tone, as though Greene is merely going through the motions of setting a scene. Nothing in Querry's predicament is handled with the kind of intensity that would make the reader shudder at his fate. Even a burned-out case can inspire terror, but not if it is being depicted by a burned-out novelist.

Greene's book was based on a visit he made to Dr. Michel Lechat's clinic at Yonda, on the Congo River. He used the unimaginative pseudonym Mr. Graham during his stay and informed the doctor that he was "probably" not going to write a book about his experience, adding that he might never write another book in his life. Unlike the absorbing account of his trip to Liberia, his short "Congo Journal" is the work of a man who is watching the world with only one eye open. The reader can sense the drowsiness of the writer as he adds another brief entry to his diary about some inconsequential event. There are no riveting moments of self-discovery, only the dry observations of a weary traveler. The most bizarre reflection in the journal has nothing to do with Africa or lepers. Without any explanation, Greene suddenly complains that modern women have lost the old inhibitions about having sex during their menstrual periods. In the good old days, he reflects, the male could get several days of rest each month, but now he is lucky to have just a couple. Filling up a journal with this sort of thing is a sure sign of burnout.

In the literary labors of his early career, Greene seemed to thrive on the mechanical approach of writing a certain number of words a day. It helped to discipline his talent. But the later work often seems forced, as though Greene was simply trying to meet the day's quota. Using great chunks of uninterrupted dialogue, he was able to fill up space quickly, and many of the lines are of the "What?" and "No" variety, short responses that work well in a play or film but quickly become monotonous in a novel. Having once created great novels with strong cinematic qualities, Greene was now too enamored of writing film treatments disguised as novels.

His preference for dialogue became clear in the 1950s, when he wrote almost as many plays as he did novels. For the most part the plays were respectfully received, but they now seem turgid and pretentious. "Pain is my profession" is a typically bad line from *The Living Room,* a drama first staged in 1953 that is concerned with the too-familiar combination of God, adultery, and suicide. *The Potting Shed* is important for its autobiographical insights, but as a piece of drama it develops with agonizing slowness and overwhelms the audience with too much background information. As suggested earlier, *The Complaisant Lover* is primarily an exercise in sadism, with the principal targets being Anita Bjork and her dead husband, and Catherine Walston and her "complaisant" Harry.

Before he had finished dabbling in the theater, Greene wrote one

of the worst plays produced in London during the 1960s. Critics
gleefully tore it to pieces, but Greene stoutly defended *Carving a
Statue* (1964) as a subtle blend of tragedy and farce. He seems to
have been the only one who detected a note of farce. A sculptor
spends much of the play working on an enormous statue that is supposed to depict God or the devil, or both. To help him get the face
right, he projects slides on a screen showing various men's faces,
including that of two murderers who especially intrigue him. The first
is a Frenchman who liked to kill women and burn their bodies. The
sculptor speaks admiringly of the man's evil eyes. This slide is immediately followed by another, of a murderer photographed at Brighton
Pier. The sculptor likes him as a model because he killed his son. A
few moments later a stray slide appears on the screen, showing a little
girl's corpse lying "spread-eagled" in a road. The sculptor seems
indifferent to it, but his restless son enters the studio and seems to
become sexually stimulated by it. Later in the play the sculptor's
friend—a doctor—tries to rape a deaf and dumb girl, and he is still
casually carrying her panties in his hand after she flees him and is hit
by a car. Greene must have thought that the farcical element lay in
getting an unsuspecting public to attend the first night. It must also
have pleased him to plant another allusion to a murder in Brighton.

II

To revive the good old days of Pinkie and Raven, Greene desperately
needed to find a new devil. And, unlike the sculptor in his play, he
required more than an ugly face on a slide. He had to get a taste of
the very atmosphere surrounding the devil, yet it was not so easy to
find a really bad one in the 1960s, at least not an identifiable one who
was accessible. The world was becoming a little too civilized. Ho Chi
Minh and Castro were too friendly and well educated. But there was
some cause for hope in Papa Doc Duvalier, the bloodthirsty tyrant of
Haiti. He had taken control of the country after Greene's visits in the
1950s, but the novelist had followed press accounts of Papa Doc's
rise to power and was curious about him.

In August 1963 Greene flew to Port-au-Prince and stayed for a
couple of weeks at a large but almost empty gingerbread structure
known as the Hotel Oloffson. Aubelin Jolicoeur, a dapper gossip
columnist for a newspaper in Port-au-Prince, acted as his host, taking
him to parties and introducing him to the elite of Haitian society. In
the 1950s it was Truman Capote who had first brought Greene to

Jolicoeur's attention. In a jolly manner typical of the young Capote, he brought them together at the El Rancho Hotel with the words "Aubelin Jolicoeur, have you met the celebrated author of *The Power and the Glory?*" Greene, typically, was sipping drinks at the bar. Jolicoeur captured Greene's interest by taking him to the Oloffson, whose owner at the time—an American photographer named Roger Coster—quickly saw how to please the famous visitor. According to Jolicoeur, "Coster enjoyed taking his guests, including Greene, to a brothel run by two upper-class Haitian sisters."

As in his visits to Batista's Cuba, Greene's experience of Haiti was limited to a very narrow but lively range. If any publisher had wanted to commission a guide to the world's brothels, Greene would have been the best man for the job. On the political level, he does not seem to have made much progress. American and British diplomats had horror stories to tell him, and some brave Haitians came to the Oloffson to share their experiences of life under Papa Doc's brutal rule. But he does not appear to have made the acquaintance of the dictator. On his brief visit in 1963, he found abundant evidence of the repression in the country and observed in all corners of the city the intimidating presence of the Tontons Macoutes—Papa Doc's henchmen. Still, the devil himself remained a figure in the mysterious distance, a somber ruler in a black hat.

The poor but friendly Haiti Greene had known in the 1950s had become one big prison, where everyone lived in fear of Papa Doc. He was a voodoo version of Col. Elwood Davis and was obviously destined to join Greene's cast of characters. After returning from Haiti Greene gave the *Sunday Telegraph* of London a short article about Papa Doc's reign of terror and then began creating his fictional portrait of life under the dictator—*The Comedians* (1966). He wrote the first quarter of the novel while he was preparing *Carving a Statue* for its disastrous debut, and he found the work difficult to sustain. He was so tired of writing novels that he started looking for any reason to stop. If his play became a hit, he told Catherine, he would leave *The Comedians* unfinished. He must have known that he would have no choice but to continue it.

An odd thing happens in an early chapter of the book. Some of Greene's old genius flares back to life in a passage of stunning beauty. And the interesting thing is that the passage has nothing to do with Papa Doc and Haiti. It concerns the memories of the narrator, Brown, who owns the Hotel Trianon—a big, empty place based on the Oloffson. In his youth Brown was able to disguise himself as an adult and managed to gain admittance to the casino in Monte Carlo.

He lived out a boy's fantasy, winning a large sum of money and then going to bed with a beautiful older woman who patiently tried to teach him the secrets of love. In simple prose that reads like poetry, Brown recalls the scene in the hotel bedroom when the woman was on the verge of giving up her seduction. He was too shy and afraid, and nothing seemed to arouse him. Then, suddenly, a large seagull flew through the open window from the port below and perched on a piece of furniture, staring calmly at the humans in their bed. The woman began shaking with fear, but her young lover found the invasion exciting. With the woman in the position of vulnerability, he felt able to make love and was so caught up in the pleasure of the act that he never noticed the seagull leave, although he swears in adulthood that he sensed "the current of its wings" as he surrendered his virginity.

In this passage Greene seems so completely absorbed by the writing that there is no sign of weariness or reluctance. But, within a couple of paragraphs, Brown is apologizing to the reader for having digressed, and soon we are back in the grim world of Papa Doc. It is as though Greene wanted to write a different novel—one unconnected to his "research"—but could not bring himself to break the pattern set by *The Quiet American, Our Man in Havana,* and *A Burnt-out Case.* Not that Papa Doc is a poor subject for Greene's talent. It is simply that the novelist is too much under the influence of his work as a journalist. He cannot put the facts aside long enough to let his imagination and style take flight. All the right journalistic details are in the novel, but the novelist's independent vision is lacking. In *The Power and the Glory* Greene concentrates on the human story and uses the political realities of Mexico only as a springboard for his imagination. In *The Comedians* Papa Doc and the Tontons Macoutes are never more than the stick figures of a journalistic report.

The danger of treating Haitians in a superficial way is that it leads to racial stereotypes. The men who belonged to the Tontons Macoutes deserve to be presented as ugly thugs but not as people whose conduct is associated with blacks in general. Greene creates such an association when his narrator notices a car full of Papa Doc's gangsters and says that their "expressionless" black faces make them look like "golliwogs." The gossip columnist Petit Pierre—who is apparently based on Jolicoeur—is reduced to the worst sort of racial stereotype when Brown describes his appearance. Small, agile, and full of laughter, Petit Pierre is said to resemble a "monkey." This comparison is bad enough by itself, but Brown makes it worse when he adds a ludicrous metaphor: "He seemed to swing from wall to wall on ropes of laughter." Other characters in the novel are simply described as "a negro" or "the negro" or "boy."

In a novel of the 1920s or 1930s, such language might seem excusable as an example of the common attitude of the time, but the excuse cannot be applied to *The Comedians,* published in the middle of the 1960s. The book does, however, contain the first black characters in Greene's fiction who are portrayed as articulate, independent people. The dignified Dr. Magiot is such a character, and he is allowed a prominent place in the story. But he is more of a disembodied voice than a flesh-and-blood human being. In fact, in purely dramatic terms he is probably the most boring character in the book. Instead of engaging in normal conversation, he tends to make bookish pronouncements, and there is no sense that he belongs especially in Haiti. With some changes his words could easily be those of a man living in any of a dozen other countries. In most respects he is a token character, a political voice who represents a reasonable response to Papa Doc's insanity. But reason is not Greene's great subject, and the story as a whole does not lend weight to Dr. Magiot's views. Papa Doc's terror is more interesting, but because he and his thugs are so one-dimensional, they never begin to give the reader a sense of the real fear that gripped Haiti.

Aware of his failure to give life to this particular hell, Greene subtly draws attention to the problem. Brown refers to journalists who fly into the country for a short time, collect a few facts, then whip together articles with titles such as "The Nightmare Republic"—the exact title of the piece Greene submitted to the *Sunday Telegraph.* Greene simply could not find the imaginative power to convey more than the surface horrors of the place. *The Comedians* is a better novel than *A Burnt-out Case,* but it is still the work of a writer who knows that his best writing is behind him.

Like *A Burnt-out Case, The Comedians* uses an interesting analogy to address the question of literary failure. Brown's hotel was once a thriving establishment—the most fashionable place to stay in Port-au-Prince—but after Papa Doc came to power, the tourists were frightened away. The hotel suffered a rapid decline until finally, at the time the novel begins, there are only a couple of guests—not counting the corpse of a murdered politician in the swimming pool. Brown's sense of failure is so acute that he keeps on his desk a paperweight in the shape of a coffin, with R.I.P. written on it. And he feels a special attachment to the hotel suite named after the hard-drinking actor John Barrymore—"a great talent ruined."

When the hotel owner begins reading an old copy of Henry James's "Great Good Place," it becomes clear that Greene means to connect the failures of his own work with those suffered by Brown. James's story is about a writer who longs to escape the demands of his highly successful literary career. A burnt-out case whose life is made a little easier by a devoted servant named Brown, the writer dreams of finding peace in an idyllic retreat—the great good place where life is free from care. A similar dream would appear to lie behind *The Comedians*. The novel has all the ingredients of a good tale from Greeneland, but the author's heart is not in it. Rambling and dark, the book is not unlike Brown's big hotel. The owners of both structures have known better days and are anxious to be rid of their burdens.

It is comic to think of anyone continuing to operate a virtually empty hotel, and, to some extent, it is equally funny to see Greene trying to keep his career going with the empty "farce" of *Carving a Statue* and the journalistic treatment of Haiti in *The Comedians*. But the comedy is "black," and, as a background, Greene must have thought that Papa Doc's Haiti made the situation even funnier. From the perspective of a cynical outsider, the Tontons Macoutes and their voodoo dictator can look like extremely comic figures who have dragged the rest of Haiti into their absurd act. With their sunglasses, hats, and dark clothes, Papa Doc's gangsters appear laughable—from a safe distance. Brown can hardly conceal his contempt for the ignorant thugs, and he helps to trick them by indulging in a bit of black comedy—in both senses of the term. He puts the wanted man Jones into women's clothing, pretends they are lovers, and helps him to escape. In the film version, which Greene wrote, the "female" Jones wears black makeup on his face and arms.

Greene's black humor, including his implied pun on the phrase, indicates how little he felt for the real suffering endured by Haitians. The names of his major white characters—Brown, Jones, and Smith—indicate the paucity of imaginative effort that was applied to the story. But for Greene the novel had to be completed, and not only because his hopes for *Carving a Statue* had failed to materialize. There was an enormous amount of money at stake. While the novel was still being written, the MGM film company acquired the rights for a big-budget production. Greene's friend Peter Glenville agreed to direct the film, and the cast he assembled was the most impressive to appear in any adaptation of Greene's work: Richard Burton, Elizabeth Taylor, Alec Guinness, Peter Ustinov, Lillian Gish, James Earl Jones, and Raymond St. Jacques.

Greene profited both from the sale of the rights and from his fee as the screenwriter. The film itself did not do well. With such a cast there should have been at least a modest chance of success, but the actors could not do much with a flimsy story of a few white people flirting with violence in Haiti. Adding to the problem was Elizabeth Taylor, who failed miserably to meet the demands of the job. Cast as Brown's lover, she adopted an accent that is part Californian, part French, part English, and part Third Reich German. Richard Burton as Brown is suitably gloomy and boozy, but he looks bored in the excessively long production. Peter Ustinov fairly summarized the film when he said that it was "too strange and too long—two and a half hours with those characters is too much. It was one of those mysterious films that look marvelous in the daily rushes and everyone gets terribly excited, but when you string the whole thing together, there is a certain feeling of imbalance."

It should not be surprising that Papa Doc and his henchmen were enraged by Greene's novel and by the subsequent release of the film. Papa Doc did Greene the honor of personally reviewing the book in his own newspaper, *Le Matin*. Showing some talent for literary criticism, Papa Doc found it too journalistic. But after the film was released, the dictator decided that Greene's book deserved an extensive attack. His government prepared a glossy booklet in French and English that spells out Greene's many crimes against humanity. *Graham Greene: Finally Exposed* is also a celebration of Papa Doc's enlightened rule over the happy people of little Haiti. The text is full of photographs showing the attractive modern architecture in the country, and there is a particularly good portrait of the great leader looking thoughtful but friendly. As for Greene, no words of abuse are too strong to describe the harm he has done to the good citizens of the "First Negro Republic in the World." It is a nice twist of fate that Greene is treated in the booklet as a kind of devil. One sentence is so loaded with criticism that the propagandist loses count of his charges, using three insults to explain a "double hit": "With *The Comedians* he makes a double hit: he satisfies his sadistic instincts, vomits his negrophobia, and at the same time rounds off his bank account."

It is difficult to credit any criticism coming from a gang of murderers and torturers, but one reasonable point is made in the pamphlet: the propagandist points out that Greene's experience of Papa Doc's Haiti was limited to only a couple of weeks. Greene might have answered that a visit of two days was too long in the "nightmare republic" and that any reasonably alert observer could find more than enough evidence of evil in two weeks. But the charge does help to support the point that Greene's novel is the result of a hit-and-run journalistic exercise. After leaving Haiti in 1963, Greene never returned, not even following the fall of both Papa Doc and Baby Doc. He did meet with a few Haitian dissidents, and wrote some letters attacking the policy of the U.S. government on Haiti, but when one British journalist tried to get him to make a return visit, he excused himself on the pretext that he was too old—even though old age did not keep him from frequently traveling to Panama and Nicaragua in the 1970s and 1980s, and to Siberia in the late 1980s.

Although it is certainly true that writing about Haiti had helped to fill Greene's bank account, a financial catastrophe in 1965 meant that his account was badly in need of the new cash. Greene told Evelyn Waugh that he had lost half his savings to a man who had some points in common with the character of Jones in *The Comedians*. "Major" Jones is an enterprising fellow who never served in the army, but as a good comedian he can put on an entertaining show, charming some people into believing whatever he says. The man who lost Greene's money was a tax expert who helped his clients save money through certain investments. The only trouble was that some of the investments were less than satisfactory. At his trial on fraud charges in Switzerland, the prosecution charged that he "had used funds belonging to his clients, including Graham Greene, the novelist, to finance overdrafts incurred during construction of his £135,000 villa." The tax expert fought the fraud charges but "admitted receiving $375,000 in counterfeit money as part of a desperate final effort to reimburse investors." He was described at the trial as "a man with considerable charm, but essentially weak, lacking the moral courage to say no."

In his years as a spokesman for the downtrodden masses, Greene was often portrayed as a simple man who disdained wealth, but he made complex efforts to increase his fortune through unusual investments and tax-saving schemes, beginning with the formation of Graham Greene Productions in the 1950s and ending with the formation of Verdant, SA, a holding company managed by Swiss accountants and lawyers. Although his tax expert disappointed him in the 1960s, he was soon able to recover from the loss, especially after moving his legal residence to France. At the end of 1965, he decided that he could not tolerate the combination of high taxes from a socialist government in Britain and the recent loss of his savings in Switzerland. On January 1, 1966, he disposed of his chambers in Albany and moved to Antibes. When asked by the *Sunday Times* to say why he was leaving England, he explained that it was purely for health reasons: "My doctor . . . says that I should avoid London smog." He was referring to the lung problems that he had suffered in the early 1960s, but this was not his reason for moving. Whenever he wanted to escape the London fog, he could afford to fly down to Antibes or Capri for a break. But it was less taxing—in more ways than one—to live in France and make occasional visits to the Ritz in Piccadilly.

There was another private reason for choosing Antibes. By 1966 all Greene's old affairs had cooled, and a new one was in full swing. The lady in question was a married Frenchwoman who lived outside Antibes, in Juan-les-Pins. She was Yvonne Cloetta, a small, attractive blonde whom Greene had met in 1959, when his affair with Anita Bjork was ending. Yvonne was to remain a companion for the rest of Greene's life, although she never left her husband. It was the kind of affair he preferred, but, with Yvonne and her husband, there would be no repeat of the conflicts that had marked his relationship with Catherine and Harry. In his odd way, Greene was finally trying to settle down.

As for Catherine, she was now Lady Walston. As a reward for serving his country in various administrative capacities, Harry had been made a life peer in 1961. There was no longer any reason for Greene to expect something more than friendship from the woman whose very name had once seemed so magical to him. But friendship still left room for at least a small betrayal here and there. In his next novel, *Travels with My Aunt,* he used a very private secret of Catherine's as the basis for one episode, and in *The Comedians* he brought the magical name down to earth. Whereas he had once repeated it as an incantation, now it was only another joke in the long comedy of life. The madam of the best brothel in Haiti is called Mère Catherine.

CHAPTER TWENTY-TWO

MONSTER OF
THE CHEMINS DE FER,
OR BRIGHTON REVISITED

Greene called Yvonne his "happy, healthy kitten," or simply HHK. The term recalls the days when Vivien used to apply various kittenish descriptions to herself, but Yvonne's feline charm was not spoiled by any possessive instinct. She was content to let Greene come and go as he pleased, and she showed little sign of jealousy. Although she was the principal woman in the last thirty years of his life, he was not one to restrict his interests to only one person. Until his final year, he never lived with Yvonne, and he gave no indication that he wished to. Whenever he was in Antibes, she would come to see him nearly every day, making the short drive from her home in Juan-les-Pins to his little apartment. As was his custom, he spent the mornings alone with his work, dutifully producing his quota of words for the day. By the time Yvonne would arrive—usually at noon—he was free to enjoy the company of his "kitten."

Invariably, they had lunch at a restaurant near the harbor—Chez Félix. In the afternoons they would go for a drive in Yvonne's car or take her little dog for a walk. There was usually time for a game of Scrabble or other amusements, then in the evening Yvonne would return home, leaving behind some simple fare for Greene's dinner. It was an easy and agreeable routine for both of them. Her husband, Jacques, appeared to be content with the arrangement, and divorce seemed out of the question for both Yvonne and Greene. To one acquaintance from England—the writer Piers Paul Read—Greene showed a certain amount of pride in the "convenient way he had arranged his life." Comfortable in his sparsely furnished apartment, "he never had to live with a wife, drive a car, or have anyone to stay."

From the start of their relationship, Yvonne appreciated Greene's need for privacy. "He needed solitude," she recalled. "He needed to be alone to write, and he liked being alone. . . . When he came to the South of France, certainly there were a lot of English people settled there, and at the beginning they started inviting him out, and he said no. He refused because he was afraid that things would snowball, and he would be invited all the time." She is not the retiring type, but she never felt restless for a life with more excitement: "Before I met him I had been living in Africa for seventeen years, and there, my goodness, with all these cocktail parties at the embassies and what not, my goodness, we had so much social life I think I was fed up with it."

It was in Africa that Yvonne first saw Greene. In 1959 she and her husband—who worked for Unilever—were living in Cameroon, and Greene paid a brief visit to the country on his way home from Dr. Lechat's leper colony in the Congo. Yvonne and Jacques met the novelist through some friends who gave a party in his honor. For Yvonne, who was approaching her thirties at the time, it was not love at first sight, but she was intrigued by the reserved manner of the famous writer and was flattered when he showed an interest in her. After asking her out for a drink, he confided that he would like to see her when she was next in France. As it happened, she was returning there later in the year, and she agreed to his proposal.

By the beginning of the 1960s, they were seeing each other frequently. With her two young daughters—Brigitte and Martine—Yvonne settled in Juan-les-Pins, going back to Africa only during school holidays. Greene would stay at a hotel in Antibes for weeks at a time, exchanging visits with Yvonne. Occasionally he would take her to Capri, where some of the local people were under the impression that she was his secretary, an impression Greene found convenient to sustain. In the beginning their relationship was based very much on physical attraction. In fact, any conversation was difficult, because she knew very little English and his French was poor. Over time both of them improved, especially Yvonne, who became quite fluent in English. Gradually Greene realized that he could have the kind of life that he wanted in Antibes, and his financial crisis in 1965 gave him the incentive to settle there.

Almost from the beginning of the affair, Greene was on close terms with Yvonne's daughters, especially Martine, who was a young teenager in the 1960s. Greene said that he became like an uncle to Martine, although it is odd to think of him seeking out that part. He was never close to any of his real nieces and nephews, or even to his own children. In the 1970s he went so far as to say that his books were his real children. But he must have found something especially appealing about Martine. In 1984 he called her "my greatest friend." He was protective of her and was ready to go to great lengths to help her. After his own daughter left Canada and settled in a village near Vevey, Switzerland, Greene helped Martine move to the same place. This warm relationship between "niece" and "uncle" did not please Vivien: "I was upset that Graham came and bought a house for Martine in the same road that my daughter lives in. And brought her along to my daughter—you know, he used to come for two or three days at Christmas—he would bring her and Yvonne. He got a job for the daughter at his lawyer's . . . in Lausanne. I thought it was not good taste to get his mistress and daughter involved with the family." Yvonne and Martine valued his care as a kind of "fortress" and, in Yvonne's words, felt that "inside these big walls we were safe."

In turn, Yvonne helped to protect Greene, providing him with steady, loyal support in a town where he had no other close friends. Part of the attraction of Antibes, at least at first, was that he was not recognized there. He could live a very private existence. He had many reasons for liking this situation, but he and Yvonne discovered that his literary fame soon spread even to the remote corners of Chez Félix: "He said that for the sake of his work, he had to be anonymous, he had to be able not to be watched but to watch the others. That was the problem at Félix in Antibes, that restaurant which was a real home away from home for him. At the end [of his life] a lot of people knew he went there, and people used to come and ask to take a photograph of him." In the early days, however, it was an almost perfect hideaway.

For most of his career Greene had enjoyed using Brighton as the seaside retreat where he could easily disappear in the crowds and watch others without being watched. But fame spoiled that. As he lamented in the 1960s, "I am too well known in Brighton nowadays." Antibes was a second Brighton, and for many years everything worked out well there. The local people left him alone, and the French government honored him in 1969 by appointing him chevalier of the Legion of Honor. And then, at the end of the 1970s, he ran into trouble. He made enemies and received death threats. He began keeping weapons handy for defense against sudden attacks.

He wrote angry letters to the press about his enemies and urged the French authorities to deal sternly with them. When action did not come quickly enough to suit him, he made the grand gesture of returning his Legion of Honor to the government, then threatened to make all involved pay for their crimes and misdemeanors by exposing them in a book. And what was the cause of all this extreme action? A charge of plagiarism? A feud with anarchists? Massive gambling debts? No, it was something much worse. Martine's safety and honor were in jeopardy.

As her protector, Greene turned a minor divorce question into a major international feud. When she was in her early twenties, Martine married a property developer in Nice, and after only a few years the relationship began to turn sour. She was granted a divorce and was given custody of her small daughter, but her husband—Daniel Guy—managed to persuade the courts to revoke the judgment and give him custody of the child. All kinds of accusations were thrown back and forth between the unhappy couple. Guy was alleged to have behaved violently, and he in turn tried to cast doubts on Martine's character. The only reason that this rather unpleasant marital dispute was covered by the international press is that Greene had entered the fray, protesting that all the trouble was Guy's fault. Martine's reputation was spotless, Greene argued, but he charged that Guy was a miscreant who had used his ties with the underworld in Nice to intimidate Martine and her family. He took it on himself to be her companion when she was forced to do battle in court. Yvonne explained:

> He was very fond of my daughter, as she was fond of him, right to the end. He used to accompany her [to the court], where she used to come out crying like anything, saying that she hadn't been allowed to open her mouth, either herself or her lawyer, in front of a judge. There, Graham himself would go with her to the [court], not inside, because he was not allowed, but he would wait outside, and he saw with his own eyes what was happening. It was not through me or anyone else. He wanted to be a witness of what was going on.

It is best for outsiders to stay clear of speculating on the rights and wrongs in divorce cases, but once Greene was deeply involved in the matter, he would not tone down his campaign against Guy. Realizing that a merely personal problem would not attract substantial attention, Greene widened the dispute by claiming that corrupt officials in Nice were protecting Guy. In the pages of the *Sunday Times,* Greene urged tourists to stay away from Nice. As everyone suspected at the

time, and as subsequent events have proved, the longtime mayor of
Nice—Jacques Médecin—was involved in some shady dealings. In
1991, after being sentenced to prison for misusing public funds,
Médecin fled to Uruguay and became a T-shirt vendor.

But the problem of corruption in Nice obscured the real question.
Was Guy a crooked man who had mistreated his wife? After spreading that allegation far and wide, Greene set out to demonstrate his
case in detail. In May 1982 he published a pamphlet that he called
"*J'Accuse:* The Dark Side of Nice." From the look of the title, one
would assume that Greene meant to launch a major attack on the
criminal element in Nice, but the surprising thing is that he barely
mentions the subject. Médecin's name comes into the work only a
couple of times, and no specific evidence is presented to back up his
claim of pervasive corruption. The title is wildly inappropriate for a
pamphlet that is mostly concerned with a blow-by-blow account of
Martine's divorce and custody battles. It is absurd for Greene to suggest a comparison with Zola and the Dreyfus case; indeed, it borders
on obscene—given his history of anti-Semitism. But it would seem
that, even in the middle of fighting what he deemed a serious battle,
Greene could make jokes. Médecin's nickname in Nice was Jacquou.

Before he issued the *"J'Accuse"* pamphlet, Greene had never publicly mentioned his relationship with Yvonne, except to dedicate
Travels with My Aunt to HHK. He was thus faced with the difficulty
of explaining why he cared about Martine's case. With his usual talent for such things, he came up with a good story, which every journalist accepted without question. As the *Saturday Review* explained
to its American readers, Greene had become friends with Yvonne and
her husband in Africa: "Six years later, when he moved to Antibes, he
discovered the family was living not far away in Juan les Pins. They
renewed their friendship, the wife became Greene's secretary, and the
daughter, Martine, a surrogate niece." In other words, Greene and
the Cloetta clan were one big happy family. Uncle Graham knew how
to use his pen for maximum publicity when he wanted to.

Guy was warned that Greene would strike at him in print, but the
young man was not worried. His property business was prospering,
and he was perfectly capable of taking the novelist to court. The
interesting thing is that Greene was completely defeated on the legal
front. Guy won a decision in a Nice court to ban the book in France,
and later, in a Paris court, he won libel damages of 52,000 francs
against Greene and his publishers. Thanks to large sales of *"J'Accuse"*
in Britain and elsewhere, Greene was more than able to pay the damages from royalties.

Legal defeat did not prevent Greene from fantasizing that Guy was Pinkie Brown reincarnated. When an interviewer asked whether he would write a novel about Guy, he said that he had already told the story in *Brighton Rock*. This, however, is an insult to Pinkie, whose deeds are far more wicked than anything Guy was accused of doing. Greene had spent his entire career describing events much worse than this petty divorce and had led readers to sympathize with ruthless villains. Yet *"J'Accuse"* fails to find any virtues in Guy's alleged disloyalty. As Jonathan Raban noted in a review of the pamphlet, "Greene was able to anatomize Pinkie with studied calm in a book . . . when he meets his counterpart in real domestic life he responds with a degree of moral bluster that would do credit to a maiden aunt." But perhaps, in this case, Greene really wanted to identify *himself* with Pinkie. The defensive, nasty tone of the pamphlet suggests a portrait of the artist as a vindictive Pinkie defending Kite's memory against the onslaughts of a rival gang. In this drama Médecin would presumably play Colleoni, and Guy would assume the part of a minor associate such as Crab.

Greene's impassioned attacks on Guy suggest a deep personal grievance that went beyond the circumstances outlined in *"J'Accuse."* As the *Sunday Times* remarked, "It is fair to say that Greene sincerely hopes *J'Accuse* will destroy Daniel." The writer reached this conclusion after Greene confided that he had been thinking of Guy when he wrote the short novel *Dr. Fischer of Geneva or the Bomb Party,* which came out in 1980. It is the tale of a rich man who uses his wealth to hurt others but who is eventually undone by his own schemes. Although Greene was not exactly poor, he resented what he thought was Guy's extravagant display of riches. He claimed that the man had a Rolls-Royce, a BMW, a motor boat, a gold watch, and a platinum bracelet. (Guy pointed out that the cars belonged to his company and were bought secondhand.) But even this kind of luxury does not put Guy in the class of the superrich Dr. Fischer, and, in any case, it is difficult to see specific parallels between the young man of property and the old doctor. Perhaps the only connection was Greene's hate for someone in a dominant position. His hero in the novel is a modest but brave Englishman who lives in Vevey and who is in love with the doctor's attractive daughter—despite the fact that he is old enough to be her grandfather. It is obviously a tale that has little to do with Greene's explanation of his fight in *"J'Accuse."* As he insisted, his anger was merely that of an outraged friend of the family.

After the libel case was concluded, Greene decided to keep his

silence on the matter, but he continued to fear for his safety in
Antibes. In the course of pursuing Guy, he had made some powerful
enemies in Nice, and he worried that an accident might be arranged
for him one dark evening. "If they get me, I will give them a good
fight," he told Yvonne. "No, if they get me, it will be so obvious, and
then he [Daniel Guy] will be put in prison, and then everyone will
have peace." Journalists who interviewed him in Antibes came back
with stories that he was armed with everything from a pistol to a gas
bomb. But he stayed in the town, on and off, until 1990, and no one
ever attacked him. Once he stopped trying to drag all the politicians
and gangsters of Nice into his affair, the atmosphere grew calmer. It
also helped to have Martine at a safe distance in Vevey, where she settled after the pressures became too difficult for her in the South of
France.

The dispute did nothing to clean up Nice, but it should have indicated to readers that Greene's battles were almost always personal
ones, and that he preferred publicity stunts to substantial long-term
action. He knew how to make headlines, and the press was so eager
to assist him that no one tried very hard to probe either the nature of
his motives or the truth of his allegations. How could the great
Graham Greene have anything but the purest motives? For his uncritical admirers, the episode also had the attraction of being a real-life
adventure from Greeneland, with our hero courageously battling
mobsters from the seamy side of the Riviera. After Greene had finished all his interviews, written his letters to the press, and published
"J'Accuse," there was not much attention given to the conclusion of
the episode in 1983, when the court threw out every one of his
charges. By that time the story had been largely forgotten, and the
press was ready to be used again. In 1984 all the papers in the
Western world performed wonderfully well by breathlessly reporting
the discovery of Greene's "lost" novel, *The Tenth Man*.

II

When Greene returned the Legion of Honor, the French were good
enough to send it back, explaining that it belonged to him for life—
unless a court convicted him of a criminal offense. But, for Greene, it
was the gesture that counted. If he felt offended or unappreciated,
he liked to use resignations to upset and embarrass authority. He
proudly claimed that he had resigned from five London clubs—
including White's—and he enjoyed making publishers squirm by

threatening to take his books elsewhere, or by making fun of them in the press after they had crossed him in some way. He left Heinemann in the early 1960s, when his friend A. S. Frere, the managing director, lost favor in the firm. He complained bitterly that no one at Heinemann properly appreciated him or Frere, and there was some truth to his accusations. He made the Bodley Head his new publisher and was happy there under the care and supervision of another friend, Max Reinhardt. But when Reinhardt's power was in jeopardy in the 1980s, Greene again went on the attack, using the pages of *The Times* to air his complaints against the conglomerate that controlled the publishing imprint. This put Greene in the odd position of criticizing his own nephew—Graham C. Greene—who was the principal shareholder in the conglomerate. Toward the end of his life, Greene became the mainstay of a little publishing company set up by Max Reinhardt—Reinhardt Books. Under the protection of this imprint, he was able to do whatever he wanted without having to defer to any corporate chiefs.

He exercised his new publishing power in 1989, when he arranged for Reinhardt Books to bring out a first novel by an Irish writer named Vincent McDonnell. *The Broken Commandment* is a weak novel with some similarities to *The End of the Affair,* but Greene was sufficiently impressed by it to give it his full support. This noble act was soon spoiled, however, when Greene worked unfairly to guarantee that McDonnell also received a major prize. In 1989 Greene was appointed the supreme judge for the new GPA Book Award in Ireland, whose cash award was a very impressive 47,000 pounds. Greene's appointment was considered a great boon for the new prize, offering it immediate importance and distinction in the world of letters. A panel of three judges were given the job of selecting a shortlist; it was expected that Greene would name the winner from this list.

The talented poet Seamus Heaney and the promising novelist John Banville were among those on the list, but Greene threatened to ignore them and give the prize to McDonnell, who was not in the running. There was much speculation about what the great novelist would do and considerable tension as everyone waited for his final decision. Fay Weldon, who was one of the judges, remarked with cool restraint, "This might make some of us feel we were wasting our time." Greene forced the issue until a compromise was reached. Banville received the top award, but McDonnell was given a special "first fiction" prize of £19,000. One of the sponsors later said of Greene, "He twisted our arms and we agreed to the extra prize." Greene turned the whole affair into a farce, demeaning the significance of Banville's prize as well as McDonnell's. He proved once again that it was always dangerous to trust him.

Once in a while Greene's defiant gestures failed to make the right impression on the appropriate authorities. By far the funniest example of this kind was his resignation from the London Library in 1962. He had been in the habit for some years of sending his secretary to collect books from the library, which was only a short walk from Albany. In the late 1950s a new secretary named Josephine Reid joined him, and she began making routine visits to the library on his behalf. But one day a librarian informed her that she could no longer check out books unless she submitted a letter of authorization from her employer on each visit. As an official later explained, "It has been a custom in the library for many years for members to send their secretaries or staff for books, but only members are allowed into the book racks. We cannot have anyone roaming around."

This explanation infuriated Greene, and he immediately resigned his membership. The press soon learned of the story, which caused the library to issue polite statements of policy and to inform the ex-member that he was welcome to rejoin at any time. Greene had made his point and seemed on the verge of enjoying another successful exercise of intimidation, but then someone at the library decided to have a look at the membership records. The search revealed a surprise, which was quickly communicated to the *Daily Telegraph*. On November 6, 1962, the paper reported: "The London Library may well say that Graham Greene, who stopped his subscription when his secretary was refused access to the shelves, is welcome to rejoin tomorrow. In fact, Mr. Greene has never been a member. The subscription, taken out in 1943, was in the name of his wife." It was not often that one of Greene's games was so successfully, and swiftly, exposed.

In 1970 Greene resigned from the American Academy, Institute of Arts and Letters, and, at first glance, this may seem a serious gesture, because he claimed that it was in protest against the Vietnam War. But a closer look at the letter reveals that it is just Greene having fun again. He was hoping to spark a mass resignation from the academy and had started a letter-writing campaign to accomplish his goal. It looks suspiciously like one of his plans to bankrupt the post office or to force mass political resignations from governments. He compares his honorary membership in the American Academy with an honorary place in the German Academy of Arts and Letters under Hitler. One might be tempted to take such a letter seriously if Greene had done anything besides write letters on the Vietnam War. But he never bothered to carry his protests directly to America or Vietnam, and he played no significant part in any antiwar movement.

At the height of the Vietnam War, he was safely lost in the farcical world of *Travels with My Aunt,* a novel that is an extended version of the entries he submitted to various "Graham Greene" writing contests. The book is nothing but a parody of his life and works. Aunt Augusta and the mild-mannered Henry Pulling visit Brighton, take the Orient Express, keep company with a man from Sierra Leone, attend a cremation, run into smugglers, and meet the daughter of a CIA agent who is escorted by a young Vietnamese. Aunt Augusta recalls a visit to the Shanghai Theater in Havana, Henry's father is said to have slept with a young woman named Rose, and a whiskey-drinking priest's escape is delayed by women asking to make their confessions. There is a reference to Zachary Macaulay living on Clapham Common (in the same house that Greene and Vivien shared in the 1930s), a bad pun about a woman named Dorothy and her gloves, and a description of a hotel in Paris called the St. James and Albany. One of Greene's favorite books from his youth, Marjorie Bowen's *The Viper of Milan,* is alluded to in the character of Mr. Visconti (the duke of Milan was also called Visconti), and for good measure the character is nicknamed the Viper.

For anyone who knows all Greene's books, the abundance of in-jokes is too much and serves as a constant reminder that he is merely toying with imagination and memory, turning everything into farce. For readers who know nothing of his personal life, the seemingly pointless allusions to such figures as Macaulay can be irritating. But there are some good comic moments in the novel, the best of which is Aunt Augusta's recollection of the doggies' church in Brighton. She helped to run the place with a Rev. Curran, who did his best to hold services over the din of barking dogs. By the time he reached his last prayer, he would often find the dogs had been subdued by the service and would gaze contentedly at them as they "peacefully licked their parts." A strict moralist, he was opposed to divorce and refused to sanction it within his canine congregation. The church was doing well until the police began to investigate it for violations of the Blasphemy Act. Unable to prove any specific points of blasphemy, the police finally settled for an easier and more obvious charge against the minister. They arrested him for harassing young women.

Although the novel was written in Antibes and Capri, the spirit of earlier days in Brighton hangs over the book. But instead of the old nightmares and violent hatreds of *Brighton Rock, Travels with My Aunt* takes a milder, less serious view of life. Like Greene, his hero wants to slow down, and it is only the wild nature of Aunt Augusta that keeps him on the move. He would gladly stay home and tend his garden. But her energy revives him and draws him back into the hectic world. Greene found some of the same energy in the Dottoressa Moor, his friend on Capri, who always kept him entertained with extravagant stories about her past life and with gossip about the lives of their fellow residents on the small island. She knew many of his secrets and was one of the few people who could come to and go from his villa as she pleased. Although they never traveled the world together in the manner of Aunt Augusta and Henry, they were often together in the self-contained world of Capri, wandering the streets late at night, visiting the Dottoressa's friends and patients, and enjoying long dinners with lots to drink at their favorite restaurant, a small place tucked away in a dark corner of Capri.

Her memoir, *An Impossible Woman,* provides several candid glimpses of Greene. One night in the late 1940s she was having dinner with Greene in Capri town, and they were joined by the film director Cavalcanti and a local friend named Aniello. At the end of the evening, the conversation turned to a forthcoming Italian election. Suddenly, Greene announced in a loud voice, "We will hold our own elections, and you, Cavalcanti, will be a candidate for the Communists because you have just come from Czechoslovakia and you, Aniello, will be for the Christian Democrats, and I will be for the Anarchists." Inspired by too much drink, Greene gave a speech in favor of Anarchism, which—given the tense political mood of the time—was a rather unwise thing to do. According to the Dottoressa, everyone quickly left the restaurant except one man. "Be quiet, Graham," Aniello warned, "that is the Chief of Police."

Like Aunt Augusta, the Dottoressa had many strange adventures. She had a secret habit of burying dead cats. It seems that her dog was extremely good at killing any cat who wandered into the Dottoressa's garden. Her neighbors in Anacapri were very fond of their cats and would have been distressed to learn why so many of the little creatures had mysteriously disappeared. To get rid of the evidence, the Dottoressa made occasional nocturnal excursions to bury the bodies in remote parts of the island, and one night her accomplice was Greene. They put the body in a large bag and went in search of a good hiding place, but every time they found a promising spot, a car would appear, and they would have to keep walking. They wandered the island for hours before accomplishing their mission. "Never had there been so many cars at night," the Dottoressa lamented.

One section of the memoir is called "The Anacapri Murderer." A barber in the town had strangled his wife and dumped her body in a cistern. It was a crime of passion—he was in love with another woman—and the sympathetic authorities required him to spend only a dozen years in prison. When he finished his sentence, he came back to Anacapri and worked once again as a barber. "This murderer," the Dottoressa explains, "was a friend of Graham Greene's." Whenever he was on the island, Greene always had his hair cut by the murderer, and he liked to sip a glass of wine while the barber did his work. One night Greene gave a party in Anacapri for Catherine and a few other friends, including the murderer. But it was not a success. The murderer drank too much whiskey and pulled Catherine's hair. The Dottoressa was so offended by his rowdy behavior that she decided to slap him as hard as she could. Her aim was off, however, and another man received the blow.

Travels with My Aunt must contain many clues to Greene's life that will never be detected, and there is at least one allusion no one may be able to explain. After recalling some of Aunt Augusta's conversation from their stay in Brighton, Henry thinks that she might enjoy a visit to the Louvre, but she hates the idea. She cannot stand the thought of seeing all those famous sculptures—all those torsos, the "naked women with bits missing," as she puts it. The reason for her aversion to such things is that she has never quite overcome the memory of a friend who died at the hands of "the Monster of the Chemins de Fer." The female friend was traveling on a train from Paris to Calais, presumably headed for England. The murderer happened to share a compartment with her and decided to kill her because he thought she was a loose woman. He was heavily influenced by the darker side of Catholicism and later argued that his murders were carried out from "a misplaced devotion to virginity." He decided that his murders were actually for the good of the world, and a few people who agreed with him organized a cult to support his mission. But they soon lost their leader to the guillotine, which was a particularly appropriate way for him to die. Aunt Augusta's friend was cut up so that there was nothing left of her but a torso, which was presumably left somewhere along the railway. The whole business gave Aunt Augusta a permanent dislike of torsos of any kind—literal or artistic— and it continues to haunt her when other troubles have long since faded from her mind. She refers to the murderer early in the book, then brings him up again toward the end.

In a novel full of obscure personal references, Greene brings us back to the most obscure subject in his biography—his attraction to the murder and dismemberment of the young woman in Brighton. In one place or another, all the important elements of the murder are present in his writing—the railway, the trunk, the torso, the awful stench of the corpse, the speculation that the victim was a prostitute or some kind of "loose woman," and the association of all these things with Brighton. There is also a hint of some connection to France, not only in *Travels with My Aunt* but also in *Brighton Rock*. For no obvious reason the narrative of the earlier novel keeps reminding the reader that Brighton faces France: when the waves hit the shore, we are told that they have come from France; on clear days people strain for some glimpse of France; and at one point Pinkie leans against a rail and stares for a long time at the sea, "towards France," as though he is searching for something in the distance. Similarly, a connection between France and Brighton is made in *Carving a Statue,* when the slide of the French murderer of women is replaced by one showing another murderer leaning against a rail at Brighton.

Greene would not have continued to return to the subject of the Brighton case unless it occupied an important place in his mental landscape. Thinking about such a crime was obviously a major obsession, and the images must have held some special significance for him—as did Clapham Common, Dorothy Glover, St. James's Street, Albany, the Dottoressa, and *The Viper of Milan.* Perhaps it symbolized for him the worst that human beings could do to each other. Or perhaps he found a reflection of the Brighton monster in his own heart, especially because he had "dreamed" about committing a trunk murder before the actual event.

But of all his allusions to the murder, those in *Travels with My Aunt* are the most disturbing simply because he turns them into a joke. In the farcical world of Aunt Augusta, even the things that haunt her cannot be taken seriously. She is supposed to be funny, and her fear of torsos is only another one of her comic eccentricities. From the horrifying vision of Kite with his razor and his cold phrase "Such tits," Greene descended to the burlesque level of Aunt Augusta worrying about the torsos in the Louvre. Perhaps his references to such a murder were always meant to be humorous—a private joke that might mislead a curious critic or biographer. But the final indignity is that Greene would find cause for laughter in such a crime. The case of the real woman who was dismembered in 1934 will probably never be solved. In February 1935 the authorities in Brighton buried her remains in an unmarked grave. Her killer destroyed not only her life and that of her unborn child but also her identity.

Despite its bad jokes, *Travels with My Aunt* was a success. It sold well, particularly in America, where it was a main selection of the Book-of-the-Month Club. And, of course, there was the inevitable film—in this case another expensive MGM production, with George Cukor directing and Maggie Smith playing Aunt Augusta. Greene was spared the public humiliation of commercial failure, but as an artist he had definitely turned his back on the example of his hero Henry James, who took the path of most resistance in old age, producing *The Ambassadors, The Wings of the Dove,* and *The Golden Bowl.* Greene may not have been able to reach such a level of achievement, but the point is that he never really tried. In the 1960s he wasted six years on *The Comedians* and *Travels with My Aunt,* all because they promised to produce instant income. And there was no one close to him who could push him in a different direction. Isolated for much of the year in Antibes and Capri, he could avoid the challenges and pressures of the literary world, loftily addressing it from time to time in letters to the press or through carefully arranged interviews.

Greene addresses the curse of fame and fortune in an essay written in 1964. The ostensible subject is the career of the popular author Edgar Wallace, who was once the most widely read novelist in England. Greene had always admired Wallace's *The Four Just Men,* but in his essay he takes the writer to task for failing to develop his promise and for preferring instead to enjoy the wealth provided by his indulgent audience. But the most interesting thing about the essay is the explanation that Greene gives for this artistic failure. On three different occasions he blames it on Wallace's desire to "escape," by which he means a retreat from the awful "knowledge of the world." This reason may not actually apply to Wallace, but it does seem to fit Greene, whose success allowed him to pursue all the ways of escape that he could imagine, including an escape from the greatest demands of his craft and from the darkest truths about himself and his world.

In the middle of the essay, Greene pauses to reflect on the reason that a painter of obvious skill will stop at a certain level of achievement. He thinks of the landscape painter who can capture the look of a sunset or a mountain but who will not stretch his talent beyond what comes easily. Although he can provide no satisfactory answer to the problem, what fascinates him is that moment when the artist surrenders to failure. There is always the mystery of how much more he could have accomplished. In any case, the artist's admirers will still buy his work, and perhaps many critics will praise him. They see only the finished product. But the artist's eyes are always on that point at which he surrendered.

CHAPTER TWENTY-THREE

DOWN THERE
ON A VISIT

In 1976 Greene found a dictator he could love. The affair began when Gen. Omar Torrijos invited the novelist to visit Panama and sent him a first-class air ticket. After he arrived at one of the general's houses, he was kept waiting for a short time, but, when Torrijos appeared in all his splendor, Greene fell for him immediately. The general made his entrance with his beloved Sergeant Chuchu, and both of them were attractively dressed in robes and underpants. Apparently, they had just come from bed—Chuchu was wearing bedroom slippers, and Torrijos was barefoot. Greene found the sergeant looking pleasingly "plump" and the general lean and fit, with a boyish forelock. Greene liked everything about Torrijos—who was then in his forties—but was especially smitten by his "give-away eyes." Fate seems to have brought them together. Fifty years earlier, when Greene had been so fascinated by the Carlist wars, he had developed a special liking for the doomed figure of a Spanish general named Torrijos.

In their first conversation Greene worked hard to win a smile from the Panamanian dictator, who was initially a bit shy, but their relations soon grew warmer as they exchanged information about their childhoods. It was a delight to learn that they shared a common bond—both their fathers were schoolmasters. The more they talked, the more relaxed they became, and soon they were happily discussing their favorite writers and their favorite brand of whiskey. The general did not have much to say about politics, but Greene liked the basic philosophical tone of his conversation. In one moment of deep thought, the great dictator observed that any village with uncut grass in the cemetery must be bad. If they neglect the dead, he said, they will also neglect the living. With the enthusiasm of an innocent schoolboy, Greene repeats such pearls of wisdom in *Getting to Know the General*. He is equally fond of Chuchu's sayings. "If shit was worth money," the sergeant remarks, "the poor would be born without arses." As Greene proudly notes, Chuchu was a former professor of Marxist philosophy at the University of Panama.

At the nonpolitical level, *Getting to Know the General* is mildly funny, although it is not always clear whether the humor is intentional. Although Greene's love for Torrijos is supposed to be the driving force of the book, it is clearly Chuchu who steals the show, prancing through Panama with the writer in tow. As an earlier chapter pointed out, the adventures of the sergeant and the novelist are depicted as a gay romp. Torrijos seems to have been preoccupied with government business and was therefore unable to join Greene and Chuchu on many of their outings. Because the sergeant spoke English fluently, he had no problem communicating with his new friend, whereas Torrijos knew nothing but Spanish. And, despite having traveled widely in Mexico, Cuba, and other Spanish-speaking countries, Greene spoke only a few words of the language.

In the book Torrijos and Chuchu are repeatedly identified as friends of the common people, but they seem to spend most of their time getting drunk with their cronies, talking about sex, and taking small planes to various fun spots in Panama. Thanks to the generosity of his hosts, Greene is kept well supplied with whiskey, rum punches, and expensive meals. He becomes so spoiled by the luxuries showered on him that he begins to make ungracious complaints. His hotel room in Panama City is too large, and his flight home on the Concorde is uncomfortable. Shortly after making a brief comment on the slums of Panama, Greene describes his trip aboard the supersonic plane and laments the airline's failure to provide its passengers with a selection of good cheeses. While the poor in the slums struggle to survive, the rich novelist dismisses the Concorde's supply of Camembert as meager and stale.

Between 1976 and 1981 Greene made four trips to Panama. He learned important details of Torrijos's negotiations to regain control of the Panama Canal and accompanied the general's delegation when the canal treaty was signed in Washington. As a way of thumbing his nose at the United States, he traveled to the treaty ceremony on a Panamanian diplomatic passport. Before the Sandinistas came to power in Nicaragua, Greene met some of their leaders in Panama. Chuchu, who was born in Nicaragua, encouraged Greene to take an interest in the country. When the Sandinistas overthrew Somoza, the novelist helped to celebrate their victory in Managua, flying there on Torrijos's private jet. In all these adventures it can be assumed that he shared valuable information with his intelligence contacts in London.

As a good double agent, Greene served Torrijos by speaking out in favor of the general's rule and by criticizing the tendency of the United States to meddle in Central American affairs. Ignorant of Greene's history of writing political propaganda for hire, *The New York Review of Books* accepted his long tribute to the general, "The Country with Five Frontiers." Published in February 1977, the piece praises Torrijos for his vision and courage, and holds him up as the great hope for democracy in Central America. In terms of charisma Greene compares him with Castro and Churchill, and says that he has given all Panamanians a strong sense of pride. Grateful for such praise, Torrijos authorized Chuchu to translate the article and publish it in a Panamanian newspaper.

In the article as well as in *Getting to Know the General*, Greene pretends that Torrijos seized power to sweep aside a corrupt "oligarchy." In fact, he overthrew an elected president—Arnulfo Arias—for essentially personal reasons. In an attempt to purge the National Guard, Arias had ordered Torrijos to take a post as military attaché in El Salvador. Rather than leave Panama he organized a coup and shipped President Arias off to Miami. Less than a year later his troops abducted his chief rival in the National Guard and bundled him into a plane headed for Miami. Torrijos became "Maximum Leader of the Revolution without Dictatorship and of Liberty with Order"—in other words, Panama's dictator.

His loyal henchman throughout his rise to power was Manuel Noriega, whom he had protected on several occasions in the past. A sadistic hoodlum, Noriega beat and raped a prostitute in Peru in the early 1960s, and a few years later he was accused of raping a thirteen-year-old in Panama. His commanding officer at the time—Maj. Omar Torrijos—saved him from the rape charge, and, after the coup of 1968, the Maximum Leader promoted Noriega to lieutenant colonel and put him in charge of military intelligence. With Noriega's help some 1,600 political prisoners were locked up, and a few trouble-makers were permanently taken care of. In 1971, for example,

Noriega's men abducted and beat Father Hector Gallegos, a young priest from Colombia, then threw him from a helicopter flying over the ocean.

To keep Noriega and other military cronies happy, Torrijos tripled the size of the National Guard and increased its budget tenfold in ten years. Money was no problem after Torrijos helped to create a set of new banking laws that made Panama the "Switzerland of Latin America." Secret accounts allowed gangsters throughout the world to launder their money in Panama. In a matter of a few years, almost one hundred new banks were established to handle the overflow of illegal cash. Calling Noriega *mi gangster,* Torrijos was happy to play the smiling dictator while the brutal colonel took care of dissidents and helped to smuggle drugs and weapons into other countries. Anything was for sale. Noriega peddled intelligence to the Cubans as well as to the CIA. And when the shah of Iran needed a hideout from the Iranian revolutionaries, Torrijos allowed him to enter Panama, assigned Chuchu as the monarch's bodyguard, and let Noriega extort millions from him in protection money.

Greene was well aware that Torrijos was a thug, but the corruption and violence were a great part of the dictator's attraction. The most extraordinary scene in *Getting to Know the General* takes place at a party in 1980, when Torrijos pulls Greene aside and offers to help him deal with Daniel Guy. Chuchu had told his boss about Greene's fight to help Martine in Nice. Showing his true colors, Torrijos proposes that he send someone to France to take care of the problem. The implication is that one of Noriega's goons would beat Guy or probably kill him. Greene says that he turned down the proposal, but he could hardly have said anything else in print, especially after having lost his libel battle in the French courts. All the same, merely reporting his refusal is bad enough. It was a message to Guy that Greene had friends who could help him get even. As far as Guy knew, Greene had not definitely rejected Torrijos's offer and could take it up at any time in the future. One way or the other, Guy could not have been pleased to hear that Panamanian hit men were available for his adversary's use. That fact also undercuts any idea that Greene was an entirely innocent victim in the *"J'Accuse"* battle.

As *Getting to Know the General* makes clear, Greene did not lose all his clout in Panama after a plane crash claimed Torrijos's life in 1981. He returned to the country for at least three more visits, and during the first of these he undertook a mission for Noriega. It was important for the colonel to show Fidel Castro that Panama's relations with Cuba would continue to be friendly. So he sent the general's famous friend to Cuba with a message of friendship, and the mission proved completely successful. As an added benefit Greene was able to stop in Nicaragua and speak to Lenin Cerna, the Sandinista chief of secret police, who asked the novelist to give Noriega an invitation to Managua. In 1985 Greene had a long meeting with the colonel in his office and gave his assessment of President Reagan's strategy in Central America. In 1987 he shared a platform at a new stadium with Noriega, who embraced him as a friend. He then gave the colonel a present—a hammock from Nicaragua's Daniel Ortega. A few days earlier he had enjoyed a good laugh with one of Noriega's fellow officers, who described how a political opponent had been silenced by a threat to kill the man's son.

As Greene's private travel diary reveals, he knew that Noriega and his men were heavily involved in drug and weapons smuggling. Chuchu had a piece of this action and did not try to hide it from Greene. He showed him one of his secret airstrips, and he made it clear that cash was no problem in his business. On December 3, 1985, Greene describes how Chuchu stopped at a bank and made an apparently routine withdrawal of $29,000 in cash. On December 10 Greene recalls Chuchu's story of how Panama profited from smuggling goods to Nicaragua and Cuba, in violation of the U.S. embargoes. Noriega had set up several companies to facilitate the smuggling, and Chuchu explained how the colonel took his share of the profits from each enterprise. Instead of exposing Noriega's various crimes, which were much worse than the activities of the underworld in Nice, Greene continued to stand by Panama. In 1983 a grateful Panamanian government honoured him with the Grand Cross of the Order of Vasco Núñez de Balboa. In addition he was given a solid gold Rolex wristwatch. When a reporter from *The Washington Post* asked Greene about Noriega in 1988, he pretended at first that he hardly knew the colonel but then avowed that he would support him, explaining, "An enemy of my enemy is my friend. And my enemy is Reagan."

Of course, Noriega's position as an enemy of Reagan was a bit compromised by his lengthy employment as a CIA informer. But there is no point in trying to make a logical analysis of Greene's remarks on Central America. As usual he was simply trying to create as much trouble as possible while having some private laughs and some interesting adventures. Once Noriega was in a U.S. prison and was exposed as a major drug dealer, Greene developed a serious case of amnesia about the colonel. In perhaps the last interview of his life, he told the publisher of *Harper's*—John R. MacArthur—that he vaguely remembered having a drink with Noriega once, but he could not think of a single thing from their conversation. "He was completely uninteresting," Greene insisted, conveniently overlooking his mission to Castro on Noriega's behalf and his several meetings with the colonel. He did admit, however, "There was something about him that I didn't like."

For dissidents, the days of Torrijos and Noriega were not all that amusing, and they had little sympathy for Greene's antics. The associate editor of Panama's *La Prensa*, Guillermo Sánchez Borbon, was one of those who tried to tell the truth about Torrijos and Noriega, and who suffered as a result. He was twice imprisoned and was forced to live in exile for a long period. In happier days he was a friend of Chuchu, but he parted company with him over the dictators. Noriega hated him for revealing details about the murder of Dr. Hugo Spadafora, a courageous adversary whom the colonel's troops had beaten and mutilated, driving a pole up his rectum and ripping out his nails. Sánchez Borbon's verdict on *Getting to Know the General* is simple: "I can't forgive Greene for writing that book. He was a good writer, but he didn't know shit about Panama."

One might think that old age would have kept Greene from running off to Central America all the time, but he could not resist the intrigue and comedy created by the dictators, Communists, spies, quiet Americans, and the inimitable Chuchu. After Torrijos's death he spent so much time championing the cause of the Sandinistas that they gave him a special award—the Order of Rubén Darío. During the award ceremony in Managua, Greene called Nicaraguans "the first defenders in a war between civilisation and barbarism." His citation praised his contribution to literature and his "struggle against imperialist domination." The word *struggle* must have been used in a purely poetic sense. While the Sandinistas were actually fighting to take over Nicaragua, Greene stayed far away, limiting his contribution to financial donations. And when he visited Managua after the revolution, he spent a lot of time in the company of a Torrijos substitute—Tomás Borge, the tough minister of the interior.

When the journalist Richard West approached a bar in Managua one evening, he was warned not to go in. "It's full of gunmen," he was told. The reason for all the weapons was the presence of Borge, who was surrounded by "a bevy of strong-arm men, like a gangster boss from old Shanghai or Chicago." West went into the bar anyway and was surprised to find Graham Greene seated in the middle of all the gunmen, with Borge beside him. It was a shock for the journalist, who could not understand why his hero Greene would be on friendly terms with such characters. Borge's idea of combining Christianity and communism was to declare that "State coercion is love." He also had a soft spot in his heart for terrorism and wrote a spirited defense of a Sandinista group that hijacked a plane in 1970. "It troubled me," West wrote in 1989, "that a man of whom I have stood in awe since childhood, and now regard as the greatest living English writer, should be such a friend of the Sandinistas, consorting with men like Borge, whom I regard as a terrorist."

Greene was also friendly with Cayetano Carpio, a fierce guerrilla leader in El Salvador. When he first saw Carpio in 1980, he made the mistake of telling a *Time* correspondent that the leader had "merciless eyes." When he met him again in 1983, he hastened to apologize for his unkind description, fearing that it would be held against him. But the leader was full of forgiveness and charmed Greene with his candid discussion of guerrilla tactics and strategy. He was even kind enough to present the novelist with a copy of his book *Kidnaped and Hooded*. Three months later this kindly fellow killed himself after being implicated in the murder of the woman who had served as his second-in-command. When her body was found in Managua, it was covered with eighty stab wounds. Of this killing, the *Washington Post* correspondent Christopher Dickey wrote: "When even Cayetano's friend, Tomás Borge, refused to play along with this atrocity and confronted Cayetano Carpio with his apparent complicity, the sickly and humiliated rebel leader was left little choice but to commit suicide."

With the protection of Torrijos, Noriega, and the Sandinistas, Greene had a comfortable seat from which to observe a world of incredible violence and corruption. It was the best spectacle he had encountered since his visit to Haiti in 1963. He had been denied the privilege of watching the terror in Haiti from Papa Doc's vantage point. The voodoo dictator did not warm to foreigners and was not the sort of fellow one could joke with over a bottle of whiskey. Papa Doc was too far over the edge to realize the value of courting a prominent novelist with parties, lavish dinners, and a free flight on the Concorde. But the Central Americans handled Greene beautifully, and he repaid their hospitality by saying all the right things to the outside world. With Greene things have to be turned upside down to understand them. From a conventional perspective, his interest in Central America looked like a form of political commitment. No one guessed that he simply wanted to be a passive Pinkie, happily watching his gangsters stealing and bullying.

If he had been a younger man, Greene might have turned some of this material into a good novel. For years he flattered Chuchu by telling him that he was going to write a novel about him, but nothing came of this until 1988, when he brought out the slim novel *The Captain and the Enemy*. It is a confused story that tries to combine the world of Berkhamsted with that of violent Panama. For Greene all roads led back to the terrors of his father's school, but it is too awkward to cram bits of Berkhamsted and Panama into one small novel. By the time the action moves to Panama, the reader is more than halfway through the book. The richly evil atmosphere of Noriega's rule fails to emerge from the story, although Greene makes an effort to show that any kind of treachery is possible in Panama.

In the end Greene was more attracted to the idea of a love story, and he borrowed part of the romantic plot from his first novel, *The Man Within*. Just as Carlyon took Andrews from his school and gave him an exciting but guilt-ridden life as a "smuggler," the Captain takes young Jim Baxter from school and eventually draws him into shady activities in Panama. Some of Greene's activities with Chuchu are incorporated into the story. Like the sergeant, the Captain has his own secret landing strip. And Jim's love for the Captain reflects the romantic attitude toward Torrijos and Chuchu in *Getting to Know the General*. True to form, Greene must finally destroy any hope of a complete love between two men. The Captain dies in a fiery plane crash and leaves Jim wondering about "the nature of love. . . . I wish I had seen him once more."

At the end of the novel, a Panamanian colonel tries to figure out what Jim and the Captain were really up to. His only important clue is the name King Kong, which he believes is part of a special code used by the two. He thinks the name must have some political significance, and, as the novel ends, he is seen diligently working to uncover its meaning. He will never crack the code, though, because he is looking for the wrong answers. Just as Greene's admirers believed that his interest in Torrijos and Chuchu was entirely motivated by politics, the fictional colonel in the novel cannot conceive of a non-political meaning for the code. But its only message is that of repressed love.

After the Captain takes Jim from his school, they go one day to see the film *King Kong*. In part the Captain is looking for a place where he and Jim can be alone. He complains bitterly that England makes it too difficult for boys and men to enjoy a little privacy. It is simply impossible for a man to "talk quietly to a boy under age." In France, he says, they manage such things much better. In a nearly empty cinema they sit close together at the front, and soon the Captain's eyes fill with tears as he watches the beast struggle to fight the world with his female "burden" clinging to him. In his innocence the boy asks, "Why doesn't he drop her?"

This episode brings us back to the shadowy territory of "Yes and No." Can the man and boy drop women and forget the world's views? Women love them and are easy for them to pick up, but what they really want is each other. Although the idea of love is present throughout their discussion of the film, they cannot bring themselves to say that love is the thing they want from each other. Nor can they acknowledge the sexual energy that pulls at them, a force only too obvious in the image of the oversize ape with its squirming captive. Greene is also alluding to a fear of male sexuality. In *The Man Within*, Andrews repeatedly compares Carlyon to an ape and at one point calls him the "heroic ape."

Breaking the code is relatively easy. Discovering Greene's point of view is the hard part. In the case of Padre Pio, for example, the conventional assumption would be that Greene was drawn to him by some mystical religious feeling. But when one understands Greene's sexual obsession with wounds, it becomes clear that Padre Pio is a kind of pinup attraction for him—the ultimate wounded man. Likewise, it is logical to think that Greene identified with the political thinking of the Sandinistas. But all he really wanted was a chance to play with Chuchu and a reasonably safe way of immersing himself in a violent society. After a good dose of Chuchu and revolution, he could go back to Paris, Antibes, Capri, or the Ritz, then return for another taste of the tonic in a year or so. He drank deep, but it was not at the fountain of Marx and Lenin.

II

Near the time that he began traveling to Central America, Greene became acquainted with perhaps his most ardent admirer—Father Leopoldo Durán. The priest had studied Greene's novels for many years in his native Spain, where he taught English literature at the University of Madrid. When he decided to write a doctoral thesis, he took as his subject the "theology" in Greene's work, especially in relation to his portraits of priests. Greene took a look at the thesis and commended the priest for his efforts, telling him that he was particularly grateful to have his theological support. In the early 1970s they met and began spending time with each other in Spain. They would load up Father Durán's small car with cases of wine and roam through the countryside for days at a time, drinking and talking.

Father Durán seems to have done much of the talking. When a BBC producer interviewed him in 1992, the priest talked for hours, praising Greene in the most extravagant fashion and recalling holidays when his conversations with the novelist would continue for as long as fourteen hours a day. Wine helped to keep the mouth from going dry. According to the priest, he and his friend replenished their supply by visiting a certain cellar in Galicia "many dozens of times." In addition to their fondness for a good drink, Father Durán thought that he and Greene enjoyed a mutual trust, which allowed them to speak openly to each other: "Graham realized that with me he could talk about everything, and I wouldn't be, you know, surprised by anything." Father Durán also thought that the novelist appreciated his ability to keep a secret: "I think that Graham wanted to travel, to be friendly with a priest who was a kind of . . . I would say a priest ready to joke, ready to laugh, ready to talk about his books . . . ready to be a secret person because Graham had many disappointments with some priests."

In his enthusiasm for the novelist's company, Father Durán would try to find something funny or profound in almost everything Greene said, and he kept a detailed diary of their conversations. The priest may have liked a good joke, but he tended to respond with great seriousness to Greene's religious and political pronouncements. From time to time he was inspired to write an essay on some new insight into the theological significance of a certain novel or story. He usually published these pieces in the *Clergy Review*. As far as he was concerned, Greene was clearly on God's side, and the novelist's achievement was to create one long testament to the divine "mastery" over good and evil.

Greene must have been greatly entertained by his friend's earnest attitude. He could always count on a sincere reaction to any provocative remark. Father Durán was a character waiting to be used, and Greene did not pass up the opportunity. Their relationship became the basis for *Monsignor Quixote* (1982), a novel filled with pages of dialogue that seem to have been pulled straight from their conversations. Greene put Father Durán's name at the top of his dedication page, and the priest was delighted to find that he had inspired a new creation from his friend's noble mind. He was proud to see a bit of himself in the eternally innocent Father Quixote.

Like Cervantes's great hero, Father Quixote prefers to see the world in a romantic light, taking everything at its highest value. With a friend he calls Sancho—a former mayor with Marxist leanings—he wanders from place to place in a temperamental old car, talking end-

lessly about the ways of God and humankind. A great deal of time is
devoted to discussing contraception and other sexual questions. "Has
sperm a soul?" is one of the pressing questions the two men debate.
Another is whether coitus interruptus can be considered a form of
masturbation. Because Father Quixote's replies are predictable, the
fun of the debates lies in pushing the priest to make increasingly difficult efforts to defend not only Christianity but the general qualities
of optimism, innocence, and goodness.

By comparison with his previous writings, Greene's satire on Father
Quixote is mild. Nevertheless, every opportunity is taken to place the
priest in positions that compromise his moral character. He is
involved in a police chase, spends a night in a brothel, mistakes a con-
dom for a balloon, watches a blue film, and hears a confession in a
lavatory. The priest endures all these tawdry experiences without fully
realizing what has happened to him. He assumes that the film—*A
Maiden's Prayer*—is supposed to have some sort of religious message
and is more than a little confused by all the nude bodies moving up
and down. As he leaves the theater, he remarks to Sancho, "What a
lot of exercise they were all taking." This sort of comedy is easy
enough to achieve, but Greene does not take it anywhere. There is no
great passion behind his satire, no bite. In artistic terms, *Monsignor
Quixote* resembles a respectable painting that has been defaced by a
clever adolescent with a box of crayons. In a suitably subversive gesture, Greene donated the novel's Spanish and Latin American royalties to two extremely different organizations—a Trappist monastery
in Galicia, which he had visited with Father Durán, and the guerrilla
army in El Salvador.

With such uncritical companions as Father Durán, Yvonne and
Martine, and Chuchu, Greene was not likely to be told that anything
he wrote was inferior. His small circle of friends was always ready with
a soft murmur of approval. In the last thirty years of his career, there
are only two books that seem worthy of comparison with his best
work. The portrait of Dr. Plarr in *The Honorary Consul* is powerfully
rendered, and *The Human Factor* is perhaps his most polished creation, a novel with elegant prose and flawless organization. In *The
Human Factor,* one is given a glimpse of a resurgent genius. It is the
sort of work that Greene might have produced earlier if he had stayed
on the path set by *The Third Man* and *The End of the Affair.*

Published in 1973, *The Honorary Consul* is the story of a botched
political kidnapping in South America. Ideas for the setting and plot
came to Greene after he visited Paraguay and Argentina in the late
1960s and early 1970s. Rebels mistakenly abduct Charley Fortnum,

Britain's honorary consul, thinking that he is the American ambassador. But neither Charley nor the rebels are as interesting as the lonely doctor who is having an affair with Charley's wife. Dr. Plarr has a lot in common with other devoted adulterers in Greene's work, but what sets him apart is the completeness of his isolation. Unlike Scobie in *The Heart of the Matter,* he has grown accustomed to living in a world where all the choices are the wrong ones. He faces the emptiness of his life with stoic pride, but he is not a burnt-out case. In dim regions of his brain, there is a flicker of warmth. He wants to love, but the flicker simply cannot be coaxed into becoming a bright flame. Or as he puts it, with the accuracy afforded to a character in a post-1950s novel, "I know how to fuck—I don't know how to love."

The first part of his declaration is no idle boast. Greene is not known for creating graphic sex scenes, but *The Honorary Consul* shows Plarr pursuing his talents to the limit. While he is on a visit to the home of a mistress, she tells him that her husband is taking a nap in an armchair but that they will not wake him if they keep up a steady chatter in the background. Any sort of talk will do. Willing to give the game a try, Plarr has sex with his mistress as she is sitting astride him. He provides the necessary verbal background by reciting the story of the Three Bears. As his partner bounces on his lap, he does his best to follow the story line: "And then the third bear said in his gruff voice, 'Who has been eating up my porridge?' " Near the moment of climax, however, his memory fails him, and he must fall back on an emergency substitute: "This is the way the postboy rides. Gallopy, gallopy, gallopy."

Using a finely balanced mixture of comedy and tragedy, Greene brings Plarr to life in a way that makes the reader care about his fate. It is quite an accomplishment, because Plarr is essentially a cold man. Life has taught him that it is easier to keep his emotions in reserve. Sex with strangers or married women is less painful than a real love affair. Prostitutes are best because the memory of the contact is quickly canceled by the next man for her and the next prostitute for him. But Charley Fortnum's plight helps to thaw Plarr's emotions. Although Fortnum's wife is his mistress, he is not consumed by hate for the husband, nor does he seem to fear an attraction to him. Motivated by some long-buried sense of heroism, he tries to save Charley's life. He fails and is killed, but his death is perhaps the most moving one in Greene's work.

In *The Human Factor,* Castle's case is similar. Trapped inside a world of bewildering codes and conflicting loyalties, he has taught himself to guard his emotions and to live cautiously, avoiding friendships and any contact that might endanger his security. But the human factor cannot be completely tamed. During an assignment in South Africa, he falls in love with a black woman named Sarah and is given a brief reprieve from loneliness when he marries her and adopts her son. This reprieve is, however, costly. As the epigraph from Joseph Conrad warns, "He who forms a tie is lost." The threat of disaster hangs over Castle from the beginning of the novel. Greene does a fine job of keeping the reader guessing when and how the ax will fall. Despite the connotations of his name, Castle can mount no defense against the Cold War mentality that thrives on suspicion. He wants to guard against every contingency, but there are too many traps waiting for him. Sooner or later he must fall into one.

Greene began writing this novel in 1967 as a kind of tribute to the "virtues" of Kim Philby's treason. Castle is a traitor, but the reader is supposed to recognize that he has "good" personal reasons for being a double agent. His allegiance to his wife and son gives him sufficient excuse to betray his country. Philby had no such family concerns to hide behind, but they make it much easier for Greene to cast his hero in a sympathetic light. After Philby's *My Silent War* appeared in 1968, Greene put Castle's story aside, worried that it would be too closely identified with the real traitor. But he could not put the draft out of his mind and finally came back to it in the mid-1970s. When the book was published in 1978, it enjoyed the greatest commercial success of any Greene novel, selling especially well in the United States, where it stayed on the *New York Times* best-seller list for six months.

The action is set in the 1970s, but Greene drew his material primarily from his wartime memories of office life at Section V's headquarters in Ryder Street. He wanted to show the bureaucratic routine that characterizes most espionage work, and his only real experience of that life was in the 1940s. The advantage of this circumstance is that Greene was obliged to set much of the action in a place that he knew better than any other—central London. Since *The End of the Affair* Greene had avoided London as an important setting in his novels, but *The Human Factor* is a reminder of how well he could handle its urban landscape. Vivid details blend smoothly with the action and create an intimate sense of place. The night porter is glimpsed as he scrubs the steps of Albany, the old red bricks of St. James's Palace glow in the winter afternoon, a young woman giggles into a telephone at Piccadilly Circus station, and prostitutes lurk in the doorways of Soho. The effortless evocation of Greene's favorite parts of London makes one wish that he had never ventured into foreign parts.

This novel also takes Greene back to Berkhamsted, and he describes it without any of the bitterness that spoiled the view in *The Lawless Roads*. Whereas the young Greene yearned to escape from the town's boundaries, the old novelist depicts it as a temporary refuge from the dangers of the spies in London. It is the one place where Castle can find some measure of peace. All the familiar sights are present in the novel—the canal with its willow trees, the old school, the long High Street, the wilderness of the Common, and—significantly—the ruined castle. Like the hero of the novel, the castle failed to withstand all assaults. The fragmented walls seem to be an omen for Castle, a sign of the bleak future awaiting him when he will have to flee Berkhamsted for Moscow.

The only senior officer whom Castle respects is Colonel Daintry— in charge of internal security. He is not merely another cog in the bureaucratic machinery but a sensitive man who abhors heavy-handed tactics. Although he is dedicated to finding the "mole" in the service, he is not willing to solve the problem at any cost. His "human factor" makes him reluctant to trap Castle. He knows the pain of loneliness and has felt the disappointment of broken relationships. In a scene that has parallels with Greene's life, the colonel visits his estranged wife's home and feels overwhelmed by her collection of china owls. They seem to be hiding in every corner of the place, and he keeps bumping into them until he does the unforgivable thing— he breaks one. His wife's passion for surrounding herself with a collection of inanimate objects embarrasses him and makes him feel that he has never been anything more than an object in her fantasy world.

Despite his understanding of the human factor, Daintry can do nothing to save Castle. Each officer is hampered by the code of secrecy, which makes misunderstandings and betrayals inevitable. The great evil in the secret service is secrecy itself. It not only breeds suspicion but creates an atmosphere in which the innocent can easily be mistaken for the guilty. Davis, Castle's colleague, is guilty of nothing but idleness and stupidity, yet his minor flaws are magnified under the close scrutiny of his bosses. They seem to need a scapegoat, and Davis suffers when his incompetence is made to look like treachery. In the interests of secrecy, the case against him is never aired openly, and he goes to his death without being able to defend his innocence. He is simply disposed of, quietly and cleanly.

Although much of the book is informed by Greene's own experience in the secret service, he knew of no attempts to silence an officer by killing him. The episode was invented not only for dramatic purposes but also as a way of embarrassing the service. It was his little touch of betrayal in a novel devoted to the subject. And he went to great lengths to make the method of the killing seem authentic. He asked his brother, Dr. Raymond Greene, to tell him how a murder could be disguised as a death from some natural cause. After doing a little research, Raymond found the perfect solution and conveyed the details in a letter to his brother, who put them into the novel almost verbatim. The evil medical officer of *The Human Factor*—Dr. Percival—explains the procedure to Sir John Hargreaves, the head of the service. Percival plans to poison the hard-drinking Davis with an undetectable drug that will attack his liver. Known as Aflatoxin, the drug is derived from moldy peanuts. It destroys liver cells and usually proves fatal within a week. In a man who is known to abuse alcohol, the death can appear to be the result of overindulgence. Percival relishes every detail of his plan and carries it out with precision, administering just the right dose for the job.

As a cold, calculating representative of authority, Percival has none of the human qualities that distinguish Greene's passionate murderers. There is no glory in his villainy, but his power is godlike in the worst sense. For Castle, the only protection against such characters is to devise a good method of escape. When the walls of the fortress are stormed, there must be a secret tunnel that will lead to safety. In *The Human Factor* the tunnel of escape leads straight to Moscow, but it is doubtful whether there is anything safe about the final destination. It is merely another place of suspicion and betrayal where more traps are waiting, and Castle's isolation there is much worse than anything he has known before. In his dangerous game of playing double agent, he learns that no authority is worthy of his allegiance. Both the Soviet and the British spymasters are shown to be cynical, self-serving frauds who will exploit anyone for temporary gain. In such a world disloyalty is the only virtue that makes sense.

Maurice Oldfield and other members of SIS were offended by Greene's treatment of their world. They could accept the comic vision in *Our Man in Havana,* because no one thought it would be taken seriously. But *The Human Factor* showed too much disloyalty to the old firm, and too much sympathy for Philby. But Greene was able to talk his way out of the trouble, giving his spy friend Nicholas Elliott the old excuse that he was simply a storyteller who meant no harm. Even Oldfield decided to forgive and forget. In 1979, when Greene went to Oxford to receive an honorary degree, he saw Oldfield at a reception and was welcomed with an embrace from the old spymaster. Another guest—the historian Alistair Horne—asked Oldfield why he had embraced Greene and was told, "No point nurturing grudges." With much greater success than Philby, Greene had charted numerous escape routes, none of which led to a place as dismal as Moscow. His system allowed him to pop up anywhere. Everyone could be betrayed, and no one could trap him.

But what was the good of remaining so elusive? It brought him money and fame and a certain security, but it was also a trap that cut him off from too much of the world and that encouraged him to squander his talents on bad books. His pace in the 1930s and 1940s had to slow down, and the passions of those years were destined either to cool or to burn out. But one cannot help thinking that another Greene might have emerged from the turmoil, perhaps a Jamesian craftsman specializing in subtle short novels. Most of all, one wishes that he had been able to go beyond disloyalty and pain. He took that combination as far as it could go and was left with no substitute when the fires had dimmed. All he could do was repackage old themes in duller hues. A complete retirement would have been preferable to the sad failures of *"J'Accuse," Monsignor Quixote, Getting to Know the General,* and *Dr. Fischer of Geneva or the Bomb Party.*

The flicker of warmth in Dr. Plarr and the confident artistry of *The Human Factor* show that a new path could have been forged, one without any easy escapes or clever tricks. In the last dozen years of his life, Greene had enough energy to fight Daniel Guy and play bandits with Chuchu. That same energy could have gone into one or two good books. Art was his only salvation, and, as long as he was going to write anything, he might as well have made it worth the effort. But no amount of speculation will alter the facts. The long despair of failure was his fate, and it was perhaps the inescapable price of a life spent too close to the edge of pain. In the end, he could not adopt a brighter shade of Greene. He was always a prisoner of that enemy within, the one who was angry with him, the one who caused him to yearn so much for escape.

THE LAST WORD

The Human Factor might well have been Greene's last novel. In 1979 he underwent an operation for intestinal cancer. Such an operation for a man of seventy-five was risky, and there was always the chance that the spread of the cancer would not be stopped. But he recovered rapidly and never suffered any more trouble from the illness. For a man who ate whatever he wanted, never took regular exercise, and drank too much, his body was amazingly resilient. Even so, he claimed that he was ready for death. When people asked about his chances of winning the Nobel Prize, he liked to say that he was expecting a better reward—death.

Catherine Walston's constitution did not prove as strong. Hard drinking robbed her of her looks and then hastened her death. She developed pancreatic cancer in 1978 and died before the end of the year. After he heard that Catherine was dying, Greene asked to visit her, but she did not want him to see her looking so ill. When she made one of her last trips to the London Clinic, Greene happened to be staying at the Ritz. Mabel Dawes, one of the Walston family's longtime employees, took Catherine to the clinic and then paid Greene a visit. She told him about Catherine's weak condition, and he ordered flowers for Mabel to take back to her. The real end of the affair came as Greene watched Mabel take the flowers away in a car.

Not long afterward the news arrived that Catherine was dead. She was sixty-two. Only a year after she was gone, Harry Walston married again.

Greene's health remained good until he went to Ireland for the GPA Book Award in November 1989. The trip—and the fuss he raised about awarding a prize to Vincent McDonnell—left him exhausted, and he was never the same again. "He always said that Ireland killed him," Yvonne recalled, "but, in fact, he was very tired before he went there, and he was treated very well there indeed. They sent a special plane to fetch us at the Nice airport. Until then, more or less, he was strong." In December, while he was staying at his daughter's house in Vevey, he collapsed and could not get up. A local doctor decided to test his blood, and the results showed that his red cell count was extremely low. He was immediately given a blood transfusion and was required to come back for further transfusions every two weeks. The new blood helped, and for a while he seemed to be making a steady recovery.

He kept quiet about the nature of his illness and its treatment. In 1990 he decided to leave Antibes for good and move to an apartment in Corseaux, a small village above Vevey. Yvonne came with him, so he had the benefit of her full-time help, as well as the assistance of his daughter and Martine, both of whom lived only minutes away. The apartment was not large, but it had a magnificent view of Lake Geneva, with the Alps and the brown hulk of the Castle of Chillon in the distance. Greene also had the comfort of knowing that Henry James was fond of the area. The first half of *Daisy Miller* is set in Vevey.

He received his transfusions at the Hôpital de la Providence, on the eastern edge of Vevey. Yvonne would drive him down at nine in the morning, pick him up at three in the afternoon, and repeat the process two weeks later. At first he took only magazines to read, but then he suddenly developed a passion for one book, which had been in his collection for many years. After taking it to one of his transfusions, he always insisted on having it with him for each treatment. It was *The Letters of Ezra Pound, 1907–1941,* which was published in 1950. At the end of his life Greene was going back to the early days of his career, when Pound was one of his heroes. The volume of letters is distinguished by the sheer exuberance of the young American poet's campaign to free literature from the tight grip of the Victorian patriarchs. It is also tainted by the poet's outbursts of anti-Semitism. And, occasionally, the letters say something that seems especially appropriate to Greene's career. In 1922 Pound wrote, "If the poets don't make certain horrors appear horrible who will?" If the aesthetic merits of *Brighton Rock* needed defending, Pound's comment would make a good starting point.

By March 1991 it was clear that Greene's transfusions were losing their effectiveness. He grew more lethargic and pale. Near the end of the month, he could no longer move beyond the confines of the apartment. Yvonne spent three sleepless nights watching over him; then she tried to get some rest one night while Greene's daughter stayed with him. On Sunday, March 31, at five in the morning, Lucy woke Yvonne and told her that Greene had taken a turn for the worse. They sent for an ambulance, and he was rushed to the Hôpital de la Providence. He was fully conscious for two days but knew that he was dying. "Don't stop me," he told Yvonne. "I want to go. Let me go." Martine told him, "You will be immortal. Your body will die, but your works will live on."

Through Lucy, Vivien asked to be allowed to come to Vevey. She wanted to see her husband one more time, but he refused to give his consent. According to Vivien, he was also reluctant to see his son: "He didn't want to see Francis, but eventually they persuaded him that he ought to." The last time that Greene and his wife and children had been together in the same room was Christmas 1958. Vivien remembered the exact date because she used a diamond ring to scratch it into a windowpane of her house in Oxford.

Since leaving home in the 1950s, Francis had led such a quiet life that it is difficult to say much about him. Like his father, he managed to travel to some distant places, although the reasons for some journeys seem obscure. In 1968, during the middle of the Vietnam War, the *Daily Telegraph* reported that Mr. Francis Greene had been "detained by the military authorities in Southern Laos." No explanation was given for his detention, but Francis was said to be "collecting material for a book." If such a book exists, it has escaped this writer's notice.

The doctors did what they could to save Graham Greene, but he lapsed into a coma on Tuesday and did not awaken from it. Yvonne clearly remembered his last words: "Why must it take so long to come?" She called Father Durán in Madrid and asked him to fly to Switzerland. In her recollection, Greene was not conscious when the priest arrived, but he was still breathing when Father Durán gave him the last absolution. According to Durán, "there was one thing worrying [Greene] most at that time. It concerned his work for the secret service, and how it would be judged."

Just before noon on Wednesday, April 3, Greene died. The cause of death is not given on his death certificate. For the past fifty years Switzerland has not required that such information appear on official records available to the public. The hospital has the information but will not release it without the consent of his family. In an interview given shortly after Greene's death, Yvonne was unable to give a name to the illness that killed her companion of thirty years. It was not leukemia. She could describe it only as a blood disease in which the bone marrow fails to produce enough red cells.

After a long career of fantasizing about cremation, Greene left instructions that his body be given a proper burial in Corseaux's little cemetery. Prominent among the sixty mourners were Vivien and Yvonne. It was the first time that they had seen each other. The service was conducted by Father Durán, who said good-bye to his friend with words from Greene's favorite Shakespearean drama: "Good night, sweet prince, / And flights of angels sing thee to thy rest." Ever the optimist, the priest declared, "My faith tells me that he is now with God, or on the way there."

The subject of Greene's final destination goes beyond the limits of this biography, but everything in his life seems alien to the concept of heaven. At his requiem mass in Westminster Cathedral, a noble attempt was made to place him on the side of the angels, and evidence was brought forward to verify his good deeds. Muriel Spark spoke of her gratitude to him for sending her money and bottles of wine when she was a struggling young novelist. Father Roderick Strange, the former Catholic chaplain at Oxford University, said, "He had a great respect for the teaching of the church, even if it was a teaching which he couldn't always live up to."

In an article for the *National Review,* which appeared a month after Greene's death, the film director Peter Glenville portrayed the novelist as a friend of the "underdog" who had little interest in wealth, fame, or power. To illustrate his point, he said, "Although he was personally quite fond of Sir Alexander Korda, he had a strong distaste for his yacht and all its fine appurtenances." Of course, what Glenville failed to add was that Greene's "distaste" did not keep him from accepting enormous sums of money from Korda for film work or from cruising the Mediterranean on numerous occasions as Korda's guest. And his fondness for the underdog did not keep him from launching strong attacks on Korda's "Semitic" art in the 1930s.

It is all very well to praise a friend who has recently died, but there is no point in creating an idealized portrait of Greene. His friends and admirers did their best to make him look gentle and humane, and in old age he often gave that appearance. He charmed many people, and showed kindness and generosity to some. But trying to find moral excellence in his life is not a helpful way to honor him. There is too much evidence to the contrary. Only his best writing can plead a case for the value of his life. Books made him, and books must sustain his reputation. After all the voices have been heard, Art will have the last word.

SELECT BIBLIOGRAPHY OF GRAHAM GREENE

Babbling April. Oxford: Blackwell, 1925.

The Man Within. London: Heinemann, 1929; New York: Doubleday, 1929.

The Name of Action. London: Heinemann, 1930; New York: Doubleday, 1931.

Rumour at Nightfall. London: Heinemann, 1931; New York: Doubleday, 1932.

Stamboul Train. London: Heinemann, 1932; *Orient Express*. New York: Doubleday, 1933.

It's a Battlefield. London: Heinemann, 1934; New York: Doubleday, 1934.

England Made Me. London: Heinemann, 1935; *The Shipwrecked*. New York: Doubleday, 1935.

The Bear Fell Free. London: Grayson, 1935.

The Basement Room. London: Cresset Press, 1935.

Journey Without Maps. London: Heinemann, 1936; New York: Doubleday, 1936.

A Gun for Sale. London: Heinemann, 1936; *This Gun for Hire*. New York: Doubleday, 1936.

Brighton Rock. London: Heinemann, 1938; New York: Viking, 1938.

The Lawless Roads. London: Heinemann, 1939; *Another Mexico*. New York: Viking, 1939.

The Confidential Agent. London: Heinemann, 1939; New York: Viking, 1939.

The Power and the Glory. London: Heinemann, 1940; *The Labyrinthine Ways*. New York: Viking, 1940.

British Dramatists. London: Collins, 1942.

The Ministry of Fear. London: Heinemann, 1943; New York: Viking, 1943.

The Little Train. London: Eyre & Spottiswoode, 1946; New York: Lothrop, Lee and Shepard, 1958.

Nineteen Stories. London: Heinemann, 1947; New York: Viking, 1949.

The Heart of the Matter. London: Heinemann, 1948; New York: Viking, 1948.

Why Do I Write? London: Percival Marshall, 1948; New York: British Book Centre, 1948.

The Third Man and *The Fallen Idol*. London: Heinemann, 1950; *The Third Man*. New York: Viking, 1950.

The Little Fire Engine. London: Parrish, 1950; New York: Lothrop, Lee and Shepard, 1953.

The Lost Childhood. London: Eyre & Spottiswoode, 1951; New York: Viking, 1952.

The End of the Affair. London: Heinemann, 1951; New York: Viking, 1951.

The Little Horse Bus. London: Parrish, 1952; New York: Lothrop, Lee and Shepard, 1954.

The Living Room. London: Heinemann, 1953; New York: Viking, 1954.

The Little Steamroller. London: Parrish, 1953; New York: Lothrop, Lee and Shepard, 1955.

Twenty-one Stories. London: Heinemann, 1954; New York: Viking, 1962.

The Quiet American. London: Heinemann, 1955; New York: Viking, 1956.

Loser Takes All. London: Heinemann, 1955; New York: Viking, 1957.

The Potting Shed. London: Heinemann, 1958; New York: Viking, 1957.

Our Man in Havana. London: Heinemann, 1958; New York: Viking, 1958.

The Complaisant Lover. London: Heinemann, 1959; New York: Viking, 1961.

A Burnt-out Case. London: Heinemann, 1961; New York: Viking, 1961.

In Search of a Character: Two African Journals. London: Bodley Head, 1961; New York: Viking, 1962.

A Sense of Reality. London: Bodley Head, 1963; New York: Viking, 1963.

Carving a Statue. London: Bodley Head, 1964.

The Comedians. London: Bodley Head, 1966; New York: Viking, 1966.

Victorian Detective Fiction. London: Bodley Head, 1966.

May We Borrow Your Husband? and Other Comedies of the Sexual Life. London: Bodley Head, 1967; New York: Viking, 1967.

Collected Essays. London: Bodley Head, 1969; New York: Viking, 1969.

Travels with My Aunt. London: Bodley Head, 1969; New York: Viking, 1970.

A Sort of Life. London: Bodley Head, 1971; New York: Simon & Schuster, 1971.

Collected Stories. London: Bodley Head and Heinemann, 1972; New York: Viking, 1973.

The Pleasure Dome: Collected Film Criticism, 1935–1940. London: Secker & Warburg, 1972; *Graham Greene on Film.* New York: Simon & Schuster, 1972.

The Honorary Consul. London: Bodley Head, 1973; New York: Simon & Schuster, 1973.

Lord Rochester's Monkey. London: Bodley Head, 1974; New York: Viking, 1974.

An Impossible Woman: The Memories of Dottoressa Moor. London: Bodley Head, 1975; New York: Viking, 1976.

The Return of A. J. Raffles. London: Bodley Head, 1975; New York: Simon & Schuster, 1976.

The Human Factor. London: Bodley Head, 1978; New York: Simon & Schuster, 1978.

Dr. Fischer of Geneva or the Bomb Party. London: Bodley Head, 1980; New York: Simon & Schuster, 1980.

Ways of Escape. London: Bodley Head, 1980; New York: Simon & Schuster, 1981.

Monsignor Quixote. London: Bodley Head, 1982; New York: Simon & Schuster, 1982.

J'Accuse: The Dark Side of Nice. London: Bodley Head, 1982.

Yes and No. London: Bodley Head, 1983.

For Whom the Bell Chimes. London: Bodley Head, 1983.

Getting to Know the General. London: Bodley Head, 1985; New York: Simon & Schuster, 1985.

The Tenth Man. London: Bodley Head and Anthony Blond, 1985; New York: Simon & Schuster, 1985.

The Captain and the Enemy. London: Reinhardt, 1988; New York: Viking, 1988.

Yours Etc.: Letters to the Press, 1945–89. London: Reinhardt, 1989; New York: Viking, 1989.

The Last Word. London: Reinhardt, 1990.

Reflections. London: Reinhardt, 1991; New York: Viking, 1991.

A World of My Own: A Dream Diary. London: Reinhardt, 1992; New York: Viking, 1994.

The Graham Greene Film Reader: Mornings in the Dark. Manchester: Carcanet, 1993; New York: Applause Books, 1994.

AUTHOR'S NOTE:
GRAHAM GREENE AND
BIOGRAPHY

Graham Greene's unusual career and complex personality may put off certain critics, but these qualities could not fail to attract the interest of biographers. A few began submitting proposals to him as early as the 1950s. Yet when the author of *Lord Rochester's Monkey* became famous enough to be a worthy biographical subject himself, he was a well-established man of letters with lots of secrets to keep, and was understandably reluctant to have someone prying into his life and speculating on his motives with the abandon that he had used in Rochester's case. When he wrote the poet's biography, he was a nobody and felt free to tell stories without worrying that one day stories would be told about him. As late as 1949, he was planning to write another biography—the proposed subject was his distant cousin Robert Louis Stevenson. But he abandoned that idea and soon developed a narrow view of the biographer's art. He began claiming that he had a "copyright" on his life and warned people not to infringe it. In this matter, he was perfectly serious and was willing to use legal means to frighten away potential biographers.

In 1975 he decided to appoint an official biographer, someone who would tell his story with a certain degree of sympathy, admiration, and restraint. In return, he would provide access to papers, introductions to friends and family, and the right to quote without restriction. It was a big job and one that would require years of research. And by the time the project was complete, many people from Greene's past would be dead, their testimonies available only through interviews conducted by the official biographer. History would be recorded, but it would be one writer's version.

Greene found the biographer he wanted in the person of Norman Sherry, who was then professor of English at the University of Lancaster. A respected expert on Joseph Conrad, Professor Sherry was ready for a new challenge. He took to the job with enthusiasm and great devotion, spending more than a dozen years on the first volume of a projected three-volume work. Periodic reports of his progress reached Greene. Visiting the grand old man in 1985, the novelist David Lodge found that Greene "seemed to derive a mischievous glee from the tribulations that poor Norman Sherry had suffered in trying to retrace Greene's every step."

Sherry's first volume appeared in 1989, only two years before Greene's death, and his second volume came out in Britain in 1994. His biography does a great service in providing abundant evidence from restricted documents. Sherry did not produce the kind of whitewash that Greene seemed to expect. Within his generally sympathetic narrative, he found room to expose some of Greene's less pleasant qualities. But his dedication and official backing did have the effect of deterring potential rivals.

Anthony Mockler, the author of a book on Emperor Haile Selassie, is one biographer who tried to challenge Sherry's monopoly. Mockler managed to produce a partial biography based on unrestricted materials at the University of Texas. Before this work could be published, however, Greene's lawyers threatened to take Mockler to court. Greene also used the press to attack his adversary, accusing him of using "false pretenses to gain access" to the Texas material. This was a good line of attack because the general public could not be expected to know that any scholar can use the archive in question, with or without pretenses. In 1989, with the backing of the *Sunday Telegraph,* Mockler was able to publish a few excerpts from his work in the newspaper, but the book itself did not appear until 1994. *Graham Greene: Three Lives* bears the imprint of a small press in Scotland (Hunter Mackay), is barely 200 pages long, and covers Greene's life only to the age of forty-one. Fearful of being sued by the Greene estate, Mockler cut many of his quotations from Greene's work, and used a long preface to beg the estate not to take legal action against him.

After Greene's death, representatives of his estate took strong measures to discourage any new biographers from entering the field. The announcement that this book was in preparation brought—among other things—a stern letter to its author from a law firm with a charming Dickensian name. Of course, it is important to respect the legal rights of others, and I have tried to abide by all laws governing the sale and distribution of literary biography. The majesty of the law is not to be trifled with, as Greene himself learned— at considerable expense—when he had the misfortune to lose a libel suit brought against him by the representatives of Shirley Temple.

The courts say that it is impossible to libel the dead, so no one will now be able to do to Greene what he did to Shirley Temple. But this legal point will not stop some people from saying that a biographer should take a strictly respectful attitude toward the recently departed. Strangely enough, even in writing about a poet whose friends and family had long since turned to dust, Greene was not spared the accusation that he had maligned the silent dead. One high-minded reviewer took him to task for daring to question the honor of Lord Rochester's wife. Given the earl's tendency to roam far from home, Greene rightly wondered what the attractive wife was doing to occupy her time, and he mentions that her mother-in-law had some doubts about the lady's fidelity. Greene merely raises the question, carefully avoiding any appearance of forcing a firm conclusion. This is proper and necessary, but the reviewer called his action "a gratuitous indecency," and protested that Greene should not have allowed his thoughts to wander into private, uncharted territory. In other words, safeguarding the virtue of a woman who had been dead for three centuries was more important than allowing a living mind to sort out the flesh-and-blood aspects of history— the very things that make history worth knowing.

As Greene well knew, he did not have a copyright on his life. He gave that up when he chose to make a public spectacle of himself, which is exactly what he did each time that he published a new book. These occasions turned into news events, complete with interviews, commentaries, promotional displays, new photographs by Karsh, even an occasional piece of misleading advertising. And from all this exposure he profited greatly. Whether he liked it or not, he was an object of curiosity, someone readers wanted to understand, just as he had wanted to understand Lord Rochester. And once this process begins, there is no way to stop it. Making it easier or harder is possible, but stopping it is out of the question.

It is not a good idea to have only one complete biography of Greene. Given the novelist's fondness for deception, a biographer can profit from undertaking a thoroughly independent study. There are unrestricted materials available in a number of places, including some that are still in private hands, and there are many surviving friends and associates who have more than one story to tell. Above all, there is the large body of Greene's published work—much of it uncollected or issued only in limited editions. Interpreting the significance of all that work is a task that is big enough for at least two biographers. In any case, the story of Greene's life seems to merit an unofficial approach, one that might even allow an occasional "gratuitous indecency." This extravagantly imaginative, passionately disloyal novelist deserves nothing less.

SOURCES

Papers held at two university libraries have been particularly useful in the preparation of this biography. The Harry Ransom Humanities Research Center at the University of Texas, Austin (hereafter referred to as Texas) has a large and diverse collection of material on Graham Greene, including manuscripts of his books, diaries, letters, and film scripts. The library has more than 500 letters from Greene to his wife. I was kindly allowed access to all the items I wished to see—some of which were still being cataloged. I cannot praise highly enough the efficiency and courtesy of Dr. Thomas Staley and his staff. The Lauinger Library of Georgetown University (hereafter referred to as Georgetown) also has an impressive collection of Greene's papers, although it is impossible to describe its entire range of holdings. The library refused to let me see certain papers, citing restrictions placed on the material by Greene and his estate. Nevertheless, the Catherine Walston Papers at Georgetown are available for study, and this collection helped to enlighten me on many aspects of Greene's life. There are at least 1,000 letters from Greene to Catherine, and they cover more than forty years, beginning in 1946. Reading through all these letters was a fascinating experience, and I am grateful to Catherine's oldest son, the Hon. Oliver Walston, for alerting me to the existence of this vast collection.

I have tried not to burden the reader with extensive references to source material. Specialists who wish to know more about Greene's life should consult the holdings of the libraries at Texas and Georgetown. It may be many years before a reliable edition of Greene's letters can be published, and some documents may remain restricted until a distant date in the next century. Moreover, copyright laws will make it possible for his estate to restrict the right of quotation until at least the year 2041. I have not been allowed to quote from his unpublished work or correspondence.

Titles of Greene's books are hereafter listed without full publication details, which are provided in the select bibliography.

Greene's autobiography, *A Sort of Life,* and his volume of autobiographical pieces, *Ways of Escape,* are a subtle blend of fact and fiction, but they are indispensable works and have helped to inform my account of Greene's life.

CHAPTER ONE

DECEPTION AND DETECTION

John Updike's comment appears in *Odd Jobs: Essays and Criticism* (New York: Knopf, 1991). Faulkner's comment is a blurb that he gave Greene's American publisher, Viking.

The text of "The Virtue of Disloyalty" can be found in Greene's *Reflections.*

The public response to "The Destructors," as well as Greene's reply, can be found in *Picture Post,* August 14, 1954. Vivien Greene's comment is taken from the author's interview, June 1992.

For information about Lord Rochester, I am indebted to Jeremy Treglown's excellent *Letters of John Wilmot, Earl of Rochester* (Oxford: Basil Blackwell, 1980). Greene's factual mistakes in his biography were pointed out in a scholarly review by David M. Vieth, *Philological Quarterly,* Fall 1975. Also see *The Complete Poems of John Wilmot, Earl of Rochester,* ed. David M. Vieth (New Haven: Yale Univ. Press, 1968). The "expert" who claims that Rochester became a Catholic is Greene's official biographer, Norman Sherry.

Greene's comment about Henry James's "legend" appears in "The Young Henry James," *Reflections.* In *The New York Times Magazine,* February 26, 1978, V. S. Pritchett referred to Greene as "genially subversive." "The Revolver in the Corner Cupboard" first appeared in the *Saturday Book* (October 1946), ed. Leonard Russell (London: Hutchinson, 1946). One person who did notice the detail about the blanks in the revolver is John Carey in his introduction to the Everyman edition (1993) of *Brighton Rock.*

Information about the Anglo-Texan Society comes from the author's interview with Gillian Sutro, April 1993; John Sutro's "Greene's Jests," *Spectator,* September 29, 1984; *Picture Post,* August 14, 1954; and Graham Greene, *Yours Etc.*

Greene's comment about *The Tenth Man* is taken from the *Sunday Times,* April 14, 1984. The letter of March 30, 1967, was written to Mrs. Jill Phillips, of London, and a copy is available at Texas, along with a copy of *The Tenth Man* typescript. Also see *Graham Greene: A Bibliography and Guide to Research,* ed. R. A. Wobbe (New York: Garland, 1979). For background information on *The Tenth Man* "discovery," I am indebted to

Professor David Leon Higdon, of Texas Tech Univ., who has seen the original copies of letters from Mrs. Phillips in the files of Laurence Pollinger Ltd., Greene's former agents.

CHAPTER TWO

I SPY

For details on the career of Sir William Graham Greene, see his entry in *Dictionary of National Biography, 1941–1950*. Herbert Greene's remarks are taken from *Secret Agent in Spain* (London: Robert Hale, 1938). The best account of Benjamin's Greene's case can be found in A. W. Brian Simpson's *In the Highest Degree Odious: Detention Without Trial in Wartime Britain* (Oxford: Clarendon, 1992).

Claud Cockburn writes about the surveillance at the Berkhamsted School in *In Time of Trouble: An Autobiography* (London: Rupert Hart-Davis, 1956). The comment about an "army of women" is quoted in Michael Tracey, *A Variety of Lives: A Biography of Sir Hugh Greene* (London: Bodley Head, 1983). Peter Quennell recalls the statement about "unmentionable vice" in *The Marble Foot: An Autobiography, 1905–1938* (London: Collins, 1976). For general background information on the school, I am grateful to the late Peter Quennell.

Details of Charles Greene's early career are taken from *A History of Berkhamsted School, 1541–1972,* a work that was written by former headmaster B. H. Garnons Williams and was printed for the school in 1980. Claud Cockburn discusses Charles Greene's craving for chess, and his own desire to break rules, in *In Time of Trouble.* I am indebted to the late Peter Quennell for information about the Armistice Day incident. See also Norman Sherry, *The Life of Graham Greene, Volume One: 1904–1939* (London: Cape, 1989; New York: Viking, 1989). Cockburn's book quotes Charles Greene on "the pernicious and destructive doctrines."

Information about Herbert Greene's relationship with his brother is available in Graham's letters to Herbert at the Pierpont Morgan Library, New York City, and from his letters to Vivien, February 24, 1926; March 10, 1926; May 31, 1926. This second group of letters, as well as all others to Vivien that are mentioned hereafter, are held at Texas and are quoted at some length in Sherry's biography.

Paul Fussell's remark can be found in "Can Graham Greene Write English?" *New Republic,* December 27, 1980. In *A Sort of Life* Greene says that he went to Estonia. Greene's comment about being in Prague by accident is taken from Allain, *The Other Man* (London: Bodley Head, 1983). Greene wrote to Catherine on February 16 [1948]; n.d. [February 17, 1948]; and February 23 [1948]. These letters, as well as all others to Catherine mentioned hereafter, are held at Georgetown. Greene mentions the figure of 44,000 miles in *In Search of a Character.*

Information about Greene's espionage career comes not only from the official briefing arranged by the Cabinet Office but also from the author's

interviews with several former and current members of the intelligence community. For more information about Greene's contacts with Maurice
Oldfield, see Anthony Cavendish, *Inside Intelligence* (London: Collins,
1990); and Richard Deacon, *"C": A Biography of Sir Maurice Oldfield*
(London: Macdonald, 1985). Greene mentions his voyage with Korda in *A
Sort of Life*. William and Babe Paley, and Slim and Leland Hayward accompanied Greene and Korda on the summer cruise in 1952. See Slim Keith,
Slim: Memories of a Rich and Imperfect Life (New York: Simon & Schuster,
1990).

Details about Korda's espionage activities can be found in Karol Kulik,
Alexander Korda: The Man Who Could Work Miracles (London: Virgin,
1975; 1990); Martin Stockham, *The Korda Collection* (London: Boxtree,
1992); and Anthony Read and David Fisher, *Colonel Z: The Secret Life of a
Master of Spies* (New York: Viking, 1985). The remark about Prince
Metternich is in Orson Welles and Peter Bogdanovich, *This Is Orson Welles*
(New York: HarperCollins, 1992). The information about Korda and
Claude Dansey is taken from the author's interview with Anthony Read and
David Fisher, May 1993, and from their excellent biography of Dansey,
Colonel Z.

Evelyn Waugh speculates on Greene's spying in a letter to Ann Fleming,
September 5, 1960, *The Letters of Evelyn Waugh,* ed. Mark Amory (London:
Weidenfeld & Nicolson, 1980).

For information about the financial arrangements of the magazine, see
Night and Day, ed. and with an introduction by Christopher Hawtree
(London: Chatto & Windus, 1985). Victor Cazalet's comment is quoted in
Richard Griffiths, *Fellow Travellers of the Right: British Enthusiasts for Nazi
Germany* (Oxford: Oxford Univ. Press, 1980; 1983). Douglas Jerrold
praises Franco in "Spain: Impressions and Reflections," *Nineteenth
Century,* April 1937. And the phrase "real Toryism" is used by Sir Charles
Petrie, *A Historian Looks at His World* (London: Sidgwick & Jackson,
1972). Greene's comment about the general election of 1945 is quoted in
Norman Sherry, *The Life of Graham Greene: Volume Two, 1939–1955*
(London: Cape, 1994).

On Greene in East Berlin see his "Letter to a West German Friend,"
Reflections. The Soviet praise for *The Quiet American* is quoted in "When
Greene Is Red," *Newsweek,* October 1, 1956. Greene's use of opium is
attacked in the *Saturday Evening Post,* October 6, 1956.

Greene's letter to *The Times* (September 4, 1967) is reprinted in *Yours etc.*
Mervyn Jones tells his story in *Contemporary Authors Autobiography Series,*
Vol. 5, ed. Adele Sarkissian (Detroit: Gale Research, 1987).

The introduction to Philby's memoir is reprinted in Greene's *Collected
Essays*. Greene uses the phrase "spying for spying's sake" in *A Sort of Life*. In
an interview with Christopher Burstall, Greene referred to himself as
"Quisling's son," *Listener,* November 21, 1968. "A rage of personality" is
used by Henry James in "The Jolly Corner" and is discussed by Greene in
"Henry James: The Religious Aspect," *Collected Essays*.

CHAPTER THREE
SECRET GARDEN

Greene's letters to Catherine Walston, n.d. [February 18, 1952, and February 25, 1952], and a letter to Herbert Greene, March 3, 1952 (Pierpont Morgan Library) shed light on his fondness for Harston. His mother's visits to the nursery are recalled in *A Sort of Life*. Ave Greene Barham commented on Marion Greene and general family matters in the author's interview, August 1992. Mrs. Rivers, the parlor maid, spoke to the author in June 1993. I am grateful to the present owners of Harston House—Terence and Iris Armstrong—for showing me the house and garden, and for sharing information about its history. Greene's quotation about the family's self-sufficiency is in *The Other Man*.

Bonté Duran spoke to the author in July 1992 and shared a copy of her letter about Ernest Northrop, n.d. [Summer 1952].

Greene's illness is discussed in Allain, *The Other Man;* in Greene to Evelyn Waugh, June 22, 1960 (British Library); and in the *Evening Standard*, November 28, 1975.

The Raffles tale is Ernest Hornung's "Ides of March," *The Amateur Cracksman* (London: Methuen, 1899).

Julian Symons discusses the revolver episode in "The Strength of Uncertainty," *Times Literary Supplement*, October 8, 1982.

Greene's *Spectator* piece about Anne Greene—"Book Market," July 14, 1939—was later reprinted as "George Moore and Others" in *Collected Essays*. Anne Greene did indeed have a final *e* in both her first and last names, but Graham Greene's essay drops the letter from both names. For the clue about Anne Greene, I am indebted to Philip Stratford's excellent essay "Unlocking the Potting Shed," *Kenyon Review,* Winter 1962. Despite its title, the essay says nothing about Harston and has only a brief mention of Greene's many references to sheds.

The Civil War story may be loosely based on Lord Nugent's *Some Memorials of John Hampden* (London: Murray, 1832), although Greene may also have had in mind a more popular account of Hampden's death in some twentieth-century periodical or pamphlet.

CHAPTER FOUR
YES AND NO

For more information on Kenneth Richmond, see *W. E. Ford: A Biography,* by J. D. Beresford and Kenneth Richmond (London: Collins, 1917); and Richmond's *Evidence of Identity* (London: Bell, 1939). I am grateful to Ave Greene Barham for background information about Greene's stay at Richmond's house.

For Greene's denial of homosexual activity at Berkhamsted, I am indebted to Lady Selina Hastings, who interviewed Greene in December 1987. In *The Other Man*, Allain asked about Greene's duality. He recalled the origin of his autobiography in his interview with Lady Selina. His knowledge of Strauss's homosexuality is confirmed in a letter to Catherine, n.d. [February 18, 1952].

For information about Ted, I am indebted to Pat Wallace Frere, the widow of Greene's friend and publisher A. S. Frere. A copy of Ted's photo is in the possession of her son Harry.

The comment about syphilis is quoted in Elisabeth Moor, *An Impossible Woman* (London: Bodley Head, 1975).

Norman Douglas's interest in children is evident in his memoir *Looking Back* (New York: Harcourt, 1933); also see Richard Aldington's comments in *Pinorman* (London: Heinemann, 1954). Roger Senhouse's comment is taken from a BBC interview of April 29, 1958. The comment was not broadcast, but a transcript of the interview is available at the Lilly Library, Indiana University. Nancy Cunard's request for help is described in Ralph Lindeman, *Norman Douglas* (New York: Twayne, 1965). To study more of Douglas's verses, see *The Norman Douglas Limerick Book* (London: Blond, 1969). Background on Greene's dispute with Aldington is provided in Charles Doyle, *Richard Aldington: A Biography* (Carbondale: Southern Illinois Univ. Press, 1989). In March 1966 *The London Magazine* published Greene's review under the title "Poison Pen."

The present owner of the Villa Rosaio, Signor Riccio, kindly gave me a tour of the place in May 1993. Information from Gitta Bittorf is taken from author's interview, August 1992. The quotation from Michael Richey appears in *The Tablet* (London), September 10, 1994. In *An Impossible Woman* the Dottoressa spells the baron's name Von Schacht, but the correct spelling is given in James Money's *Capri: Island of Pleasure* (London: Hamish Hamilton, 1986). Attilio Scoppa is a native of Anacapri and still lives in the town; information from author's interview, June 1993. For information about Greene's honorary citizenship, I am grateful to Raffaele Vacca, who spoke to me in June 1993. Also see the pamphlet *Graham Greene Civis Anacapreensis* (Comune di Anacapri, 1980).

CHAPTER FIVE

OXFORD: A TOUCH OF THE POET

Anthony Powell's comments about Balliol are in *To Keep the Ball Rolling* (Harmondsworth: Penguin, 1983). I am also grateful to Powell for speaking to me about Greene. Evelyn Waugh's impression of Greene is given in *A Little Learning* (Boston: Little, Brown, 1964). Cyril Connolly's comment on Greene comes from *The Evening Colonnade* (New York: Harcourt, 1975). Peter Quennell's remark is made in *The Marble Foot*. John Betjeman's lines are from *Summoned by Bells* (Boston: Houghton Mifflin, 1960). Waugh's joke about the dean of Balliol is described in Quennell, *The Marble Foot*.

Greene discusses his work for the Germans in *A Sort of Life*. He recalled his attempt to spy for Ireland in the *Irish Independent,* July 1, 1989. See

Conversations with Graham Greene, ed. Henry J. Donaghy (Jackson: Univ. Press of Mississippi, 1992).

Information about Claud Cockburn in Spain is taken from Cockburn, "Serving in Spain and Elsewhere," *A Grand Street Reader,* ed. Ben Sonnenberg (New York: Summit, 1986). Information about his work for the Comintern can be found in Hugh Thomas, *The Spanish Civil War* (Harmondsworth: Penguin, 1965; 1986).

In *A Little Learning* Waugh comments on the Hysteron-Proteron Club. John Buchan wrote to Graham Greene on October 29, 1923 (Brown Univ. Library).

A. L. Rowse describes his feelings in *Friends and Contemporaries* (London: Methuen, 1989). On Greene's description of Monkhouse see Graham Greene, "Poetry by Wireless," *Oxford Chronicle,* January 30, 1925. Publishing figures for *Babbling April* can be found in R. A. Wobbe, *Graham Greene: A Bibliography and Guide to Research.* The book was reviewed in the *Times Literary Supplement,* May 21, 1925. Harold Acton's review is in *Cherwell,* May 9, 1925. The biographical critic is John Atkins, *Graham Greene* (London: Calder, 1957; 1966). Greene replied to Harold Acton in *Cherwell,* May 16, 1925.

Pound's comment on imagism comes from *The Letters of Ezra Pound: 1907–1941,* ed. D. D. Paige (New York: Harcourt, 1950). Arthur Calder-Marshall's essay "The Works of Graham Greene" appeared in *Horizon,* May 1940. Cyril Connolly's remark about Eliot is in *The Evening Colonnade.* Eliot's essay "Baudelaire" can be found in *Selected Essays* (New York: Harcourt, 1950).

For a description of the Pound rally, see Donald Hall, *Their Ancient Glittering Eyes: Remembering Poets and More Poets* (New York: Ticknor & Fields, 1992).

CHAPTER SIX

TIES THAT BIND: VIVIENNE

Greene found it difficult to forget Gwen, recalling her name more than fifty years later in an interview with John Mortimer. See Mortimer's *In Character* (London: Lane, 1983). "The Godly Distance" is included in *Babbling April* and was published two days after the radio symposium in the *Weekly Westminster,* January 24, 1925.

Ave Greene Barham's comments come from the author's interview, August 1992. The family history was written by Eva Greene, Graham's aunt, and is in the possession of John Lindgren, who lives in the village of Harston.

The Swinburne Letters were edited by Cecil Y. Lang, and the reference to Carleton Greene is in volume 1 (New Haven: Yale Univ. Press, 1959). Greene's comment about genes appears in Allain, *The Other Man.*

Much of the information about Greene's relationship with Vivien is based on the author's personal interview with her in June 1992 and on subsequent telephone conversations with her in 1993 and 1994, as well as on Greene's letters to her. For consistency I refer to her throughout the notes by the shorter version of her first name. The surviving letter from Vivien's mother was written in October 1925 (Texas). The kitten talk is in Vivien's letter to Greene, February 9 [1927] (Texas).

In the late 1940s Greene prepared a list of the prostitutes he had known in the 1920s and 1930s. The list is now in the Catherine Walston collection at Georgetown. In an interview with Alex Hamilton (*Guardian,* September 11, 1971), Greene mentioned that the prostitutes were discussed in an early draft of his autobiography.

Joseph Macleod was interviewed by Norman Sherry for his biography of Greene, but Sherry did not find any connection between the friend and *The Man Within,* nor did he raise the issue of a homosexual attraction.

Hugh Greene said that his father had stopped reading Graham's work after *The Man Within.* See *Evening Standard,* September 18, 1984.

I am grateful to Quentin Falk for discovering the quotation about the "queer bits." See his excellent *Travels in Greeneland: The Cinema of Graham Greene* (London: Quartet, 1984).

CHAPTER SEVEN
HEAVEN CAN WAIT

Kenneth Bell's letter is quoted in *A Sort of Life.* Cecil Roberts recalls his meeting with Greene in *The Bright Twenties* (London: Hodder, 1970) and *Books and Bookmen,* October 1971.

For information about Father Trollope, I am indebted to Margaret Quinn's "Graham Greene's First Priest: Father George Trollope," *Clergy Review,* December 1984. Greene's comment about measuring his evil against the Church was made to the screenwriter Guy Elmes and recounted in the author's interview with Elmes, March 1993. Greene's review of *After Strange Gods* was published in *Life and Letters,* April 1934. Eliot's comment about the spiritual quality of evil can be found in *After Strange Gods* (New York: Harcourt, Brace, 1934). Greene's essay on Mauriac is included in *Collected Essays.*

"The Trial of Pan" appeared in *Oxford Outlook,* February 1923; "The Improbable Tale of the Archbishop of Canterbridge" was published in *Cherwell,* November 15, 1924.

Greene criticized Belloc and Chesterton in *The Spectator,* August 11, 1933. His quotation from 1951 can be found in *Time,* October 29, 1951. His remark about a "moral treatise" is quoted in Donald Costello, "Graham Greene and the Catholic Press," *Renascence,* Autumn 1959. His comment on *The Potting Shed* is taken from the *Evening Standard,* January 25, 1957. Father Gardiner is quoted in Costello, "Greene and the Catholic Press."

David Lodge spoke of Greene's influence in the *Times Literary*

Supplement, April 12, 1991. Greene described himself as a "Catholic atheist" in V. S. Pritchett's interview, *New York Times Magazine,* February 26, 1978, and he referred to the Vatican as the "politburo" in *The Times,* December 17, 1985. The episode in the confessional was related to the author in an interview with Guy Elmes, March 1993.

Greene's suicidal threats were made in a letter to Vivien of January 18, 1926.

The comments of Douglas Jay were made in an interview with Donald Sturrock, producer of the BBC *Arena* series on Greene, which was broadcast in January 1993.

Greene described "The Episode" in the *Sunday Times,* January 16, 1966. His lies to Vivien are given in two letters from November 1925.

CHAPTER EIGHT
THE MAN WITHIN

Publishing details for Greene's books have been taken from Heinemann's files. The sales figures provided in this biography differ considerably from reports in biographical sources that have used Greene's version of his sales history. I prefer to rely on the official records. For assistance with Heinemann archives, I want to thank Joan Holah, the group librarian of Reed Books, and her deputy, Jean Rose.

Greene's resignation letter to *The Times* is quoted in "Our Man Within," *The Times,* April 5, 1991. His desire to witness civil unrest is conveyed to Vivien in a letter of May 4, 1926. His comments on the French occupation of the Rhineland can be found in "The French Peace," *Oxford Outlook,* June 1924.

Hugh Greene's remarks on the Nazi concentration camp can be found in Michael Tracey's biography. Graham Greene's encounter with Stefan Lorant is described in Norman Sherry's biography, but without any explanation of Lorant's identity or any discussion of Greene's anti-Semitism. "Notes from a Journal of the Blitz, 1940–41" appeared in *The Month,* November 1952.

Couto's interview with Greene is included in Maria Couto, *Graham Greene: On the Frontier* (London: Macmillan, 1988).

Orwell's remarks on Dalí are taken from "Benefit of Clergy: Some Notes on Salvador Dalí," which was written in 1944 and is included in *Collected Essays, Journalism and Letters of George Orwell* (London: Secker & Warburg, 1968; New York: Harcourt Brace, 1968).

Waugh's review of *The Name of Action* was published in the *Graphic,* October 25, 1930.

The New York review of *Rumour at Nightfall* appeared in the *New York Evening Post,* January 30, 1932.

According to Sherry, Greene's interest in Swinburne's whipping establishment is recorded in his diary, February 25, 1932.

CHAPTER NINE
MAKING ENDS MEET: *STAMBOUL TRAIN*

The comment about the devil looking after his own appears in *Ways of Escape*. Blunden's offer of help is recorded in Greene's diary, June 7, 1932. In "The Dark Backward: A Footnote," *Collected Essays,* Greene attacks the Book Society as something beneath the dignity of Henry James.

Cyril Connolly's comments on reviewing are taken from *The Condemned Playground: Essays, 1927–1944* (London: Routledge, 1945).

Greene's remarks on childhood terrors can be found in *The Spectator,* June 30, 1933. His piece on Beatrix Potter is reprinted in *Collected Essays.* The voice raised against "biocriticism" is that of John Atkins in his *Graham Greene* (London: Calder & Boyars, 1957; rev. ed., 1966). Pritchett's remark on Greene and Potter is included in his *Complete Collected Essays* (New York: Random House, 1991). "Pigs, Be British" appears under the title "The British Pig" in Greene's *Collected Essays;* the same volume includes a reprint of his essay "Portrait of a Lady" under the title "Portrait of a Maiden Lady." His comment on *Tobacco Road* can be found in *The Spectator,* October 6, 1933.

Sherry's biography cites evidence of Greene's desire to give up his child for adoption. Greene's trip to his mother-in-law's funeral is described in his diary, May 24, 1933 (Texas).

Greene comments on his sexual relations with Annette in his diary, August 4, 1932 (Texas). The unnamed "lover" spoke to the author in July 1993; for legal reasons I have not identified her. Alan Ross spoke to the author in June 1993.

Comments from Vivien are taken from the author's interviews.

The dream about murdering someone and leaving the body in a railway station and the poem about the raped woman are recorded in Greene's diary on January 4, 1933, and November 21, 1932, respectively (Texas). Sherry's biography quotes the poem as well as the words describing the dream.

The game Hating People was described to the author by Guy Elmes, March 1993.

Information about Raymond Greene is taken from his autobiography, *Moments of Being* (London: Heinemann, 1974).

CHAPTER TEN
JOURNEY WITHOUT MAPS

All details about Greene's contacts with the Foreign Office man Mr. Thompson are taken from documents in the Public Record Office, Kew.

Background information about Col. T. Elwood Davis is available in I. K. Sundiata, *Black Scandal: America and the Liberian Labour Crisis* (Philadelphia: Institute for the Study of Human Issues, 1980). Lady Simon's views on colonialism and Africa can be found in Kathleen Simon, *Slavery* (London: Hodder, 1930). Greene's contacts with the Anti-Slavery Society are documented in papers available at the Rhodes House Library, Oxford. Sir John

Simon's remarks about Liberia are quoted in Sundiata's *Black Scandal*. Sir John Harris's letter to the Colonial Office is held at the Public Record Office, Kew.

Moura Budberg's career as a Soviet agent is discussed in Robin Bruce Lockhart, *Reilly: The First Man* (Harmondsworth: Penguin, 1987).

The letter to the *Times Literary Supplement* was published July 18, 1966.

Barbara Greene was interviewed by the *News Chronicle* on January 4, 1935. Her book *Land Benighted* was first published in 1938 and was reprinted by Penguin in 1990 as *Too Late to Turn Back*.

Otto Preminger's comment is taken from his *Preminger: An Autobiography* (New York: Doubleday, 1977).

Dr. Harley's career is discussed in Winifred J. Harley, *A Third of a Century with George Way Harley* (Newark, Del.: Liberian Studies Association, 1973).

Greene's speech is summarized in the *Anti-Slavery Reporter and Aborigines' Friend,* October 1935. I am grateful to David Ould, of Anti-Slavery International, for sending me a copy of this periodical.

CHAPTER ELEVEN

THIS GUN FOR HIRE: MOTION PICTURES

The best collection of Greene's film reviews is *The Graham Greene Film Reader: Mornings in the Dark,* ed. by David Parkinson (Manchester: Carcanet, 1993).

Sir Raymond Carr wrote to *The Spectator* on April 22, 1989. Francis King commented on Greene in the *Evening Standard,* August 22, 1994, and in author's interview, June 1994.

The satiric portrait of Louis B. Mayer is offered in Greene's "Film Lunch," in *The Lost Childhood.* The Jewish reference is missing from the version reprinted in *Collected Essays.*

Anti-Semitic references in Greene's film criticism can be found in *The Spectator,* June 5, 1936, and April 7, 1939; and in *Night and Day,* October 21, 1937.

Information about Greene's financial dealings with Korda can be found in the Korda papers at the British Film Institute. I am deeply grateful to Janet Moat for introducing me to this impressive collection.

CHAPTER TWELVE

BRIGHTON ROCK

Greene's plans to bring down the British cabinet are explained in Walter Allen, *As I Walked Down New Grub Street: Memories of a Writing Life* (London: Heinemann, 1981). Greene's notes on pornographic magazines are contained in the diary entries that *Granta* published in autumn 1985, "While Waiting for a War."

In an interview with J. W. Lambert, *Sunday Times,* January 16, 1966, Greene explained why he failed to take part in the Spanish Civil War. His article on Tennyson and Hallam is reprinted in *Collected Essays* as "The Apostles Intervene."

For information on *Night and Day,* I am indebted to Christopher Hawtree's collection of pieces from the magazine and to Richard Pennington, "*Night and Day:* A Contribution to Literary History," *Contemporary Review,* November 1991. Shirley Temple Black comments on Greene in *Child Star: An Autobiography* (New York: Warner, 1989).

Greene's criticism of the Technicolor film appeared in *The Spectator,* April 17, 1937.

Greene's comment on literary people occurs in his interview with Martin Shuttleworth and Simon Raven, *Paris Review,* Autumn 1953. For information on Greene's friendship with R. K. Narayan, see "A Friend in Malgudi," *Guardian,* April 11, 1991.

Walter Allen's description of Greene is taken from *As I Walked Down New Grub Street.* The memoir by Julian Maclaren-Ross is included in his *Memoirs of the Forties* (Harmondsworth: Penguin, 1965; 1984).

Greene commented on his relationship with his children in an interview with Lady Selina Hastings, December 1987. Vivien's comments on Lucy Caroline are taken from author's interview, June 1992.

Eliot's idea of damnation and salvation can be found in his essay "Baudelaire."

The three views on Pinkie belong to Harvey Curtis Webster, "The World of Graham Greene," and Nathan A. Scott, "Graham Greene: Christian Tragedian," both in *Graham Greene: Some Critical Considerations,* ed. Robert O. Evans (Lexington: Univ. of Kentucky Press, 1963); and Paul O'Prey, *A Reader's Guide to Graham Greene* (London: Thames & Hudson, 1988).

There are many accounts of the Brighton murders of 1934, but the best is by Jonathan Goodman in *The Railway Murders* (London: Allison & Busby, 1984). Goodman interviewed Chief Inspector Robert Donaldson, the Scotland Yard detective who led the investigation of the torso murder. I am grateful to Mr. Goodman for discussing the case with me, although I must emphasize that my conclusions about its significance are strictly my own. I have also consulted the many articles about the case in *The Times,* from June 1934 to February 1935, and I have consulted the official files of the case in the archives of Scotland Yard, Public Record Office, Kew.

Selections from Greene's "dream diary" were published as *A World of My Own* (London: Reinhardt, 1992).

A limited edition of *A Quick Look Behind: Footnotes to an Autobiography* was published in 1983 by the small California printing firm Sylvester & Orphanos.

The bizarre little story published in 1965 is "The Over-night Bag." See Greene's *Collected Stories.*

CHAPTER THIRTEEN
ACROSS THE BORDER: *THE POWER AND THE GLORY*

The early publication history of *To Beg I Am Ashamed* is explained in the Routledge files at Reading University. Greene reviewed the book in the *New Statesman*, November 21, 1953. Helen Neville reviewed the book in *The Nation*, July 16, 1938.

On May 23, 1938, *The Times* reported the remarks of the lord chief justice. Vivien Greene's recollections of her trip to America are taken from the author's interview, June 1992.

Judith Adamson's *Graham Greene: The Dangerous Edge* (London: Macmillan, 1990) contains excellent background information on Mexico in the 1920s and 1930s. A good contemporary article on Tomás Garrido Canabal is "The Scourge of Tabasco," *Collier's*, February 23, 1935.

Greene's Mexican travel diary is held at Georgetown.

The review by Gervase Mathew appeared in *Blackfriars*, June 1939. Greene's comment on Mexico and Catholicism appears in an interview with Maria Couto, *Graham Greene: On the Frontier*. The essay on Herbert Read can be found in Greene's *Collected Essays*.

All information about Greene's confrontation with the Vatican is taken from papers held by the Westminster Diocesan Archives. I am grateful to Father Ian Dickie for supplying me with copies of this material. Evelyn Waugh wrote to Greene on May 2, 1954, *The Letters of Evelyn Waugh*.

CHAPTER FOURTEEN
BREAKING UP

Vivien Greene's comments on Dorothy Glover are taken from the author's interview, June 1992.

In *Dear David, Dear Graham: A Bibliographic Correspondence* (Oxford: Alembic Press with the Amate Press, 1989), David Low tells the story of Greene and Dorothy serving in the ARP.

The Heinemann archives reveal that Dorothy Craigie and David Craigie are the same person. David Low relates Dorothy's hopes for the future in *Dear David, Dear Graham*. Lady Rothenstein recalled Catherine Walston's remark about Dorothy in the author's interview, March 1993. Judy Taylor, formerly of the Bodley Head, recalled the fate of Dorothy's illustrations for Greene's books in the author's interview, June 1992.

Derek Verschoyle's review was published in *The Spectator*, September 22, 1939.

Lauren Bacall's comments are taken from her autobiography, *By Myself* (New York: Knopf, 1978).

Penelope Houston's *Went the Day Well?* (London: British Film Institute, 1992) is an excellent introduction to the film. Dilys Powell's review was published in the *Sunday Times*, November 1, 1942.

Greene's remark on *Went the Day Well?* is taken from Quentin Falk's *Travels in Greeneland*.

Greene wrote to John Lehmann about "Men at Work" on June 5 [1941] (Texas).

Greene recalled the blitz in interviews with John Mortimer, *In Character*, and Maureen Owen, *Mail on Sunday*, September 9, 1984.

Rose Macaulay's comments are taken from *Letters to a Friend, 1950–52*, ed. Constance Babington-Smith (New York: Atheneum, 1962).

"At Home" is included in *Collected Essays*.

Vivien's experience in Crowborough is recalled by David Low in *Dear David, Dear Graham*.

CHAPTER FIFTEEN

TOP SECRET: OFFICER 59200

Details about Greene's secret service career have been taken from the author's Cabinet Office briefing and from information provided by former and current members of the intelligence community.

Greene describes his stay at the North Oxford Nursing Home in a letter to John Betjeman, October 18 [1941]. The letter is held at the Univ. of Victoria, Canada.

The diary entries in *In Search of a Character* describe Greene's sojourn in West Africa in 1941–42. The complete diary for this period is held at Texas.

Garbo's story is told in Michael Howard, *British Intelligence in the Second World War*, vol. 5 (London: Her Majesty's Stationery Office, 1989). The wartime activities of Norman Holmes Pearson and James Jesus Angleton are discussed in Eliot Weinberger, "Tinker, Tailor, Poet, Spy: Tales of Literary Espionage," *New York Times Book Review*, October 4, 1992. Also see Humphrey Carpenter, *W. H. Auden: A Biography* (Boston: Houghton Mifflin, 1981).

Muggeridge discusses Philby in *Things Past* (London: Collins, 1978).

Greene's quotation about meeting Philby in Moscow is taken from the *Sunday Telegraph*, May 10, 1987. Cited in Phillip Knightley, *The Master Spy: The Story of Kim Philby* (New York: Vintage, 1990).

The quotations from Philby's private papers are taken from Geraldine Norman, "The Last Effects of Treachery," *Independent on Sunday*, April 24, 1994.

Copies of Greene's French literary magazine, *Choix*, are available in the Political Warfare Executive archives at the Public Record Office, Kew.

CHAPTER SIXTEEN

ODD MAN OUT: KIM PHILBY AND *THE THIRD MAN*

For background information on Philby's life and career, three sources have been especially valuable: Andrew Boyle, *The Climate of Treason: Five Who*

Spied for Russia (London: Hutchinson, 1979); John Costello and Oleg Tsarev, *Deadly Illusions* (London: Century, 1993); and Knightley, *The Master Spy.*

Hugh Greene's broadcast to Germany is described in Tracey, *A Variety of Lives.*

Otto John tells his story in *Twice Through the Lines: The Autobiography of Otto John* (New York: Harper & Row, 1972).

Allen Dulles's quotation about saving lives is taken from Klemens von Klemperer, *German Resistance Against Hitler* (Oxford: Clarendon, 1992). In his introduction to Hans Gisevius, *To the Bitter End* (London: Cape, 1948), Dulles discusses the possibility of ending the war in 1944.

Hugh Trevor-Roper (Lord Dacre) wrote to the author on February 8, 1993. See also his *The Philby Affair* (London: Kimber, 1968).

For information about Peter Smolka, I am grateful to his wife, Lotty, and his sons Tom and Tim.

Anthony Glees discusses Smolka in *The Secrets of the Service: British Intelligence and Communist Subversion, 1939–51* (London: Cape, 1987).

Elizabeth Montagu's comments are taken from the author's interview, June 1993.

Quotations from Eric Gedye and the Austrian journalist (E. H. Cookridge) are taken from Knightley, *The Master Spy.*

Greene's comment on helping Philby escape is taken from the *Sunday Telegraph,* March 12, 1978. Philby explains his desire to protect Greene in the *Daily Express,* February 20, 1988.

A superb account of the production of *The Third Man* can be found in David Thomson, *Showman: The Life of David O. Selznick* (New York: Knopf, 1992). Greene's interview with Quentin Falk appears in *The Graham Greene Film Reader.*

The scholarly article about *The Third Man* is "Looking for the Third Man," by Judy Adamson and Philip Stratford, *Encounter,* June 1978.

CHAPTER SEVENTEEN
THE UNDISCOVERED COUNTRY: *THE HEART OF THE MATTER*

Douglas Jerrold's comments are in his "Pleasure-Hater," *Picture Post,* March 15, 1952.

Greene's comment about the film version of *Brighton Rock* is taken from Quentin Falk's *Travels in Greeneland.*

Vivien Greene's comments are from the author's interview, June 1992. John Rothenstein's recollections can be found in his *Time's Thievish Progress* (London: Cassell, 1970).

Orwell's review of *The Heart of the Matter* appeared in *The New Yorker,* July 17, 1948. Waugh's review appeared in *Commonweal,* July 16, 1948.

Mother Mary Angelica's comments are quoted in Costello, "Graham Greene and the Catholic Press."

CHAPTER EIGHTEEN
THE THIRD WOMAN

Much of the information in this chapter is drawn from the Catherine Walston collection at Georgetown.

Evelyn Waugh's comment about Catherine's party was reported to Diana Cooper, August 15, 1952, *Mr. Wu and Mrs. Stitch: The Letters of Evelyn Waugh and Diana Cooper,* ed. Artemis Cooper (London: Hodder, 1991). Waugh's remark about Catherine's personality appears in his diary, September 28, 1948. On Catherine in Capri, Ann Fleming wrote to Waugh on June 10 [1960], *The Letters of Ann Fleming,* ed. Mark Amory (London: Collins Harvill, 1985).

The recollections of Frances Donaldson can be found in *A Twentieth Century Life* (London: Weidenfeld, 1992). Information about Catherine's early years has been taken from the author's interviews with her sisters, Bonté Duran (July 1992) and Belinda Straight (October 1992). John Rothenstein describes Catherine in jeans in *Brave Day, Hideous Night: Autobiography, 1939–65* (London: Hamish Hamilton, 1966).

The IRA lover was Ernie O'Malley, and the American general was Lowell Weicker, Sr. In the author's interview with Catherine's friend Diana Crutchley, August 1992, she recalled the story that Catherine and Greene had "committed adultery behind every high altar in Italy." Perhaps this claim is an exaggeration, but it is easy to accept that such a sacrilegious activity would appeal to a man who relished the idea of having sex with his goddaughter. Pat Frere recalled Lady Huntingdon's comment, author's interview, July 1991. Information confirmed by Lady Huntingdon's daughter, Lady Selina Hastings.

Bill Walston recalled Father Gilby in the author's interview, March 1993. Bonté Duran's letter about Father Gilby was written to her husband, Gustavo, on June 5 [1952]. Brian Wormald's comments are taken from the author's interview, March 1993. Guy Elmes's remarks were made to the author in March 1993.

Norman Douglas ridiculed Padre Pio in an unpublished BBC interview at the Lilly Library, Indiana Univ. Greene's interview with *The Tablet* was published on September 23, 1989.

Greene refers to Catherine as Kate Croy in a letter to her of June 7, 1948. Catherine's diaries are available at Georgetown.

Catherine's letter to Bonté about Greene's shyness was written on March 13, 1950. Her letter about his kindness and suffering was written on May 22, 1950.

Quotations from Edward Sackville-West are taken from Michael De-la-Noy, *Eddy: The Life of Edward Sackville-West* (London: Bodley Head, 1988).

Bonté's description of Greene's anger was written to her husband, n.d. [1952]. Father Turner's comments are taken from the author's interview, March 1993. Dorothy's comment about Catherine is in a letter to Greene, April 18, 1948 (Georgetown).

Greene's remark about Padre Pio was made to Graham Lord, *Sunday Express,* August 7, 1988.

Information about Jean Stafford's relationship with Greene is taken from Donald Roberts, *Jean Stafford* (Boston: Little, Brown, 1988). The quotation from her review is also taken from Roberts.

Richard Crossman's experience is recorded in his *Backbench Diaries* (London: Hamish Hamilton and Cape, 1981). Derek Patmore recalls his conversation with Greene in an unpublished essay held at Texas.

The Catholic Literary Award was given to Greene in 1952.

CHAPTER NINETEEN
RED MENACE

Lucien Bodard's brilliant book is *The Quicksand War: Prelude to Vietnam* (Boston: Little, Brown, 1967). Greene's *Paris Match* article appeared July 12, 1952. His interview with Ho Chi Minh appeared in the *Sunday Times,* May 8, 1955. In a letter to Catherine, November 7 [1951], Greene describes smoking opium.

Greene's articles on Kenya appeared in the *Sunday Times,* September 27, 1953, and October 4, 1953.

Howard R. Simpson's remarks are taken from his letter to the author, and from his *Tiger in the Barbed Wire* (Washington: Brassey's, 1992).

Louis Heren's memories of Greene are set forth in a letter to the author, October 15, 1992.

Greene's "Malaya, the Forgotten War" came out in *Life,* July 30, 1951. Henry Luce's statement of faith in American destiny is quoted in Lloyd Gardner, *Approaching Vietnam* (New York: Norton, 1988). Greene's "Assumption of Mary" appeared in *Life,* October 30, 1950. Emmet Hughes's correspondence with Greene is held at Texas.

Douglas Bolam wrote to the author, September 1993. Some details of Trevor Wilson's activities in Vietnam can be found in the Public Record Office, Kew. "The General and the Spy" appeared in *London Magazine,* August 1954.

Greene's activities on behalf of SIS were described in the author's briefing from the Cabinet Office.

Greene discusses his troubles with the McCarran Act in the *New Statesman,* November 22, 1952. *The New Republic* defended Greene on February 11, 1952. His interview of 1953 was given to Kenneth Tynan, *Harper's Bazaar,* February 1953. The position of the Department of State is spelled out in a memo of December 14, 1956, addressed to the Immigration and Naturalization Service.

The comment about Leo Hochstetter was made to John R. MacArthur, *The Progressive,* June 1991, although Greene did not identify the man by name. Greene's comment about the diplomatic officer is taken from an interview with Gloria Emerson, *Rolling Stone,* March 9, 1978.

The quotation from Joseph L. Mankiewicz appears in Quentin Falk, *Travels in Greeneland,* as does the critic's comment about the American "martyr."

A. J. Liebling's review appeared in *The New Yorker* on April 7, 1956. I am indebted to Lisa Vargo's "The Quiet American and a Mr. Lieberman," *English Language Notes,* June 1984. Nora Sayre's recollection of her encounter with Greene was published in *The Nation,* October 7, 1978.

CHAPTER TWENTY

ANTIC DISPOSITION

Greene's interview in the *Paris Review* was published in autumn 1953.

Quotations from Jocelyn Rickards are taken from an unpublished memoir, which she kindly loaned to the author, and from the author's interviews, as well as comments made to Alex Kershaw of the *Guardian.* See also her autobiography, *The Painted Banquet* (London: Weidenfeld, 1987).

A good account of Greene's confrontation with John Gordon appears in Christopher Hawtree's notes to *Yours etc.*

Evelyn Waugh's comment about Olivier is reported in *Yours Etc.*

Greene's habit of looking for car numbers is described in Evelyn Waugh to Nancy Mitford, September [1951], *The Letters of Evelyn Waugh.* His interview with Waugh's biographer—Selina Hastings—took place in December 1987. His comment to Tynan was published in *Harper's Bazaar,* February 1953.

John Sutro shared his memories in *The Spectator,* September 29, 1984. Otto Preminger's story is told in *Preminger: An Autobiography.*

Anita Bjork's comments are taken from her letter to the author, September 30, 1993. Michael Meyer's stories about Greene and Anita Bjork can be found in *Not Prince Hamlet: Literary and Theatrical Memoirs* (London: Secker, 1989). Meyer is the source of the comment about Stig Dagerman's suicide attempts.

Peter Lennon's article appeared in the *Guardian,* April 8, 1991.

Greene's stay with Truman Capote is described in a letter to Catherine of August 30, 1954. Capote's comments on Greene appear in Lawrence Grobel's *Conversations with Capote* (New York: NAL, 1985). Noël Coward's remarks appear in *The Noël Coward Diaries,* ed. Graham Payne and Sheridan Morley (Boston: Little, Brown, 1982).

The article on Greene's China trip was published in *The Times,* May 27, 1985, and was reprinted in *Reflections.*

Hugh MacDiarmid's comments are taken from his *The Company I've Kept* (London: Hutchinson, 1966).

Greene's letter to Catherine of August 31, 1956, shows that he planned to set his spy novel in Lisbon.

Quotations from Lisandro Otero and Nydia Sarabia are taken from Tom Miller, "Sex, Spies and Literature," *Washington Post,* April 14, 1991.

Greene expressed his point about communism and puritanism in conversation with David Lewin; see the *Daily Mail,* April 4, 1991. The *Havana Post* article appeared on April 17, 1959. Greene made his comment about Hemingway in the *Observer,* November 16, 1969. The Shanghai scene is described in *Horizon,* November 1959.

CHAPTER TWENTY-ONE
TO TELL THE TRUTH

The letter from *To Tell the Truth* is at Georgetown and was sent to Greene in November 1957.

The "Congo Journal" was published as one part of *In Search of a Character.*

Aubelin Jolicoeur's comments are taken from his article "How a Local Character Found His Author and Immortality," *Guardian,* April 12, 1991.

Peter Ustinov's opinion of *The Comedians* is quoted from Tony Thomas, *Ustinov in Focus* (London: Zwemmer, 1971). See also Falk, *Travels in Greeneland.*

A copy of *Graham Greene: Finally Exposed* is available at Georgetown.

Greene's explanation of his decision to leave England is given in the *Sunday Times,* January 16, 1966.

Greene wrote to Evelyn Waugh on January 6, 1966, and explained the resemblance between the financial adviser and the fictional Major Jones (British Library).

TWENTY-TWO
MONSTER OF THE CHEMINS DE FER, OR BRIGHTON REVISITED

Piers Paul Read's remarks are made in an obituary notice of Greene, *Evening Standard,* April 3, 1991.

Yvonne's comments are taken from the author's interview, August 1991. Greene discusses his relationship with Martine Cloetta in the *Sunday Times,* April 1, 1984, and *Newsweek,* February 15, 1982. In *The Other Man* Greene says that his books are his real children.

In late January and early February 1982, the *Sunday Times* gave prominent, and sympathetic, attention to Greene's personal feud. Greene's lament about Brighton appears in an unpublished essay by Derek Patmore, Texas.

The *Saturday Review* explanation of *"J'Accuse"* appeared in May 1982.

Jonathan Raban's review was published in *The New York Review of Books,* November 4, 1982.

Fay Weldon questioned Greene's view of the GPA award in the *Evening Standard,* November 28, 1989. The complaint of the GPA sponsor was reported in the *Guardian,* November 29, 1989.

Greene's resignation letter to the American Academy, Institute of Arts and Letters, is included in *Yours etc.*

The essay on Edgar Wallace is in *Collected Essays.*

CHAPTER TWENTY-THREE

DOWN THERE ON A VISIT

I am grateful to Guillermo Sánchez Borbon and R. M. Koster for talking to me about Torrijos, Chuchu, and Panamanian politics. Their book *In the Time of the Tyrants: Panama, 1968–90* (New York: Norton, 1990) is a passionate and thoroughly convincing account of the pervasive corruption and brutality that existed under Torrijos and Noriega. Other interesting books on the subject include Kevin Buckley, *Panama: The Whole Story* (New York: Simon & Schuster, 1991), and John Dinges, *Our Man in Panama: The Shrewd Rise and Brutal Fall of Manuel Noriega* (New York: Times Books, 1991).

During Greene's life one of the few critics to challenge his views on Panama was David Pryce-Jones, whose review of *Getting to Know the General* is a brilliant piece of analysis. See his "Graham Greene in Panama," *Encounter,* February 1985.

Greene's private travel diary for his trips to Panama is available in the Manuscript Room of the British Library.

The *Washington Post* interview was published on September 20, 1988. John R. MacArthur's interview appeared in *The Progressive,* June 1991.

Greene's award ceremony in Nicaragua was reported in the *Guardian,* April 24, 1987.

Richard West's comments can be found in *Hurricane in Nicaragua: A Journey in Search of Revolution* (London: Michael Joseph, 1989).

Christopher Dickey's remark is in *The New Republic,* October 15, 1984.

Father Leopoldo Durán's recollections of Greene were given to Donald Sturrock in an interview for his BBC *Arena* series on Greene. I am indebted to him for a copy of the transcript of this interview.

I am grateful to Alistair Horne for describing Maurice Oldfield's reaction to Greene's appearance in Oxford.

THE LAST WORD

Mabel and Lionel Dawes spoke to me about Catherine in March 1993.

I am indebted to Yvonne Cloetta for detailed information about Greene's last days. She spoke to me in August 1991.

The *Daily Telegraph* piece on Francis Greene appeared on March 9, 1968.

Father Durán's comment about Greene's espionage work is quoted in *The Times,* September 24, 1994.

John Ezard gives a good account of Greene's funeral in the *Guardian,* April 9, 1991.

AUTHOR'S NOTE
GRAHAM GREENE AND BIOGRAPHY

David Lodge's comment about Greene and Professor Sherry can be found in "Graham Greene: A Personal View," *Times Literary Supplement,* April 12, 1991. Greene's attack on Anthony Mockler is reported in the *Daily Telegraph,* March 11, 1989. The phrase "gratuitous indecency" was used by R. T. Jones in his review of *Lord Rochester's Monkey,* in *Essays in Criticism,* October 1975.

ACKNOWLEDGMENTS

As a biographer, I have benefited greatly from the kindness of strangers. It never ceases to amaze me that people will take great pains to provide assistance of all types. And some good souls expect absolutely nothing in return. They answer your questions patiently and directly, share their letters and photographs, and accept your freedom to tell the story in your own fashion. No strings are attached. These are the angels of biography, and without their generosity, this book would have been much more difficult to write.

I am happy to list the names of the many people who made an effort to assist me. Some were eager to talk, some refused to answer certain questions, and some had second thoughts about giving their help, but I am grateful to everyone who wrote or spoke to me, including Judith Adamson, Christopher Andrew, Terence and Iris Armstrong, Father Noël Barber, Ave Barham, Felicity Behrens, Gitta Bittorf, Anita Bjork, Jill Black, Douglas Bolam, John Bright-Holmes, Vincent Brome, Anthony Cave Brown, Sally Brown, Euan Cameron, Father Caraman, Laetitia Cerio, Yvonne Cloetta, Mary Cowgill, Diana Crutchley, Lionel Dawes, Mabel Dawes, Teresa De Gregorio, Frank Delaney, Father Ian Dickie, Frances Donaldson, Bonté Duran, Barbara Egglesfield, Nicholas Elliott, Guy Elmes, Quentin Falk, David Fisher, Harry Frere, Pat Wallace Frere, Richard Gekoski, Vivien Greene, Ed Guillion, Lady Selina Hastings, John Hawkesworth, Louis Heren, Leon Higdon, Mrs. Leo Hochstetter, Mark Holloway, Bill Igoe, Alan Judd, Alex Kershaw, Francis King, R. M. Koster, Peter Levi, John Lindgren, Georgianne Marcinkovich, Rubina Mariniello, Janet Moat, James

Michie, Anthony Powell, Peter Quennell, Anthony Read, Jocelyn Rickards, Michael Richey, Mrs. Rivers, Alan Ross, Lady Rothenstein, Sánchez Borbon, Attilio Scoppa, Howard R. Simpson, David Sherratt, Janet Adam Smith, Lotty Smolka, Tim Smolka, Tom Smolka, Belinda Straight, Philip Stratford, Donald Sturrock, John Debenham Taylor, Judy Taylor, Saundra Taylor, Hugh Trevor-Roper (Lord Dacre), Father Vincent Turner, Elizabeth Montagu Varley, Bill Walston, Oliver Walston, and Brian Wormald.

I also want to recognize the personal help and encouragement given to me by Ronald Baker, Diane Breeden-Lee, Richard Cohen, John Coldstream, Cressida Connolly, Tom Derrick, Mary Ann Duncan, Helen Fraser, Bill Hamilton, Mark Hamilton, Rhonda Hughes, John Lee, Deirdre Levi, Jeremy Lewis, Kate Medina, Mary Burch Ratliff, Dr. Wesley Ratliff, Jack Rollins, Emma Rhind-Tutt, Nicholas Shakespeare, June Shelden, Stuart and Sophie Sperry, Dorothy Stowe, and Tom Weldon.

As always, I owe my greatest debts to my strongest supporters—Sue, Sarah, and Vanessa.

INDEX

ABOUT THE TYPE

This book was set in Galliard, a typeface de-
signed by Matthew Carter for the Mergen-
thaler Linotype Company in 1978. Galliard
is based on the sixteenth-century typefaces of
Robert Granjon.